Elena N. Zaretskaya

RHETORIC. The Theory and Practice of Speech Communication

MIR COLLECTION
New York
2007

ELENA N. ZARETSKAYA

Rhetoric. The Theory and Practice of Speech Communication

Publisher Mark Chernyakhovskiy
MIR COLLECTION Publishing House
8700 25th Avenue, Suite 6G
Brooklyn, NY 11214
Tel./Fax: (718) 449-6245
E-mail: MIR8700@ yahoo.com

Computer design: Rudolf Furman

Copyright © Elena N. Zaretskaya

All rights reserved.
No part of this book may be reproduced or utilized in any form or by any means, electronic or mechanical, including photocopying, recording, or by any information storage and retrieval system, without permission in writing from the Author.

Library of Congress Cataloging Number
2007900440

ISBN – 1-893552-45-4

Printed in the United States of America

MIR COLLECTION
PUBLISHING HOUSE

Elena N. Zaretskaya, PhD, Doctor of Philology, Full Professor of the Academy of National Economy under the Government of Russian Federation. Vice-president of Moscow Department of the Russian Scientific Association. Member of the International Faculty Development Program IFDP (USA-Spain-France-Italy). Member of Association of International Amnesty.

Courses conducted: Speech Communication, Business Ethics, Rhetoric, Speech Logic, Management Communication and Leadership.

Education: Moscow State University, Philological Faculty (graduated 1973).

Work experience:

1973–1989 – Academy of Science of Russia, Scientific Research Institute of Information. Position – Chief Science Assistant.

1989–2002 – Academy of National Economy uder the Government of Russian Federation. Position – Head of the Department of Social Sciences and Humanities.

Publications: 42 articles on the topic of Theoretical Linguistics, Rhetoric and Speech Communication;

Books: "Speech Logic" (1997); "Verbal Forms Synthesis Typology" (1998), "Rhetoric. The Theory and Practice of Speech Communication" (1998), "Business Communication", 1, 2 vol. (2005)

International Conferences on Linguistics, Psychology, Management Communication Participant. International Exchanging Educational Programs with USA, UK, France, Spain, Sweden Universities.

Address: 23, Sadovaya Kudrinskaya Str., Apt. 17a, Moscow, 103001, Russia.
Telephone: +7.495.254.5815
E-mail: elezaret@mail.ru

The book RHETORIC. The Theory and Practice of Speech Communication is based on Professor Zaretskaya's lectures at the Moscow State University and the Academy of National Economy.

The monograph treats problems of what can be conventionally described as the science and art of communication. Rhetoric, science of purposeful speech, is its pivotal part as speech is the principal component of human communication.

The book is intended for experts on, and students of speech conduct – teachers, parliamentarians, lawyers, businessmen, and anyone who is eager to find the right tone in communication.

CONTENTS

Introduction 7

Part I
THE CHARACTERISTICS OF ORAL COMMUNICATION
Chapter 1. The Ethics of Speech 13
Chapter 2. The Position of the Listener 17
Chapter 3. The Conscious/Unconscious and Lie in Oral Communication 22
Chapter 4. The Three Types of Information Reception and Transmission 34

Part II
THE GOALS OF SPEECH
Chapter 5. Ritual Speech 45
Chapter 6. Provocative Speech 57
Chapter 7. Imperative Speech 71
Chapter 8. The Categories of "Coercion" and "Persuasion" as Realisation of the Power Urge 78
Chapter 9. The Motivation of Professional Speech 86
Chapter 10. Classification of Speech Goals 99

Part III
THE CONCEPT OF SPEECH
Chapter 11. Logical Proof in Speech 103
Chapter 12. The Thesis 109
Chapter 13. Argumentation 141
Chapter 14. Deductive Demonstration 162
Chapter 15. Inductive Demonstration 186
Chapter 16. Analogical Demonstration 200
Chapter 17. Additional Kinds of Demonstration 229
Chapter 18. The Art of Public Speech and Discussion 248

Part IV
THE TEXT
Chapter 19. The Text as Sequence of Symbols 289
Chapter 20. The Communicative Expressive Force of the Trope 339
Chapter 21. Irony in Speech Communication 368
Chapter 22. The Expressive Force of Figures of Speech 384
Chapter 23. The Body Language 399

Bibliography 414

INTRODUCTION

> The rich content of speech depends on the richness of thought.
>
> *Victor Hugo*

The culture of speech conduct is within a sphere wherein lie the answers to the following four questions:
1. What for are we speaking?
2. What do we want to say?
3. What means are we using for that?
4. What is the response to our speech?

The answer to the first question determines the goal of the speech, G; the second, the concept of future utterance, C; the third, the particular oral or written text of our speech, T; and the fourth, the adequacy of the listener/reader's response to the speaker's goal, R. The goal must certainly be achieved, or speech is wasted.

The goal, G, is the motivation underlying whatever speech. The concept, C, is the information you intend to pass to the listener as this information promotes the achievement of your goal. The concept consists of the thesis (the idea you want to pass to the listener) and arguments to prove it. The text, T, is the oral/written speech which reaches the ear or eye. Response, R, is the listener's behavior in speech communication. Evidently, to adequately describe speech communication, we need information of many sciences – psychology, logic, information theory, linguistics, ethics, philosophy, poetics, cybernetics, aesthetics, semiotics, physiology, and the theory of eloquence and acting.

Rhetoric, in the broader sense, is a kind of philological world–outlook which makes part and parcel of spiritual culture in civilisation. It is a set of methods in humanitarian knowledge. That is why we borrow a part of general definitions in this book from encyclopedic dictionaries, and use them without quotation marks. Rhetoric is the cultural basis of knowledge and social activity. It helps one to be citizen of the law–based community and determine the form of thought and direction of future action. At the same time, it links the human being with cultural history.

The speaker creates imagery through speech, so he usually stands to lose when he is completely sincere – his speech disorganises the audience. As every author's, the speaker's public image depends on 1) the audience, 2) the subject of speech, and 3) the type of speech. Three categories characterise the act of speech: the rhetoric logos, the rhetoric pathos and the rhetoric ethos. The rhetoric logos is the argumentation of speech connected with the understanding of reality – the awareness of the speech being not out of place, to quote Plato. The logos pertains to prognostication, to the future reality, and presupposes a change of world-outlook through speech, i.e., it forms the mental state of the audience to merge reality with imagery.

The rhetoric pathos is determined by the speaker's emotion (Aristotle repeatedly referred to the false pathos which produced a comic effect). It is a volitional category which has for its principal vehicle the desire for the audience to make a decision. The situation breeds the will to create reality with the help of the word. The rhetoric pathos is a merger of general pathos and the speaker's emotion. The general pathos may be heroic, sentimental, romantic, naturalistic and ironical. The heroic rules out inner reflection, and has a personality in a tragic situation for its hero. It is characterised by a particular, high-flown vocabulary and exceptional heroes. Aristotle advised to address heroic pathos to young audiences.

The sentimental pathos, its antipode, pertains to a reflective person who emotionally analyses the motives of his conduct. Sentimental pathos is a barrier to decision-making, and so can be used to stop creative activities.

The romantic pathos also includes reflection, yet it makes a choice necessary because of chaos evidently underlying it. Romantic pathos is good to prompt one to an energetic decision: circumstances – the motif of outstanding personality – necessity of decision.

The naturalistic pathos presupposes an audience standing on realistic positions, proceeding from the visible and the tangible. A particular name is contrasted to abstract ideas resulting in a standard and generalised perception of reality. Naturalistic pathos leads to criticism and stagnation of activity. It usually serves to impede decision-making.

The ironic pathos is democratic. Its strength lies in its destructive potential, so it is dangerous to recur to that kind of pathos as the speaker's main goal is to reach an accord with his audience through dialogue.

The rhetoric pathos is within the category of confidence, determined by the speaker's status, public image, well-wishing and sense of justice.

The sequence G – C – T – R is a systemic structure, so a change of one of its parts changes all the other.

Speech is a means of human communication stretching from person to person or to many. If simplified, the communication process proceeds on the following pattern. There is a speaker, message sender, and the listener, addressee. They enter a certain contact to pass a message which takes the form of a sequence of symbols – sounds, letters, etc. To receive the information we must have a particular arrangement of correspondence between elementary messages and reality known both to the sender and receiver. This system of message-reality correspondences is known as the language system or merely language, as contrasted to a multitude of messages known as speech. In speech, we always deal with a continuum while in language, with categories. herein lies the basic difference between language and speech.

Thus, according to Roman Jacobson, the communication process consists of the following six components:

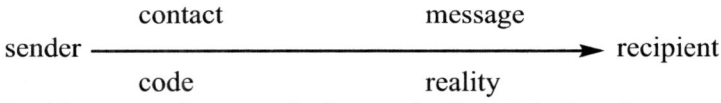

```
                  contact              message
    sender  ─────────────────────────────────► recipient
                   code                reality
```

In this connection, we single out six linguistic functions, each with a corresponding communicative reference:

1) reference to the sender, i.e., transmission of the sender's state – e.g., emotions;

2) reference to the addressee, i.e., desire to evoke his particular – e.g., emotional – state;

3) reference to the message, i.e., to the form in which it is communicated;

4) reference to the language system, i.e., the specificities of the language in which the message is communicated;

5) reference to reality, i.e., to the event which the message concerns;

6) reference to contact, i.e. to communication proper.

Reality is a continuum which every language subdivides in its own way. The problem of such subdivision can be approached from the following point. Reality is viewed as a sequence of situations – both physical, i.e., particular arrangements of objects of the physical world or the human impact on such objects, and social, i.e., human interaction. The category of situation as concrete or abstract reality is one of the principal initial categories of rhetoric. In certain instances, none but the situation determines the text as answer to the question, "What do we say in cases like this?" We can only regret that situations have never been analysed from the linguistic and, broader, semiotic point.

One thing is clear even now. The situation, especial social, must be described at the so-called level of perception or collective evaluation. Corresponding to one physical object may be totally different semantic descriptions depending on the civilisation in whose framework it is regarded. This is true not merely for the terms of immediate evaluation (good, bad) but for things, natural phenomena, animals, etc. (for instance, the cow in Europe and in India, where it is worshipped). Rhetoric proceeds from the availability of a set of situations characteristic for the mode of life and the culture of a nation speaking a particular language.

We also have to bear in mind that different linguistic means and even different languages can be used for different situations within one culture. Hence the importance of the category of sublanguage for rhetoric. By sublanguage, we mean the smallest possible arrangement of lexical and grammatical categories within the system of a particular language necessary to describe a particular material area, i.e., a particular sphere of reality.

The division into sublanguages generalises what stylistics sometimes knows as division into functional styles, and in other instances as division into terminological areas.

Only one person is always the source of speech. To be more precise, not the person speaks but his or her personality. This means that the personality can be identified by speech, sometimes against the speaker's will. That is why all countries with a high level of jurisprudence allow refusal to testify, that is, grant the right to avoid verbal communication.

There are a great many goal references of speech because they are connected with the human need of communicative influence on others – desire to persuade, move to do something, evoke a particular emotion, etc. There are also goal references which are not exactly communicative, for instance, reciting texts in solitary confinement to keep sane or not to get out of the habit of oral speech.

Every goal reference has its own linguistic and extralinguistic expressive means from the arrangement of the text and choice of vocabulary to intonation, mimics and gestures.

Any goal reference needs a moral aspect – that is, rule out conscious lie, libel, misinformation and evil in general. An immoral goal leads to false texts and, in the final analysis, to false culture or anti-culture. One ought to say only what one really believes in! Authors' disbelief in what they say or write in a multitude of false texts written and uttered under the Soviet rule created in the USSR a phenomenon unprecedented in global history – anti-culture. Perhaps, that was the worst sin of the Soviet regime, which made the entire nation a stage company in the Theatre of the Absurd. Immoral goals either directly imply false utterances or misrepresent reality.

As we regard the semantic aspect of speech, we must point out that, even with the most noble goal, it is better to keep silent when you have no ideas of your own and no precise and convincing arguments. "Improvisation is none other that a sudden and deliberate opening of a reservoir known as brain – but the reservoir ought to be full. The rich content of speech depends on the richness of thought. In fact, what you are improvising may seem new to the listener but is old for you. he speaks well who wastes the reflections of a day, week, month, or sometimes of a lifetime in a speech which lasts a mere hour," said Victor Hugo.

Many years' debates in the Russian corridors of power are crying instances of that principle shrugged off. Those debates lack an underlying idea. That is their main vice. Russia has never felt intellectual poverty so acutely as now. That is the most dire heritage of the anti-culture in which we contemporary Russians were brought up.

Speech must be arranged in such a way as to make the listener feel the speaker's competence. "You cannot be a good public speaker in all respects before you acquire a command of all essential sciences. Speech can unfold only on the basis of excellent knowledge of its subject. If there is no content underlying it, which the speaker knows and has digested, its verbal expression appears empty, childish talk." (Cicero)

Of great importance here is the speaker's family upbringing, education, erudition, and ability of logical analysis – the gifts any totalitarian regime tramples underfoot. Intellect is free by nature, and does not tolerate coercion – yet the regime kills or banishes the bearers of the most staunch intellect. Examples are close here for all to see.

The personal cultural level is an eternal value in this sense. The ignoramus cannot be allowed to rule. Likewise, he cannot be allowed to speak in public. We must not forget that "culture is reticent, ironic and self-conscious while barbarity is didactic, selfish and blood-thirsty. The ignorant start with a homily and finish with bloodshed." (Boris Pasternak)

The means to communicate a message to the reader/listener fall in two groups: linguistic (natural language means) and paralinguistic (mimicry, gestures, etc.). The former play the greater part, though a mere gesture sometimes eliminates an entire text.

Still, natural language means – phonetic, morphological, lexical and syntactic – play a far greater part. With very few exceptions, they are unique in every natural language. Much has been said about contemporary Russians' stylistic blindness and stunning bad speech. We can only regret that by glasnost (openness), the Russian mass media most often mean appearance on the air of all who want to speak as they can – while it is the media that ought to implement linguistic norms more carefully than any other.

The language recurs to all its structural levels to give expression to an idea. So, to speak correctly, we must know:

a) how to pronounce a word (the phonetico-stylistic level);
b) in what grammar form it ought to be put (grammatico-stylistic level);
c) what word or lexical combination to choose (lexico-stylistic level);
d) how to arrange the words in a sentence (syntactico-stylistic level);
e) how to arrange a coherent text out of sentences (stylistic level of supraphrasal unity);
f) how to intone the text (stylistic level of intonation).

Though the first and the last points do not concern written speech, experience shows that errors at one level are automatically accompanied by errors at others.

Man is not endowed with the gift of language by nature. He masters it in communication. Genetically, he has only the linguistic competence not performance. That is why mistakes are extremely rare in the speech of people who have been in a stylistically irreproachable milieu since babyhood. But oh, where is that milieu? Who of us has been in it since birth? Too many have to fill in educational gaps years and years too late. But never say die – that is not a task you cannot cope with.

PART I

THE CHARACTERISTICS OF ORAL COMMUNICATION

Chapter 1. **The Ethics of Speech**

> All things whatsoever ye would that men should do to you, do ye even so to them.
>
> *(Mt 7:12)*

Two problems – of speech ethics and the listener's attitude – appear at first sight to be fairly distant from each other, while really they are closely interconnected.

When man is in a particular psychological state – let say, aggressive, despondent, or depressed – which is linked to others' conduct or utterances, he is ready for aggressive action. We can hardly find a human being who would not fly into a rage in a certain situation. Yet there are social, moral and personal limits, so not every urge is followed and not every act implemented. Many die at the embryonic stage of motivation, which means that there is something in the human consciousness that allows some acts to ban others. That is the moral barrier of the personality. That barrier is certainly correlated, to an extent, with the moral level of the community, and is at the same time profoundly individual – a practical manifestation of the theory of contrary trends combined in one object. Whatever pertains to the inner moral barrier is determined by man's surroundings, by what he has seen since his birth. As moral barriers took shape in the mentality of Russians of the older and younger generations, they were amply influenced by hypocrisy, so those barriers are rather low as compared to their universal human analogues. That gives an even greater edge to interethnic communication problems. In his "Moscow Saga", Vassili Aksenov tells about a young provincial of the postwar years, who is visiting Moscow for his first time and gasps with admiration at shop windows, cars shooting past, and smiling passersby.

The boy never sees that "cruelty and lies" permeate every brick and stone in the city that has won his heart, the author says with pain. We Russians have made very small progress in our efforts to break away from cruelty and lies. That is seen the clearest as we analyse our contacts with overseas partners, which are often a failure due to a crying gap in moral standards.

As the first, and pivotal premise of rhetoric has it, speech can be addressed only to persons whom the speaker wishes well. That premise taboos a great amount of speech. If we carry it to its logical end, we see that we should not address anyone who irritates us. That is a stringent condition, and we must make it a point to observe it. Why, now, ought we not to address a person we think disagreeable?

Every action proceeds from a set of goal references known as motivation. Speech is action as any other, and a practical psychological goal always underlies it. Imagine you are addressing a man you dislike. Your address may have any purpose, for instance, to persuade him to take up French for study. You may think your goal is quite neutral, with nothing negative to it. Yet the text you produce derives from the entire range of goals you may have as you are speaking. It meets not only your basic goal, to persuade the man to take up French, but your innermost psychological goals of which you may not be fully aware.

Human intellect divides into the conscious and the unconscious, and motivations of our conduct may lie within both. We do certain things being fully aware why (conscious motivation) and we sometimes do not know why we do others (unconscious motivation). Yet there is always a goal. Unconscious motivation bases on emotions of which we sometimes are unaware, and which occasionally urge us to do unexpected things, for instance, go to a certain place at a certain time for no visible reason at all. That is the work of the unconscious, which motivates a particular part of the goal. It is usually impossible to conceal the unconscious in communication – that is the way man is made. The unconscious is a traitor – it is always open. All your inner emotions toward your interlocutor are seen and heard, whether you like it or not. They are seen better than heard because the Body Language (mimicry, gestures, countenance, pose, eyes, etc.) is the semiotic system of the unconscious. That system coexists in speech with natural language, i.e., acoustic waves reaching the listener's eardrum. Natural language is the semiotic system of the conscious, so its implementation is liable to intellectual correction. For instance, you can misinform someone when you deem it necessary. The Body Language cannot deceive – your face, eyes, pose, etc., reflect whatever you feel. Every teacher knows how easy it is to see the impression his speech makes at every pupil in class. That point concerns all participants in a communication process. The listeners, too, can make easy conclusions on the speaker and his opinions of his audience and of his own speech. Here open the non-standard opportunities of human communication.

Thus, there is no chance to conceal the unconscious. So, if, against the background of a reasonable goal, to persuade someone to study French, you feel prejudiced against the man, just now or for a long time, your feelings will be visible during the conversation. Whatever the topic of your talk may be, you tell the other, even despite your will, what you think of him. If he is a good listener and a clever man with an acute power of observation, your prejudice will certainly be unveiled. That is a first reason why you ought not to address people you dislike. Every goal requires fulfilment. You may be posing only one goal, consciously, but the entire range of unconscious goals are met at the same time. So you may receive in response what corresponds to the emotional unconscious (sometimes nothing else) instead of meeting your basic conscious target. You may be coaxing a man to join a French language class, and he will listen to you for a long time, but he will see only that you dislike him.

Rhetoric is a science of purposeful speech. It is pointless to address people you dislike – certainly with the exception of situations when you cannot avoid addressing, let say, a boss you hate like poison, or your husband before divorce, when you have to settle financial and other problems. One ought to reduce such ticklish instances to the minimum. Society has worked out sufficient remedies. For instance, you can have your lawyer negotiating with your husband as a neutral person whose speech purposes have nothing negative to them.

There is another reason why you should better not address people you dislike. It is purely moral, defies formalisation and even cannot be proved – you either accept it or shrug it off. It says that you must avoid doing bad to others if you can. There is too much evil, as it is. Then if you do someone bad, your evil will return on you sooner or later.

A second rhetorical premise, which follows from the first, says: orient your speech on the good – which means that a reference to kind feelings which you are eager to bring to those around you must necessarily be among your goals in your inner motivation. Now, what is good? the categories of good and evil belong to general philosophical categories which defy precise definition. All their dictionary definitions are conventional, imprecise and far from absolute. At the informal level, however, they are understood by all, though each and every has his own conception of those categories. Good is preternatural and appeared before evil, says the Bible. Evil is contrasted to good. Evil is what you do not wish for yourself. [This definition is universal in theology. "All things whatsoever ye would that men should do to you, do ye even so to them," says the Gospel according to St. Matthew. "Do not do upon the other what thou wishest not for thyself" (Confucius), "Do not do upon the other what harmeth thee" (Talmud), etc.] Every human feels it, and it is extremely important to realise that such feelings are individual. As we address someone, we ought to think whether he would like to hear what we intend to tell him. A large part of our prepared speech will be immediately discarded because all too often, we do not want to hear what we want to say.

Here is a simple and, alas, a very frequent instance. A young man has an affair with a girl. Her friend sees him in a restaurant with another woman and rushes to the girl to tell. Who would like to hear the news? In conformity with the second rule, rhetoric forbids such speech because it is evil by definition, and good intentions do not excuse it as they pave the road to hell. When two people meet, it is an encounter of two boundless universes. Their touch is so sophisticated in an attempt to penetrate each other that the situation is conflict-laden from the start on the personal plane. Conflict lies in its very nature. True, there are instants of harmony, but only instants as the other side of a dialectical contradiction. Private life is always a conflict situation. If a third world invades, even with good intentions, this intricately conflict situation, it can only destroy the unity of the former two, which was reached at a great price. Any attempt to influence private life from without, be it by a rival, parent, friend, teacher, father confessor – anyone, always leads the two to a bad end. You should not tolerate whatever penetration into your private life, and attempts to influence it. Man receives his fated portion of suffering by himself, and needs no help in that.

Here is a convincing practical example. A young woman was enthusiastically saying to her workmates, again and again: "My husband is working at his thesis. He stays into morning in the State Public Library night reading room!" As it really was, the library closed at half past nine every night, and had no round-the-clock reading room – but the loving woman did not know it till a well-wishing lady friend advised her to look up the library working hours. Divorce was the closest result of her utterance. More fruit came later – the woman's misery, her husband's broken career, and two neurotic children madly loving their father. A few words destroyed four or even more lives and the two kids' future families as a child who grows in a shattered household develops bad complexes, which his children are doomed to inherit. Even a short utterance can do great evil. The tongue is the most destructive of all weapons known to man. Moral education in love and compassion for the neighbor must start at home in the tender age. Later on, man's eyes can open to it without bidding from without. Once you make a profound and unbiased analysis of any human, you soon develop a realisation of life as sequence of suffering – and love and pity come to your heart unasked.

Instances as the above are extremely rare in many countries. It is typical in Russia not because we Russians are born scoundrels but because we grew in an atmosphere of cruel and false communication which totalitarianism forced on us – an atmosphere in which utterances like that are within the moral standard. Did any of us ever hear as a child that such things are better left unsaid because another may find it painful to know them? Yet this is a norm of the civilised world, whose basic law is non-interference in another's privacy. Speech communication is called to provide a beneficial psychological situation. Such communication is learned and trained in childhood.

Speech must benefit not harm people. Treat your partner in a conversation as God's own child on earth, entitled to the utmost love and respect. Does anyone grant us the right to break into another's privacy and judge it? Are we allowed to influence matters of another's vital interest? No one is judge unto another. That is why contemporary society has elaborated a ramified arrangement of regulations which help people to coexist. Each of us is obliged to follow those rules.

Chapter 2. **The Position of the Listener**

> What is a reliable basis for
> something is not for me to decide.
> *Ludwig Wittgenstein*

The listener is the one you must not hurt, the object of your speech. The listener comes into the foreground in the pair, speaker-listener. He has priority in speech communication. His priority has two aspects—psychological and physiological.

Let us start with analysing the psychological aspect. We arrange the system of speech communication as a chain of four links: goal – concept – text – response (see above). The concept of speech is connected with the listener's position and individual psychology the closest. Imagine you want to call someone to spend an evening with you at the theatre in connection with your goal. You can use diverse arguments to persuade him to go: 1) the play is very interesting; 2) it was staged by sensational Roman Viktyuk; 3) the theatre bar always has Tuborg beer; 4) that's a good chance for a night out; 5) it is always worthwhile to shirk your duties for entertainment, etc. Understandably, one person can never perceive the entire set of offered arguments. Proceeding from your listener's tastes and cultural level, you say to one: "Come, it's a Viktyuk production!" as the only effective argument, while to another you may say: "Come, they always have Tuborghard to get it anywhere else!" and he will go to the theatre without the least attention to the play. Another, who has a hell of a life at home, will fall in for, "Come, have a nice night out!", and so on. Some people need several arguments at once. So you ought to choose your arguments depending on your listener's psychological type, age, sex, ethnicity, the language he or she speaks, intellect, present psychological state, and health. That was a simple example, but the principle underlying it works in defending even the most sophisticated premises on which human lives or major research problems may depend.

The listener's personality alone determines the choice of arguments, which accounts for his priority. So, before you start speaking, you have to make painstaking analyses, especially when you address a stranger—for instance, a pretty girl, somewhat exotically dressed, whom you have never seen before and about whom you do not know anything. The girl may look provocative, but she really is clever and well-read, does not like beer, and has seen all Viktyuk productions. You offer to drive her home in your car while her Volvo is parked round the corner. You choose the wrong arguments and do not get your end. As extra response to your speech, you get a witty, biting verbal rebuff after which you long cannot get to your senses.

Analyse your listener's personality before you speak, or your arguments will not strike home, and your speech will be not to the purpose with an unpredictable result. Many go through that. So intellectual work to evaluate your listener before speaking is a necessary job. In spontaneous speech communication, You do the most thinking when you have to enter a dialogue with a complete stranger: you ought to pay attention to his or her age, sex, clothes, tone of voice, the presence or absence of stylistic errors in the very first words your interlocutor utters, and the place where you meet – here, it makes a world of difference whether it is a conservatory concert hall or a communist rally. Analyse everything you see, and then start unobtrusively to tune in to the other, avoiding categorical utterances and attentively watching the response to every word you say. Such psychological sounding is part and parcel of the model of obtaining communicative priority at the level of an initial contact on the pattern, one speaker/one opponent.

A more complicated communicative situation comes with one speaker/many opponents, that is, speaking to an audience. How can you rule a gathering of many people, all with differing value orientations, some of mutually contrasting convictions, and all in different psychological states? You cannot do that before you realise that when many congregate in a particular place at a particular time, they must share the reason to come there. If we designate the space of one person with a circle, we have the many circles crossing at a point to see what they share.

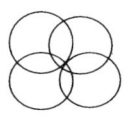

Speech to an audience must orient on the crossing zone, which we have to spot beforehand through logic, that is, guess what is bringing all those people together. It may be their duty to come, as an obligatory college lecture, or interest in the speaker or the topic of his speech, and many other reasons.

There are difficult and easy audiences. Student audiences are among the easiest as consisting of people who share a motivation level, language, national culture, age, career priorities, etc. Difficult audiences can be exemplified by a constituency rally a parliamentary hopeful is addressing. The nominee wants to be heard by as many as possible. Underlying that goal may be a variety of reasons – power urge, patriotism, thirst for publicity, and so on, and so forth. A thesis emerges at the concept level: "I am socially useful. If they vote for me, people will get the chance to live a better life." That thesis is proved to the many voter groups through a set of arguments – the pre-election programme. The arguments are oriented on most diverse social groups – soldiers, professional people, disabled persons, and many others. If the candidate visits a disabled persons' shelter to tell them in detail about his programme concerning the army – be it soldier welfare or reduced conscription service term – he will never catch his audience's attention, and his speech will be pointless. One cannot interest people in anything that does not concern their own interests. The candidate will also be an utter failure if he speaks about disabled persons' plight in a military cantonment. That is evident. But how to arrange a pre-election address in a polling station conference hall, where all kinds of people gather – of different age, income, social status and education – some in an unruly psychological state? That is an extremely unwieldy audience, and it may seem that such a gathering cannot be persuaded in anything. That is wrong – any audience can be persuaded. That is a matter of intellectual priority – you have given thought to the situation while the people on the audience are totally unprepared – they have not been thinking about you. Now think why they have all come here, as this is a voluntary gathering. Each may have many reasons of his own, but one, even small, has to be shared – they are all dissatisfied. The rich and complacent do not go to listen to parliamentary hopefuls. They all must feel robbed. Sometimes, their problems are personal not social, yet such problems are unconsciously sublimated into a sense of social wrong. Uncertainty and dissatisfaction has brought all those different people together. What is the speaker to do in that situation? Go into the centre of the room, stand there – or sit down, which will produce a better impression, and try to bring home to the audience the following: "It's a hell of a life – with me, too." The speaker must become part of the area of psychological crossing for a confidential talk about despondency and shattered illusions which have brought them all together. You can talk to people only about their concerns, Emotional solidarity gradually reconciles the audience to the speaker, and they become friends. The candidate does not need to make practical promises – his audience gets what it has gathered for. The people are feeling better because shared grief seems easier to bear. The chance to see that life is tough on others, too, helps to cope with stress. So the speaker gets his end – his audience's votes.

The listener's priority to the speaker is also rooted in the physiological aspect of speech communication: it is harder to listen than to speak.

What the speaker does is known as speech synthesis according to a preset message, in conformity with which the speaker synthesises his speech. The zone of meaning known as semantic representation, *SemR*, is at a deep level. This set of information nuclei, or semantic quanta, has no linear arrangement. They are present in our mind as a sophisticated multi dimensional structure, while speech is linear at the implementation level – a word endowed with meaning is followed by another word. That is why we have to arrange a linear sequence out of a multi-dimensional semantic environment. Coping with that duty is a syntactic block, or syntactic representation, *SyntR*. Syntax is a linear arrangement of semantic units, an arrangement not yet divided into words, not government by rules of grammar – for instance, a pattern on which the meaning of the plural is attached to the word as a grammar index in Russian, and a separate word in Chinese. That is the mission of the morphological representation, *MorphR*, that is, grammar, which divides linear units into word-forms. At the uppermost level, the divided morphological units – words – come up in a text at the level of sounds, when articulated, or letters when written and read. That is the phonetic representation, *PhonR* in oral speech and graphic, *GraphR* in written.

Speech synthesis is a transition from the meaning to the text, where an arrangement of phonetic or graphic units is meant by text:

SemR ➤ *SyntR* ➤ *MorphR* ➤ *PhonR (GraphR)*.

Textual analysis, the listener's duty, is the same sequence the other way round. A sound wave reaches the acoustic analyser at the moment of listening next to be divided by the brain into meaningful units as words are identified in an unbroken stream of speech. That is the morphological representation. Words are perceived in speech as linearly arranged, and understanding, e.g., of the speech subject and object, emerges in conformity with that arrangement. That is the syntactic representation. Then comes the exit into the zone of ideas which are not linearly arranged, have no precise associative system, and are individual in every human mind. That is a movement reverse to synthesis:

PhonR (GraphR) ➤ *MorphR* ➤ *SyntR* ➤ *SemR*.

The priority of synthesis to analysis is not evident from the point of evaluating the structural complexity of the two sequences. Both procedures are comparable in terms of the complication of their implementation. It is movement in opposite directions along the same root.

Why, then, is analysis harder than synthesis? When you speak, you are not harassed by noise. First, you are unaware of physical noise as the human larynx and organs of articulation are very close to the ear, which always controls man's own speech. They are so close that only a very bad noise can harass the speaker. This means, in particular, that classroom noise harasses the teacher less than anyone else – he hears himself in any situation. Thus, the speaker is performing outside physical noise, and outside intellectual noise, as well. You cannot think about one thing and speak about another – that is the way the human brain is made. Anyone who attempts to do that loses the string of thought, and cannot produce meaningful speech. That means that the speaker enjoys a unity of thought and speech, and so the inner – psychological and intellectual – noise does not bother him. The listener, unlike him, is decoding the sound wave, which is a difficult thing to do, especially when the speaker does not articulate well – an instance in which speech decoding is at its hardest. More than that, any noise interrupts the sound wave to remove a part of units from it, so the brain has to decode the meaning proceeding from an incomplete outer expression. Still, it decodes even when the hearing is bad. If the topic catches the listener's interest, he will ask to repeat. That is why students who talk or noisily fumble their papers in classroom harass those who are listening. The latter get nervous fatigue and develop a headache toward the end of the class. There is another aspect – inner noise at the time of hearing. A haunting idea is always present at the back of one's mind, so two actions often go on simultaneously: you think of your problem as your brain is decoding a sound wave aimed at your acoustic analyser. That is why mental activity is far more complicated in speech analysis than synthesis. The two processes are comparable for labor consumption but conditions in which the two are implemented defy comparison. That is why priority in speech communication belongs to the listener.

Chapter 3. **The Conscious/Unconscious and Lie in Oral Communication**

> To be is the surest way to seem.
> *Socrates*

As we said above, the human intellect divides into the conscious and the unconscious. Behavioral motives may lie in either, and both are manifest in a particular human action, in particular, speech.

Let us regard the problem in detail as applied to a peculiar kind of speech communication – attempt at deception.

When one speaks, especially when you see the speaker, he is transmitting 1) information proper, which is usually within the sphere of the conscious; 2) his attitude to that information;3) his attitude to the people to whom his speech is addressed. As a rule, the speaker wants to conceal his attitude to information and other people as he is not always well-wishing enough to his listeners, while he treats his information as unreliable if he means to deceive. It is difficult to divulge his true attitude to information and his interlocutors in written speech at the level of the natural language, *NL*, while there is a negligible chance to conceal it in oral speech as the Body Language, *BL*, symbols demonstrate his unconscious desire to conceal emotional information. It ought to be understood that when the listener catches you on a lie, he does it only within his mind and will not say out loud that he does not believe what you say. If you are deceiving him, he will feel your negative attitude to him, if that is really the matter, and will give a relevant emotional response (see the chapter, "The Ethics of Speech". Indicatively, he receives that information unconsciously, as a rule, i.e., he feels inner dissatisfaction with speech communication, and will produce a response extremely undesirable to you. Thus, the *BL* is in itself the traitor of the human unconscious. That has to be so, in all probability: if there is sin there must be punishment (this dichotomy is necessarily present in human communication as dialectical opposition).

The natural language and the Body Language as systems of signs thoroughly differ from each other. The basic difference lies in the linear arrangement of *NL* while *BL* is a vertically arranged paradigmatic column with many symbols realised simultaneously while it is impossible to arrange a consecutive text. This coexistence of two functioning sign systems in the human conduct is striking from the point of evaluation of the human intellectual potential. To see how it is all complicated, we need merely to try to make thoroughly different things with the right hand and the left – for instance, horizontal movements of the right and stabs by the left. This hard task demands special mental training as it is difficult for the brain to send different impulses to the different parts of the body, i.e., coordinate different activities of one body. As to oral speech, two different sign systems are constantly at work within it, yet man does not feel marked discomfort. This means that all intellectual efforts at that time are concentrated in the conscious: man thinks hard about what he is saying, while the *BL* system is functioning spontaneously to betray him even worse as he has no intellectual force to spare for control of it. We really cannot keep that elemental power in control. Even when we do not forget that they have to control our countenance in certain situations, we do not cope with the task well enough. Professional training of actors, spies and others is very long and hard. It is difficult to demonstrate *BL* signs in conformity with a particular inner scheme.

Apart from information proper and the interlocutor, emotions transmitted through *BL* may be addressed to the speaker himself. That is, speech can express the speaker's inner state irrespective of particular speech – a state which continues preceding developments and in which the speech started. Such emotions also find expression through *BL* signs.

The speaker's attitude to his interlocutor can change with the change of the latter's response during talk. The sight of boredom on the audience's faces can evoke his negative response, and the speaker changes his tone or, partly, the content of speech to catch the audience's attention, and sees more vivid response, interest lighting in the eyes, etc. The speaker responds in his turn with a better mood, and his speech becomes even more expressive in a chain reaction. So, when we refer to attitudes to the partner in speech communication, we also mean the preliminary attitude, formed before the start of speech – for instance, when the speaker has been connected throughout his lifetime with the person whom he addresses, and the changeable attitude which arises in the speech process. Sometimes, a serious conversation spectacularly improves problem-laden relations between people, and a wave of well-wishing overflows them. We can only regret that contrary developments are most often the case.

Thus, the psychological situation which connects you with your partner in communication can change for other *BL* signs to show your body and face in an uncontrollable process. Because of that lack of control, you can ask an essential, long-pondered question, and your partner does not reply at once but in ten seconds or so – but you know the answer immediately from his blush, shrug or look. Even when the belated verbal reply is not what you expect from the bodily response, that reply is not truthful. A psychologist would correct the known warning, "Beware of the first moves of your soul – they are the most noble," into "Beware of the first moves of your soul – they are the most sincere." Response at the BL level cannot be concealed. It is the truth. Vexation is discernible more clearly than other emotions though it is carefully masked when speech starts a few instants later. Joy and displeasure are also rather visible, especially when they are aroused by your appearance. A wealth of contradictions and incongruities against the initial and most spontaneous response become evident as soon as the conscious *NL* system starts working. What ought to guide our subsequent conduct – the initial response or the speech that follows? It is hard to say. On the one hand, you now know the true response from BL signs; on the other hand, the man has his own hidden goals and may later act in keeping with a decision with which he benefits and which he takes at the logical level, rather than proceeding from his true, emotional response. So you have to judge whether to reckon with the listener's initial, spontaneous response for every particular instance. A statement of yours, let say, vexes your listener but he overcomes his emotion and, for some inner reason, determines to go on talking to you. The knowledge of his vexation, however, is food for thought as you choose the following communicative tactic, and ought to be reckoned with.

A psychological state usually survives for a long time. When you bicker with your family in the morning or are in a traffic shock, you sometimes enter speech communication in the same mood all day long. *BL* signs reflect your state, not in the least correlated with what you say. That is very awkward to the speaker. You come to your office or institute after a home scene, and see a man who interests you and whose acquaintance benefits you. Unable to bridle your emotions, you manifest your exasperation in the conversation without mentioning the morning scene. The man sees a range of negative emotions – grief, wounded pride, malice – in your face, and unconsciously puts it on his own account. It will be very hard later to explain the misunderstanding. That is how lives take the wrong turn. A man obsessed with a bad health or career problem is always gloomy and prepossessed when he meets with the woman he loves. The woman blames herself for his gloom. One of the reasons for pathological, informationally deformed communication lies in the inadequate state of people entering such communication. That state has no bearing on concrete speech but manifests itself in that speech to evoke a transformed or false impression in the listener. Even a top-notch professional commands BL only to an extent. You need time to control yourself, give yourself commands concerning bodily movement, countenance and the expression of the eyes, and you can gain that time with a communicative pause.

You also ought to see that a man obsessed by emotion often does not want it to go. He needs it. Really, the human psyche is paradoxical and surprising. You may welcome even negative emotion. When an embittered man is being consoled, inner resistance often starts as he is loath to leave his emotional state. Understandably, one is even more reluctant to quit a complacent or euphoric mood.

In all those instances, you ought to regain self-control and conceal your psychological state in speech communication lest you are misunderstood by the listener at the unconscious level. They will be under the impression that your state concerns them – and will be wrong. Positive response is, in a sense, worse than negative. When you are euphoric, for instance, thanks to requited love, everyone who communicates with you thinks your exaltationis addressed to him – a dangerous turn as man is capable of evoking congruent emotion in others. That is why you have to keep your mood secret by an effort of will. It will be perceived correctly and transferred to another object, again to find expression in BL signs. When you are in an emotional excitement, you ought to mix as little as possible with people who bear no relation to your state. Many see that point intuitively. That is why lovers do not need communication with others. When you are angry, you also would not like strangers around. Being under strong emotion is not the time for communication with people to whom you do not owe that state. People must be spared.

People greatly differ in that respect – some are reserved, and do not impose their emotional state on those around; others, obtrusive, are always eager to shift their psychological problems on you, and you find it hard to shed that burden. Imagine only people of the latter kind surrounding you. Can you survive under an emotional press of, let say, twenty people, even when they are your near and dear or, at least, close acquaintances? Each of us ought to display an extent of communicative modesty, though emotions sometimes take the upper hand, and man needs help to overcome them in such an extremity.

Personal attitude to information is also an emotion, and is transferred by the BL arrangement as any other emotion. That issue is related to the categories of the true and false in speech communication. It is typical for people to deceive each other because, in the inner motivation, a lie is sometimes regarded as the best way out of a predicament. From times immemorial, disputes have been going on about the morality or immorality of deception. Has man the right to lie, and how a lie is to be punished are eternal questions, the answer to which is unknown to this day. What, now, is a lie in speech? First, we ought to see what is the truth and what the untruth – when is true to reality and what is not. Here a contradiction arises carried by man due to the natural limitations of his potential. The world around him is arranged in a particular way. Man has visual, acoustic, tactile and olfactory analysers with whose help he perceives the world. Is there a guarantee of correct perception? There is none, and none can be. The answer to that question, which, in fact, concerns the cognoscibility of the world, divides people from times immemorial in two camps, depending on their materialistic or idealistic approach to the world outside. If our analysers perceive the world adequately, it is cognisable, and we can pose ourselves the task of ever closer approach to knowledge. If our analysers largely distort the world outside, the question of cognoscibility ought not to be posed at all. If the world perception is badly distorted through analysers' errors, is this distortion universal or individual? As the subjective idealistic concept sees it, every man has a world perception all his own. So there is no adequate human perception of the world, and human mutual understanding is conventional. This categorical conclusion may be not far from the truth.

Let us regard an example. To each of us, other people are among the facts of the outer world, which consists not only of seas, plains, mountains and woods but of humans. Take a man, M, acquainted with, let say, 500 other people, and ask them what kind of person M is. We shall certainly receive 500 diverse descriptions. Some of them will closely resemble each other, and some mutually contrasting, though they all concern one and the same person. That proves inadequate performance of our analysers, and the fact that the information wave which reaches our brain decoded after the analysers perceive it produces an inadequate analysis of impressions from the outer world. This is understandable as analyses largely depend on man's personal experience and system of associations and values. If perception were adequate, a situation would be ruled out in which there are so many opinions of one and the same person. Surely, opinions coincide more often on objects simpler than man—yet this does not cancel the problem for evaluating complicated objects.

The problem of adequate world perception has a pure linguistic aspect, as well. We can say about every natural language unit that it repeatedly occurs in speech, that is, the speech flow divides in repetitive elements. The first type of articulation concerns sounds in oral speech and letters in written, i.e., units which in themselves have no meaning (one-sided units). The second type concerns meaningful parts – units endowed with meaning, or double-sided units: morphemes, words and phrases. For instance, *m-e-d-i-a-t-i-o-n* is the minimum articulation of the first type, while *med-ia-tion* of the second. We can assuredly say of every unit obtained as the result of articulation – of the first and second types alike – that it has repeatedly occurred in diverse variants.

Articulation of speech is part of a more general concept of discreteness. What is continuity? A mathematical function is continuous when sufficiently small changes of the argument lead to infinitely small changes of the function. Pressure continuously changes when we are pumping a balloon. Discreteness determines not continuous but intermittent changes from one object/state into another, which leads to simplification. Thus, the telephone time service was saying "eleven forty" throughout the minute in the recent past. Dependencies in which infinitely small changes of the argument lead to finite changes of the function are known as discrete. The principle of discrete dependence is deep in Nature – the cell can be in one of the two states, calm or irritation. There is a barrier below which is calm, and above, irritation. The transition from the one state into the other is not gradual but abrupt. The discreteness principle underlies all sign systems. Take the traffic light. Whatever shades of red, yellow and green it may have, our response reduces to the three basic states, which means that this particular system has three classes to which all the colours are reduced.

Natural language bases on the discreteness principle. As, for instance, we regard the phonetic system of speech, we see a vast variety of, let say, [a]. This multitude of shades is perceived similarly – everyone understands it is an [a] irrespective of the voice, its tone, etc. The discreteness principle saves a vast amount of energy. Herein lies its tremendous significance. We ought to realise, at the same time, that discreteness is in the projection of the numerous, sometimes infinite (e.g., a segment) on the unitary (e.g., a point). A large number of similar objects – let say, tables – form in the language user's mind a generalised concept fixed by one lexical unit, the word "table".

The human consciousness divides an infinite in its changes color spectrum into sections, each has its name: "yellow", "green", "blue" and so on. Obviously, that information can be transferred with the use of a linear text only, if the text consists of discrete unites. At that the transmitted information considerably simplifies the actual pattern of the reality (in the direct proportion of bringing the section to the point). It is interesting that the natural languages perform this simplification in different ways. For instance, the Russian language divides the color spectrum into seven sec-

27

tions; the English language does it into six sections and the not written tone language – into two sections. (Upon the evident uniformity of the visual analyzer the native speakers of these three languages think that the rainbow has seven, six or, correspondingly, two colors; they perceive the set of the rainbow colors exactly in this way.)

Tone language	Colors of warm tones	Colors of cold tones
English	red orange yellow	green blue purple
Russian	red orange yellow	green blue purple light blue

The language does not repeat the inner organization of the material world. The freedom lies in the basis of the senses organization; they are independent. The natural language is connected with the world not directly, but through its organization. At that the organization in different countries varies. The Russian native speaker clearly perceives any object in a single or plural form, however there are many languages (for instance, the languages of the South-Eastern Asia), wherein it is not necessary to tell the number, it is considered to be a facultative factor (compare, please, with the unnecessariness, say, in the Russian language, to say "little" or "big"). The Japanese or Chinese languages do not distinguish the persons of verbs, but at the same time they distinguish with the full grammatical strictness the degrees of respect to the interlocutor. The English, French and German languages impose on the native speakers the category of distinctness/uncertainty, which is expressed by the article: "A house is on the hill" (uncertainty), "The house is on the hill" (distinctness).

As various languages divide the reality in different ways, there is a grounded assumption that the native speakers perceive the surrounding world in accordance with the said division, which is imposed by their native language. According to the concept, called a hypothesis of the linguistic relativity, the language structure determines the thinking structure and the method of the outer world comprehension. American linguists E. Sapir and B. Whorf elaborated the hypothesis within the framework of the ethnolinguistic. Under this hypothesis the language determines the logical order of thinking. The character of the reality structure depends on the language in which the comprehending subject is thinking. The people divide the world into parts; they organize it into the definitions and distribute the meanings in this, not that way, since they are the participants in a certain agreement, which is valid only for this language. The comprehension does not have any objective and common character: "Similar physical phenomena enable one to create a similar pattern of the Universe only upon the similarity or at least upon the correspondence of linguistic structure" (B.J. Whorf). "The people live not only in the objective world, and not only in the world of public activity, as they usually suppose, but to a large measure they stay under the influence of that concrete language, which turned out to be a means of expression for this concrete society. It would be wrong to assume that we can comprehend the reality in full without using the language, or think that the language appears as an accessory means of solving some special problems of communication and thinking. In fact "the real world" to a great extent unconsciously is constructed on the basis of the linguistic norms inherent in a certain group of people... We see, hear or differently perceive the reality in this, not that way, as the linguistic norms of our society predispose to a certain choice of interpretations", i.e. "they propose a certain form of expression" (E. Sapir).

So, one cannot say about an absolute adequacy of the outer world projection onto the human consciousness. If it is so, then what is the lie, when our reaction to the outer world by itself is of a distorted character? The lie appears as one of the communicative functions. The lie in a speech is said to be a distrust of the man to the verity of the things that he speaks about. Neither the objective lie, nor the objective truth, but the trust is given to the man in the knowledge. It is interesting that nobody knows what is the lie; however, when a man lies, but he always understands it this is a lie. The category of a trust is not formalized; the object of the trust cannot be either proved, or disproved, however, every person feels it in his sole. Under this category one ought to understand the trust in the God, trust in the verity, trust in the fairness and so on, and, correspondingly, the distrust in the God, verity and fairness... It is a factor, which psychological foundation lies deep in the unconsciousness.

It does not seem possible to determine the category of a lie from the terminological point of view; the dictionary interpretations do not give the understanding, however, every person knows what it means. However, this knowledge is absolutely individual (Compare, please, the definition of the category of evil, which is different for every person). In the same way the lie represents that thing, which the person by itself considers to be a lie, i.e. the thing that he does not believe in. Such categories as "good", "evil", "lie", "truth", "happiness" and so on can be determined only functionally, not in a static way. They appear as functions of a certain argument, wherein under the argument one ought to understand every concrete person, and depending on the fact what kind of an argument is it (i.e. what kind of a person is it) the function value may vary. With no doubt, such categories shall exist: if they do not, the people would live in the dogmatic world of absolute truths that is absolutely not inherent in the human consciousness, which is dialectic by its nature.

What is the mechanism of communication upon the lie? The speaker transmits a disinformation, i.e. information, which he considers as wrong. Together with the disinformation in spite of his will he transmits by the BL sings his relation to the disinformation and to the speech communicant. What kind of relation is it? An inner relation of a person to the disinformation is negative: the brain painfully perceives any intellectual inadequacy; the nervous system comes to the state of stress. All lie detectors are constructed on the basis of this principle. A lie detector perceives nervous impulses, i.e. the excitation of the central nervous system. When a person lies, his nervous system finds itself in the state of stress and the analyzers fix it. The listener perceives the same negative state of an excitation through the BL sings without any help of a lie detector. It is interesting that when lying the person feels so strong psychical discomfort that it influences on the irradiated informational bio-emanations, which not only people, but also plants like begonia can perceive. An American investigator Carlson and a Russian professor V. Pushkin carried out very interesting experiments in this respect. The probationers were asked to go through a test by a lie detector. But the investigators did not attach any analyzers and apparatus, usually used in similar cases; they left to begonia to determine how truthful were their answers. The operator chose a number from 1 to 10, but he concealed it. He said "no" to each of the called numbers, i.e. one of the answers was false. As to the contrast of the operator's energetic emanation intensity the plant exactly determined the target number, showing a characteristic wavy line on the tape of the encephalograph.

In addition to the information, which the listener does not know about either it is a truth or a lie; he fixes the interlocutor's nervousness and his internal anxiety.

When speaking about the relation to the speech communicant, one ought to notice that it is negative at the moment of lying. When we mislead somebody, we dislike him. It is very important to understand. Maxim Gorkiy in his novel "The Life of Klim Samgin" says about the fact that we like people for that good, which we did for them, and dislike for that evil, which we brought to them. It is psychologically founded. If a man did something good to another person, the communication with him every time reminds him of his mental grandeur and therefore stimulates strong positive emotions. "I am a so noble man that did a good to you for nothing. I love you for that thing, since you symbolize by yourself my nobleness. And if I brought the evil to you, you become a reproach for my depravity. And if you are a reproach, then what for shall I love you?" – that is a mechanism of the self-estimation in the communication.

When a person is misled, of course, they do evil to him. As the outer world projects itself on our consciousness to a great error measure, every crumb of the truth takes on a special value: it helps the human being to orient himself in the surroundings. When you mislead him you deprive him of the useful for him information. The world pattern in his consciousness jumps even more. It is compared with a blind person, who came into a strange room with three windows with the one of them open. If you deceive the blind person that the room has only two windows, having felt them he will get quiet and very possibly he will die falling out from the third window. Thus, upon the deception one can face the following communicative situation: The listener 1) perceive the information without knowing either it is true or not; 2) feels the irritation of the speaker's central nervous system, it puts him on his guard and provokes his reciprocal nervousness; 3) feels that he is treated badly. The reciprocal reaction is the same: what is transmitted, that is received (by analogy with a boomerang). As information 2) and 3) is transmitted by the unconsciousness block, then it is received by the unconsciousness block too. The person even does not understand that he formed the reciprocal negative relation, however it happened and he will proceed to act in accordance with his mental state. The subtlety of this matter lies in the fact that both participants in the communication do not realize it. An inner psychological state is transferred from one participant in the communication to another and it returns, coming into the sphere of those inner spontaneous motives, which determine the human behavior. The listener will return all the evil that he received. By what means, a priory, it is hard to assume, but not always through the lie. It is also is not known when, may be after a long time, but he will return it, for sure.

It is understandable that the more a person is subjected to the lie, the more is his reciprocal reaction. The judicial psychiatry has a fixed case, which proves it. A married couple lived together 10 years. He was always unfaithful to her, but he did it so skillfully and cunningly that she never unmasked him: every time when leaving the house, he found convincing reasons for his absence. The wife never expressed her suspicious at the speech level, though she was subjected to the lie for ten years. They lived quite a happy life and had no particular conflicts. One day the husband was found dead – his wife poisoned him. During the investigation sobbing she admitted that she poisoned him, but she could not explain why she did so. Or she thought out a certain ridiculous reason that, actually, did not appear as a reason, instead it represented a substitution of the true reason, which lay much more deeper. The woman behaved so strangely that it was necessary to call for a psychiatrist. The psychiatrist made up a conclusion that she was perfectly healthy. And only psychoanalytic (an expert on the unconsciousness zone of the human psychic) was able to explain the motive of the crime: a reciprocal aggressive reaction of the unconscious to the prolonged deception, which the conscious failed to disclose. (Fortunately, the reciprocal reaction is not always so ominous). The woman was asked how she felt herself in this marriage. She thought that it was not so bad, but then it was revealed that she was often depressed. No one, including herself, was able to explain it. However, there was a reason: the woman constantly was subjected to the disinformation and always felt negative relation to her. In such cases the crime is conceived by the unconscious long before its realization. At first one can feel an unconscious interest to drug stores, then to special drugs that can be bought in the drug store, then one of such drugs is bought for some purpose and surely concealed somewhere in the house, then to be used one day.

The psychoanalysis of quite many criminal cases is similar. Any evil that a man brings transmitting a disinformation returns to him in this or that way. Onus understanding this fact one can decide for himself to what extent it is expedient to deceive other people.

We have discussed the speech communication under the conditions of the undisclosed lie. Upon the situation of the disclosed lie the communicative model looks somewhat different. At this moment the speaker faces very dangerous situation, connected with the full loss of the authority in the opinion of not only the man, who caught him in a lie, but also of all those who were present at the moment of disclosure. The speaker loses the trust also in addition to the authority loss. The authority and trust belong to the categories, which are hard to obtain, but easy to lose and practically it is impossible to renew them. It is quite a common case when in the beginning of the mutual life one of the spouses deceived another and it was revealed. He/she was forgiven, but after that he/she was treated with distrust for the whole life. Because it seems impossible to renew the lost trust, then if you were caught in a lie, you would better never enter into the communication with this man (most likely he/she will leave your surrounding or may keep formally staying with you; there will be no more such warm and trustworthy relations with him/her).

The public exposure of a lie is a big disgrace. As usual the person has a hard time upon this and he remembers it for the whole life. Everybody, whose speech conduct is based on a lie, lives with a threat of such a disgrace.

The moral aspect appears as an important aspect of the discussed type of communication. The lie is an evil in respect to the speech communicant and every time, when a man lies, he ought to think over to what measure he wants that this evil to be directed towards him. No one likes to be deceived. From the moral point of view one should not deceive people. However, the moral barrier represents such a barrier that every person set for himself/herself; it cannot be imposed from without. Therefore to what extent you presume a sinful relation to other people, you permit yourself to enter into the false communication with them.

Of course, there are such every day life situations, when it seems that the person shall be deceived due to the thoughts of humanism ("white lie"). As a diffused example they usually provide an example of a hopelessly sick person, to whom nobody says about the irreversibility of his disease, instead, they say that he is recovering and today he looks much better than yesterday. Shall one act in this way? It appears that the "white lie" represents a function, with the personality of the sick person as an argument. Depending on the personality of the person, to whom you are addressing, you are able to estimate the relevancy or irrelevancy of the deception. If you face a strong person, who used to take independent decisions (it is a well-known fact that to take a decision one needs a trustworthy information), by the deception you bring him evil, depriving him of the perception of truth and of an adequate decision-making. The person wants to sum up the results of his life and you deprive him of the possibility to understand that the time has come. By hiding the true information you do not enable him to realize in his life the things that he intended to do. As a result we have an unfinished book, unfinished film, unfinished song and so on. If the person believes in the God and as an average man he sinned a lot, he needs some time to repent. The time for repentance is not that hour, which the priest spends at the bed of the dying person, it is a time and the person shall have this time. (Why do the verily faithful people categorically raise an objection to the death penalty for even the most terrible criminals? Since if a person dies a violent death, he won't have time for repentance, and if he is leaved alive he will find time to do it.) It is not the only cases, wherein the thought about the "white lie" as a good does not seem so obvious. One ought to remember about the purely medical factor. There are fixed cases of a considerable energization of the human organism's protective forces: if a person is directly said that he is dying, the organism finds out an internal reserve, which wins the disease that cannot be won in ordinary circumstances. So strong is a thirst for life. When the diseases are incurable, the human immune system fails to control it. It is known that the bioenergetics method of treatment is based on the stimulation of the protective forces exactly of the immune system. The words of truth can turn out to be such a stimulator. So, one ought to treat the thesis of the "white lie" with a great care and quite individually.

Chapter 4. **The Three Types of Information Reception and Transmission**

> One shall not consider the weakness in helping himself with a word as to be not disgraceful, since the use of words is more typical to the human nature than the use of the body.
>
> *Aristotle*

What does a man speak for? What for does he need an apparatus that is to produce a speech flow or a text? The answer is to transmit information. The universal designation of any speech is to transmit information. A certain meaning underlies the flow of sounds or letters as the language is arranged in this way. A meaningless sequence of sounds (even verbal) does not produce a speech or a text. Meanwhile, a meaningful sequence of sounds transmitted by a speaker and understood by a listener produces a text. More over, a text that is clear to the transmitter (the speaker) and meaningless to the receiver (the listener or reader) cannot be referred to be a text in proper sense of the word. For instance, the people who speak Russian do not consider the following phrase said in Swahili to be a text: "Anawasifu watoto wa wageni wangu" that means, "He praises my guests' children". This phrase is incomprehensible and it cannot be comprehensible since they do not know the Swahili language.

An individual is empowered with the linguistic competence to comprehend the natural language and communication in this language. The natural language as a semiotic arrangement has semiotic structure and it provides by itself an optimal tool to transmit information. When using the natural language an individual pursues two objectives: first, to transmit information, and second, to comprehend the world. Consequently, the language is taken as a means of comprehension. What does the comprehension mean? As the term, the comprehension can be referred to as information reception; however, it is not its proper definition. One ought to say that the natural language serves information reception and transmission. Except that the function of thinking is to receive and transmit information, it is precisely the thinking that solely deals with information reception, evaluation and transmission. Such a view enables one to consider thinking and the language to be a single essence. Over many years the linguistics as a science identified both definitions for a certain extent. A wealth of books and articles were published having in their titles the words of "language and thinking". These texts have arguments in favor of double-headed essence of the objective (in particular, Noam Chomsky' s famous book "The language and thinking". Noam Chomsky is the founder of the leading linguistic concept of the 20-th century – the theory of transformative producing grammars. This book is fundamental for the contemporary linguistic science development. See Chapter "Demonstration by analogy"). The natural language seemed long to be an ideal model for thinking. Until recent years the linguistics kept to the issue that intellectual activity projects itself onto the language and vice versa, thus making a single essence.

When you hear somebody' s saying like "in ideal model" or "ideal arrangement", it is wise to ask a question – What is it compared with to decide that it is the best one? Since, as a rule, when you want to recognize the advantage of a certain object you shall compare it with the others present. This is a usual practice when you want to achieve a result through comparison. However, it is not a single method to evaluate objects of the outer world. In the 20-th century the science came close to comprehend that there are some objects exist whose ideal essence should not be established through comparison. The point is not that the ideal essence of the objects is hard to be established, but their exception, as ideal should underlie the theory basis and share its axiomatics. This idea is a conceptual conquest of the natural science, not the linguistics.

It is notable, that many people guess this idea on the every day life level. Let us have a trustworthy example. A young man saw Andjei Waida' s film "The ashes" with Beata Tyshkevich who is a wonderful Polish actress and very beautiful woman staring in the film. The young man wanted to share his impression of the film with his friend:

– Yesterday, I watched a film and I saw the most beautiful woman in the world.

– Well, did you compare her with all other women? How can you say that she is the most beautiful woman in the world if you did not see the main mass of women?

– She is the most beautiful, indeed, because no one can be more beautiful. There is no need to compare.

Such seasonings are informal and they cannot be proved. You may refuse to accept them but the contemporary science approbated their methodological rightfulness. Such postulates underlie plenty of scientific results.

So, a priori, some ideal arrangements are in existence. In case when we refer to the natural language, this is not a single arrangement but a class of arrangements (i.e. multitude), and, initially, they appear for a certain objective (communicative goal) as ideal. All natural languages existing in our planet share this class of arrangements. It is important to understand that there are no more or less complicated, expressive, better or worse languages; every natural language is useful to express the deepest thought. In particular, such scientific argument destroys the theoretic basis of the racialist concept. It is another matter that the languages differ considerably by their arrangements: some of them are more complicated in vocabulary, the others – in grammar. If one language (for instance, English) has a special term for a certain object and the other language (let say, Papua) has not, it does not signify that it is impossible to express the meaning. The term will be expressed in a descriptive manner by the use of many words, so the listener will catch the idea quite adequately.

When you recognize the natural languages as the initial ideal communicative arrangement, however, it is reasonable to ask the following question: Do the means of the natural language always underlie the information reception and transmission as the function of thinking or does the human being have some other capacities to do it? (Here we refer not to the semiotic arrangement of the body language, since it follows the speech, but to the natural language.)

It turns out that in addition to the natural language two more methods, at the minimum, exist to receive and transmit information. These methods correspond to two intellectual capacities of the human being: image-bearing thinking and sensory perception. The image-bearing thinking means the world perception in picture form. A painting or a sculpture can be also defined as a certain text (with special features) that bears a considerable informative burden. Every man is aware of thinking by visual objects, for instance, when he refines an episode of his life in memory, provided thus episode is not divided into words, but it is fixed in memory as a picture.

The sensory perception means a bioenergetic method of information exchange, wherein the speaker says and demonstrates nothing (he may be out of observation at all), bit in so doing he transmits information and his interlocutors receive such information.

Thus, upon a painstaking analysis it becomes clear that people have three different forms of thinking: the natural language, image-bearing and sensory thinking. We constantly observe how the natural language operates in speech and communication: a linear arrangement, one word follows the other, each word has its meaning; altogether they establish a summarized meaning(true enough, the sum is conditional, it does not result from a simple summation of all components).

How does the image-bearing thinking function? When asking this question we shall remember that it underlies fine arts, in particular. The world perception takes place through a single picture not in divided images. It is impossible "to read" a painting as a liner text, it cannot be divided into segments. The painting is perceived as a whole. The human being receives more information not through shifting his gaze from the left side of the painting to the right, but when he pays more attention to the whole painting. So, this is a fundamentally different form of perception, as compared with the natural language. Undivided pictures in some kinds of arts may create a linear sequence(cinematograph, comics, etc.), but it is important to understand that complicated and combined images always rank among the elements of such sequence.

We shall say that some people share the image-bearing thinking to a greater extent than the others. Parents are often surprised when their child responds to a regular question in an unusual way:

– *How do you feel?*
– *I will draw it for you now.*
– *Do you like the doggy?*
– *I will model it.*
– *What kind of a present did Papa make to you today?*
– *Oh, I will show it to you.*

The natural attempt to enter into verbal communication with such child faces an evident predominance of image bearing thinking over verbal. This phenomenon, to one side, is innate and it seems to be not inherited, on the other side. It is proved by a well-known fact that children of famous painters are not so talented as the parents.

It is interesting, that professional painters, who combine work with teaching, determine the capacities of a man to paint by the following words:» He or she has a good eye, he or she is capable to see." What does it mean to have "a good eye"? It means the capability to see in a picture more than other people can see, it is an ability to transmit through an undivided arrangement more information than other people can do it. In such a manner the ability to draw, let say, a horse does not mean painting and drawing. It signifies the ability to express a complicated and profound meaning through a visual method instead of verbal. Of course, the difference is principal. Dmitri Merezhkovsky in his trilogy "The Christ and Antichrist" puts into Leonardo da Vinci' s mouth the following words: "The eyes give more perfect knowledge of the Nature to the human being than the ears. What is seen is trustworthier than what is heard. Verbal descriptions contain only a set of individual images that follow one another, whereas in picture, all images and all paints appear together, combined into one unit like sounds in an accord..." People with the developed image-bearing thinking perceive the world in a different manner than those who have the predominant linguistic thinking.

As to the sensory thinking one ought to notice that the issue is discredited by many cases of profanation. Unfortunately, the scientific investigations of bio-sensory perception were harmfully affected by simple tricks that many people pretend to show as sensory influence. Nevertheless, there is still by far a method that helps to receive and transmit information without any analyzers that are familiar to the scientists.

It seems like the basis of this phenomenon shall be looked for at the deepest cellular level. It turns out that a cell is capable to demonstrate a phenomenon pertaining to clairvoyance, prognostication and retrospection. Take notice that the cell has no embryonic stage of nervous system or any other receptors. This phenomenon is called "cellular telepathy".

In the year of 1965 the Academician V. Kaznacheev's laboratory in Novosibirsk began experiments on communication between isolated cells. The principal scheme of the experiments was very simple. Similar one-cell cultures were placed into two hermetically sealed transparent crystal spheres. The cultures had no biological, chemical or physical contacts. They just could "see" each other. The investigators inserted a pathogenic virus into the first sphere and all cells died. Then, an amazing thing came to the light: cells in the other sphere became sick and then died, though any possibility of accidental exposure of the virus was ruled out. It turned out that if a third sphere with healthy cells was placed near the second sphere with died culture, the latter, in their turn, had the same fate. During the experiments the investigators made a line of fifty spheres and the chain reaction stretched over the whole line, step by step. You can extend the process to the infinity, but the result will be the same. So, there is a question: What is the reason of the cells death, if the virus, as a material subject, was safely isolated in the first sphere? The only answer is the mortal information. So, what is the way of its transmission? The cells have no optical receptors to gain the information from the transparent sphere and in this case all other known channels of perception were excluded. It means that the information can be transmitted only through bio-field that is produced even by a single cell, let alone every living thing. Academician Kaznacheev underlines: "When studying cells conduct, mechanism of their reproduction, interinfluence upon no contact except visual one, after thousands of experiments we came to a thought that the true nature of the living things shows itself in the interinfluence, not in isolated life. We must recognize the existence of bio-fields. Our work also proved a hypothesis according to which there is a "cosmic" life apart from living cells." It is interesting, that the existence of bio-fields is not only a feature, but a necessary condition of a living human organism existence: a man can stay in a magnetic isolation chamber not more than half-an-hour, since after that his brain is threatened by irreversible effects. The reason is seemed to lie in the fact that within four billions of years the living matter never was in the state of isolation from magnetic field. The fields were turned out to be a necessary term of its conservation and development.

It is proved that a man is able to effect without contact upon activity of biological objects having different levels of arrangement, such as cells, microorganisms, animals and people. When a person with extrasensory abilities (extrasensor) brings his hands near a test tube with one-celled animals, one can see in microscope how they start moving up and down the tube and they return to the previous condition only in an hour. Relying on this experiment a trustworthy method was developed to evaluate people' s extra-sensory abilities and now it is very easy to detect those who still pretend to have such abilities.

When an extrasensor has a mental purpose to stimulate growth of microorganisms their developing is many times of greater intensity, whereas if the purpose is to deprive – their activity in the average decreases to one third. Experiments on animals show that when an extrasensor within two weeks gives several performances of medical irradiation on artificially produced inflammation of white rat' s leg, it heals up three times quicker then the same of the other controlled rats. Since such experiments exclude any suggestions or self-suggestions, the influence of biological energy that is generated by the extrasensor and bears information upon the brain processes shall be considered as the only factor. Most probably it differs from any known kinds of energy, since it affects inanimate objects, as well. When addressing the skeptics one ought to quote Clod Bernard, the famous physiologist, –"...when you find out a fact that is in conflict with the predominant theory, you shall recognize the fact and forget about the theory."

It is clear now that there is a possibility to model the bio-sensory influence and one can learn how to do it. In fact, there are some institutions that develop every kind of information reception and transmission, and sensory abilities, as well. Sensory perception includes telekinesis, telepathy parapsychological phenomena. It pertains to the cases when a man being in a special psychological state, so called "trance", sees a picture of a crime in which he did not participate, and takes certain information about it. And no one can explain what means he uses to receive this information. It seems that all explanations are not conclusive. It is important to understand that it cannot be explained in terms of general meaning. It cannot be explained by means of the natural language. Sometimes, it can be drawn (it explains the fact that many people with developed bio-sensory perception are wonderful painters). Such presupposition underlies the scientific hypothesis. The case in point is three discussed means of information reception and transmission that stay in unequal interaction. The verbal apparatus and auricle analyzer localized above the neck are used as a means of the natural language. The image-bearing thinking is generally connected with the visual analyzer, but, in addition, our hands that can model and draw are also used in the channel of information transmission. It seems that the whole human body serves as the analyzer upon bio-sensory influence. The production designer of Anton Chekhov's play "Cherry Orchard" shown in the year of 1994 in St. Petersburg's Dramatic Theatre wrote the following words: "My attention, as the painter, first and foremost is drawn by a mood that is hard to express in words, but I feel it by the skin of my back.» Do not look for a metaphor in this text. There are no reasons to presuppose that in such cases solely the brain receives the information. Another method of information transmission through laying hands over is quite common. Localization of the body zones that participate in information reception and transmission by means of the natural language, image-bearing thinking and bio-sensory perception is absolutely different; whereas the image-bearing thinking is closer to the natural language, the bio-sensory perception – to the image-bearing thinking. The bio-sensory perception is well off the natural language so that one is hardly able to explain one by a means of the other.

The science of the XXI-century will study how to correlate the types of thinking. Nowadays the issue goes through the stage of formation.

So, the following statements have a certain hypothetic feature:

1. Every man has three innate types of thinking.
2. Distribution of the types of thinking in different people varies in percentage.
3. The priority of one type of thinking leads to the reduction of other two.

When you are watching the people who are professionals, for instance, in painting, it is noticeable that many painters can speak well and even know several languages, but they are not so much interested in it. These people, as a rule, find hard the procedures of strict logic transitions (because the transitions are linear) this is why in school years they were among the backward pupils in such disciplines as algebra.

The people empowered with evident sensory abilities are usually men of few words; they just do not need chattering.

4. All types of thinking can be developed. The congenital distribu-

tion of these types is not fixed for the life period. There is a tendency to deviation. The distribution itself is not a static arrangement; it can stay fixed only in a unit of time. Of course, the power of people's comprehension is progressing within the lifetime, but the progress is not spontaneous. If you do not stimulate the progress you will face degradation. More over, if every thinking form is not used it is liable to abolishment. This fact has evident proofs by the cases of lost children so called "Mowgli", whereas the lack of human communication even for one year does not allow psychologists, linguists, logopedists and doctors to reconstruct the speech in spite of all their collective efforts. The speech is affected in a short period of inaction: one can loose the verbal capacities in full.

Let us presume that a man is empowered by nature with the strong image-bearing thinking, but for a variety of reasons he failed to stimulate its progress. For instance, his interests were far from fine arts. (One ought to notice that not every kind of fine arts helps to develop image-bearing thinking, for example, music that like speech has a linear arrangement. Instead, painting, modeling and architecture increase the level of imagery in the world perception.) In the school he studied languages and mathematics, thus changing his patterns to the first type of thinking that resulted in obvious reduction of the image-bearing thinking. Though in the beginning he perceived foreign languages in images, he tried to memorize texts in pictures.

There are two terms: "fitness of an organ" and "non-fitness of an organ". If you do not train a certain organ it will atrophy. There are no reasons to suppose that it does not spread to thinking.

The above rule is general. To prognosticate the result of a man progress one shall consider his innate distribution of all three types of thinking. For instance, two men (A and B) may have the following distribution:

Type of Thinking	**Distribution in Percentage**	
	A	B
Verbal	40	18
Image bearing	40	80
Sensory	20	2

As a result of unfortunate development the A may have the image-bearing thinking reduced to minute sizes, whereas, the B will have lesser reduction, since he has a higher starting percentage (80 %). When we deal with the general rules we shall keep in mind that they apply to a different extent to various people: they are true for one, they are partly true for another, and the third person may find them doubtful. The humanics as the science of a man (and all people differ) is of a probability nature and no conclusions may be considered absolute.

Shall we speak about a harmonic concord of the types of thinking; for instance, the concord of the natural language with the image-bearing thinking is inherent in poets. The semiotics (the science of semiotic arrangements) has a rule stating that harmony can be achieved in the framework of a certain arrangement, since symbols gain their definition only in such arrangements. The symbols have no meaning beyond the concrete arrangement. The arrangement shall be used at its best, since it affects the harmony. It is a common point of view that is still considered true, because no serious investigations were made to demonstrate the effect produced by joint operation of several semiotic arrangements. For instance, the conjunction of a performance with the author's text (novel) – (novel is a linguistic method of information transmission and a performance is basically image-bearing.) Do they complete or disturb each other? Producers know well that, as a rule, the author's text disturbs the performance that is why they make an independent production by using different means. The idea of analogy by itself looks illegal. Such evidences demonstrate that one semiotic arrangement "disturbs" another. Investigations in the field of such difficult semiotic arrangements as fine arts are very arduous and today's science goes through the stage of tasks formulation. (The works of Y. Lotman on culturology and semiotics made a considerable contribution to the issue.)

5. We shall not exclude the fact that the correspondence of three types of thinking to a certain degree is in connection with the racial features; it does not refer to civilization, but races. It is wise to suppose that the natural language as the most evident form of thinking activity turns out to be the privilege of the white race. Since it is true for the white race that speech has a priority over other means of information reception and transmission. So, if the history of the mankind for the last thousand of years was suppressed by the culture of the whites, that is why the following idea was widely spread out saying that the natural language is the only and optimal thinking arrangement. All the above said is exclusively associated with the culturological authority of the white race.

The yellow race mainly uses the image-bearing thinking. In some way the written language proves it (hieroglyphs demonstrate a certain kind of pictures), as well as, a specific combination in the cultural tradition of any fine art (for instance, poetry) with a visual raw (drawing). The Europeans complain about considerable communicative problems arising from the lack of mutual understanding between them and, let say,

Japanese people. It impedes contacts even in such a universal sphere as business.Japanese people are considered to be very reserved; they rarely disclose any secret information to foreigners. But may be the point is that they find hard and strange the verbal method that is habitual for us, whereas we, the Europeans, do not understand the visual images – symbols (stones, flowers, gestures, etc.) so typical in the East.

The culture of the black race so insignificantly explored riddled the investigators a plenty of riddles. For instance, how do they transmit information from one tribe to another through impenetrable jungles for many hundreds of kilometers? Why does the chief of the tribe have extra-sensory capacities? Ho do aborigines know about white missionaries much more than they say? We may presuppose that the bio-sensory method of information reception and transmission is more typical of the black race. With no doubt, it is still only a hypothesis. However, it remains to be interesting to the scientists.

The priority of unequal types of thinking shared by different people has a great significance for the practice of communication. When you enter a speech communication with another person (private, business, official) together with the thorough psychological analysis of the interlocutor' s personality you shall have a grasp of his prevailing type of thinking and try to get round him at his level. Since, the listener always occupies the main communicative position, the speaker shall tune himself to the listener not only in the individual respect and in the respect of priority in argumentation, but in the respect of the said distribution. Imagine, that you are sitting in a restaurant with a person whom you like and want to impress. You want to transmit your own emotional state to him or her and you keep speaking for the whole meeting. Meanwhile, you interlocutor has an evident sensory abilities, he or she is a perfect receiver who sharply feels another person without words. (1)

---

(1) Such people are usually known by their wonderful intuition; however, it is noticeable, that the definition of intuition is absolutely informal. Under intuition one can understand an analytical analysis of information: analysis of the current situation and understanding of a high degree of probability that the situation will progress in a certain direction. In all probability, one can predict the result. There is nothing energetic in it. A journey with time is quite an apposite phenomenon. (If a journey with space is possible at the energetic level, why won't be there a journey with time, i.e. along the forth coordinate axis?) In accordance with Einstein's theory of relativity nothing impedes the transition from the past to the future and vice versa.) Allowing for such a possibility, one ought to recognize signals coming from the future; so, the intuition can be referred to as the reception of such signals. Such phenomena are called "proscopy". The term "intuition" ought to be recognized as polysemic, since it is spread to the first and the second.

With no doubt, you will failure to reach any emotional goal that you set for yourself in this situation. It is better to keep silence and glance at each other (rhetoric has an expression for it – "to hold a pause"). The procedure is very difficult for the people who are empowered with a developed verbal thinking, however in such a case you would better hold a pause exchanging with insignificant phrases. If your interlocutor is a painter and you are telling him about your visit to Florence and your impression of Michelangelo's David trying to describe this genius sculpture, he, as professional, will not understand how one can explain a work of art. In so doing you may only provoke his irritation. It is better to show him a picture of the sculpture and his conscious will have its own associations. Two persons with strong image-bearing thinking can enjoy the meeting by showing each other the drawings they make on napkins and they will be happy. (To some extent it corresponds to the communication of deaf and mute people. Notwithstanding the fact that their language is linear and remains to be an analogy of the natural language, the meaning of words is not transmitted by sounds, they use gestures, whereas the eyes serve as analyzers to receive information. So, one may presuppose a certain deviation of the image-bearing thinking.)

There are not a few people who do not like loquacity: if you ask them to do something in five words they will surely do it, if you ask them in ten words they will think before they do something, if your request contains twenty words they won't do it at all. You just began saying and suddenly you hear in reply: "Do not proceed, I guessed the idea." Still, when you have a meeting with a man who has evident verbal thinking and if during the meeting you are very shy to converse and your only action is to node in reply to his stories, the goal of communication will hardly to be obtained.

The above examples of verbal communication are based on inequality of the distribution (of the types of thinking) in the psychic of a single person. You will face a communicative failure for sure if you don't analyze your interlocutor from this standpoint beforehand and if it is impossible – upon the conversation. This is a pure psychological aspect.

PART II

THE GOALS OF SPEECH

Chapter 5. **Ritual speech**

> A man of wisdom shall regard the community (specially, the state and the culture) friendly but with restrain.
>
> *Epicure*

As it was mentioned above, the information transmission takes place upon every verbal action. The natural reply to question like, what is the reason a man speak for, as to transmit information, is a tautology. As any tautology such a reply is not constructive. Another question suggests itself: For what reason does a mat transmit information? The analysis of speech goals is intended to realize why this person transmits this information to exactly these people and in this time.

Let us analyze the speech conduct of a person since he wakes up. There is a regular saying like "Good morning" or "How do you do". Since every man does everything for a particular reason, his every action is motivated, including his every verbal action, as well, so one ought to analyze the reason our mutual greeting. It is evidently, that we do it not for a well wishing (to the Russian tradition it means to wish a good weather or health), since we also greet the people whom to whom we don't feel well. The above meaning usually does not refer to the greeting. Every man greets because it is a typical rule and refusal to do it will result in negative attitude of the neighborhood.

In every historical time unit each civilization has a special set of ceremonies (or rituals) that impose a definite conduct under certain terms and conditions upon the human being. It is so called "the rules of play" that are customary among the definite group of people. (In a like manner, when playing a preference you shall keep to the rules, otherwise you will be ruled out.) All rules that are made by people split into two groups: the first one – laws and the second one – etiquette. The rules of the first group are defined as prohibitory, i.e. they put a veto upon a certain activity; the second group comprises suggestive rules, i.e. the ones that recommend people what to do or not to do under certain circumstances. The human is the author of the laws and etiquette that were made for comfort and regulation of common being. Why do people as the community members usually try to obey the rules? Otherwise, the community will try to get rid of infringers. (Those who infringe the laws are called in English outlaws.). The community transfers infringers to another human space both physically and spiritually (deportation, jail, etc.).

An etiquette disturber is not physically transferred to any place, he faces another treatment – the surrounding people just go away. Try not to greet others and within three or four days you will stay alone. It turns out that a secession from the human space is crucial the human being. It leads to deep depression nervous stresses. Why so? The reason is that every man was borne egocentric. He/she perceives the world as a thing that is functioning around him. So, people work only for themselves and for others as derived from their work. For instance, a person saves up money to become rich and to make his family wealthy; as a result, his work and efforts lead to the society development, etc. But how can a person be egocentric when there is no one around him? Can we use such terms as egocentric of egoism if we refer to an island with a man living on it? The dialectic view of the world leads to understanding of the fact that a man can be selfish only if other people surround him. He works his way up in a certain human space and if there is no such a space then there is no psychological basis for such advancement. It looks like a man with the innate selfish character looses the ground under his feet, since all his activity entails inner competition with other people. Such a competition underlies the source of his perfection, as well as, the perfection of other people, i.e. it refers to each individual and the community, as a whole. In such a manner, an individual can be selfish if he lives in a community. It is a dialectical paradox. When moving to a new human environment the individual from the beginning must create such environment around him. To gain such an environment one shall work hard for many years and often it is a thankless task. This is one of the reasons why emigrants when placed to a new human environment usually feel a psychological discomfort. They need to spend much time and efforts before it becomes possible to appear as a special individual in such an environment. There is a common regret of an average Russian emigrant: "In past days I thought that our Moscow laboratory where I worked before was full of stupid people and informers and now for some reason I miss all of them." The phrase does not reflect a certain re-evaluation, as well as, it does not mean that the former colleagues seem better then they were before. The only meaning is that he misses the environment where his individualities were formed and where he learned how to work his way up leaving some one behind. Now he needs to do the same from the beginning and he finds it to be very hard to do. The intuitive and inner understanding of this drama (and it is a drama, of course) forces an individual to play upon the rules imposed by the community where he was borne and grown up. It is doubtless that a new-borne child is not aware of laws and etiquette, but he/she is open to such knowledge and his/her parents, teachers and surroundings teach him/her these entire rules from the first days of life. Of course, each of us possesses such rules, but partially and at the level that is sufficient for communication.

The greeting as a type of speech refers to a kind of speech upon the rules of etiquette (not laws, of course). Though, there are quite a few of criminal laws that imply conviction of speech including some laws that convict of slander, insult and sending somebody to suicide. So far as the meaning of etiquette is in relation with the meanings of a ceremony and a ritual, so the speech is called ritual.

The goal of the ritual speech is to stay in the community. "I remember the rules of play and I observe them." Everybody greets for the same purpose. It is an exchange of signs of the membership, i.e. it is a reminder of yourself that you are a member of the community. (1)

By virtue of the fact that the greeting has no more information except the reminder of the membership, the texts like "Good morning" and etc. lost their direct meaning. Such linguistic phenomenon is called **desemantization**. In Greek the word "sēmasia" signifies the term of "meaning", "idea" (The word "Semantics" comes out of the same root. The semantics signifies a part of the linguistics that studies meanings of words and word-combinations.) "De" is a Latin prefix for a reverse

---

(1) One ought to notice a mysterious regularity that is a subject of scientists's reflection for many years (See works of Karl Jung, K. Levi-Strauss, V. Propp, V. Toporov): A man greets another one once a day and he does it for sure if he has not seen him before the actual meeting today; i.e. in our conscious the border of human communication lies in the framework of 24-hours. Is there somebody who determined that we should greet each other every day, not every hour or once a week? There is nobody. Nevertheless, this rule is typical to every country and every nation. It signifies that our psychic divides the world exactly into 24-hours, where the night symbolizes death and the morning reflects the symbol of a new life. So, a man greets in his new life everybody whom he meets along his path and whom he knows in the previous life. The man does not have such a division into week, month and year periods; the division into 24-hours period is principal to him.

moment. So, the desemantization signifies disintegration, diminution and reduction of the meaning. The desemantization is a process according to which a certain text begins to loose partially or fully its meaning. In fact, the meaning exist, you can find it in a defining dictionary or reconstruct it in your conscious, but it does not manifest itself in the speech (in concrete verbal communication). The speaker does not transmit this meaning (for instance, well-wishing in the first half of the day) and the listener does not receive it.

If a text is spoken in the same situation too frequently it goes through the process of desemantization. If a text is repeated for many times, it begins to loose its meaning not to increase it. This is one of a few universal rules that practically have no exclusions.

For instance, Russian people many times saw placards of the past Soviet years like "Glory to the CPSU (Communist Party of the Soviet Union)", "People and Party are United", "Communism is a Radiant Future of the Humankind". They saw and read them many times, the more so as they were written in large letters. Who and when did reflect upon the meaning of the texts? In fact, those texts reflected by themselves the meaningless symbols, since the process of desemantization in full affected them.

As we have mentioned above, the phenomenon of anticulture in the former Soviet Union lasted for 75 years and it resulted in the mass of false texts received by the human eye and ear. It sent many people to intellectual decline, because upon perception the brain does not analyze the information that it recognizes as a false one. Desemantizated texts make the same effect. When we hear the same text for many times our brain stops decoding the source information as the previously decoded one and takes a brake. It is very dangerous, because an average person never uses his intellectual resources by more than 17 percent, so his mental activity needs a constant stimulation.

The process of desemantization extends over the texts of everyday life communication. Remember the fact of your life; when you came home too late and your parents began to abuse you. You felt perfectly impressed. When it was the tenth case in your life you merely did not hear their lectures. It is an easy case to explain. The texts that the parents directed towards you had time to desemantizate. If you tell your child once: "Eat the porridge and you will be strong as Schwarzneger", he will believe you. If you repeat this phrase every day the child will stop eating the porridge and will treat you with hostility; the more so the text that you are addressing him has no true meaning.

The ignorance of decemantization frequently leads to pedagogical failures when one uses the method of multiple repeats of the same statements for their better understanding and learning them by heart. From the scientific point of view this method is the most ineffective among the other possible methods. So far as the above pedagogical method is quite common in Russian schools, the students have a loath for some disciplines like the Russian classical literature. The teachers choose one and maybe a splendid text and repeat it as often as they can. You may try yourself to take one of Alexander Pushkin's poems and read it aloud fifteen times in succession and you will see the effect: beginning from the third time no one will listen to it and no one will perceive it from the semantic point of view (or as linguists say "read the theme out of the text"). Later on, the listeners will feel a psychological separation from the text, as such. One ought to be perfectly aware of that even the most refined texts are subjected to the process of desemantization. When you are through private relations with some one try not to make a rough communicative mistake, do not repeat the same for many times (for instance, "Why don't you shave before going to bed?")

The decemantization underlies the meaning of a "cliche". The abbreviation of the CPSU was associated with the word of "glory" for many years, and one hardly could separate the both definitions: they unified into something inseparable. The phrase "People and Party are United" could be written in one word without gaps, considering that the inner division into semantic unities was lost. Alas! Such examples are still common; they remain to be a part of the conscious of many people.

The process of desemantization corresponds to both oral and written speech. If your utterance was lame either oral or written and the meaning failed to reach the interlocutor's conscious, the second attempt, as a rule, will just worsen the situation. You have lost the speech and the repetition won't help, it worsen it even more. That is why every word that you are saying is so important and valuable: said once it should be remembered for long. One should pronounce it in such a way and in such time that it would last in the listener's conscious for long. That is exactly what the oratory means.

Many of those who learned foreign languages know that a text with a striking information is memorized in a moment, as well as, the similar statement is true for a separate word if it is pronounced with a special intonation, played up or heard in stressful circumstances. In particular, it means that an emotional provocation shall underlie the methods of the foreign languages teaching. The nervous system of a student shall be driven to such a state that enables to memorize the text at once. Why is it believed that a student will learn a foreign language very quickly if he is "immersed" into the country or a community where this language is spoken? Because he stays in a stressful situation for all the time, especially, when there are no people around him who speak his native language. He stays constantly alert, mobilized, frightened and feeling discomfort. Such alertness mobilizes his intellect in such a way that he memorizes every text received by his acoustic analyzer. Every activity in some way connected with the intellect and memory shall include an act of provocation. The best way to force a student to memorize is to force him to guess by himself. What is the easiest way to let a student to learn the demonstration of a theorem? Don't write it on the blackboard, please. Let him to prove the theorem. Help him to guess, i.e. provoke his thinking and the student will memorize the theorem for the whole life. When somebody says that repetition is "the mother of learning", it is wrong from the psychological point of view; it is a scientific nonsense.

It is a different matter that the communication is often accompanied with misunderstanding and incomprehension. Such situation dictates the necessity of repetition: the brain will analyze the information until the comprehension is achieved. As soon as the speaker guesses that he is understood there is no need to repeat.

There are some so complicated texts that require multiple repetitions before they can be understood; such texts require certain "cipher texts". They include, with no doubt, canonical theological texts. The text of the Bible is repeated for several thousands of years and its meaning opens up more and more; still there is a presupposition for one to comprehend the meaning. The culturologists think that every ritual goes through two stages:

1) The text of the ritual has a clear meaning; the meaning is absolutely clear to the ritual performers;

2) The ritual goes through the process of decemantization. It serves only as the confirmation of a community between the ritual performers. It is a stage of degeneration. If a man repeats a pray multiple times and he never ponders over its meaning, it is the man's failure, not an indication that the text is desemantizated in the framework of the ritual.

In special cases when the ritual preserves the actual form and the meaning, it does not degenerate upon daily repetition within hundreds of years. Obviously, it is true only for "coded" texts.

It is important to understand, that the decemantization is not a result, it is a process; and as any process it may be partial, considerable, nearly full and etc. In every concrete case the process of decemantization reaches a certain level; full decemantization is a rare thing. In ritual speech the level of desemantization is very considerable due to its constant repetition.

When playing upon certain rules the people quite often need to be sure that the rules of the play remain the same, since the rules may change upon the development of one human life (in a similar way as with the development of every national culture).

Take a notice how painfully the people react to fact that you failed to greet them. They will then ask you about it, for sure. Every man needs a constant reminder that he stays in one social environment with you. When living together with a dear person you try all the time to make certain that he or she still loves you and you can count on the reservation of your emotional status quo.

There are rules of etiquette and laws that are universal for the whole humanity and there are some rules that are isolated for concrete civilization, ethnos or nationality. Punishment for murder that exists practically in all countries may serve as an example of such a universal rule (however, there are some exclusions of the rule: sacrifice that is typical for some nations, vendetta and some others). Greeting is a universal rule of etiquette: people greet each other all over the world, even in their own way. There is an etiquette rule that is specific for a national culture: to serve cheese after desert (in France). Forget about the next party, nobody will come if you omit to serve cheese after desert.

So, the first precept of the etiquette: play upon the rules that are common in the territory where you live. In Cockney's market (Cockney is an area in London, Great Britain) you should behave like it is used to there. Ignorance of this precept leads to the failure in communication. Unfortunately, Russian people frequently forget about the rule when they go abroad. You can see a Russian tourist a mile off; he lives upon the laws that he used to live upon, he behaves upon the rules that he was taught in the childhood. He does not feel obliged to know the behavioral rules that are common in the country where he now stays. That is why Russian emigrants keep staying eternal emigrants: except rare exclusions they do not incorporate into the surroundings. They begin to establish their own rules that is impossible to do, because the neighborhood lives in a different way. Nobody will accept the rules of a newcomer. A person who lives upon his own rules that differ from the rules common in the neighborhood always remains to be a stranger: he can be employed, he can have a house and a car, but he is still an eternal foreigner, he feels as a foreigner and sometimes it is very hard to stand. Though the reason is very simple: this person failed to make it obligatory for himself to live upon the laws and rules of the country. He may like or dislike them, it is up to him, but if he decided to live there, he must play upon the common rules: to eat the common food, and to do it in the time that is set for, especially, if he shares a meal with someone; to greet in the typical way; to do official paperwork, to make an appointment; to make presents that are typical and avoid making untypical gifts, and so on. There is no other form of communication. That is why before going to another country (even if it is a short official or friendly visit) do not forget to learn the rules of etiquette common in this country.

Foreigners when visiting Russia shall observe the rules common in this country. One ought to notice that not only Russian people, but Americans, as well, may disregard the traditions of other nations. Americans think possible to live upon their own rules in any country, even if such rules are inadmissible, let say, in Europe. That is why Europeans often despise them. It is a standard of behavior to know the language of the country, which you intend to visit. If you don not know the language you shall feel guilty and it shall be seen. Americans rare feel guilty, they think that the American English is the language of the humanity and it is quite sufficient for communication of all people living on the Earth, and it is not understandable at all what is the use of French, German, Sweden and all other languages.

It is amazing since the United States is the country of emigrants and unlike other countries it has the meaning as "a culture in the culture". The whole areas in the United States look like different civilizations that belong to other nations: there are Latin, Chinese, Jewish and Italian districts where people live upon the rules of the countries they came from. They usually speak their native languages. The American culture exists on the background of such micro-cultures and it has its own rules. How do the people living in such national areas feel themselves? This is one of the mostly complicated problems of the United States. The people feel themselves belonging to their own nations, on the one hand, and business relations force them to leave their enclaves, on the other hand, and frequently it leads to misunderstanding and conflicts. The general rules of American behavior were established by a philosophy of the end of the XIX-century that is called "pragmatism". The philosophy is associated with the names of the famous American philosophers as Pierce and James. In the year of 1878 Pierce wrote the following: "To define the meanings of the common sense it is necessary to analyze what practical results can be reached if required from the truth of the meanings. Summation of the results determines the definition of the meanings." Jams developed the idea: "The philosophy of pragmatism recognizes as the acceptable truth only such thing that controls us in the best way, the thing that is best adapted to every part of the life and enables to unify with the joint experience at the best."Pragmatism is a philosophy of usefulness and success (in Greek pragma and praxis mean action and practice). Its main thesis is the following: "true things are among advantageous and comfortable things" (bellow we discuss it more closely). As a consequence the rules of American etiquette are intended for the comfort of mutual living. They are simple, unaffected and not obtrusive. In small national communities (like in Italian) the rules are stronger than in the whole country.

The true psychological reason of emigration seems to lie in the impossibility for a certain man to live upon the rules that are common of the neighborhood and in his incompatibility with the outer micro world.In another country he will feel himself in comfort only if he learns to accept its norms and rules as the reasonable ones. The ritual speech is among such norms and rules.

The nomenclature of ritual speeches varies since it includes all types of communication determined by strict regulations and rules: greetings, congratulations, excuses, farewells, wishes, condolences and so on. There are some more complicated types of ritual speeches: phone calls, official salutations and speech ceremonies. For instance, wedding ceremony represents such a ceremony that in addition to symbols includes a certain consequence of rituals, as well as speech ones. The ceremony is taken upon a certain scenario, it includes a plenty of rituals and desemantizated texts, though some words are very expressive, they agitate both the newly-weds and their relatives.

Ritual ceremonies include folklore and civil ceremonies in addition to church ones. Protocol speech is among the types of the ritual speech. It is peculiar with a high degree of decemantization and strict arrangement; it goes through a certain scenario and bears little information.

Various official papers, orders, instructions and so on may serve as examples of the ritual speech in literature genres. For instance, the banner of an application that includes the names of the addressee and the addressor and the name of the document (herein "application") represents a clichй. When you try to send in an application with no banner they will not accept it:"It is written against the rule". If you try to write down the application according to all rules exchanging the information of the banner into something abstract (as a joke), they may accept it, because, as a rule, nobody reads the banner, especially, if they know the applicant.

Synopsis of a thesis is also a stereotype ritual written text and if you fail to underline the parts of it as "Theme", "Actuality", "Novelty", "Basic Statements" and so on, nobody will treat it as a synopsis, because the arrangement will break the rules. The synopses are usually read from the fourth page.

Every blank form is a clichй, in which the typed information is well known and only the information that is filled in is considered to be essential. There is a risk: imagine that you sign a blank of bilateral agreement and the other party changed a few words in the typed text. The essence is changed (sometimes considerably), and you sign the document without reading the text. It is not the same document that you intended to sign. Sometimes, a clichй may be informative.

If we say that legislative and behavioral norms and rules really exist, than every nation can be determined as law-abiding and law breaking in accordance with their execution. Perhaps, today' s Englishmen are in the list of law-abiding nations and Russian people vice versa. The reasons that lead a certain nation to the state of law-abiding or its absence in one historical unit are very complicated and meaningful. In Russia it is a common rule to plume for law breaking: they see in it a certain national "chic" (you make an appointment by six and there is a great possibility that you will meet the man at eight on the next day). It is well to know that the absence of law-abiding impedes the communication between people. Each of us spends too many nervous cells. The absence of obligingness at a higher level (and it is the derivative of the law breaking) leads to a total nervous stress. Owing to this Russian people live a worse and shorter life. The human communication in Russia is more difficult unlike in many other countries, and, sometimes, it could result in the lack of mutual understanding with the foreigners. Let us give a trustworthy example.

A Russian woman had a relationship with a Swede. He had to leave for Indonesia to an expedition for many months. When leaving in September he told her: "At seven o' clock on the 12-th of April I will be at your door." The woman did not receive any information from him till April and as an every Russian woman she thought that he would never come back. What kind of amazement she had when on the 12-th of April at seven o' clock he came to her with a bunch of flowers and the offer of his hand and heart. She could not help hiding her amazement and he understood it in the wrong way (he decided that she did not wait for him and he is not long-wished for), because as to his point of view there was no reason for amazement. Only the death could make him free of the given promise. That is a behavioral standard in Sweden. A Swede' s notebook is full of appointments made for a year in advance and he lives upon such a calendar as on the divine code of rules. The marriage, alas, was failed.

There is one more example. In the year of 1990 two Swedish cinematographers came to Moscow for negotiations with a local producer who had an office in the "Mosfilm" film studio. They asked to bring them directly to the film studio from the airport. There was a sing on the gates of the film studio – "No entry", but everybody drove in. To the right of the gates there was another sign – "No parking", and there were plenty of cars parked just under the sign. The street-door welcomed with a sign – "No smoking", and there was a crowd of people smoking nearby the door. The reception hours on the table of the office door gave them a hope that they could meet the producer immediately. But the door was locked with nobody in. They decided to have a lunch and went to the "Pekin" restaurant. They saw a line at the door, though only two tables in the restaurant were occupied. When studying the menu they found out through an interpreter that half of the dishes indicated in the menu were absent. The Swedes decided that they came to the Wonderland. They took offence at the Russian colleague, since they thought that he invited them and played a trick with them from the first moment of the meeting at the airport. They booked tickets on the nearest flight and came back to Zurich on the same day.

Civilized people refer to law breaking and pluming on it as a nonsense that makes intercommunication impossible. It seems to me that the life is easier if everybody parks his car in the parking places and does not park where it is prohibited.

Below there are more examples of ritual speech:

1. *Dear Chairman,*
Dear Mr. Vranitsky, Chancellor of Austria,
Dear Ladies and Gentlemen,
First of all I want to express our sincere gratitude to the leaders of Austria for the hospitality and wonderful arrangement of our meeting.

The leaders of Russia attach a special importance to it. I was authorized to transmit their following appeal: "To the participants in the meeting of the leaders of States and governments – members of the EPCE in Austria. Dear colleagues, I am greeting the participants in the meeting of the leaders of States and governments – members of the EPCE.

The leaders of more than 40 states from Lisbon to Vladivostok, as well as, the representatives of many competent international organizations came to Austria. This is an evident proof of the EPCE's capabilities and potential as a means to strengthen democracy, stability and peace.

Recently, we have done many things. The EPCE comes close to be a valuable European organization. Today, it pays its attention to practically every significant matter of the European development. Our organization has on its credit side a detailed discussion on the European security as a model for the XXI – century and a possible economical program of the European development in the XXI – century. Our organization plays a significant role in providing the human rights on the European continent.

Nevertheless, there is still a problem of what path for our continent to choose. There are plenty of matters remaining unsolved. Europe stays on the eve of the most paramount decisions. We shall not permit a new alienation and confrontation. We shall determine our position on the most significant matters of the European security, development of the disarming process, as well as, we have to determine our attitude to the OBSE and the North Atlantic Treaty Organization (NATO).

Exactly in Vena we shall start a practical work over these paramount issues and establishing a common space of security and economical zone.

Our task is to make decisions that will in full signify our nations' common interest in establishing united, peaceful and democratic Europe.

The time period passed after the Luxemburg summit advanced us to this goal. First of all it resulted from the fact that people in Europe do not die in international and civil wars. The efforts were made to cease the bloodshed in many regions of Europe: in former Yugoslavia, Abkhazia and Nagorny Karabakh. The maintenance and reservation of peace in Yugoslavia are mainly based on the efforts of the EPCE. Many European countries face problems of national minorities and our organization plays a significant role in dissolving such problems. We shall not stop at this. There are a few countries where the human rights are violated and our goal is to stop it.

We shall meet the demands of the end of the last century and the beginning of the new millennium. At the end of the century we are facing a new global problem. It is an international terrorism. Hundreds of innocent people die every year due to terrorism. None of the countries can solve this problem solely. No only European countries, but the whole world shall join their efforts to struggle successfully against terrorism. The EPCE shall be the first organization, which will start to realize this idea. We shall enter the XXI – century as a valuable organization that will play an important role not only in Europe, but in the whole world, as well. Our goal is a flourishing united Europe.

The fulfillment of all the above tasks is possible only upon our active work.

Dear Chairman, dear colleagues, ladies and gentlemen, I am sure that you will hear many constructive announcements made on this tribune. All together they will constitute a model of future Europe that we shall establish in cooperation. I sincerely wish you a success in this work. It is very important for all of us. Thanks for your attention."

2. "*Dear ladies and gentlemen,*

We gathered here on a quite important occasion, better say a reason, since we have plenty of occasions to meet. It is a solemn occasion and at the same time, I would say a nostalgic one. Today, we attend the well-earned seeing-off of our much-esteemed colleague – Akakiy Akakiyevich. He worked in our collective more then forty years. His stainless diligence, discipline and modesty were always an example for all members of our solidary collective. I am perfectly sure that I will express the feelings of almost all those attended and not attended our meeting, if I say that we will miss our dear Akakiy Akakiyevich, we will always fasten our eyes on his empty table. The sorest feeling it will be when we see his table occupied by another officer who will come to the place of Akakiy Akakiyevich (it is inevitable), especially, if he is very young with some so called "new ideas and imagery about the high meaning of discipline". The God save us if he will bring distemper to our solidary collective. Akakiy Akakiyevich never distressed us in this way.

We don't say solemn words praising that the memory of Akakiy Akakiyevich will always live in our hearts. No, we don't. It is too early. We don't say you – farewell for ever, we say – we see you again. We don't part with him forever, we will think of our dear Akakiy Akakiyevich and he will think of us. We will congratulate him on all holydays, make phone calls and see him.

Let me on behalf of our collective congratulate, and I insist exactly on such wording, our dear Akakiy Akakiyevich with this solemn occasion in his life. Let me tender him thanks (I won't read the Directorate's order) and make a gift in the form of an inkstand, set of pens and pencils, blanks and other papers that our dear Akakiy Akakiyevich in his long-wished free hours and days could have a dream about the time when he worked here by vocation. We are sincerely glad of you and we recommend you our dear Akakiy Akakiyevich to be pleased, not to regret. We all join you there (on a pension)!"

Chapter 6. **Provocative speech**

> If there were no speech no one would know about good or evil, truth or lie, satisfaction or disillusionment. The speech makes all the above understandable. Reflect upon it.
>
> *Upanishads*

There are some cases when a man speaks not to transmit information, but to receive it. Usually, he chooses such a construction that is specially designed to receive an answer. This construction is interrogative. However when addressing a man in an affirmative form you can force him to give an answer.

There is an example:
– You cannot win this match.
– Yes, I can. I had a set of trainings with special loads and now I am in a very good athletic shape.

We can signify the first phrase as a "provocation. Such a speech is called provocative. A provocative speech is defined as a special type of speech internally designed to receive some information in reply or to get some information known by the provocateur or to get some new information (such cases are called as "to try to discover" new information).

Let us study first a category of the issue. The interrogative construction represents itself as a linguistic universality. Linguistic universalities are defined as linguistic phenomena (characteristics, qualities) that are common to all (or practically to all) languages of the world. It is wise to propose that the linguistic universalities are connected with the general psychic peculiarities of the human conscious. Only genetic components inherent in the man by nature may be evident in the speech of any native speaker of any language, i.e. all people irrespective the place and time of communication. The study of linguistic universalities leads to the understanding of the human being' s psychic structure (See chapter 19 "The text as sequence of symbols")

The interrogative construction is a linguistic universality; it means that a need for a question naturally pertains to the conscious of every human being, so, consequently, the provocative speech is of a genetic character (unlike the ritual speech that the human being learns in accordance with the rules common to the society; only the instinct of self-defense is of a genetic nature (both physical or psychic) that comes to light in the form of a fear of the loneliness).

The provocative speech is intended to cause a direct influence on other people; it is being known that the influence is of a suppressing nature: you force somebody to transmit you some information against his will. It means that a need to force another man to do something is a component of the human nature; i.e. a certain component that is inherent in every man from the birth. We are designed in such a way that makes us to try to force other people to act in certain circumstances according to our will.

The interrogative construction in the Russian language has its own characteristics. This fact is proved by a syntactic error typical for written texts: wrong placing of the question mark at the end of a sentence. Even intelligent native speakers of the Russian language omit the question mark in many places where it should by placed in accordance with the rules, and, vice versa, they place the mark where they should not. It is an indication of hypercorrection as a phenomenon that provokes the writer to put the question mark, that long is absent in the language, into the wrong place in imitation of a certain standard, whereas the writer actually does not know where to put it. (For instance, in the written monuments of the XVII – century plus quam perfect is placed instead of aorist) The hypercorrection of the question mark indicates that the person does not refer to the essence of the sentence as to an interrogative one, so he omits the mark. It is evident that every language has two types of questions: questions by the meaning and questions by the construction. It is wise to initially propose the existence of symmetry: a specially designed construction is chosen to transmit a certain meaning, which it is not. (2)

The Russian language makes possible the following situations:
I. Question by implication – question in form.
II. Question by implication – affirmation in form.
III. Affirmation by implication – question in form.
IV. Affirmation by implication – affirmation in form.

The table consists of four cells. The first square contains the question by implication and at the same time – the question in form (phrases like: *"What is the time, please?"*). Such a question needs a reply; it is expressed by an interrogative construction that is ended by the question mark in writing. This is the first and the simplest situation that could be the only one in respect to the common sense, which it is not. It turns out that the question by implication can be expressed by an affirmative construction (second cell). In phrases like: *"I would like to know where you were yesterday."* This phrase represents itself as a compound sentence that in accordance with the Russian punctuation shall be ended by a dot. In oral speech it has no interrogative intonation. There is no doubt that the semantic question is inherent in such phrases, since they demand (provoke) a reply in communication.

The third cell includes phrases with an affirmative meaning expressed in an interrogative form like: *"Who does not like beautiful women?"* In the Russian language it is an interrogative questions; in writing it is ended by the question mark and in oral speech it is followed by an interrogative intonation. It is an affirmation by implication with no demand for a reply. The phrase: *"Who does not like beautiful women?"* is equal by implication to the phrase: *"Everybody likes beautiful women."*

---

(2) The similar cases prove the linguistic law, which is called by S. Kartsevsky as an "asymmetric dualism of a linguistic symbol" (Refer to Chapter 19 "The Text as Sequence of Symbols").

It is an example of syntactic synonymy (the synonymy at the level of a text that is larger than a collocation).

In the fourth cell presents the phrases in which the affirmative meaning is presented symmetrically in an affirmative form like: *"The novel of Fyodor Dostoyevsky "The Karamazov Brothers" was finished in the year of 1880."* The fourth cell was put into the table not by a coincidence. Nevertheless, it is composed of the phrases that have neither a semantic question nor an interrogative construction, i.e. they make null constructions in terms of the problems of the issue. However, it is a significant null.

When considering linguistic categories, if it turns out that a certain category in certain positions did not realize either by implication, nor in form, such information shall be considered significant and quite important for a linguistic description, as well.

The definition of a significant null exists both in the linguistics and in such sciences as mathematics, logics and so on. Long known are the sentences that are affirmative by implication and interrogative in form; they are called rhetoric questions. Consequently, a **rhetoric question** represents an interrogative construction with an affirmative meaning. The presence of rhetoric questions means that in some cases the affirmation is expressed by unusual means, though the linguistic arsenal has a special affirmative construction and this construction is very common. Inasmuch as everything in the language is motivated, it is wise to propose that a rhetoric question together with the function of information transmission bears an additional communicative load. When analyzing texts, beginning from antic, one may eventually comprehend that the atypical structure of the rhetoric question is the main reason of its designation to provoke the attention of listeners and readers.

In the Middle Ages in Europe the following action was quite common: a preacher stood on the top of a hill and his flock that consisted of citizens of many villages and small towns, gathered on the hillsides to hear the sermon. The preacher, of course, spoke about the matters that were important and stirring to the people: wars, harvest, and epidemics, breeding of children, moral issues, interpretation of the Words and many other things. There were plenty of listeners; some of them hindered others from hearing, looking aside and making a fuss. The preacher spoke without a microphone addressing to many thousands of people and he had to arrange his speech in such a way that enabled him to draw people's attention within several hours. It is understandable how hard the task was and how brilliant orator one should be to attract people's attention for a long time in such circumstances. The rhetoric question is one of the tricks that were necessarily used in such types of the speech (it is still used now in public speeches) as a means to make the speech reception more effective (Refer to Chapter 23 "The Expressive Force of Figures of Speech"). The interrogative intonation by itself is very atypical; it agitates the human attention. Everything atypical activates the communicative function. Aristotle wrote: "It is nice to feel a change, since changes are in conformity with the nature of things. An atypical way of behavior is especially important if the speech is a long one, since the limits of the human perception are insignificant." (3)

That is why it is so important to the speaker to stimulate in his speech the listeners' involuntary attention, that appears as if by itself with no volitional purpose of the speaker. The involuntary attention may appear in respect to a strong, contrast or a new unexpected irritant, which is considered to be significant or may result in an emotional response.
Imagine a speaker who suddenly begins dancing when he sees that the public is getting tired. The fact of such non standard behavior agitates the listeners renewing the public attention in such a way. It is a rough trick, but it works. The more elegant method is to influence by an intonation contour that distinctively differs from a typical one, i.e. it means the use of a more emotional and distinctively interrogative intonation instead of a quiet narrative one. Thus, the rhetoric question is used to provoke attention and interest to speech.

When analyzing classical philosophic texts one may notice that the headlines of some articles often look like interrogative constructions. Why do they use such a form? Since the question provokes both the attention and the need for reflection. As soon as the man hears an interrogative intonation, he feels an intuitive desire to give an answer that, as a rule, follows by reflection and formation of a certain point of view. Even if it is an affirmative sentence, still it stimulates the reflection on the given

---

(3) The word of attention means the direction and concentration of the conscious on certain objects (for instance, on the speech). There are two types of attention: arbitrary and involuntary. The arbitrary attention, i.e. conscious concentration on certain information, asks for volitional efforts, the exhaustion comes in 20 minutes. In addition, the human brain every 6-10 seconds switches off the reception of information for a fraction of a second that results in the lost of some information.

The figures correspond to the depth of the human short-term memory, which ensures that the information once presented for a short period of time to be memorized. Then, the information can be forgotten completely or be transferred to the long-term memory. The short-term memory is restricted by volume, it may hold on average 7+ 2 units. This a magic formula of the human memory; i.e. an average man is able to memorize from five to nine words, numbers, figures, patterns, parts of information within 6-10 seconds. Then, his brain needs some rest.

if it is an affirmative sentence, still it stimulates the reflection on the given theme. So, the construction being affirmative by implication and interrogative in form resolves an additional task: to force the human being to think and feel an interest to the topic of conversation.

The analyzed asymmetry in the Russian language causes the appearances of syntactic errors in the use of the question mark: it appears where there is a question by implication, not by form. The human being treats the following situation as a typical one: when he needs to know something, he asks a question and, consequently, put the question mark. The native speakers do simply not interpret a question in form upon the absence of a semantic question as an interrogative construction that is why they do not put the question mark. The inner feeling of the human being reflects the interrogative construction as a semantic construction. Though, the aforesaid table represents that the question mark does not always correspond to the question by implication and the question by implication can be executed without the question mark.

One ought to accept that the question mark in the Russian language, as well as, the interrogative intonation does not have the meaning of a question. Misunderstanding of this fact puts a man into an awkward situation: as soon as he hears an interrogative intonation he begins answering thus making an ass of himself. For instance, in reply to a common greeting "How do you do" he confides his problems in details and looks foolish, since this phrase represents an affirmative, not an interrogative text (it is an example of the ritual speech). Every time when you hear an interrogative intonation, you shall first think it over and understand if it is a question or not, if they want to know something of you or not, or if they just want to tell you something in this way. It helps you to avoid awkward situations. Ill-wishers intuitively understanding the hidden possibility to compromise a person on talks, upon defending a thesis, or at a scientific conference, and so on (i.e. on serious and important events) will try to use the possibility in their favor. They ask such a man a question that in fact contains no question by implication and if the man is confused of upset he won't be able to understand it immediately and he will begin answering thus making an ass himself. As a result he is compromised not as a personality but as a man of intellect: he is short on brains if he is not able to get that there is no question in it.

One ought to analyze the above communicative situation in details understanding that he has a reliable (and ethic, that is very important) method to put somebody in his place: it is a very powerful rhetoric trick, since as a result the interlocutor by himself may demonstrate short brains and low reaction.

Let us analyze an altered communicative situation. A man knows that you had some troubles and he is not interested in. But from the ethic point of view he asks you: "How is you problem go on?" You shall give a short and polite answer: "Still the same" or "A bit better". If you start telling him in detail about your private and serious matters, you will show your hands before the man who is not interested in. You will open your heart to a man who does not need it: he might be in a hurry or be bored, but he will be compelled to keep up the conversation. You may bring about his abhorrence of yourself. More over, the awkwardness is usually seen not only to the interlocutor, but to accidental witnesses of such conversation: you may comprehend without hearing that one of the interlocutors is exhausted and only his politeness or some other reasons makes him to keep up the conversation. You ought to consider one of the most important communicative postulates: nobody is obliged to participate in any verbal communication, no one should be forced or required to do it.

The above asymmetry of the semantic and formal sides of interrogative constructions is typical to the Russian language. It marginally projects on other languages (for instance, English, German and Arabic languages that have more symmetry, hence it follows that the speech communication is easier).

The Russian language, Russian mentality and Russian culture belong, to all appearance, to the most complicated ones in the communicative respect and the Russian literature demonstrates this conclusion perfectly. If one compares, say, the dialogs in the works of Fyodor Dostoyevsky with the dialogs in the works of any western greats, it becomes evident that the Russian word communication has special complicative characteristics: usually, it has several semantic levels (for instance, "undercurrent" as a speech standard in the texts of Anton Chekhov); it is often coupled with provocation, oversaturated with disinformation; it efforts an opportunity to confuse the interlocutor and so on. Businessmen know that talks with Russian partners are among the most complicated ones: it is very hard to understand anything by the text, since it bears several levels of hardly decoded subtexts. All this extremely complicates the decision-making by the partner. The civilized business is established on the basis of confidence whereas the confidence derivates from understanding. The psychology law says: "Trust is function of understanding".

An effort to receive information can be realized not only by a question, which is usually asked when the speaker pretends to get an easy answer, as assumed to be non-confidential for the listener. However it is evident, that people do not want to disclose all information. In this case the provocative speech gains special features: it bases itself on craftiness, superiority over the interlocutor, intents to take power in hands; and it uses special tricks for it. The first of them is to set the theme, i.e. to hurl a remark into the communicative space with the purpose to hear what people or a concrete person think about it. Talk shows as a TV genre are based on such a principle; usually the presenter simply sets a theme and then together with the audience he watches how the invitees communicate and behave in the TV studio.

One ought to consider that the inner motive of any provocative speech is to get true information; i.e. it should be such information, which seems to be true to the transmitter (See Chapter 3. The Conscious/ Unconscious and Lie in Oral Communication). Every opinion is always subjective, that is why it is so important to choose a right man to whom you want to address with your provocative speech: the man is assumed to be more competent and informed in a certain field of knowledge than you. For instance, you want to know the future rating of US dollars for the next six months. How do you set a theme to provoke experts and force them to express their estimates? To achieve this objection it is better to say in confident and peremptory tone something provoking that goes against the common sense. The human brain is designed in such a way that it aggressively responds to any lie and stupidity (as a matter of fact, lie and stupidity irritate the people). At the first moment when the person does not realize that he should avoid from showing his irritation, as well as, his knowledge, he begins rejoining and discloses the needed information. For instance, you are interested in future inflationary prospects in Russia. You may say: "I am satisfied with all that comes about the Russian financial system within the last years, especially, with the process of inflation." Most likely they will explain that you are absolutely wrong and adduce arguments in support of their point of view, and among such arguments you will hear the prognostication of the future rating. So, you will achieve the objection, you will provoke public reflections of an expert on the theme that you were interested in.

Not every remark is worthy of your respond. You shall do it carefully, with great attention: the remark can be provocative and when expressing your opinion you may find yourself under the threat of saying more than you want, i.e. you may disclose yourself in some way.

There are special speech genres that are intended to say less and to hear more (for instance, diplomatic speech). Who is the winner in the dialog of two diplomats if both have the same inner goal? The one always wins who is trained better and more intelligent. That is why the diplomatic work demands people who have a high IQ in addition to other capacities. The diplomats quite often need to obtain some new information from their colleagues of other countries. One ought to present such information as obviously known trying to prognosticate it beforehand wherever possible. You will fail if you guess wrong, but if you guess right just a part of it, then they will speak with you confidentially as with a man who is familiar with the subject. The bluff as the best kind of provocation underlies such speech conduct. Clever people bluff very often in their speech; the morals do not prohibit it directly. The bluff differs from the lie: you have to pronounce your opinion even if you have doubts as to its reliability. Such examples are quite often in day-to-day speech: a person declares his knowledge of the subject willing to obtain some information; he declares it naturally with no doubt in his voice. Of course, there are things, which people think out for themselves through their experience and observation; however, the use of provocative speech demands special training. There are different kinds of people: trusting watchful and suspicious; but one ought to remember that every man has another one to whom he yields. This is one of such theses that do not have exclusions. The cleverest person can meet another one who will be found more intelligent, better trained, with better psychological shape in a certain situation, more prepared for a talk and who will a priori win. One ought to keep it in mind before trying to provoke somebody: your provocation may turn out to become a public disgrace to you, if he discloses your intentions, he will have an aversion for you. They may treat you very roughly, even more so that our society, alas, cultivated speech unruliness: some times we allow telling each other such things, which are basically tabooed in a respectable community; in our society the rough speech is almost universal.

The roughness results from three various reasons as to the psychological point of view. The first, it testifies the man's personality: the man is ill mannered, since he was bred in unintelligent circumstances, he was unlucky. The second, the man has an inner aggression, which means that you were able to touch him on the raw and witnessed his coming off second-best; he demonstrated his weakness in your respect. The third, the man is insufficiently intelligent. One ought to remember these three reasons before he wants to say rude things. Because when being rude you demonstrate that you have unintelligent parents, the interlocutor is more intelligent than you since he made you angry and you are short on brains to win. Those who want to win the speech shall omit any roughness. In this connection we treat as special the situation wherein you have an inner desire to quit communication with a certain man. It is the only case that allows saying rude things. If a drunken scoundrel sticks to you and you, naturally, want to get rid of him, it is expedient to say rude things, even strike, in some cases, since your goal is to quit the communication. However, such situations are not common.

When you address a man with a negative provocative intent to force him to give you some information, which he does not want to disclose, whereon he understands your intention and in respond says you rude things, such a situation demonstrates an example of the communicative situation wherein none of the interlocutors wins, both are losers. If your interlocutor unmasks your provocation and instead of saying you rude things makes an ass of you before other people just merely demonstrating your incompetence at a certain moment of the communication (not necessarily right away after your provocation), it will be a deserved counter to your attempt to provoke him.

Demonstration of your incompetence or insolvency, especially, before the people whose opinion you value, is a more striking blow than the demonstrated superiority. Roughness is among the smallest weapons: when a man has nothing to say he begins crying and saying rude things. It projects the helplessness; the people who always win in communications, usually, speak in low tones (sometimes, a bit louder, as depends on the communicative situation), very quietly and politely, whereas their interlocutors demonstrate the states near nervous coma. The communicative victory looks in this way. When one teaches somebody to be rude, it means the same like he arms his ward with a broken gun that does not shoot or can shoot at him. If your objection is to discredit some one, just provoke him to be rude, and you will obtain it. There are not a few cases when, say, a company dissolves a problem of firing an employee: they provoke him to say rude things and oaths in the chief's presence and he loses the job due to unethical behavior, though the unethical behavior is just a cause, there is a true reason behind. In business it is a typical method to discredit some one through provocation. One possibly needs a power of observation to understand this fact. Many people of the ruling class struggle for the place under the sun, and exactly the provocation is one of the mostly effective means. You do not say bad things about a man to discredit him; you put him in such a situation wherein he discredits himself. The provocation is a strong, elegant and powerful method of influence; usually, people do not suppose that some one wants to provoke them to a wrong and inexpedient action.

Many of us have plenty of enemies, more than we suspect, since the inner world of other people is a closed book. The conscious of other people is a part of the outer world, which we percept quite conditionally, with a large portion of an error. It is always a secret how other people treat us and sometimes the provocative method helps to lift the veil of secrecy. Inasmuch as one does not know well how other people treat him, the caution prompts to proceed from the fact that the treatment is more negative than it is seen. The human being lives under constant threat and the provocation is one of them. Everybody should learn how to defend himself against the provocation. Of course, not all of the people are able to make a full provocation, but quite many of them; and every person considers it by himself. There is no absolute gradation of "able – unable", rather some people are able to do it to a lesser degree, some of them – to a greater extent; some of them are able to do it in respect of all people, some of them – in respect of a certain man. People differ from each other depending on the values learned in the childhood, since their moral values, laid in the period preceding the conscious ages, when a child learns to speak, are steady and keep a tendency to permanency. Every man knows better than others about his limits determined by the inner moral barrier.

The provocative speech does not always serve the negative purpose; it is true only in the cases when the interlocutor does not want to disclose the required information. It is the only case when the provocation has a malevolent intention. The interlocutor may be quite loyal to you inside, but he may need terrifically the information that you have; sometimes the need is so terrific that it may seem to him that even his faith depends on such information. It often happens in private relations. In such a case he may obtain the required information affecting the call of compassion.

Why do people use the provocative speech so frequently in the social sphere? Since in the social hierarchy the first who obtains information gets into the privileged position. Efficiency is one of the prime methods of information reception. Journalists and businessmen know well about it. Naturally, the more people know the wider is their information space that enables them to take optimal decisions.

The speech conduct defined as "to angle for compliments" is typical to many people. Young girls, grown-ups, both women and men have a soft corner for compliments (it looks funny when it regards men). It is a simple and harmless case of provocative speech and if a man fishes for a compliment you must pay a compliment to him.

Bellow there is an example of such a case:
– *I do not gain enough understanding of the matter, it requires a more competent expert, I do not have the appropriate training.*
– *Well, if you do not have the training, who has such training at all?*

Journalists like to use a play in compliments during an interview as a good beginning of conversation, because it wins the interlocutor' s favor.

When summing up all the aforesaid one ought to say that the provocative speech represents one of the most complicated and meaningful by interpretation types of speeches. It requires both interlocutors to mobilize in full their intellectual and volitional resources.

The following are the examples of the provocative speeches:

1. *An owner of a big motorcar company "Prr" needs to know certain information on the project that a company "Www" is to realize. He authorizes an officer of the company to obtain this information. The officer decides that the best way to execute the task is to meet a person who has the required information and enter into the conversation with him. So, he began realizing the plan.*

– I' m sorry, are you Mr. John Sauber, a vice-president of the "Www" company?

– Yes, it is me. I am John Sauber. Where do you know me from?

– I am your future partner.

– Yes, I remember, it seems that I was told about you. Your name is Ron Denis.

– You are perfectly right.

– Nice to meet you. Sorry, that I did not do it before. A great deal of work. We work on our project from the morning till the night.

– Nice to meet you, too. I heard a lot about you, and only positive things. I hope that we shall cooperate successfully. I heard abou the project, but I am skeptical to it.

– Do you think it is unsuccessful?

– Yes, I do.

– It seems to me quite the contrary, I think that it is a very perspetive deal. It can bring us a tremendous profit. This industrial branch is underdeveloped in this country. It exists, of course, but a half of motorcar plants either stand idle or produce cars that became obslete almost ten years ago. So, we are going to sign a contract wi the "TF" company and start producing our own cars. According to approximate calculations the cost of the cars will be about 11 000 $, i.e. it is equal or even a bit cheaper then their cars. We interrogated the people of several regions and we found out that they are ready to by "Www" cars if we adapt them to local conditions. The talks are on. Almost all points are agreed upon except two of them. Their part insists on, as I have said, adapting the cars to local conditions. But we consider it unnecessary, since on the streets of Neiwa and other cities you can see plenty of cars of foreign brands that are not adapted to their climatic conditions and roads. There is one more problem. We came into a deadlock trying to decide which model is to be produced in the assembly line of the "TF" company. The company's representatives insist on the latest model and we object it. I hope that we will be able to reach an agreement on these issues in our favor. They have no choice. No one wants to invest in this industrial brunch,at least. We see our task only in delivery of spare parts for car assembling at their plant.

– When do you suppose to sign the contract and to proceed to its realization?

– It is hard to say now. We can sign the contract even tomorrow, but we have to incline them to our terms and conditions. I think that we can do it in a month. We will start realizing the project not earlier then in two years.

– I do not think that you will face any problems with its realization; more over there should be no problems with your competitors. As far as I am informed in the near future none of the firms is going to undertake anything similar to your project.

– You are inspiring me. I hope that our cooperation will be succesful and we will be able to find a common language. It was nice to meet you.

– Me too. Good luck.

This information gave the "Rrr" company a chance to take the lead over the "Www" company. In three days they signed a contract on the assembly of the latest model adapted to the local conditions.

2. On the 10-th of December Mr. A, manager of the "Z" company, as usual, worked in his office. He tried to busy himself with various things, but one thought was persistently after him. The point was that accidentally he received confidential information proving that its competitor – the "Y" company was on the verge of bankruptcy. If he managed to buy the controlling block of shares of that company, he would be able to change the "Y" company from his powerful rival into his good partner, then the joined company would be able to take under its control more than 50 % of the market. The idea was worthy of being seriously thought over. But the problem was that Mr. A had his doubts as to the truthfulness of the information about the bankruptcy.

Mr. A saw the only way to clear up the real state of affairs in a conversation with Mr. F, who was a member of the exchange group. Mr. F's group was engaged in prognostications. It received all information about the bankruptcy of any company in three days before its official announcement at the exchange. These three days could give Mr. A a tremendous advantage over all other potential buyers, he could properly get ready to score a victory. Mr. A perfectly understood that notwithstanding the fact that they previously met, Mr. F would not directly give the required information, still he decided

69

to take a risk. He found out where Mr. F intended to spend the evening and he went to the same small club in the center of Moscow.

In the club:

Mr. F: Mr. A! By what chance? I did not expect to see you here. How are you getting on?

Mr. A: Fine, thank you, Mr. F. I am glad to see you. Today, I decided to take a day-off and I did not find the better place where I can spend the evening than this club.

Mr. F: Yes, right you are. It is very cozy here. I do not come to this place very often, but when I am here, I find peace of mind.

Mr. A: Won' t you keep me company? We will have a chat.

Mr. F: I will join you with great pleasure. It is so good to be in silence after a hard working day. Frankly speaking, I feel myself like a squeezed lemon.

Mr. A: Oh, yes. I feel myself awfully tired, too.

Mr. F: I can imagine, you manage a huge company, aren't' t you?

Mr.A: Yes, a big company is like a big ship. It is less handy and it is easier to her to stumble on reefs and to run aground. But you know, how it is sad to see others sinking, especially those with whom you ploughed the seas.

Mr. F: I don't quite understand you.

Mr.A: I speak about the "Y" company. Yesterday, I spoke with Mr. K, a manager of the company. He told me everything about the approaching bankruptcy. You can't imagine how it was pity to hear such bad news.
(Here, we shall say that Mr. A bluffed. Actually, not only he did not speak with Mr. K, but also he knew him very little as well)

Mr.F: I did not think that you know everything.

Mr. A: We are friends with Mr. K.

Mr. F: Yes, it is very sad. In three days the "Y" company will be declared bankrupt. And you perfectly know what it is followed by: stocks will decline at the same day, until any magnate buys them all at a funny price and turns out to be the new owner of the company. We can only express our sympathy with Mr. K.

Mr. A: Is there anything to be done with it to avoid bankruptcy?

Mr. F: Looks like nothing. In three days nothing can be changed.

Mr. A: Yes, you are right. By the way, let's avoid speaking about sad things.

Mr. F: After all today is our day-off. We shall not spoil it. How is your wife doing?

And they passed to talks about their families, children and future holydays, and so on.

Of course, Mr. A was satisfied by the well-handed evening. Next morning he started executing his plan and...now (after six months passed from that unforgettable day) he is a chief manager of the "Z and Y" company.

Chapter 7. **Imperative speech**

> No laugh, no cry and no hate, but understanding.
>
> *Espinoza*

The ritual and provocative speeches are not the prime ones in the speech communication. When we address a person, i.e. initiate a speech, most often we want to influence on his emotional state: to please, flatter, humble, infuriate and so on. This function of the speech is called "to provoke a feeling", i.e. to excite emotions.

First of all one wants to arouse such an emotion that he feels. This phenomenon is called "congruency" (it is a mathematic term that signifies the equality). To feel the congruent emotion means to feel the same that the speaker feels. Complicated emotional events take place in such situation, sometimes they lead us into the state of guinea pigs, since according to the known psychological pattern the people are used to exchange with their states of mind. It is a universal pattern. Why do we want to share a strong emotion with other people? Because the emotion, by itself, is very hard, it represents a heavy burden on the central nervous system. When a person shares the emotion with other people, transfers it to the outer world, i.e. "runs down", the tension falls and the nervous system comes to a more balanced state. So, the human being has a psychophysical need in "running down". It applies all of the people, not only those who have a specific character – open and frank people. It is inherent in the human nature. It is quite another matter that we have a system of strict self-restraints, which are often linked with the complexes of inferiority and vulnerability formed in the childhood. Sometimes people feel awkward to express their emotions and to realize them in their outward behavior and in this way to "infect" other people with their emotions.

The modern Russian society is less open and frank as compared with the western society, but the absence of openness is not a national strain, it results from the experienced humiliation of the human dignity and personality in the Russian history. When you suffer indignity, naturally, you are afraid of opening your emotions to other people, notwithstanding the fact that openness is inherent in the human nature at the genetic level. In which connection we shall say that together with a need to demonstrate emotions there is a capability to easily percept other people' s emotions and respond to them with the similar ones.

Such state of affairs has a significant threat, since the emotions are imposed to you against your will (by an imperative method); sometimes they are not long-wished and you are not prepared for them.

First, we analyze an amorous emotion. A person full of passion transmits this emotional information through different means. Very often it is an energetic method (See above); in addition it includes mimics, gestures, look and expression of eyes (body language), and, of course, speech. The person at whom the amorous emotion is directed perceives it very well, as any strong emotion. If you stay in a long communication with a man who loves you (especially, if all three means of communication are used, i.e. you observe each other face to face) and for the first time you fill nothing to him, then, in a certain period of time you, as a rule, begin responding to this emotion. It is one of the reasons of unexpected marriages-misalliances, when, for instance, a very interesting, rich and respectable woman by a strange reason from the standpoint of the common sense chooses a husband that is less attractive and has no position in the community. But she is in love with him.

When analyzing the experience of the above personalities one ought to come to a conclusion that the man initiated such a feeling and having a tremendous influence (predominantly, it was an energetic influence) on the woman he inspired her feeling in return. The similar psychological situation, according to the witnesses' evidence underlied the relations of Marina Vladi (a famous French actress) and Vladimir Vysotsky (a famous Russian actor and singer). The history of their relationship is the history of a strong passion of Vladimir Vysotsky that passed through many years. It was a very strong feeling, almost fanatical to a unacquainted and unknown woman (he saw her once in the film). When they met for the first time Marina Vladi found herself in a very pressing position: she felt unusual energetic and extraordinary emotional press which after awhile she could not resist in spite of the fact that her destiny and her heart as well belonged to another person at that moment.

In other words each of us finds himself in the "danger" situation if he enters into a communication (any kind of it) with a person who feels very strong emotions in our respect. If you are not psychologically ready to return the emotion, you have only one way out of it – to quit the communication at all. As if you socialize with the person too often, watch him, perceive the influence of the whole multi-channel information network that he directs on you and he cannot help doing it (it is beyond the human capabilities), you will be forced to return the feeling sooner or later. Such is one of the reasons of many changes in the people's destiny in different periods of their life. Beautiful women are rarely devoted to one person through their life as they are exposed to strong emotions of many men who come to take each other's place as a result. The reason does not lie in a frivolous behavior of the woman. The reason is that she, as any other person, perceives the emotional information that are directed to her more often than to other persons, and she cannot help returning it. The provocation of congruent emotions is a common mechanism of human relations. It underlies many phenomena of the public life. The speaker feeling nervous and overexcited (from the medical point of view) addresses the public with a burning speech and in awhile he "infects" it. Contagiousness in this situation is very dangerous: people may attack each other in a hysteric state, being slow to grasp what they are doing, or they may form evident aggressive intentions. The tragic European history of the 20-th century knows quite a number of such examples.

In a simpler case the speaker communicates his bad mood to the surroundings in such a way provoking the congruent emotional state. The people often share their negative emotions. One ought to notice that a strong compassion most likely belongs to negative emotions. (In psychiatry the emotions are not divided into positive and negative; the gradation differs: whether the emotion stimulates a depressive or a maniacal state). The human being finds a strong passion to be a torture; it shows the seventh heaven just for a moment. When somebody loves you very much, especially, if the love is unrequited, he shares his torture with you. The negative emotion is easier and it is better assimilated. In fact, we are the potential victims of negative emotionality. The need in sharing negative emotions often occurs in the unconscious.

We will show an example, which may look unexpected, but it is psychologically trustworthy. When an older child comes home late failing to warn his parents about his being late, quite often the parents give him a talking-to in a rough and harsh form. Even a dilettante understands that the cry won't help to reach anything except a negative reaction in respond, and the unconscious objective of the cry is exactly such a reaction: "I am nervous all the evening, I am going mad – now, it is your turn to suffer!" The psychological mechanism looks like that.

One can communicate not only a congruent emotion, but also any special emotion prescribed by the speaker at the conscious or unconscious level. Most likely it refers to a sinful than an ethic influence. The conscious provocation of the sense of shame is very common. Alas, it is a typical conduct of a secondary (especially, primary) schoolteacher who finds moralities in respect of slow and undisciplined pupils to be the only pedagogical method. At that "the judgment" takes place in public, since the teacher has a task to shame the pupil before the classmates (he asks the pupil to go to the blackboard and to stay in front of other pupils) or senior pupils, if they have authority over him. The emotion of shame is provoked at the speech level, i.e. orally. It is one of the strongest and the most painful emotions, which one can feel. If an adult person provokes such an emotion of another person, who cannot respond adequately, who is helpless, two times shorter, three times lighter, in the language of ethics such a public humiliation cannot be called differently than "sadism". One ought to say that people remember such humiliations for life; they return their steady abhorrence to those who abused them and they thoroughly dissemble this abhorrence. A Rolan Bykov film "Chuchelo" (scarecrow) produced in the year of 1984, for the first time rose the problem of shame and humiliation suffered by people of school age in the system of the Russian high school. Since then there have been little changes in this respect. As compared with other civilized countries children cry in school only in this country. In the western countries it is a case of criminal investigation.

There is one more strong emotion – the emotion of fear. In case when a child is defamed before the parents, the emotions of shame and fear flow together: a fear of punishment, or a fear of being expelled from the school, or fear of shame in the presence of the people who have authority over the child. This methodological method is used instead of persuasion in respect of junior pupils, as in senior classes the child won't let the teacher to jeer at him. It is quite naturally that he will take revenge for it. Sadism is one of the long persisting characteristics of the society. It is a duty of every adult person to protect children against it.

Emotions provoked by the human speech can be divided into several types. The fear of speech as such is the basic emotion: everybody is afraid of bad news. Aristotle wrote about this in his "Poetics". If an outsider is a subject of misfortune, the fear changes to compassion. The articulate speech is used for psychological compensation of negative basic emotions. It works well especially if it is elegant and melodious, since it influences on the emotion of pleasure, love or affection. In fact the speech communication as such anticipates the community and mutual understanding among the people. The aborted or specially constructed speech may provoke contrary feelings – hostility or even hatred.

The shame belongs to the ethic emotions connected with the call of duty or spiritual satisfaction. The sense of responsibility, indulgence to the weaker, and respect belong to the ethic emotions as well.

The emotions connected with the intellectual satisfaction (guess, understanding of a complicated scientific text) are appropriate for the so-called rational emotions. A pedagogical speech, in particular, is aimed at the formation of such emotions. Philosophic traditions often give the priority exactly to rational emotions. Espinoza said: "Non ridere, non lugere, neque detestary, sed intelligere." (Latin) (No laugh, no cry and no hate, but understanding.).

The human being is a critical creature: analysis, evaluation of the surroundings and himself are an integral part of his spiritual being. The speech can influence upon the feelings that are in connection with it. They are called "esthetic emotions".

The last type of emotions belongs to physiological ones. By the use of the speech one can evoke pain, thirst, erotic bent and so on. One of the most effective means is a verbal direction to a certain event; for instance, to provoke the feeling of hunger one shall tell about the holyday dinner in details.

An elegant speech may provoke the listener's or reader's subtle shades of feelings that belong to all seven types of emotions at the same time: fear, compassion, love (or hatred), ethic, rational, esthetic or physiological feelings. In the same way another speech can deprive people of an experienced emotion, i.e. one can force a person to forget the feeling, one can make him go out from a certain emotion. For instance, your friend was sad and you consoled him and cheered him up, it means that you made him forget the sorrow. It is a rare fact in case of congruency: you and some one else experience the same emotion, but you are trying to take him out from the emotion. Sometimes it occurs in private relations when two persons are in love with each other, but one (for a certain reason) tries to destroy the other lover' s feeling.

In the same way as one can make somebody feel something, he can make somebody do something. When doing this one can make somebody do something congruent, i.e. something that he does himself (for instance, to ask somebody for a dance) or congruently prohibit somebody to do something. "I do not dance and you won' t do it." It is a verbal ban for a certain activity in such conditions when the speaker does not want to do it himself. Of course, one can make somebody simply do or not do something. The humans developed a special speech form connected with the compulsion to be active or inactive: it is an order. In this country a written order as a bureaucratic document is a standard form in the management. In more democratic systems it is not so typical and an imperative, i.e. an imperative mood of this category does not sound so strictly. For instance, an order of the Russian principal of a university says: "Students shall hand the course papers over to dean' s office before..." The analogical order of, say, the British principal of a university would most likely say: "Students (have, are) to hand the course papers over to dean's office before..." The modality of recommendation has an obvious psychological advantage as compared with the modality of imperative. Of course, in such structures like, say, the army, the imperative form of an order is quite defensible and expedient, since in such structures the breach of discipline in connection with the neglect of order is punished down to the tribunal. However, in a commanding and bureaucratic system orders are typical even in those cases when they are absolutely inexpedient. Today, we are psychological victims of the routine. (4)

Example:

A guard is on watch at the university door. If you forget your pass or student card it is useless to ask him to let you pass, since a man in the uniform feels himself as to be in the army hierarchy. Even if he receives orders from a civil man (say, pro-rector of studies), he interprets it as a military command, as an obligatory function and he stays in the following disposition: "If I break the order I will be brought before a tribunal". At the level of common sense he, perhaps, understands that he shall let you pass, but at the level of the concrete problem solution he obeys the order, notwithstanding the fact that it is not the army, it is the university.

We have discussed two forms of the human representation: emotional and behavioral. The third form is intellectual. Is it possible to force the human being to think? Is it possible to organize a certain thought of the human being by force? No, it is not possible to force the human being to think, you can only persuade him. If you failed to persuade him, you may force him to take on the expression that he is persuaded. But it pertains to the category of "to force to do something". "To take on some expression" pertains to behavior, not to reflection. The human being has an innate sense of logic that makes the imperative "to force somebody to think" impossible. (5)

---

(4) All over the world the doors of universities are constantly open, even in the nighttime no one guards them. It is a certain pedagogical trick connected with an appeal for education, it is a symbol of the "openness" of knowledge. Inasmuch as the western universities are supplied with expensive equipment much better than ours.

(5) The innate sense of logic is not connected with education or any other elements of the human experience. If you meet an African aborigine who is dressed only in three plums, who never went to school, who even does not know what is the written language, and he will ask you: "Do you have a season of rains in your country?" and you will answer: "Your wife is a beautiful woman." he will immediately notice a communicative failure and he will look at you as you are a crazy man, since he ask you a question and receives a wrong answer, so, consequently, his logic is clear and you have demonstrated an ill logic.

The same thing happens with the argumentation as an influence on the innate logic of the human being (See bellow).

One cannot deny the fact that the human being can be brought into a certain psychic state in which he represents himself in the role of a zombie or a medium. Then he can be turned into the conductor of the ideas that are of the speaker's interest. However, it is a special energetic activity and it is not connected with the speech conduct. The theme is very interesting to be analyzed, but the modern science remains at the stage of the task formulation, not its resolution as regards such types of the issue. In all other cases only the persuasion makes the influence on the human intellect to be an intelligent form of activity.

One cannot force the human being to think, but he can form an intention of him, i.e. to make him take a certain decision (even against his will). Meanwhile the influence, as a rule, takes place through emotions (fear, shame and so on). For instance, one can force a spouse to decide on emigration using a blackmail of divorce. It is a common case in emigrating families, where, as a rule, only one spouse is ready to leave and the other bends to his/her will. Thus, the category of decision-making shall apply to emotional and behavioral categories, not to intellectual.

Bellow there are the examples of an imperative speech:

Lev Tolstoy
"WAR AND PEACE" (Volume 3, part 1, chapter III)
1. Alexander's letter to Napoleon after the French troops crossed the Neman river:

"Your Majesty My Brother,
Yesterday, I received a message that in spite of the frankness with which I had observed my obligations in respect of Your Imperial Majesty, your troops crossed the Russian borders, and only today I received from Petersburg a note in which Earl Loriston advises me upon the reason of this intrusion, that you, Your Majesty, consider yourself to be in hostile relations with me since the time when Prince Kurakin required his passports. The reasons on which Duke Bassano based his refusal to issue the said passports would never force me to suppose that the act of my ambassador served as an occasion of attack. And, in fact, he had no my command to do it, as he stated by himself; as soon as I knew about this, I expressed my displeasure to Prince Kurakin, telling him to execute his duties. If you, Your Majesty, do not intent to shed the blood of our nationals due to such misunderstanding and if you agree to withdraw your troops from the Russian possessions, then I will disregard all that hap-

pened and the agreement between us will be possible. Otherwise I will be forced to repulse the attack, which was not provoked by any act from my side. Your Majesty, you still have the possibility to save the humankind from the disasters of a new war.

Alexander"

2. A certain Mr. K in his letter addressed to the "Soltur-Este" company resorted to a threat of appellation to the Russian Federation Court:

TO: Mr. N
      President
      Mr. M
      Vice-president
      "Soltur-Este" Tourist Company

Dear Sirs,
My name is Mr. K and I made with your company a contract on organization of a complex tour, which terms and conditions are binding upon the both parties. In the cruise organized by your company I was injured in a car accident. According to the agreement the company was obliged to render all services called by me, including the insurance that covers the said kind of risk as a medical and surgical aid upon the sickness or misfortune at the rate of one hundred percents. However your company refused to execute the agreement. I paid all the expanses on the treatment at the place. Upon applying to the Moscow office of the "Soltur-Este" company I received no compensation of my expenses on the treatment in spite of the fact that I presented them the receipt.
In this connection I want to apply to the Russian Federation Court (in Moscow) with a claim to the address of your company in case if there is no possibility to resolve this conflict on the basis of mutual agreement, i.e. if the obligations stated in the agreement won't be executed by your company within 20 days from the moment of mailing this letter to you.

Best regards,
Mr. K"

Chapter 8. The Categories of "Coercion" and "Persuasion" as Realization of Power Urge

A prostrate idol is still the Lord
Mikhail Lermontov

Everybody knows how often he or she desires some one perform a certain deed. For instance, you desire your perfectly trained son (or brother) become a student of the Moscow State University. How can you produce such effect, i.e. how can you realize your inner desire? There are only two methods at your disposal: you can force him to enter the university or you can convince him of the expedience to be a student of the university. There is no third possibility. (In fact, he may feel his own desire to enter the university, but in such case you won't be motivated to act, since it is not up to you.)

It is possible to coerce somebody to do something against his will affecting on two strong incentives that are inherent in his mind from the birth. The first incentive pertains to fear, the second – to mercenariness. You can frighten some one, then he will do something that correlates with your will, and you can bribe him, he will do what you want, because he will find it profitable.

First, we will analyze the category "to bribe". The category "to bribe" does not always have the material character, i.e. "to bribe" does not only mean the transfer of material values (valuable things, banknotes, and so on). One can bribe a person by a more delicate method, i.e. to place him to such social circumstances and give him such a position in such circumstances, which he finds important, prestigious and advantageous, i.e. in such a case a social position may appear as the bribe. The choice of what kind of methods to use depends on the situation. It is a point of view that all people can be bribed, everything depends on the price. Many facts of the life of concrete people prove this point of view. One hardly can declare the full trustfulness of the thesis. However, it is often true, when it applies to the man's family, say, children, not to the man. There is a meaning of "mercenariness for himself" and "mercenariness for the child". The philosophic categories of "Self" and "Child" appear as two arguments of the mercenariness as a function. The child represents the physical and spiritual continuation of the human being in the eternity that is why we are connected with our children with special and exclusive relations. Those things that are of no importance to the man very often assume a special significance in his disposition if it concerns his child. Hence, they often try to act upon the mercenariness connected with the social position of the child, not the man: they coerce the man to do something meanwhile they promise to place the child (of older age) into "a good position". One can often find out and use weak spots if not of the man himself, than of his family (weak spots mean something very desirable). The human being's need in the achievement of an inner psychological goal may lead a man to the situation when he will do such things, which he did not want or intend to do. With this entire going on, the people are quite often forced to neglect their inner moralities and the code of honor. The desire of a deed performed by another person correlates with a philosophic category "power urge" that became far-famed due to the works of the German philosopher – Friedrich Nietzsche. Nietzsche interprets the power urge as the "principle of cosmic life interpretation". In aspiration for the superior execution of the power urge Nietzsche puts esthetic tasks before the man who placed himself "on that side of good and evil", who makes own laws by his own power and who yields himself to the self-made laws in the cast-ironed discipline.

However, the category of "power urge" has also a psychoanalytical interpretation (for instance, in the works of Alfred Adler) as one of the global, as compared with libido, motives of the human deeds. When Sigmund Freud wrote about a sexual attraction (libido) as an only incentive of the whole human behavior (in particular, speech behavior), he absolutized this category to some degree. The following development of the psychoanalysis theory showed the absence of the libido universality as a motivation. The human being has another prime incentive – "power urge", which is realized in the human behavior not less than the hidden or evident perception of the world (i.e. conscious or unconscious) from the position of his/her sex and the need for a sexual influence on the world. It is important to emphasize that the power urge like libido is genetically inherent in every man, not in separate personalities (tyrants, malefactors and so on). Through the power urge the man realizes his assignment as of the Lord's governor on the Earth, but at the same time, as of the Diablo's governor or the governor of the Powers for which it is typical to suppress and enslave, i.e. to affect the world by power and will. In fact, the people like to override the outer world with other people as a component of it. There are some deeds that are motivated only by the desire to strengthen one self among other people. At least, they cannot explain it in another way. (One shall not mix up the power urge with a need in authority to gain which one does not need power.) In special cases usually connected with a psychic disease, the man kills only for the reason to demonstrate his priority and power over other people. These cases are in fact pathologic, but they represent the development (to a great extent, it is a natural process) of the human being's innate need of power over other people. The power urge represents an inner, deep-laid motivation as compared with imperative or persuasion that can be demonstrated by scheme (See bellow). The categories of "persuasion" and "coercion" are the derivatives of "power urge".

So, one can force somebody to do something through mercenariness and fear. We won't specially analyze how they make somebody do something, since there is such a meaning as "an instinct of self-preservation".

When they act upon this instinct thus provoking fear for the safety of the man's own body or the body of his/her own child (philosophic dualism of "Self" and "Child" is also present here), generally speaking, they can force the man to do almost or simply everything. (6)

Of course, it is impossible to prognosticate the behavior of a concrete person in the situation when he/she or his/her child is subjected to torture. However it seems wise to suppose that in such situation the person will do everything that he/she is asked for. An act upon the fear of death is a very persuasive argument. No doubt, there are cases when a person under the direct threat of violence does things that he considers appropriate and he does not yield to the will of another person. Such cases are known. But it seems impossible to analyze to what extent the fear was adequate to the threat or depressed, which is typical to some people and can be compared with the low level of physical pain perception. It is an often case when on the background of fears the man has a feeling like: "It may be that I will get out of it…" Certainly, people differ considerably: some of them are fearful and careful; the fear controls them all the time. The others consider the self to be more important. Their prime incentive is the feeling of honor. It is highly praiseworthy.

A tragic death of a young journalist Dmitry Kholodov, which recently was widely outspoken in mass media, proves this idea to a certain extent. He was frightened for a long time since he tried to obtain such information, the possession of which was a danger to life. Nevertheless, overcoming the innate feeling of fear, he professionally and steadily did his job and wrote things that he considered to be appropriate. He did not yield to the will of other people despite their blackmail. But no one, except himself, was allowed to analyze his conscious; no one was inside of the conscious. So, no one can say for sure that Kholodov did not sincerely hope to defeat his enemies and did not underestimate the danger. No one learned to measure the fear and it is unknown whether the humans learn to do it at any time or not.

So, it wise to state that subject to the instinct of self-protection works adequately the human being does not stand the force pressure in extreme situations, it is beyond his powers. The imperative category is very tough, so, first an individual shall learn to understand when he is forced to do something (elegant verbal tricks are of frequent use in this respect), and second, he shall refrain from the similar acts upon the people, if possible.

---

(6) Of course, the instinct of self-preservation realizes itself through not only fear, but through mercenariness as well. "I want to preserve myself" – pertains to fear. "I want to preserve myself in a better shape" – pertains to mercenariness.

Verbal imperative acts are of common use in any totalitarian system, since such a system is founded on fear. The category of mercenariness serves also as the basis for the construction of human relations in a totalitarian society. The people at the same times are threatened and bribed, they are treated in accordance with the saying: with the stick and the carrot. (This saying as many others reflects the psychological state of the people under the conditions of a certain interaction.) The Russian history, at least, the history of the 20-th century, knew the periods when the fear prevailed, however, there were also periods when the bribery prevailed. In such situation the massive amount of people served as a proving ground whereon a concrete man or a concrete group of people realized their power urge. In which connection if we say about the Stalin period the situation was complicated by the fact that the bearer of this category was undoubtedly a pathological (in a psychic respect) man, in whom the feeling of power had a boundary character (as they say in psychiatry), i.e. it was considerably displaced in respect to the standard. The more terrible thing is that such situation lasted in the USSR within a quarter of the century! So, in the Stalin period the power urge was mostly realized through fear, and, say, in the Brezhnev period – mainly through mercenariness (and only partially through fear): large amount of people played upon the dictated rules performing meaningless and sometimes criminal deeds and in return for it they got state premises, personal cars, nomenclature positions, allowances and so on. The whole hierarchic state structure was founded on the small and large bribery and everybody strived to hold such a place that was not so much determined by his inner need of the human self-actualization, as it gave him the listed privileges in such conditions, whereon he, generally speaking, could have many things, doing nothing in exchange. It is an absurd system, which does not lead to the realization of the inner emotional and intellectual potentialities of the people and every single man. It was such a society in which we lived "drawing near the radiant future of the humankind" by the inanity of our existence. Today we face the reflexes of that time.

One ought to emphasize that the basic psychological category of "power urge" does not belong to the characteristic from the position of good-and-bad; it cannot be interpreted in such terms. The human being's inherent primary things cannot be estimated by a scales worse-better; it just exist in this way; no one will evaluate a person from the point of view of his body and say whether it is god or bad to have one neck and two eyes, i.e. evaluate the physical structure of the intellect bearer on the Earth. In the same way it is not constructive to say whether it is good or bad for a man to have libido or power urge as some special inherent characteristics. However, the realization of these inner motivational categories is liable to the moral evaluation. If the moral evaluation in imperative, as said above, has a negative character, i.e. the category of "coercion" shall be referred to as a negative form of the human activity (the result is achieved through suppression of the other will), the persuasion shall be considered to be a sensible, intelligent and positive act (it is an influence on the free will of an individual).

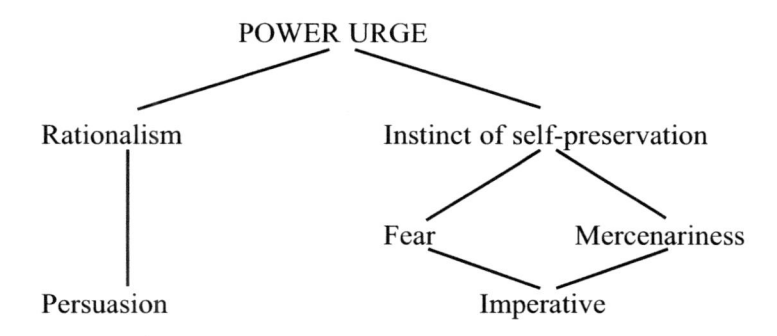

```
                    POWER URGE
                   /           \
          Rationalism           Instinct of self-preservation
              |                    /            \
              |                 Fear          Mercenariness
              |                    \            /
          Persuasion                 Imperative
```

What does the realization of the power urge through persuasion mean? Imagine, that you desire some one perform a certain deed. The persuasion represents a successful intellectual act on the conscious of this individual and as a result he comes to decision that he needs to perform the deed required by you. If in imperative he acts against his will, then you will form his will through persuasion, i.e. you do something that is more elegant and artful than an act upon the fear and mercenariness. You pronounce such a speech, that (returning to the initial example) your son begins thinking that he has a need of being a student of the Moscow State University. Further on he acts upon his own will and realizes his own desires (More frankly speaking, he acts in accordance to your will thinking that he acts upon his own.). It can be achieved only through persuasion.

The category of "to coerce" is incompatible with the definition of "to think" (See above), but the human being is a thinking creature, *Homo sapiens*, which finds natural to act upon the rational and logic nature of the conscious, not the power-based one. That is why there is no doubt that persuasion is the prime form of the speech communication: we always try to convince each other of the necessity to do something, of the adequacy of our disposition, truthfulness of our ideas and so on; it is typical to the human being's behavior.

In spite of the fact that we constantly try to prove any thing before each other, we don't know how to do it; that is the problem. In order to teach some one to convince other people, one has to teach him purely intellectual and logic priority over thinking and clever people who intellectually resist his ideas. It is the hardest task, so the considerable part of this book is devoted to the analysis of this issue (Part III. The Concept of Speech). The human intellect by its nature strives for self-preservation to a certain degree. On the one hand it strives for the movement and changing through the movement, but on the other hand it aims at a certain status quo and static balance. It is a pure dialectical contradiction. Of course, the human intellect tries to consolidate its grip on the current state. It means that if you have a certain system of convictions your intellect will constantly convince you of its consistency. When another intellect with a different system of convictions enters into communication with you, then your intellect at the first stage of communication resist any imposed views. It is natural process for the human intellect to resist other ideas: the ones that are new, opposite and adjoining. The human being has formed his system of convictions, he has inner argumentations in its defense and all of a sudden he meets a stranger who wants to change this system of contradictions, break it and impose a new one that belongs to him instead of it. For sure, the intellect will resist it. Only when you have overcame the resistance, you can tell that the person is ready to apprehend your ideas. He has not been persuaded yet, but he is on his path to the persuasion. Did you often manage to convince some one of something? Certainly you did not. After all everybody who failed to do it often has not begun yet to realize his own power urge, its divine branch (in contrast to the diabolic branch that leads to the category of "to coerce"). Every individual who did not learn how to force some one to change his/her mind in the intellectual respect has not begun yet to live in the right way, since he did not learn how to realize one of the strongest (may by the strongest) inner psychic references in the right way.

What is the mechanism of persuasion? What shall one do persuade the other one? A person (P^1) has a certain system of convictions (SC^1). A person (P^2) has a certain system of convictions (SC^2) You want to transfer your own system of convictions (or a view on a certain matter) to the conscious of another person. First, you shall take a considerable, or to be more exact, an adequate number of arquments ($A^1,...,A^n$), which can prove the insolvency of your speech opponent's point of view. It is called "supplanting". You supplant your opponent's system of convictions from his mind. After the supplanting your opponent's brain is free; it is pure vacuum there. At this moment you may begin filling it with your system of convictions through a new system of arguments ($A\text{-}1(^1), ..., A\text{-}n(^1)$). The second stage and the second procedure are called "substitution". You substitute the empty place in the conscious of another person with your concept. So, it is called "to persuade". The people rarely know how to do it without special training. They still can find arguments in defense of their point of view, but they almost never destroy in the beginning the other people's point of view (irrespective of their own point of view).

One ought to understand that supplanting and substitution reflect two absolutely different procedures; they can be organized one after another and they cannot be realized at one time. Both procedures are founded on a single method connected with argumentation. As it was previously said in the beginning one shall take arguments that can destroy the opponent's point of view, then he shall take the opposite arguments that can prove the trustfulness of his point of view. For instance, you are suggested to go to Sochi (a Russian resort) for a vacation, and you want to go to the Arab Emirates. First, you shall prove that a vacation spent in Sochi is a mess (supplanting). If you managed to do it, then there is a puzzling question (sometimes, unspoken): "If not go to Sochi, then where to go?" From this moment you shall go on to the second procedure, i.e. to convince that there is no other better place for a vacation than the Arab Emirates (substitution).

It is clear that the both procedures connected with argumentation are extremely complicated. However, there are certain tricks and possibilities that help to realize them (See Par III. The Concept of Speech). Using such a means one can convince the other people of any thesis: partially displaced, adjacent, similar and even opposite.

Certainly, it is usually easier to force some one to do something than to persuade. That is why the people realize the power urge through violence, which is understandable; it is simpler to pursue. It is more difficult to persuade some one, but the persuasion has a considerable advantage over *an imperative*. A man listens to you by order only within the moment when he is affected through fear or mercenariness. As soon as you stop frightening or bribing him, he frees himself from your influence and you are incapable of extending the act of your own will upon him. The power-based act has a transient character. The persuasion represents the power over minds; it is a constant category. If you made your own thought be a part and parcel of another person's mind, he begins considering them to be his own thoughts, often for life, so he will live under your permanent influence. Even if by virtue of certain unfortunate conditions your authority will crack in his eyes, the following truth will remain valid: "A abandoned temple is still the Temple, a prostrate idol is still the Lord!"

Chapter 9. **The Motivation of Professional Speech**

> Much wisdom brings much sorrow, the one who enriches his knowledge increases the sorrow.
>
> *Tsar Solomon*

One and the same text in fact results from the whole series of inner psychological goals, not a single one. The people are empowered with the knowledge of setting themselves multiple tasks and solving all of them by one (simultaneous) act, which demonstrates the perfect capacity of the human mind.

The professional speech serves as the best example of it. What professions are directly concerned with the speech activity and oratory? There are plenty of such professions. Say, a barrister or a public prosecutor. With no doubt they reach their professional objectives through the speech (all other actions represent a preparatory work for it), which they win or fail to win at the legal proceedings. It is a professional oratory. Our attempts to find out true court orators, as a rule, send us back to the 19-th century, to such famous names of the Russian post-reformed court as A. Kony, F. Plevako, K. Arsenyev, V. Spasovich and so on. In the court pretending to justice, the public prosecutor needs to prove the validity of accusation, meanwhile, the barrister has a real possibility to convince the judges of the truthfulness of his arguments. The speeches for the defense and the speeches for the prosecution, as well, shall contain the moral argumentation of their position, they shall demonstrate the methods of analysis and evaluation of the proofs; the speech shall be image-bearing and moving, direct, adequately judicious and cautious. It requires the mastership, since the court decides the people's fate. So, the general level of the oratory in court demonstrates the degree of respect for the human personality in the society as a whole.

The activity of a politician also represents the professional oratory connected with the attaching of the people to a certain ideology and social concepts, which the politician declares. To our regret many of the modern Russian politicians do not manage the oratory, so they are less effective in accomplishing their tasks as the politicians. Just a few political figures are capable today to address their nationals in writing or orally and to persuade or appeal them to do something. After all Plato wrote: "I state that if an orator or a physician come to any city and if in the Peoples' Assembly or in any other meeting there is a dispute whom to chose to be a physician from two of them, no one would even look at the physician, they would chose the one who is talented of speaking. If he would desire... The orator is able to speak in public against any enemy and for any reason in such a way that he will persuade the crowd sooner as anybody can..."

The same political figures who are empowered with innate oratorical capacities and at the same time in contrast to the others they have specialized education, sometimes, irrespective the ambiguity and even scandalousness of their behavior they enjoy wide popularity among the people. As professional orators such politicians do the same: they tell the people what they want to hear and desire, so they tell to different people different things, directing their efforts to the mentality of concrete listeners that is typical to the oratorical principle of the speech appropriateness. Quoting Cicero: "Really, the most difficult thing in the speech, as in the life, is to understand what and in what case is appropriate... The philosophy has plenty of wonderful directions and this subject is worthy to be learned; if you do not know it you pretty often make mistakes... . Moreover, the orator shall care for the appropriateness both in thoughts and in words. After all not every position, every dignity, and every authority, every age and, of course, not every place, time and the public allow holding by the same kind of thoughts and expressions for all cases. No, they don't. Every time and in every part of the speech, as in the life, one shall take care of the appropriateness in respect of both the subject that is spoken about, and the interlocutors, the speaker and the listeners."

The preacher is also a professional orator; his task is to preach the word of God to the folk and to strive for the moral perfection of the listeners.

Any teacher is also a professional orator, since his work is to address his pupils with a speech. Let us analyze the professional speech of a teacher in detail, because all people who ever studied or taught better know it. A university professor enters the auditorium wherein the students gathered waiting for him at the time determined by the time schedule, and if it is a lecture, not a seminar, he delivers a monologue. What for? With no doubt, there is a totality of goals, which he sets before he starts speaking. Of course, he wants to transfer his knowledge, i.e. information. Every speech situation is connected with the transfer of information. The *goal of speech* represents an inner motivation of the human personality. If the professor transfers the knowledge to the students, it means that he has a deeper than a simple transfer of information goal, according to which he wants the students to possess such information. What is this desire to share the knowledge based on? Everybody wants to have like-minded persons in his life; it is inherent in every thinking human being. So, the first goal is to create like-minded persons. Certainly the circle of intellectual like-minded persons is formed not only in the students' auditorium, but as well as in scientific conferences and symposiums, wherein giving a report and declaring his concept of a certain problem solution the man strives to reach a consent of his colleagues to the fact that his concept is worthy of note. What does the conscious of like-minded people in the scientific surroundings distinguish from the conscious of like-minded people in the students' auditorium? Why is it more successful in the students' auditorium? Herein one may find out the prime motivation of the human personality. We shall discuss it in detail.

The human being wants very much to be surrounded by like-minded persons, who at least are 20 years younger than he is. Each of us in this world behaves in the way like he/she intends to live forever. Take a notice how the human being lives. He collects material values within the life period; he organizes his relations with other people in a complicated way and tries to make them more successful; he spends a lot of efforts to obtain concrete objectives, though sometimes he is destined to leave this world with everything left behind. However, the human being has an inner feeling of the infinity of his path (of course, it is an illusion), he tries to join to the eternity, that is why, in particular, it is not given to him to know the date of death. Just imagine, that a man knows for sure that exactly at the age of 50 years three months and 4 days he will leave the world. Would he still try to get those things, which he will lose at this date forever? He tries to get more and more not for the reason of a happier life (joyful periods in one's life are quite rare things); in fact he does not believe in his finiteness, his psychic is organized in this way. Though he attends funerals... What capacities are at the human being's disposal to prolong himself in the space and time? He has two of them: biological prolongation of himself in the surrounding world and spiritual (intellectual) prolongation. His/her children represent the biological prolongation of the human being. The reproductive instinct is based upon it. That is why the coercion of the child (See above) often turns out to be more significant for a man than the coercion of him: if he dies he still have the descendants; it looks like he turns out to be transferred to the future and thus he becomes a nonfinite creature on the Earth.

But how can one transfer oneself to the future in the spiritual way? Only through the people, who will share your opinions and views on the things, subject to these people are younger than you. The human being hopes that his spiritual and intellectual "self" given to the pupils will be transferred by them to the future along the time axis. In this situation the pupils' intellect serves as the analogue of written monuments that are preserved in the human civilization for a long period of time. So, it is necessary for every person to create like-minded persons for prolongation, i.e. to prolong his intellectual essence in the space and time. The scientific symposium presents such a prolongation only in the space; the students' auditorium in addition does the same not only in the space, but in time also.

One ought to emphasize once again that a concrete human personality realizes his goals in his speech; the speech is motivated and expedient only in respect of this personality: speaking represents a selfish behavior, is this situation the man performs only such deeds, which he considers necessary.

Let us analyze the second reason: the man speaks only for the reason that they want to listen to him. It is especially true for the students' auditorium taking into account the saying: "Students vote by legs"; only those students attend the lecture that want to do it.

If a person performs a deed that is considered to be necessary by other people, it means that the goal of "to do good" underlies his actions. The goal of "to do good" is unselfish: when giving the people the things that they want the man performs a good deed. It is no doubt that the unselfish doing well is inherent in the human being, however the philosophic and psychological aspects of this phenomenon do not have a single meaning. The first concept is connected with the following interpretation: at the moment when a person performs a good and unselfish deed he begins feeling an extraordinary respect to himself and senses his spiritual priority over other people, which is one of the methods that helps to realize the power urge (See above). So, a good deed is considered to be a derivative of the power urge realized through spiritual intents. There is a more tough opinion: "Though everybody considers the mercy to be the virtue, sometimes it is caused by vanity, quite often by laziness, often by fear and always by the first, second and third." – said François De La Rochefoucauld.

Irrespective of the categories of good, the power urge is an obligatory thing in the speech of a university professor, since he constantly convinces students of the truthfulness of his ideas. A university professor is an intellectual idol of his students.

In accordance with another concept sometimes a person starts playing a role of a medium, which transfers the thoughts and will of God to the people. The person's will is not used; the God speaks by his mouth. It is moments of a mental irradiation, when the person realizes the God's will, not his. Since the God's will is unselfish and humane, than the man's mouth pronounces and his hands do something unselfish and humane. It is a diffused opinion.

According to the third concept (a sort of "a theory of rational egoism") the human being performs good deeds and avoids evil because good meets good and evil is responded by evil, and of course, the people will treat such behavior in a better way.

Every person based on his/her Weltanschauung (world view) chooses an intimate interpretation. It is a refutable fact that people are capable of performing unselfish deeds.

The transfer of knowledge represents another realization of a desire to do well. This postulate requires a separate discussion. There is a famous saying of Tsar Solomon: "Much wisdom brings much sorrow, the one who enriches the knowledge increases the sorrow." So, the truthfulness of the thesis: "knowledge is a good asset" is not evident. One ought to remember that we speak about a concrete man, not an abstract one. This concrete man is a university professor. He belongs to a certain kind of people for whom the intellectual activity is the only possible righteous activity on the Earth, since these people chose the intellectual activity and accumulation of knowledge as the prime business in their life. Otherwise how did the man become a university professor? Sometimes he understood that the knowledge by itself is a wonderful thing and he arranged his destiny on this basis. He had an individual choice. We are discussing the kind of people who sincerely think that the knowledge is a good asset. It is very important to understand. If a man does not agree with the thesis of "knowledge is a good asset", he is not able to be a teacher, since he loses an inner psychological motivation of his professional activity, which, as it was previously said, has an egocentric character and the man realizes the other people's goals only if he considers them to be necessary. A real, well delivered lecture for sure forces people to think, it stimulates thoughts, i.e. it realizes "an intellectual storm" (brain-storm). From the point of view of a man for whom it is typical to think, the provocation of intellectual activity means to do well. If the professor sees that his students during the lecture really start thinking, he considers that he performs a good deed.

An intellectual storm requires a special oratory and, generally speaking, a special talent. One can say for sure that the wonderful Russian linguist, Academician A. Zaliznyak is empowered with this talent; within several years he delivers lectures with the same brilliant result at the Philological Department of the Moscow State University. At these lectures students sometimes feel an intellectual shock. The Academician organizes his lecture by the principle of a classic detective story. The final goal of the plot is to achieve the truth; but if in a detective story it is to disclose the killer's name, at the lecture it is to comprehend a certain scientific problem (X) or to determine a complex (sometimes, undefined notion) notion (Y) or a category (Z). The lector tells almost nothing. He opens the lecture with the following words: "Let us discuss a notion (X). Who can tell anything in this respect?" Some of the students take the risk of speaking the first and in reply the Academician in a few words explains that the said opinion does not look like a truth in accordance with the following reasons (and he accounts the reasons). Then, another student, after a certain reflection about the idea, specifies the first definition in the required direction. The Academician says that the second definition is better, but still it does not comply with this or that. The third student trying to find out a definition that may comply with the said requirements considerably goes forward in precision, but he also comes into a new problematic or logical trap, which the lector immediately reveals. The auditorium slowly, by common efforts comes closer to the adequate definition of the notion. And just in a few seconds before the ring bell one of the most quick-witted students or the Academician, himself, delivers the true definition, the one for which the lecture was delivered. The work in search of the truth is extremely exiting; from the reader of a detective story you change into an investigator who clues the secret, which is not criminal, but scientific. The intellectual shock of the discovery may be so strong that the man forget about the quarrel with the beloved person, misfortunes, financial problems and so on, he forgets all of that; he keeps in such a state till he falls asleep (if he is able).

In the Moscow State University they know that the Academician' s lecture shall be the last one in the schedule, since on this day the students won't be capable to perform any other intellectual activity: it will be only one theme in their heads. As a rule, the students do not make appointments for the evening. Those who heard the lecture feel themselves intellectually spellbound, almost hypnotized. This state diminishes by the next morning as a rule. Everybody who heard the Academician's lecture understood forever that it is useless to explain somebody something, the man shall be forced to find the truth himself. The man shall figure everything out for himself; the teacher's task is only to stimulate the thoughts, i.e. to pursue an intellectual storm.

The above principle of the lecture represents a private case of the so-called concentric method. In accordance with this method the lecture is organized around one center represented by the given problem. Upon the delivery the lector all the time keeps an eye on the problem; he returns to it little by little going deeper and developing the proposed statement. The concentric method opposes to a step-by-step method designed for a sequential delivery of the problems, wherein it looks like the lector step-by-step turns from one step of the theme to another. The step-by-step method can be based on the chronological (historical) or spatial principles. The chronological principal is more convenient and natural at a lecture devoted to the history of a matter; the spatial method helps to transmit the facts by visual demonstration, graphically, in their dynamics and interaction.

The category of good in the discussed professional speech is realized through one more method. The people who entered the institution of higher learning, as a rule, want to get a certificate of graduation. If not to be cunning, it is clear that people enter the university not only for the reason to get the knowledge, but the certificate of graduation, as well, since it allows its holder to occupy a certain position in the community in future. Theoretically it is not necessary to attend lectures to get it, one can make ready to take an external degree in the library. However the scientific thinking is better formed in the auditorium, and the lectures save the students' time and make preparation for the examinations and tests easier, which is the basis to get the certificate, i.e. to obtain the objective that the students set for themselves.

The university professor delivers lectures for his students for one more reason: it is his job in accordance with the labor contract, which is made between the teacher and the university administration. The teacher takes obligations to deliver lectures, conduct seminars and so on (i.e. to conduct a professional speech activity), and the administration is obliged to remunerate his work in the amount that will enable him/her to keep the deserved living standard. The labor contract is based on the financial relations.

One more inner goal of the university professor is to preserve his social statute. With no doubt it is very prestigious to be a university professor. It is important to emphasize that in the professional activity the social statute is more significant than any financial relations, that is why university professors all over the world earn lesser money than, say, lawyers, physicians and etc., not mentioning businessmen. Consulting services provide the experts in consulting a considerably better material well being than teaching. However the prestige of a university professor is huge: it is one of the most prestigious positions to be occupied by a man. The people differ from each other considerably with regard to their priorities: money or social position. When analyzing the imperative category as the realization of the power urge we determined that quite often it is realized through the mercenariness: both material and social. The social mercenariness often turns out to be more important for the human being than the material. The person who chooses the position of a university professor finds the social statute to be more priority-driven than long shillings. At the same time there are plenty of wonderful experts – graduates of the best universities in the world, who were able to make themselves a splendid scientific or pedagogical career (they had all the capacities), but they chose another scope of activity (like business), since they found money to be more important. First of all the human being tries to accomplish those inner tasks, which he considers as more significant. It is a matter of a personal choice.

The next goal is similar to the category of social statute. It is well known that the speech helps to win authority. Jean Jacques Rousseau wrote: "Owing to the eloquence you can be captivated by a person whom you usually don't pay your attention to. The intellect does not only animate the body, but in some way renews it; rotary feelings and thoughts refresh the face and give it this or that expression; the reasonable speech for a long period of time compels your attention to the same person." Students turn out to be an ideal human space to form the category of authority. The communicative situation itself puts the professor into a higher position as regard to the intellect and individuality.

However, on shall not mix up authority with authoritarianism, which represents a special behavioral characteristic that is perceived as a negative one. The teacher executes a certain function in the community: this function is to translate the culture. At the same time some teachers all of a sudden realize themselves as living examples of the culture. Such concept of a teacher is typical to an authoritarian culture (the Middle Ages are the most brilliant example of it). Consequently, those teachers who realize themselves in this way can communicate only in the authoritarian way. The pedagogic task turns into the breading of a pupil who will look like the teacher. The modern European culture is called syncretic or dialogical (communicative): there are many samples, ways of life and ideas of the human being, so its prime value consists of a dialogue and striving for understanding. In the syncretic culture individuality and individual conscious appear as the central aspects. It is a principally democratic culture. These capacities of the modern culture shall be reflected in the pedagogical self-conscious. The teacher is not a sample, he is individuality, personality, which wants to be understood and at the same time to understand other people, each of them is a personality having an indefeasible right to speak and think. In such situation it is untimely for a teacher to be authoritarian, meanwhile his personal authority is possible and natural.

A university professor is a man, to whom it is typical to perform mental activity, including a scientific one. The pedagogical activity derivates from the scientific activity: first of all the professor is a researcher. Any person to whom the mental activity is typical, all the time keeps in the state of an intellectual dissatisfaction; it is a typical sign of reflection. At the depth of his conscious he casts doubt on even that statement that he finds reasonable. To be doubtful is a normal state of a thinking person: *"Dubito ergo sum"* (Latin) ("I have doubts, so I exist"). It is a precept of any professional thinker. So, the teacher is a professionally thinking person who gains wages for his reflections. In various companies of many countries one may find an established post called "a thinking engineer". The thinking engineer draws nothing and, generally speaking, does nothing; his task is to observe and analyze the work of all departments. His task is to optimize the production not at the level of concrete calculations, but at the level of observation and reflection on the expedience of every operation (meanwhile he is internally tuned up to a negative evaluation of the seen; he must dislike everything; he has such a psychological reference). It is the mostly high-paid engineering (sometimes, administrative) position in the company.

Actually a person thinks till he casts doubt on the truthfulness of his conclusions. It is an impulse to further thinking, since as soon as a person internally agrees upon the unambiguity of his own conclusions and ideas, and then it is no use of their further development.

If a person casts doubt on his thoughts he requires an arbitrage, i.e. he needs people who can disprove or confirm these thoughts. The need in arbitrage determines one more inner goal of the teacher. A person needs to deliver his point of view to other people in order to check its truthfulness by himself. Students are exactly right for this task. First, because they are young, unprejudiced people with clear, fresh brains. A person in his twenty years of age is able to notice a logic discrepancy, but when he is a 60 years old man he may omit it, since his brain becomes less receptive and alert. Second, because they are critical due to the existing psychological opposition to the one who confronts them in the auditorium (face to face), and every opposition gives rise to irritation. A group of students will never excuse a stupidity: notwithstanding the welcoming atmosphere there is for sure an element of aggressiveness. That is a psychological disposition of roles. The aggressiveness is also provoked by the fact that the teacher has the right to officially evaluate the students' knowledge during the examinations and in this way he can influence on the living situation of the students. The opposition is set for and it is very advisable for the teacher, since it allows realizing his every failure very quickly. Especially, if the group is large, since there will be for sure some ones who will demonstrate their reaction to any failure of the teacher. The students' auditorium in this respect is very merciless (and at the same time, thinking), owing to which the teacher has a real intellectual arbitrage: the auditorium reaction helps him to understand whether he managed to convince his listeners or not, whether he was conclusive or not.

When a person is forced to speak in the way to be understood, he, refining the formulations, actually refines his thoughts, which is extremely advisable for any teacher. Only precise knowledge gives the exactness of formulation that is why the word represents an incentive of the mind to some extent. J.E. Renan wrote: "To speak well means just to think well loudly." To make a text understandable for other people, first of all, one ought to clearly understand it by oneself. Quoting Tacitus: "The one cannot be and never was an orator, who like a warrior entering the battle fully armed did not come to a forum possessed of all the knowledge." Understanding is not static and, more over, it is not given from the birth. It is a process and sometimes a long one. At the moment of information transmission the person is forced to structure and organize his thoughts; only in such case he can make his speech understandable. So, one more goal of the teacher can be called "specification of thoughts".

If the professor delivered the lecture successfully and he understood that he was carefully listened to, his emotional tone rises considerably. There are quite many of teachers who attend their own studies with greater pleasure than, say, theaters (providing that they like the theater). The pedagogical activity brings joy and pleasure. Aspiration for pleasure is an inner need of the human being.

Let's analyze in detail this prime psychological postulate, since it has an imperishable importance for one to comprehend the bases of the human communication (in particular, speech).

The history of philosophy fairly appears as the history of development of the human conception of happiness as a goal of the human existence, on the one hand, and as a moral criterion, on the other. Socrates considered a deed, which brings a true advantage and at the same time a real bliss to be a true moral deed. Epicure joining the perception and attainment of pleasure by a causal effect told that the perception of nature is not an end in itself; it releases the person from the fear of superstitions and also from the fear of death. This release is necessary for the happiness and bliss of the human being, since their essence appears as a pleasure, but it is not a simple sensible pleasure, it is a spiritual one. Though, generally speaking, any kind of pleasure is not wicked by itself. However a spiritual pleasure has a more stable character, since it does not depend on external troubles. Owing to the mind (a gift of Gods) the man's urges shall be driven to a harmony (symmetry), which supposes a pleasure, whereas one can at the same time achieve a peace of mind and coolness (ataraxia), in which the real piety consists, being not disturbed by unpleasant feelings.

An ethic school considering the bliss and happiness to be a motive and goal of all aspirations is called eudemonism (in Greek *eudamonia* means bliss). The followers of eudemonism considered such a person to be happy and well-doer, whose spiritual and physical capacities can develop with no hindrance, who gives pleasure to himself and other people owing to the comprehensive development of these capacities in such a way, that ensures him the contemporaries' respect and the descendants' noble memory. The greatest brains of the world, not counting Socrates and Epicure, Espinoza, Leibniz, Shaftesbury, Feuerbach, Duhring, Spenser and others represent the eudemonism. A social eudemonism or utilitarianism (in Latin *utilitas* means utility) was also widely spread. The founder of utilitarianism Jeremiah Bentham thought that "as many as possible people shall strive for as many as possible happiness". All the virtues of a separate individual, in the same manner as the State, its institutes and events are meaningful as long as they serve for this goal. The moralities and laws can be determined as an art of the people's deeds regulation in such a way that they could bring as many as possible happiness. *("The great is possible quantity of happiness")* Bentham's ideas were developed in the works of James Mill, and others.

Another philosophic and ethic school was developing on the background of the eudemonism – hedonism (in Greek *hēdonē* means pleasure), that considered joy, pleasure and enjoinment to be a motive, goal or proof of the entire moral behavior of the human being. The founder of hedonism was Aristippus from Cyrene. The virtue means a capacity of taking pleasure, but only an educated, penetrating and wise person is able to take pleasure in the right way; he does not blindly follow every nascent lust, and if he takes pleasure he is not captured by it, but it stands over and holds it. Helvetius, Lamettrie and others were hedonists.

Immanuel Kant determined a psychological and personal aspect of the philosophic and ethical category of happiness as follows: "The physical virtue as a superior among the possible ones in the world and the ultimate aim of our aspirations is defined as the happiness, under the objective stipulation that the man agrees upon the laws of moralities as a virtue of being happy." The capacity of being happy belongs to the value of a personality, since the one who is capable of being happy owing to his example increases the value of life and preparedness to recognize and carry on the ethic values as such.

The meaning of pleasure merges into the processes of perception; it is "a coloring" or "an accent" of the perception as a process. Stoics called a pleasure by the name of permission and a sense of value, as well. The sense of satisfaction comes upon realization of a desire (often unconscious). As it was said above, the human behavior contains very high percentage of unconscious motivation (some of scientists, for instance, W. Atkinson think that it reaches 90 %). Our unconscious "It" (a term of S. Freud) yields to the principle of pleasure, i.e. the psychoanalytic theory regards the pleasure and happiness also as the main objectives of the human life. A transition to realization of any desire in fact represents a pleasure. The pleasure refers to the desire as an asserting form of the consciousness.

If a person does not get pleasure out of the pedagogic activity, he shall not do it. The people if possible shall do in their life only such things, as they like. One shall not wrestle with oneself doing unloved things; it will make the life joyless, meaningless and immoral as well as regards the ethic traditions. One of the teacher's speech goals is to strive for pleasure.

The pedagogical professional speech brings pleasure not only owing to the increase of emotional tone, but as well as due to an energetic replenishment, which the teacher receives from his students. The young people gathered in a closed auditorium (especially, if there are plenty of them) emanate a lot of energy; it improves the speaker's psychophysical state considerably; sometimes such replenishment is enough for 24 hours. If the teacher and auditorium are in contact and the auditorium welcomes the teacher and his speech, the entire energetic flow is directed to him. In addition, it is one of the methods of life prolongation. Of course, a speaker loses a lot of energy, but if he is carefully listened to, he takes much more in return. There is a diffused error that it is easier to conduct a seminar with five – six attendants. It is wrong: it is easier to deliver a lecture in public to a mass quantity of people. It is quite another matter that one ought to be able to do it. A successful lecture may evoke such an intensive energetic flow that it heals a sick person, lowers the body temperature and releases the pain. Many people know that if you having a toothache and overcoming the pain under the press of circumstances and you have to address somebody with a 20-minutes emotional speech, the toothache will be over. By the end of the lecture the body high temperature of the teacher falls down two degrees. Of course, it may arise again, since it is not a full recovery, it is a temporary one due to the energetic replenishment. An actor playing in front of a large auditorium feels the same. Even an older artist, physically weak, for whom it is very hard to play a big role, sustains it on the scene, since the audience supports him energetically.

Certainly, the university professor feels himself responsible for his professional activity, but much more he feels pleasure, irrespective the fact that it is a hard work, which requires constant intellectual and physical efforts. In fact, only those who can do it well like the professional speech activity. With no doubt, in addition to a specialized education it requires certain innate capacities. Cicero said: "The first and the prime condition for the orator is to have an innate talent... Since the eloquence requires a special kind of the mind and senses vivacity, which helps easily to find arguments, makes evolving and adorning lavish and memorizing accurate and lasting. At best the science can wake or stir up this mind vivacity, but the science is powerless to put it into or to present, since all the entire represent the gifts of the nature. I do not want to say that the science is almost incapable of licking that or this orator into shape. However, there are people whose tongue is so irrotational, or the voice is so false, or the expression and gestures are so clumsy and rough, that no capacities and knowledge will help them to become an orator. And on the contrary, the nature presented some people so generously, that it seems that not a coincidence of the birth, but the hand of a god created them on purpose for eloquence." Not every person is able to be a university professor; it is a destiny of the elite.

Summing up all the above, we shall say that the purposeful area of a university professor's lecture appears as a system, which includes the following elements:

    1) Creation of like-minded persons;
    2) Prolongation of spiritual existence;
    3) Realization of power urge;
    4) Performance of good deeds:
        a) To perform a deed desirable for other people,
        b) To transfer knowledge,
        c) To conduct a brain-storm,
        d) To help in studies;
    5) Activity in accordance with labor contracts
    6) Preservation of a high social statute;
    7) Winning of authority;
    8) Intellectual arbitrage;
    9) Specification of thoughts;
    10) Getting of pleasure:
        a) Increase of emotional tone;
        b) Energetic replenishment.

A lector sets as minimum ten different goals. They represent inner psychological goals of the human being. All of them are realized in one text. It is reasonable to divide this multitude of goals into conscious and unconscious. The energetic replenishment may appear as an unconscious motive. Sometimes, upon the absence of experience one may fail to realize the increase of emotional tone. Some people unconsciously set the goal of creating like-minded persons as a derivative of the need for an intellectual "eternity". However, none of the above goals can be generally referred to the unconscious. Practically all of the goals of the analyzed professional speech may be conscious. The people surely differ from each other as regards the correspondence of conscious and unconscious in the motivation of their deeds. The more thinker is the person, the wider is the area of his consciousness and the narrower is the area of unconsciousness. The person's need for an analysis of his behavioral motives (including speech) connected with a question addressed to himself: "Why do I do this?" widens the area of consciousness considerably. A university professor is a thinker, at that he is a professional thinker; otherwise he won't be able to work in such intellectually developed and hypercritical auditorium as the students'. That is why most of his speech goals are withdrawn from the area of unconsciousness and have a statute of a conscious motivation.

It is hard to obtain all of the goals set in the speech; any of them may fail to be realized. With no doubt one and the same professor sets different goals at his different lectures. Sometimes he manages to do something better, sometimes not. And, certainly, all the teachers differ from each other considerably depending on to what extent they may obtain the set goals. But the purposeful area is the matter that the person wants to realize in his speech conduct and which he desires; it is the task that he sets himself. And how he realizes this task relates to the matter of his oratory.

Chapter 10. **Classification of Speech Goals**

> Sometimes a spectator happens to be either an ordinary listener or a judge.
> *Aristotle*

We have discussed a ritual, provocative, imperative and persuading speeches, as well as the concrete goals of the professor's lecture as an example of a professional oratorical activity. Among the entire goals there are some ones that can be recognized as the universalities that common to all mankind: creation of authority, performance of a speech deed for the welfare of other people; transition of spiritual "self" to the future; formation of intellectual allies and so on. There are some specific goals, typical to a certain circle of speeches: preservation of a social statute, execution of terms of the labor agreement and so on.

The goals can be divided into three large groups by a means of realization in speech:

Imperative, which constitutes the basis of an a u t h o r i t a r i a n speech; it is a power-based method of influence through the speech (order, threat, verbal sadism, etc.)

Persuasion, which constitutes the basis of a d e m o c r a t i c speech connected with an effort to impose own system of views on another person through argumentation (proof, explanation, etc.)

Provocation, which constitutes the basis of a l i b e r a l speech connected with a need for getting information (organization of discussions, inquiring speech, etc.)

In accordance with the influence on various aspects of the listeners' consciousness the speech goals may form certain spheres of effectiveness such as:

1) Provocation of emotions;
2) Attraction of attention;
3) Propagation of knowledge;
4) Creation of intentions;
5) Inducement to action;
6) Formation of habits.

All speeches can be divided into single (oratory) and continuing (homiletics). The basis of oratory is made up of the following speeches (by Aristotle): advisory (about the future), judicial (about the past) and epideictic or demonstrative (about connection of the future and the past). "There are three types of rhetoric, since there is the same number of types of the listener. The speech is composed of three elements: the orator, subject of the speech and the listener; the listener appears as the ultimate aim of the speech. Sometimes a spectator happens to be either an ordinary listener or a judge, and furthermore the judge of something that happened or something that will happen... So, there are naturally three types of rhetoric speeches: advisory, judicial and epideictic. The advisory speeches are assigned to persuade or dissuade, since both the people who have to advise in the private life and the orators who deliver speeches in public, do one of two things (either persuade or dissuade). As regards the judicial speeches, they are assigned to accuse or discharge, since the litigants always do one of two things (either accuse or justify themselves). The epideictic speech is assigned to praise or reproach. As for the tense, which every of the said types of the speeches means, a man holding a consultation means the future: when dissuading from something or persuading of something he advises in respect of the future. A litigant deals with the past tense, since always one accuses and the other defends in respect of the accomplished facts. An epideictic orator considers the present tense to be more important, since everybody says praises or abuses in respect of something present; however in addition orators use other tenses, remembering the past or supposing in respect of the future. Each of these classes of the speeches pursues different objectives, so if there are three classes of the speeches, there are three different objectives: a consulting man pursues the objective of doing good or evil; one gives an advice persuading the interlocutor into doing good, the other man dissuades from doing evil; any other considerations like fair or not, beautiful and disgraceful recede to the background.

The litigants aim at the fair and unfair, however they can add to it some other considerations.

The people who say praises or abuses aim at the beautiful and disgraceful, however they can attach to some other considerations." (Aristotle)

From the standpoint of persuasion and coercion the homiletics looks like the most powerful type of the speech, since the orator delivers the same theme to the same people many times.

The prime goal of an oratorical speech is to achieve the efficiency of coercion based on the necessity "to win" the speech. The prime goal of a homiletic speech is to influence; it aims at the winning of authority and trust for the future.

The oratorical genres in addition to judicial, advisory and demonstrative speeches include dialogue, rumor and folklore. The homiletics includes sermon, educational speech and propaganda. The oratory and homiletics all together constitute philology. The following genres constitute written literature: documents, manuscripts, belles-lettres, scientific literature and publicism.

Mass media refers to the mixed oral-written type of literature (radio, cinema, TV, press).

Every speech genre has its own spheres of efficiency, i.e. the prime goals stipulated by the nature of this or that genre. The table shows the efficiency of different speech genres (for details refer to the works of Y. Rozhdestvensky).

Class of Literature	Type of Literature	Genre of Literature	Emotion	Attention	Knowledge	Habits	Making decision	Action
Philology	Oratory	Dialogue	+	+	+	+	+	+
		Rumor	+	+	−	−	−	−
		Folklore	+	−	+	+	−	−
		Judicial Speech	+	−	−	−	+	−
		Advisory Speech	+	−	−	−	+	−
		Demonstrative Speech	+	+	+	−	−	−
	Homiletis	Sermon	+	+	+	+	−	−
		Educational Speech	+	+	+	+	−	−
		Propaganda	+	+	+	+	−	−
Written Literature	Written Language	Documents	−	+	−	+	+	+
		Manuscripts	+	+	+	+	−	−
	Literature	Belles-lettres	+	+	+	−	−	−
		Scientific Literature	−	+	+	+	−	−
		Publicism	+	+	+	+	−	−
Mixed Literature	Mass Media	Radio, Cinema, TV, Press	+	+	−	−	+	+

Spheres of Efficiency

PART III

THE CONCEPT OF SPEECH

Chapter 11. **Logical Proof in Speech**

> All human beings are mortal,
> Socrates is a human being,
> Consequently, Socrates is mortal.

A concept or a logical proof in speech appears as the second level of the speech communication presented by four elements: goal – concept – text – reaction.

A proof (in a wide, substantial plan) means a logical act in the process of which a truth of a certain thought is substantiated with the use of other thoughts. This logic act has a great importance in the process of the outer world perception and in the joint actions of people.

A proof and methods of its presentation were in the spotlight of almost all logicians and orators from the birth date of the science of thinking. Aristotle said that the people make certain more of something when they suppose that something is proved. He considered the ability to prove to be the most typical character of the human being.

Old Indian logicians studied the process of argumentation in detail. They singled out the following components: proposal, foundation, example, similarity, heterogeneity, perception and conclusion. An Arab phonic philosopher Al Farabi considered the study of argumentation to be the basis of logic.

The practice demonstrates that in the process of thoughts exchange the people are not passive in interchanging of opinions and ideas of the outer world and their own actions. During a talk, dispute, discussion and consideration to any matters of production, science and routine the people convince listeners, readers, interlocutors and opponents of the truth of their views, they advocate, prove and uphold the truth of their opinions and notions, they disprove those ideas that they consider to be wrong. In other words, during an interchange of thoughts the interlocutors substantiate the correspondence of their concepts, opinions and notions with the objects and phenomena of the outer world.

A centuries-old experience convinced people of the fact that the validity and conclusiveness are the most significant characteristics of correct thinking. It reflects in our consciousness one of the most general pattern of the objective reality – interdependence and correlation of objects and phenomena. So our thoughts about objects and phenomena of the outer world shall correlate with each other too.

However there are different correlations both in the nature and in thinking. Some of them are evident and striking upon the first acquaintance, others are peculiarly hidden. In such a way a correlation between striking water with a stick and sinuosity of the water surface is evident to everybody, but, for instance, the correlation between a sickness and its reason often is hidden.

It mostly relates to our thoughts about objects and phenomena. The correlation between separate thoughts is lesser evident, since every thought reflects objects and phenomena of the objective reality. At that we know that this reflection does not offer a simple, direct and a whole picture. Our thoughts do not reflect patterns of the nature and society mechanically, like an ordinary mirror. So, naturally, the ability to prove earnestly the necessary correlation of thoughts, which reflects the correlation of objects and phenomena of the objective world in the process of that or this discussion, appears as the extremely significant character of thinking. Unfounded statements were always considered as an empty business.

Inasmuch as any proof is a conclusion that among other notions considered being true, the debatable thought is true in fact, then it is very important to solve the next two problems:

1. What kind of thought shall be a true thought by its content, which one shall take as a reference to the proof of the thesis truth? Of course, the logic cannot explain it. In every concrete case they refer to special sciences. Really, no matter how well, say, a physicists know the logic, but to prove the truth of such a thesis like that a wave function is a static characteristic of a quantum ensemble, not of a single elementary unit, he shall know other true thoughts of the quantum mechanics.

But *what thoughts shall be taken by form* – general, particular or single notions, *what forms of correlation between the known true thoughts* taken as references to a proof and the debatable thesis shall be used, all these questions are up to the logic. This suggests the first problem: to define exactly and classify correctly the forms of correlations between a debatable thought and the thoughts used to substantiate the truth of a debatable thought.

2. The proving thoughts or as they are called, arguments, need to be proved and, consequently, they shall be taken from other true proven thoughts; the latter in their turn, if there is any doubt about their truth, shall be substantiated with other true thoughts and so on. However such process of argumentation cannot last forever, otherwise it would be impossible to prove any thesis. It follows that the possibility of proving the truth inevitably supposes the existence of such truths, which do not need a special substantiation of their verity. This suggests the second problem: to determine *what kind of thoughts* no longer needs to be proved.

People have to prove theses in different communicative situations. But for all that the content of thoughts, which required to be proved, differs in every particular case. The logic finds something general, common in all proofs irrespective that or this content of the proof.

Based on the knowledge of that common, which underlies the correlation of thoughts in the process of argumentation, one is able to derive some rules that are valid for all cases of argumentation. The following elements are common in respect of all proofs: structure and methods of argumentation, general requirements to the debatable thought and the thoughts used to substantiate the debatable statement. The structure and methods of argumentation are notable for their stability, since they resulted from long abstractive work of the human thinking; they appear as the product of labor of several centuries, of many generations.

By the method of presentation the proofs are divided into direct and indirect.

A direct proof is based on a certain doubtless statement used to derive a verity of a thesis. (1)

In the course of an indirect argumentation one shall substantiate the verity of a thesis by refutation of the contradictory statement verity; in other words, in the course of indirect argumentation one ought to prove the falsity of the proposed thesis negation and derive the verity of the proposed thesis from it. An indirect proof consists of two types: 1) apagogic proof and 2) part-time proof.

Upon offering an apagogic proof (in Greek apagoge means conclusion; apagogic means drawing aside, leading away) one offers an indirect, as if it is directed aside, proof.

---

(1) In legal proceedings the term of "direct proofs" has a somewhat different meaning. By this term lawyers mean evidences of those who witnessed a certain crime, in contrast to indirect proofs that mean evidences of the witnesses who know about the crime at second hand.

An apagogic proof is provided in the following way: we need to prove the verity of a certain thesis. Temporarily we assume that the contradictory thesis is true and derive all the following consequences from it. Since the given thesis is false, naturally, the following consequences will contradict the reality. By having this proved we demonstrate that the thesis, which contradicts our thesis, is a false one. So, if the given thesis is false, than the contradictory thesis, i.e. our thesis is necessarily right.

Such type of argumentation is also called as "the rule of contraries", that is a wrong term, since in fact it is "the rule of contradictories", since from the falsity of one contrary thesis one cannot conclude the verity of another contrary thesis; it is possible only in case of contradictory theses.

A part-time proof is used in those cases when it is known that the debatable thesis is a part of alternatives, which in full exhaust all possible alternatives in this field.

One presents proofs in the following way: step-by-step he excludes all parts of the part-time proof, except one, which in fact appears as the debatable thesis. In such a way if it is determined that a certain act could be caused by only one of the four reasons - A, B, C, D, and if in addition it is cleared up that neither A, nor B, nor C could cause it, consequently, D is the reason of this consequence.

An indirect proof represents a particular case of the rules of assumptions known as long ago as by Aristotle, which lies in the fact that the debatable thesis is derived by supposing a certain assumption. The application of an indirect proof poses a certain challenge. In the process of presenting such a proof one shall temporarily divagate from the debatable thesis and obtain additional material, at that complicating the whole process of argumentation. (2)

By the form of argumentation the reasoning may appear as deductive and inductive (See below).

To accomplish argumentation successfully in the process of substantiating the thesis verity one shall observe the rules, which provide for the derivation of the thesis verity from the verity of arguments. All rules of argumentation are determined by the rules of the logic, which reflect the rules of the outer world.

The argumentation can be both progressive and regressive. In case

---

(2) The term of "indirect proof" can be found in legal proceedings, but it has a different meaning there. Lawyers under an indirect proof mean such a proof, which certifies a desired fact by the use of other facts that directly and indirectly do not testify for or against the defendant, but taken in aggregate with other facts of the case known to the court they enable to determine one who committed that or this crime.

of progressive argumentation the train of reasoning goes from the grounds to the consequences. There are two types of progressive argumentation:
1) When the process of substantiation goes from a general statement to the debatable thought as a consequence.
    Thus, for instance, a geologist proves the belonging of a certain rock to that or this era of the Earth development based on the presence of certain peculiarities in this rock, which are typical to the era. This type of progressive argumentation is considered being common and the strongest. It is common, since our thought, as a rule, seeks a support in general considerations and statements; it is the strongest, since the thought derived from a general doubtless statement keeps always being more stable and steady.
2) When the process of substantiation goes from the debatable statement to facts as its logic consequences and the verity of the latter affirms the former. This type of progressive argumentation is used in such cases when the necessity of certain acts is proved by their utility. Thus, for instance, a constructor wishing to defend the proposed process refinement proves its future benefit.

In regressive argumentation (in Latin regredior means go backward) the train of reasoning goes from consequences to grounds. There are two types of regressive argumentation:
1. When the argumentation goes from the debatable thought to its grounds. Example: if it is required to construct a triangle similar to the given one, we recall a condition of triangles similarity, for instance, the mutual parallelism of the corresponding sides, then, drawing the lines parallel to each of the sides of the given triangle and extending them to the intersection, thus creating the triangle, we recognize that the created triangle is similar to the given one, since its sides are parallel to the sides of the latter. In the process of such argumentation it is required to prove that the debatable statement follows necessarily from the ground, which we show in our argumentation.
2. When argumentation goes from the facts as consequences to the debatable statement as a ground.

Among all types of proofs one ought to clearly identify indirect proofs, in which a certain thought is directly derived from its ground, and the ground is supposed to be true only upon a certain condition.

In such a way wishing to prove that in a certain triangle all three angles are equal to each other, we derive this thought from its ground:

mutual equality of all sides of the triangle. Then we say that the debatable thought is true with regard to the given triangle, provided all of its sides are mutually equal.

An indirect proof is based on the method of exclusion: by enumerating all particular cases in a certain thesis they prove their impossibility except one in respect of which the arguments are presented. The method of exclusion gives a true result only in the case, when the entire cases are enumerated and it is possible to substantiate the exclusion of all cases except one. Thus, the indirect proof resembles the partitive.

There are no stereotyped method or means of proof universal for all cases. Every proof has its own specifications, which is determined by the character of the debatable thesis and existing arguments. When choosing among arguments and a method of proof one ought to consider the personalities of those to whom he presents the proofs.

Any speech proof includes three blocks: thesis, argument and demonstration. A speech proof represents a triune substance with none of its elements to be withdrawn: all of them present the conditions necessary to furnish the speech proof, and upon a successful execution their ensemble is sufficient to furnish the proof. Thus, each of them is necessary and only taken as an ensemble they are sufficient for a proof.

A thesis means a thought or a statement, which verity needs to be proved in the speech. An evident opinion cannot be a thesis, since the things that are true by themselves do not require any proof. For instance, *it is hot in the room, the lights on the square were switched on, it is raining, the Volga River flows into the Caspian Sea*, and so on. To begin presenting arguments for such theses means to demonstrate the limited nature of one's mind. Since long ago Aristotle said that "the ignorance means to be ignorant of what for it is necessary to look for the arguments, and what for it is not necessary".

An argument means a thought assigned as a proof of a thesis.

A demonstration means a logic correlation between an argument and a thesis. If there is no correlation between argumentation and something that you want to prove, then the proof cannot be furnished (since, as a rule, in such a case another thesis is proved instead a debatable one).

There are different types of demonstration and the most common of them are deduction and induction (presentation of proofs correspondingly from the general to the particular and from the particular to the general).

Let us show an example of a very short proof furnished by the scheme from the general to the particular. Let's suppose that you want to prove a thesis that "Socrates is mortal". You will present the following arguments: "All human beings are mortal" (argument 1) and "Socrates is a human being" (argument 2). The first argument of "All human beings are mortal" represents a general conclusion; the second argument "Socrates is a human being" represents a particular conclusion. By using a logic correlation you can derive from these conclusions an evident consequence: "Socrates is mortal". The consecution of statements: *All human beings are mortal. Socrates is a human being. Consequently, Socrates is mortal is called a logic conclusion.* Such a conclusion cannot be called as a definitely deductive one, since only one of two arguments is deductive; there is only one general statement: "All human beings are mortal". It is an example of a combined demonstration, which joins the argumentation to the thesis.

Of course, it is the simplest example of a speech proof, which demonstrates the structure of a logic conclusion; that is all. In principle the speech proof belongs to the category of the most difficult ones in a communicative respect, so it is a rare case when some one is managed to convince somebody of something, excluding those special cases, when the interlocutor is internally ready to accept the opposite point of view and shows a very weak intellectual resistance; in such a case the proofs are furnished quickly and effectively. In another case, when you oppose a really intellectual person, who has a system of arguments in defense of his point of view, it is a very hard task to make him change his mind. A speech proof represents a two-stage procedure of supplanting and substitution (See above), wherein every stage appears as a logic trinity of a thesis, argument and demonstration. Each of three levels is somewhat restricted. All levels have their own complications in their structure and realization. A failure to meet special requirements peculiar to each of these levels is the main reason of failure to prove. One ought to notice that all the requirements are formulated in a very simple way, but they are found hard to be satisfied.

Chapter 12. **The Thesis**

> Nobody will assert that a class
> of people represents a man.
> *Bertrand Russell*

As it was said above a thesis (in Greek thésis means a clause, assertion) means a thought or a clause the verity of which is required to be proved.

Let us discuss thesis requirements. The first and prime requirement stipulates that a thesis shall be true. What does the verity of a thesis mean? We have discussed (See above) that the pattern of the outer world projecting itself on the human consciousness through analyzers and analytical work of the brain jumps considerably, so the consciousness fixes only a relative and very inaccurate pattern of the world. Keeping this in mind one can say for sure that the absolute truth is not given to the human being either in observation or knowledge. Since the truth is not given in direct observation and knowledge, but the logic operates only with the strict meanings of "truth" and "lie", one ought to have a try at settling this contradiction. Actually, on the one hand, a thesis shall be true (otherwise it will be impossible to prove it); on the other hand, the objective truth is not given to the man in knowledge. This dialectic contradiction is resolved through the category of trust. The verity of a thesis signifies a speaker's trust in the verity, at that the verity is real, inner and not ostentatious. Sometimes the trust leads to the true guessing, thus it coincides with the objective reality; however it does not always happen in this way, since if it would be a constant coincidence with the objective reality, then the people's point of view would never change, but it changes.

The second requirement stipulates that a thesis shall be clearly and precisely formulated. The precision of the thesis formulation appears as an operation that involves three procedures. The first procedure is to formulate the thesis precisely for the speaker. The second procedure is to formulate the thesis precisely for the listeners. The third procedure is to combine the first one with the second in one text. What does it mean that the thesis is exactly formulated for the speaker? It means that the speaker so well thought the theme and the thesis over, that he has no inner intellectual doubts in respect to this thesis. Frequently a person begins proving something without gaining an ultimate understanding of the theme. It is inadmissible for the category of persuasion, since in this case one makes a liberal speech instead of a democratic one. If you begin speaking with the goal of sharing your point of view with the interlocutor, whereupon you want to listen to him in order to reach a unanimous opinion, you do not set a task of a speech proof and, in fact, you are not able to do it. You will manage to convince another person only if you, as a speaker, have an inner conviction of your idea verity.

The formulation precision foresees an accurate choice of each word in a short text of a thesis (a thesis appears as a short text, as usual) and positioning of every word to the exact place in the text.

Such a language as the Russian language has a partially strict order (contrary to a diffused opinion that it has a free order): it underlies the logic of a sentence. Let us compare two phrases: *Девушка вошла* (The girl has come in) and *Вошла девушка* (Incomer was the girl). In the Russian language they have different meanings. The phrase *Вошла де-*

вушка (Incomer was the girl) means that the matter concerns exactly a girl, not a woman, not an old woman, not a monkey and so on. The phrase Девушка вошла (The girl has come in) means that the girl has come in, not run into, not fly into, not drive into, not swim into and so on. The logic accent falls onto one part of the phrase, which is connected with such a scientific definition as "an actual sentence articulation". **An actual sentence articulation** appears as a division of a sentence in a context into the initial part of the message – theme (the given), and the statement –rheme (new information). Every part (or parts) of a sentence according to the context or situation may appear as a theme or a rheme: *The paper* (theme) *is on the table* (rheme) is an answer to the question: "What is it on the table?" The components of an actual articulation are clarified mainly by their position in a sentence: usually a theme is located in the beginning of a sentence, a rheme – at the end. The clarification may be accomplished by intonation (the character of stress and pauses), distinguishing and restricting adverb (exactly, just), and context. (In the Roman and German languages an indefinite article can indicate the semantic center of the message (rheme).) A displacement of a logic stress in the same sentence gives a different actual articulation. However, the main method of clarification is based on the order. The direct order of theme–rheme prevails; it is called as progressive, objective and non-emphatic. The reverse order of rheme–theme can be found quite rarely and it is called as regressive, subjective and emphatic. It can be conditioned by the necessity of the rheme positioned compatibility with the correlative part of the previous sentence, divided rheme, rhythm and the speaker's desire to express the main opinion as soon as possible. In this case the rheme is clarified by the context – through exclusion of the self-evident theme from the sentence, which is usually omitted or moved to the end of the sentence. For instance: *A question I want to ask you. How did you find him?- An old man is he.* These examples present untypical and infrequent constructions.

A. Weill is considered to be the founder of the theory of an actual sentence articulation. Mathesius, a representative of the Prague linguistic school, developed his ideas. It was Mathesius who suggested the term. According to Mathesius' concept a theme (basis) expresses the idea, which is known upon the given situation or at least it can be easily comprehended and from which the speaker proceeds; a rheme (nucleus) appears as something new that the speaker says about the basis of his expression. A theme according to Mathesius does not express any new information, but it is a necessary element of a connection between the sentence and the contest. It is not quite true, since frequently the theme is determined by the content of the previous sentence. However, a new object, not mentioned before, can appear as a theme, and a previously mentioned object, used as an adverb, can appear in the rheme capacity, as an assertion of the theme. For instance: *Let's speak about A. Popov. It was him who invented radio.*

An actual sentence articulation is a subject of investigation from different theoretical positions. A concept of a semantic nature of the actual sentence articulation gives a priority in the theme and rhyme clarification to the factor of certainty/uncertainty, which sometimes leads to polysemantic interpretations of the actual sentence articulation in a context. A concept of a syntactical nature of the actual sentence articulation (G. Krushelnitskaya) admits its authentication with syntactical categories due to the expression of a theme and rheme by using the language grammatical means (but sometimes, only a context). A concept of a correspondence between the actual sentence articulation and the structure of a logical opinion (L. Shcherba and V. Vinogradov) gained further development in a theory of a logical and grammatical sentence articulation (V. Panfilov) – of the expression of a logical subject (theme) and a predicate (rheme) by different syntactical means of the language. Mathesius equating the theme (basis) and the rheme (nucleus) with the psychological (logical) subject and predicate also joins this concept.

Modern linguistic theories attribute the phenomenon of the actual sentence articulation to the speech and connect it with a theory of speech acts. With no doubt the understanding of the actual sentence articulation is a necessary condition of an effective speech communication. In the context of proofs first of all it is necessary at the level of a thesis formulation.

Now the simple fact that two phrases differing from each other only by the order have different meaning in the Russian language means that we cannot say about a free order, since the change of the order changes the meaning. It follows from this statement that the change of the order leads to the formulation of another thought. Of course, the choice of lexical units has a prime importance. It is called as a work at a word. Attempts to find a precise formulation of a thought lead to a multiple substitution of one word by another (sometimes, synonymic) and arise a feeling of the choice dissatisfaction. If it does not happen then, as a rule, it results in the proof failure.

The second procedure (precision and simplicity of the formulation for the interlocutor) means that your interlocutors shall adequately comprehend you. They shall be clearly aware of the subject that you want to prove. This stage frequently represents a danger of misunderstanding. First, the speaker shall use only such lexical units that are understandable for the listener. In particular it means that none of scientific theses shall be formulated without a prior explanation of all terms used in the thesis.

It is a question of those terms that are familiar to the interlocutor, since the terminological polycemy is a typical feature of the modern science. In the humanitarian knowledge every investigator as a rule, under the same term understands somewhat different, which is peculiar to him; that is why every term has a plenty of interpretation, each of them represents the factor of a concrete investigator's consciousness and internal scientific system. It would be very well, if every scientific work would be forestalled with the author's explanatory dictionary: where he would explain those scientific terms and expressions that he uses in his work. In which connection one ought to understand that such an explanation is needed both by the professionals and amateurs, who will read the work, in order to make the implication of the work be understandable. Many scientific disputes (sometimes very bitter) in such a situation may lose their actuality, since a detailed analysis of professional disputes enables one to make a conclusion that the most disputes result from a terminological discrepancy.

Unscientific speeches, in particular, everyday life speeches also frequently require the explanation of the used lexical units. Long ago Aristotle pointed out the facts that the people wishing to discuss a certain matter first shall negotiate the applicable terms and expressions in order to achieve one meaning. If the people failed to determine the initial meanings there is merely no sense to open a discussion. If one takes into consideration the fact that there are such words in the Russian language, which have not one, but several different meanings, then every one will be more aware of the importance of meeting this obligatory requirement before entering into any discussion. Aristotle formulated this requirement in the following way: "Undoubtedly that those who intend to fall into conversation with each other shall somewhat understand each other. If it does not happen what kind of participation will be possible in such a conversation? So every name shall be understandable and the conversation shall be made over only one thing, not many; if it has several meanings then it shall be explained, which of them (in your case) you mean. Consequently, if one says that this is a certain thing (and altogether it is not), he denies the subject that he asserts, since according to his words it "turns out" that the name does not have the same meaning that it has: and this is impossible."

As it was said above it is connected with the fact that a considerable informational error arises upon the information transmission and it is rather not a linguistic fact, it looks like a hardly correctable feature of the speech communication. In general form the mechanism of the information reception and transmission looks like the following: a person transmits information plus his own associations connected with this information. For instance: he tells something about a forest *(a)*. Let's suppose that in his biography he had an episode when he was lost in taiga that is why the forest arouses fear in him. This association *(a1)* is present in his consciousness, but he holds it back. Transmitting neutral information thereby he transmits not only a part of his inner intention, which is equal to *(a)+(a1)* (he does not transmit the system of associations *(a1)*). Correspondingly the listener receives only *(a)* from his inner intention. However at the same time his own system of associations appeared in his consciousness *(a2)* (for instance, if a person was born in a house surrounded by a forest, *(a2)* appears as an associative remembrances of the childhood), i.e. actually he receives the information equal to *(a + a2)*. In general form *(a1)* almost never equals *(a2)*. If it is so then the error upon the information transmission is equal to *(a1 + a2)*.

$$(a + a1) ==> (a + a2)$$

A part of the transmitted information is lost, but then not transmitted information appears in the consciousness as a "makeweight". The aggregate value of the error *(a1 + a2)* can be huge. In an optimal case it may amount to 15 percent, then the speech communication may be recognized as satisfactory in an informational respect. We understand the directed speech maximum 85 percent. In the same way the people to whom we address our speech understand us maximum 85 percent. Their understanding can be worse, in an ultimate case – quite to the contrary (it may also happen) depending on the ratio of *(a1)* and *(a2)*. This is such a standard of the speech communication. It is one of the reasons of the fact that one cannot make an adequate automatic translation: it is impossible to formalize a system of individual associations connected with every lexical unit. The elaborations of universal automatic translation systems, which looked so productive 30 years ago, came to grief, since it is hardly possible to computerize the consciousness: it requires an unlimited volume of the memory and each program finally shall correspond to the personality of every single man.

A few particular conclusions arise from a thesis, which says that the mutual understanding between people is quite relative. If a person who lived with you many years says that he does not understand you, as a rule, he tells the truth and he is not worthy of condemnation for it. One always ought to keep in mind that you also understand him partially at best. The realization of this fact leads to better tolerance in the human relations and by itself improves the communication. One ought to forgive misunderstanding, in particular, in family relations. The reason of somebody's misunderstanding occurs not because he is more stupid than you, but because he has an individual system of associations (and he has the right to have it), which keeps being steady and determines his perception, since it is a fact of his individual destiny. It is unnaturally and meaningless to trust own system of associations (because it frequently happens with two people, wherein one person is more strong-willed than the other), since the own experience remains more valuable: if once you lost your way in taiga (Siberian forest) and you were terrified, you will hardly forget about it; and if you grew up in a house surrounded by the forest, the forest represents a part and a parcel of your childhood with its joy and happiness of recognition, that is unforgettable, of course. When speaking with a man one ought to take it into account, i.e. consider it as communicative parameters.

While setting a requirement of the formulation precision and in that way the unambiguity of the transmitted information perception by the listener, in respect of each lexical unit one shall recognize the necessity of explaining his own system of associations connected with this lexical unit, especially in the cases when it represents a significant and important association. In other words if a person pronounces a thesis, which he wants to prove, first of all he shall explain what he understands under this thesis. In this case the amount of the informational error lowers to:

$$a1 + a2 ==> a2$$

The problem that the speaker faces, connected with the formulation precision, is determined by a special linguistic method, which is adopted by almost all languages of the world (and the Russian language, in particular). The matter concerns a syntactic homonymy (in this case some investigators say about a syntactic polycemy), in the result of which one and the same text can have several levels of reading, both superficial and deeper ones that are usually called as an implication. A skillful bellestress text has a plenty of interpretations, up to an individual interpretation of each reader (See, for instance, plays of the founders of absurd in dramaturgy Ejen Ionesko and Samuel Becket or novels of the metre of "the flow of consciousness" James Joyce). So, the syntactical homonymy means the multiform of the text semantic interpretation. There are simple cases of double interpretation of such phrases in Russian like: 1) *Мать любит дочь* (The mother loves the daughter) (where it is not clear who loves who); 2) *На стене висит портрет Репина* (Repin's portrait hangs on the wall)(it is not clear, is it a portrait painted by Repin or it is his portrayal there); 3) *Мальчик был одет клоуном* (A boy was dressed as a clown)(it is not clear, whether he was dressed as a clown or he was dressed by a clown); 4) *Рецензенту следовало посоветовать указать новые издания* (A reviewer is to be suggested that he should indicate new publications) (it is not clear whether the reviewer suggests to do it or he is suggested to do it); 5)*Ответ комиссии был представлен к первому октября* (The commission response was presented by the first of October)(it is not clear whether the commission was a respondent or some one else appeared before the commission as a respondent). The homonymy in the above examples is mainly connected with the failure to clarify the subject and object relations. However there are more complicated sentences that are interpreted by various people in different ways.

The lexical homonymy, in the same way as the polycemy, is frequently removed by the nearest context, since the choice of the meaning is usually determined by the compatibility with other words. Let us discuss, for instance, the aggregate meanings of the word "*a field*" 1) bare area (to collect flowers in the field); 2) cultivated land (rye field); 3) plain play-ground (football playing-field); 4) an area within the boundaries of which an action of certain powers takes place (electromagnetic field); 5) a blank strip at the back of a book or a manuscript (margin) (marginal notes); 6) brims (a hat with wide brims). The minimal context determines the realization of this or that meaning of a word.

Upon the syntactic homonymy (polycemy) the precise meaning can be determined only in a wide context, however it does not always happen.

If the text of a thesis turns out to be homonymic (polysemic) it cannot be proved. First it shall be decoded.

In such a way before one begins presenting proofs he shall execute a complicated work connected with defining the thesis formulation. The execution of this task is a necessary start condition of the speech victory in persuasion.

The third thesis requirement entails its uniformity during the entire speech delivery. There is a term of "to hold a thesis". It is quite difficult to hold a thesis. Even a teacher, if he is not quite experienced, is not able in an hour and a half to prove strictly the same thing as he began to prove at first. Since the name of the lecture actually appears as a thesis that is to be proved. Within an hour and a half an orator without a sufficient experience may digress from the thesis in his speech, he may begin presenting examples and arguments not in defense of the initial thesis (T), but in defense of the digressed thesis (T1) and the proof will fail to be furnished. It is an easier task to hold a thesis during a short speech, however it also requires certain efforts. If drugs affect a person, for instance, during a pleasant party, in principle he is not able to hold a thesis, since it is a hard intellectual work. Sometimes a glass of alcohol is enough for a person to prove something with enthusiasm and to switch over to a new thought just in a few minutes. He keeps holding his energetic state, but the vector of the speech enthusiasm direction changes very quickly.

The distinctness, i.e. the exactness and precision of the reasoning, as well as the presentation of thoughts in the speech follow from the fundamental law of the formal logic – law of identity (in Latin *lex identitatis*), which stipulates that every thought presented in the speech upon the repetition shall have the same definite and steady content. A necessary logic correlation between thoughts shall be determined only upon the condition, which stipulates that every time if a thought about an object appears in the reasoning or conclusion, the interlocutors shall think about "the same object and in the same content of its features" (Valerie Asmus). In the traditional logic the law of identity is written in one of the following formulas:

A is A;

A = A;

A is identical to A;

A ➤ A;

A = A.

In a negative form the law of identity is written as follows: *non-A* is *non-A*.

One ought to keep in mind that the above formulas represent only the symbols of the law of identity and they do not express its entire content. In the history of the logic thought development there were attempts to take down the whole law to these formulas and arrogate to the formal logic the statement that both things and thoughts are always identical to each other. However the abstract identity allows a difference inside; one shall refer to the identity as to an obligatory, but at the same time a temporary factor, if the matter concerns a definite thought.

Let us present the definitions of two fundamental logical concepts: opinion and conclusion. Under the opinion one understands a form of a thought that proves or denies something in respect of things and phenomena, their features, connections and relations, which has property of expressing either truth or lie. For instance: *A horse is an animal, snakes do not have legs.* The part of an opinion, which reflects the subject of a thought, is called as a subject (in Latin *subjectum*) of the opinion and in the logic it is marked with a Latin letter *S*, and the part of the opinion, which reflects the assertion (or denial) of the subject of a thought, is called as a predicate (in Latin *praedicatum*) of the opinion and it is marked with a Latin letter *P* (compare the concepts of theme and rheme in the actual sentence articulation). The word is (or *essence*, when the

matter concerns multiple objects) is called as a copula. An opinion can be expressed symbolically in a formula:
$$S \text{ is (is not) } P,$$
wherein S and P are variables, in place of which one can put certain thoughts about objects and their features, and the word is presents a constant.

Under the conclusion one shall understand a form of thinking or a logic act that results in a new opinion, which appears from one or a few known and in a certain way related opinions, that contains a new knowledge. The following mental operation with two opinions may serve as an example of a conclusion: *All liquids are resilient and Water is a liquid*, which results in the appearance of a new opinion: *Water is resilient*.

It may appear that the law of identity in its strictness connected with conclusions collides with the world image as something that infinitely and continuously changes, i.e. keeps to be in a perpetual motion. The motion is not to be made and not to be destroyed and the nature keeps the process of a continuous beginnings and destructions; this is the essence of being. However in the process of motion the following states are possible: temporary balance, peace or static nature. The possibility of a relative peace represents a prime condition of life. In certain periods of time objects and phenomena keeps qualitatively the same, being safe from significant and drastic changes. Every phenomenon upon the change retains the basic features, which appear as identical, i.e. equal to themselves as the same ones. Such is the dialectic law, which overrides everything in the world. The only difference remains in the forms of a relative balance and its continuation with time.

Every subject reflected by our consciousness has a qualitative and quantitative distinctness. It joins to the group of objects, family, class and type. But altogether it has definite and typical characteristics. Our consciousness shall reflect an objective character of a thing, event and phenomenon to keep the identical and the same features for a certain period of time. Of course, it is a certain inaccuracy, simplicity of phenomena, which takes place in the world, since we ignore slight changes; however this mental operation is natural, since logic functions of our intellect are directly connected with the linguistic ones, and the natural language, as it was said above, represents a discrete system based on the possibility of partial changes in an argument upon preservation of the function value (See above).

Those things that keep a relative identity are reflected in our consciousness by a stable thought, which remains to be identical during the course of our reasoning about the given object until it changes its characteristic. It is identical to the fact that objects and phenomena in the surrounding world do not mix with each other and keep concrete and definite features, in the same way our thoughts about objects and forms of motion shall reflect these features, not mix.

The observance of the thought identity during the course of the given reasoning appears as an intellectual law. Long ago Aristotle wrote in his "Metaphysics" that it is impossible to think, "if <every time> you do not think about one thing...»

If one destroys the law of identity in his reasoning, i.e. he puts a different meaning in one and the same thought; he will never get a true conclusion as a result of such reasoning. As a rule, it leads to the construction of a sophism (in Greek sophisma means fabrication, cunning), which refers to a logic trick, deliberately erroneous reasoning posed as a true one. Usually, a sophistic reasoning in form is based on the formal resemblance of phenomena, deliberately erroneous choice of initial statements, lifting events out of the general connection, ambiguity of words and substitution of concepts. Below there are a few typical sophisms known in the logic from the time of Eleats and Aristotle.

1. *– Do you know this sheeted man?*
   – No. I don't.
   – It is your father. So, you don't know your father.
   (Ancient Greek philosopher Eubulides from Miletus)
2. *The sitting one stood up. The one, who stood up, is standing. Consequently, the sitting one is standing.*
3. *– Do you know what I want to ask you about?*
   – No. I don't.
   – Do you know that the humanity is good?
   – Yes, I know.
   – That is what I wanted to ask you about.
4. *This statute is a work of art. But it is yours. It means that the statute is your work of art.*
5. *A thieve does not want to acquire anything evil. Acquisition of good is a good thing. Consequently, the thieve wishes well.*
6. *The right grammatically is better then the wrong. The peace is the best thing. Consequently, the peace is something rather gramatically.*
7. *If the wall does not breathe because it is not an animal, then it would breathe if it were an animal. However, many animals, like insects, do not breathe. Consequently, the wall does not breathe not because it is not an animal. So, the wall is an animal, although it does not breathe.*
8. *An animal is something that has a sole. Mine is the thing that I*

can possess at my own discretion. My gods were passed into my possession by the right of succession from my father and they constitute my property. The gods have a sole; consequently, they are in fact animals. So, I can do with my gods everything I want.

9. *A medicine taken by a patient is good. The more good to do, the better. Consequently, one shall take medicine as more as possible.*
10. *This dog has children; consequently, it is a father. But it is your dog. So, it is your father. You beat the dog; it means that you beat your father.*
11. *The one who teaches some one want his pupil to become wise and stop being ignoramus. Consequently, he wants his pupil to become the one who he is not and stop being the one who he is. Consequently, he wants to pass him from existence to non-existence, i.e. to kill.*
12. *Euatulas took lessons of sophistry of Protagoras upon the condition that he would pay fee only in the case if on completion of the studies he would win the first lawsuit. But after the studies Euatulas did not take upon himself to carry on a lawsuit, so, he considered himself having a right not to pay the fee to Protagoras. Then the teacher warned that he would claim to the court saying to Euatulas the following things:*

– The judges will either impose or not a fine on you. In both cases you will have to pay: in the first case due to the judgment; in the second case due to our agreement, because you will win the first lawsuit.

Euatulas who was taught sophistry by Protagoras responded by the following words:

– Neither in the first, nor in the second case I will pay. If they impose a fine on me, then I having lost my first lawsuit won't pay due to our agreement, if they don't impose a fine on me, then I won't pay due to the judgment.

The last sophism and some of the preceding are based on the infringement of the law of identity. Euatulas considers one and the same agreement in the same reasoning in different ways: in the first case Euatulas in the trial shall appear as a lawyer, who loses the lawsuit; in the second case – as a respondent, who is discharged by the court.

Let us discuss in detail a certain schoolboy sophism based on the infringement of the law of identity:

13. *2 and 3 are even and odd numbers.*
2 and 3 is five.

---

5 is an even and odd number.

The reasoning is based on the fact that both figures, separately equal to the third, are identical between each other. An exterior form of the reasoning looks to be right, however the copulative *and*, which participates in the reasoning, is not used equally, but in different meanings: in one case the copulative *and* is used in a sense of connection, in the second case – in a sense of addition, as a plus. Such an uncertainty of the content of copulative and, as well as the different senses in both cases of the predicative copulas is and *are* (in the first case they have a partitive meaning: *2 is an even number and 3 is an odd number*) lead to a wrong conclusion as a result of the reasoning.

The law of identity requiring a certainty of a thought, naturally, minds such a significant intellectual defect as vagueness and indistinctness of the reasoning. A certainty represents one of the global and common to all mankind intellectual features. The thinking beyond this boundary makes no sense. When presenting our thoughts indefinitely we will stop understanding each other, which may lead to the impossibility of informational communication between the people.

The necessity of following the law of identity within the boundaries of the said reasoning proves at best that the formal logic proceeds from the recognition of the fact that everything in the world, including thoughts, appears as the unanimity of the identity and difference; since if the formal logic saw in everything only identical things, there would be no use of warning about the necessity of keeping within the law of identity in the reasoning. The law of identity exists for that only reason that for the period of the reasoning one shall look aside and disengage himself from all different things existing in the world altogether and in the unity with the identity, which not only needed for the reasoning, but it is fraught with a wrong conclusion in the reasoning.

The laws of the formal logic do not deny the fact that things keep changing. In other words, the formal logic does not deny the existence of vaguely drawn boundaries, but it asserts that for clear reasoning one ought to draw a distinction between A and non-A. The law of identity does not exclude a possibility of perceiving the objects and phenomena changes. Quite the contrary, the changes and transitions of an object from one state to another can be perceived and described only upon the condition that one correctly fixes what is subjected to the change and what appears in the result. That is why the law of identity cannot be interpreted in such a sense that every concept shall keep its once determined certain content forever. The content of the concept can change due to the change of the subject reflected in this concept; new sides and significant showings may come out in the studied object. However after it is determined in what direction the given concept is conceived in the whole process of reasoning and in the entire system of our statement, this concept shall be taken in one sense, otherwise there will be neither distinctness, nor correlation, nor logicality in our statement. A thought about an object may and shall change. The law of identity bans only one thing:changing the content and volume of the concept ad arbitrium and without any reason. The law of identity does not ban raising a question about the term change, but if there is a system substantiation.

When infringing the law of identity a person, as a rule, destroys his own conclusions. In fact, if the interlocutor in the beginning of a conversation puts one content into the concept and then his thought shifts to another content of the concept (or a thesis), then, usually, in such a case there will be nothing to dispute about and nothing to be discussed.

The law of identity formulates a strict speech requirement: before beginning a discussion of a certain matter it is necessary to determine its clear and concrete content, then in the course of the discussion one shall stick to the main definitions of this content and avoid any ambiguity.

A superfluous examination of an object, i.e. incompetence often results in the instability of concepts. However, sometimes it is made deliberately (See below).

The observance of the law of identity is a necessary condition of a successful proof, but, certainly, not sufficient; it is only one of the conditions.

One ought to understand that a false reasoning is also expressed due to the principle of identity. The difference remains only in the fact that in a sophistic reasoning the stress is laid on an external wordy identity, but with this entire going on they feign that the matter concerns the identity by the content (See the schoolboy sophism).

The law of identity represents a law by the use of which it is possible, if required, to force your opponent to agree with your opinion.

Suppose one ought to prove that the joinery is useful:

Mechanical arts are useful;
The joinery is a mechanical art;

The joinery is useful.

In this reasoning the law of identity represents the basis: we identify the joinery with mechanical arts, and the fact that mechanical arts are useful appears as a truth, which does not require a proof. It is a positive form of using the law of identity in order to prove the verity of this or that thought. There is also a negative form used to substantiate the truth of one's views. Suppose, one ought to prove that Venus is not a luminous body. The verity of this thesis can be substantiated in the following way:

Planets are not luminous bodies;
Venus is a planet;

Venus is not a luminous body.

If a person in his proof does not observe the requirements of the exactness and semantic unanimity upon a thesis formulation, he gives rise to a logical and speech error, which is called as "a thesis loss" (in Latin *ignoratio elenchi*). The essence of the error is as follows: beginning with an argumentation of one thesis, in a while they begin proving another thesis in the course of the same argumentation, which has only an outer resemblance with the first one. For instance, wishing to prove something unfair in a moral sense, instead of doing this one starts proving something unfair in a juridical sense. In other words, the thesis, which ought to be proved, remains unproved. A thesis loss can be due to the answer to the question, which differs from one that you were asked or due to expression of the theme, which differs from one that was stated. The text can be expressed very earnestly, but it does not correspond to the given logic, that is why the proof entirely fails.

Let us show an example. A summary was taken from an interview of one famous economist (a thesis loss in the question-to-answer system). A correspondent asks: "How do you understand the term of "privatization"?" (3)

The economist answers: "Our society is not ready for privatization." It was in the air. What is the listeners' reaction to the thesis loss? It will be an intellectual discredit that provokes an ironical laughing. So it is an

---

(3) In itself the question is righteous, since every investigator understands any scientific term, as it was said above, somewhat differently. In addition, the word "privatization" represents a loan word (in Latin privatus means private). It is not a Russian term, so, upon transition from the European culture to the Russian culture it was definitely displaced in its meaning. And now, say, in the Great Britain and in Russia this term signifies somewhat different from the economical point of view.

error that has fatal consequences for the speech. Nevertheless it can be found even in the speech of the people with a high intellectual level (the matter concerns a doctor in economical sciences). Certainly, he seemed to be tired and he was not alert at the moment of recording, but several millions of listeners heard this answer. However, in fact, may by only twenty percent of them realized the error, since the level of logical knowledge in this country, unfortunately, is very low. The fact that we used to the thesis loss as to an existing standard is easily proved by simple examples, which we constantly hear:

1. – Where did you purchase this raincoat?
– It is not on the sale there.
2. – Who is called to the phone?
– Not you.
3. – Won't you tell me, please, how to get to the terminal?
– You still won't find.
4. – What time is it now?
– In any case you are late.

It is typical. We so get used to such texts that do not notice a logic error in them. Nevertheless we shall overcome this adaptation. If you hear in reply: "This raincoat is not on the sale there", you shall say: "Generally speaking I do not ask whether it is on sale there or not. I asked where it was sold. It is not the same thing." Once you put the man to his place in such a way. May be in future he will be more accurate in his speech. It is a diffused error. We may suppose that if we managed to analyze the entire massive of the Russian language texts, say, expressed and written within twenty-four hours and to process it on the computer, then the frequency of the logically erroneous texts appearance would be very high. It is a dangerous social sign. Let us show one more diffused example connected with the thesis loss, which is often found in written works, for instance, in compositions. A theme is set; a student writes down a composition that partially or in full does not correspond to the given theme. In the school practice they usually say: "The theme is not expressed." One ought to say that there are plenty of written works wherein the thesis loss is evident. More than 20 percent of entrance compositions in institutions of higher learning have a note that "the theme is not expressed"; usually, such works earns unsatisfactory marks.

If you are asked to write something down or to answer a certain question, first of all you shall analyze what in fact they ask you to write down or what answer they want to hear.

The loss of a thesis always results in a full speech failure.

Imagine a sobering-up station. It is morning time; everybody slept himself sober. A doctor is coming to deliver a lecture on the theme (the theme represents a thesis, which is to be proved): "Alcohol is a poison for the human organism". The lecture is expressed in the following way: Let's discuss the human liver. Under the influence of alcohol it widens, its functions are partially depressed and it may lead to cirrhosis (first argument). Now let's discuss the central nervous system of a man. Under the influence of alcohol it quite frequently becomes exited, it causes the redistribution of inhibition and excitement reflexes that badly affects the functioning and results in neurosis (second argument). Let's discuss the human intellect. The constant influence of alcohol will result in degradation of the personality and manifest signs of weak-mindedness (third argument) and so on." At the end of the lecture the lector all of a sudden says such a phrase: "Of course, there are such cases when one cannot help drinking, like to remove a stress (forth argument)." What happens with the patients? Everybody laughs feeling something habitual and intimate.

The last phrase crossed out the entire previous argumentation, thus the lecture turned out to be all for nothing. Where is the mistake? The lector should declare the lecture theme more precisely, like: "From all kinds of alcohol influence upon the human organism the main percentage relates to harmful and negative, and only little percentage relates to a positive effect. If the lector declared such a theme and said that a stress could be effectively removed by small doses of alcohol, no one would laugh, since the argumentation would be appropriate to the declared thesis. In the previous formulation the fourth argument disproves the given thesis, not proves it, which is the reason why the proof fails. One ought to avoid doing this. The formulation ought to fully comply with the presented argumentation. It is a serious, responsible and hard task to formulate a theme and it requires a significant intellectual work.

A thesis loss may be provoked not only by a mental failure, but it may entail a deliberate desire of a man to answer a question that was not asked, to work on a subject different from the set _one and to prove a thesis that is not the same as the formulated. Such cases are known by a thesis loss. The loss of a thesis means the deliberate loss of a thesis.

Let us show an example:

When issuing a transit visa to a Russian citizen the officers of the Finn's embassy in Sweden want to be sure that the man has a return ticket to Russia (terry-boat, train or air ticket). The man offers his passport to the officer. The officer asks him: "Do you have a terry-boat ticket?" Feigning that he does not understand the reason of the question, the man asks the officer a puzzling counter-question: "Well, are there some problems with tickets in this season?"

Those people, who make certain that they are not able to plainly prove the given thesis, more frequently use the thesis loss. Then they try to draw away the interlocutor's attention by issuing a new thesis, which outwardly resembles the given one, but with absolutely different content. At the same time they pretend to demonstrate that they prove the verity of the first thesis content.

Long speeches, as a rule, have such a logic error as "the thesis loss", when it easier to substitute one thesis by another.

The thesis loss pertains to the typical behavior of students and pupils at the exams. There is a question; it is absolutely unaware how to answer it; and the student usually answers a question that he knows, not the one, which is asked (this is a private rule). Such experiments are, as a rule, unsuccessful, since every person without any training has an innate sense of logic, which fixes without fail the loss and substitution of a thesis. Naturally, teachers always notice all the attempts to substitute the thesis at the exams. If the teacher asks the student to explain, say, the reasons of the beginning of the World War II, and the student tells him about the battles, which were famous in the World War II, immediately it is understood that there will be no answer to the asked question. The teacher may have different reaction to this situation depending on the additive goals related to the check of the student's knowledge (but it relates to the professional pedagogical secrets).

By itself the substitution of a thesis represents a typical feature of certain speeches. For instance, It is typical to diplomatic speeches; diplomats go through a special training to do it. They are taught how to substitute a thesis and how to do it elegantly, very implicitly, when it is hard to notice at the first glance that the man answers not to the question that you have asked him, or he delivers commentary on the theme that differs from the one, which he was asked to comment. It is a professional skill.

When you notice that there is a substitution of a thesis in the directed to you speech, you ought to check out whether the interlocutor is not able to answer you question or he does not want to do it. Sometimes it happens that a person was not able to answer your question due to the lack of knowledge, and sometimes due to misunderstanding. In particular, it means that when you are asked a question, you ought to take a short time-out to analyze the question. Very often a person answers a different question, since in a stressful situation he merely did not understand it.

You will hurt nobody's feelings if you ask to repeat the question or if you take a time-out to reflect upon the answer.

If you feel that the interlocutor does not answer your question because he does not know the answer, it means that you demanded more of him that he can give; you overestimated his abilities. In this situation you ought to render him some help. But if you feel that the man does not want to answer your question or he does not want to disclose a theme that you set for him it is a precedent for the reflection upon your relations with this man.

The general ignorance shall not be perceived as a vice. Reticence forces to be on the alert much more.

A civilized rule of decision-making in the management may serve as a curious analogy of the discussed situation. It is obvious, that in respect of authorized work subordinate people may find themselves in one of the four positions: (1) they are able and want to do; (2) they are not able, but they want to do; (3) they are able, but they do not want to do; (4) they are not able and they do not want to do. The administration ought to take the following decision:

→ to preserve a status quo;
→ to send to the training (for the company's money);
→ to authorize more complicated and interesting work;
→ to fire.

Different situations connected with the discussed logic error from the communicative point of view can be demonstrated as follows:

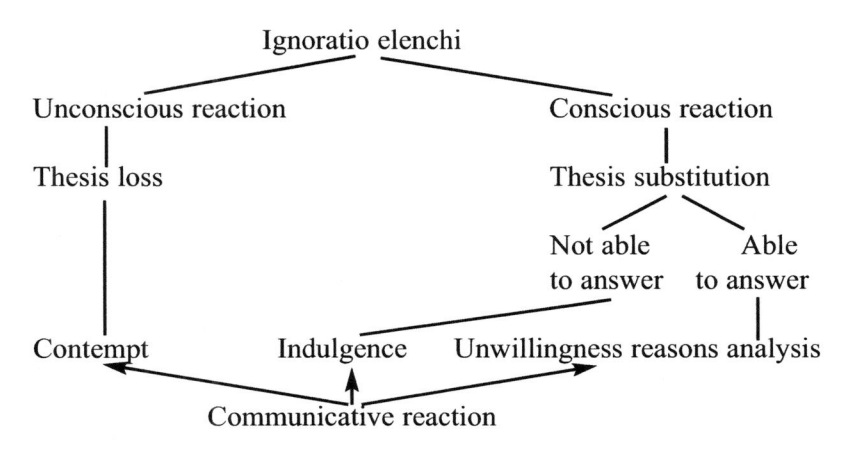

```
                       Ignoratio elenchi
                      /                \
         Unconscious reaction      Conscious reaction
              |                          |
         Thesis loss                Thesis substitution
              |                       /         \
              |                  Not able      Able
              |                  to answer    to answer
              |                      |            |
         Contempt   Indulgence   Unwillingness reasons analysis
              ←──────────↑
                  Communicative reaction
```

Such a situation is possible, when in the course of reasoning we

127

come to a conclusion that the proven thesis is a false one and another thesis is true. What shall we do in this case? It is necessary to declare that the initial thesis is false, so we shall refuse it and propose a new thesis. After the old thesis is substituted in this way, we may proceed proving the new one. Nobody in this case will be able to accuse the speaker of "ignoring" and exchanging the thesis, which is to be proved.

One can be reproached with the digression from a thesis, i.e. with a logic error of *ignoratio elenchi*, when he substitutes the old thesis imperceptibly for the other interlocutors and proves another thesis different from the initial one and at the same time tries to convince them of proving the initial thesis. In other words to avoid substitution of a thesis one ought to observe the rules of the thesis identity during the entire course of the reasoning.

Let us analyze the fourth thesis requirement. It requires inner consistency of the thesis. **The consistency** as an important feature of a logically corrected speech is defined by the requirements of two laws of the formal logic – the law of contradiction and the law of the excluded middle.

The law of contradiction (in Latin *lex contradictionis*) is interpreted in the following way: two opposite thoughts about one and the same object, taken at one and the same time and in one and the same respect cannot be true at the same time. In fact, the next two thoughts cannot be true at the same time: *This dress is white* and *This dress is black.*

In symbols the law of contradictions is drawn as follows:

It is not true that A is not-A.

This expression practically means that in the process of the reasoning, the used once thought (A) in the course of the reasoning shall not change its content (if, of course, the object reflected in the thought does not change), i.e. it shall remain to be the thought *A* and it shall not change into the thought *not-A*.

Aristotle discovered the law of contradictions and he wrote: "…it is impossible that contradictory statements taken altogether turn out to be true…" Aristotle considered that this law reflected the law of objective reality: "It is impossible that one and the same thing at the same time was and was not peculiar to one and the same thing in the same sense." Plato also expressed the idea that "it is impossible to be and not to be one and the same thing". In this case the human thinking reflects the law of universe. That is why the next two opposite opinions cannot be true at the same time: *Socrates is alive* and *Socrates is dead*, if one considers one and the same person taken at one and the same time and in one and the same respect, i.e. in respect of the physical life and death.

The definition shows that the given formal and logical law foresees not every contradiction, in general, not a dialectic contradiction, but only one of the contradiction types, namely, a formal and logical contradiction.

A word "contradiction" appears in an unstable and uncertain thought (deliberately or unintentionally) and it demonstrates that a person making logical contradictions in his reasoning in respect of one and the same matter is at variance with himself.

It is naturally, that the first logical mechanism made in the last century by an English logician William Stanley Jevons strictly obeyed the law of contradiction. He wrote: "The mechanism can discover every self-contradiction, which exists between the premises put into the mechanism; if the premises include a contradiction, then it turns out that one or a few letters-terms absolutely disappear from the logical alphabet". The law of contradiction is valid in respect of all our reasoning's, nevertheless what areas of expertise or practice they relate to. For instance, based on the fact that the Russian noun is of feminine gender, one can take a monosemantic conclusion that the noun is not of masculine gender, but the fact that the Russian noun is not of masculine gender does not allow one to take a monosemantic conclusion that it is of feminine gender. The thoughts like: *this noun is of feminine gender* and *this noun is of masculine gender* are said to be opposite thoughts. The law of contradiction regulates any operations with them. So, naturally, the one who knows the law is able to come to a true conclusion sooner in those cases when two opposite thoughts are found in the reasoning.

What is the reason in the fact that some people contradict themselves? Underdeveloped, undisciplined, eclectic and unstable thinking may cause the presence of a formal and logical contradiction in the reasoning, when some people can say something about a certain object without pondering and in a while they can say something opposite. Usually those puzzle-headed people may be at variance with themselves, who for some reasons try to defend an evidently erroneous thesis (to prove that "black" is "white").

An erroneous initial concept can give rise to a logic contradiction.

To use the law of contradiction correctly, one ought to clearly understand that it relates to contradictory statements about the object made at the same time. Different thoughts can be expressed in respect of one object in different times. The law does not prohibit to say *yes* and *no* in respect of the same matter and to combine two opposite opinions if they relate to different periods, different stages of the matter. The law not only does not forbid such combinations of contradictory opinions, but, on the contrary, it considers such combination to be righteous. One ought to keep it in mind in disputes, wherein it often happens that the opponent tries to pose a dialectic contradiction as logic one and brings an accusation of inconsistency and breach of the formal logic law. Usually it is typical to the people with an evident dogmatic thinking. Dialectic contradictions represent contradictions within a single object, phenomenon or process. The formal and logical contradiction does not have an exact prototype in the nature. Upon a logic negation two discrepant opinions reflect not the sides of a single object, but the existence or non-existence of the whole object or one of its features as a whole: a certain dress cannot be absolutely white, however at the same time it cannot be black. These are not the sides of a dialectic contradiction. The dialectic investigates the life contradictions, which breeds the development of all living creatures, and the formal logic in its law of contradiction deals with the logic contradictions, when the given thought inadequately reflects the world. It results in the appearance of strained "wordy" contradictions in the human mind.

It is also important to understand that the law of contradictions considers the utterances on a subject taken in one respect or sense. Different utterances are possible in case of different interpretations. A diffused judicial view: "Absence of a track in flagrant depict is a track" is not logically erroneous, since the word track in the first case is used in its prime meaning "a track of something on any surface", and in the second case metaphorically in the meaning of 'a symbol" and "sign".

Lack of fingerprints of a criminal on the broken lock (absence of a track) suggests an idea that it was an experienced criminal, who committed the crime (demonstration of the criminal professionalism).

In order to use the law of contradictions correctly one ought to understand that it says about impossibility of a simultaneous verity of contradictory thoughts, but it says nothing about the fact whether both of them can be false or not. Descartes wrote about this using an example of two debaters: "Every time when two persons keep to contradictory opinions about one and the same object, undoubtedly, that at least one of them is wrong and even none of them knows the truth."

It is also important to understand that the law of contradiction does not apply to deliberately false statements, though nominally they are in the state of opposition. Suppose, that there are two opinions: "Water-nymphs are warm-blooded animals" and "Water-nymphs are cold-blooded animals". It is not necessary to apply the requirements of the law of contradiction to these opinions, since both of them are erroneous.

The science pays special attention to the law of contradiction. L. Stoll wrote that it is of prime importance to determine the consistency of a theory. In many cases this problem is solved with the use of a model.

The law of contradiction has a logical connection with **the law of the excluded middle** (in Latin *les exclusi tertii sive medii inter duo contradictoria*), according to which one of the two contradictory opinions at the same time and in the same respect is certainly true.

The combination of these two laws results in the formulation of the next thesis: between contradictory opinions there is nothing middle, i.e. no third opinion (the third is not given: *terbium non dater*). Aristotle wrote: "Likewise there is nothing between two contradictory <to each other> opinions, but every single predicate about one <subject> shall be either asserted or refused." Actually, one should not express two such thoughts about a defined number at one and the same time and consider them to be true: "It is a prime number" and "It is a non-prime number", at the same time asserting that these thoughts are both true or both false. It is an easy task to determine that only one of them is true (for instance, "3 is a prime number"), the other ("3 is a non-prime number) is obligatory false, and the third possibility is excluded.

Symbolically the law of the excluded middle is drawn by the next formula:

A is either B or non-B.

It is important to understand that this formula is connected only with the logic of thinking and by analogy with the law of contradiction does not apply to the surrounding world's inner contradictions. When the law of the excluded middle is applied in contusive statements one ought to take into consideration that this law extends only to such contradictory opinions:

1. When one of the utterances asserts something in respect of a single subject or phenomenon and the other utterance refuses the same in respect of the same subject or phenomenon taken in one and the same time and in one and the same respect. The examples of such utterances are as follows: *Moscow is the capital of the Russian Federation* and *Moscow is not the capital of the Russian Federation.*

If the contradictory in form utterances do not relate to a single object, but to a class of objects, when there is something is asserted in respect of every object of the given class and the same is refused in respect of the same object of the class, then such utterances actually are not contradictory, but opposite. An opposite (contrary) antithesis is such kind of the antithesis upon which one compares an affirmative and negative opinions (See bellow) about one and the same class of objects and about one and the same feature. For instance: *All pupils of our class are excellent pupils* and *None of our pupils is not an excellent pupil.* Such opinions together cannot be true, but they both can turn out to be false, since the third opinion is possible between them: *Some of the pupils of our class are excellent pupils.* The law of the excluded middle does not apply to the opposite utterance.

Aristotle noticed the impossibility of applying the law of the excluded middle to the opinions about all objects of any class. He called such utterances as contrary, not contradictory. Aristotle wrote: "If some one in general arrogates the existence or non-existence to the common, then such opinions will be mutually contrary. Saying, "to express an opinion in respect to the common in general", I mean, for instance: "Every human being is white, none of the human beings is white". Between these opinions there is a third one: "some human beings are white".

2. When one of the utterances asserts something in respect of the entire class of objects or phenomena, and the other utterance refuses the same in respect of a part of the objects and phenomena relating to the same class. The examples of such utterances s are as follows: *All fishes breathe with gills* and *Some fishes do not breathe with gills.*

One of such opinions is surely erroneous, the other is true, and there is no place for the third one. Both utterances cannot be erroneous or true at the same time.

However, the law of the excluded middle applies to such a case when one of the utterances refuses something in respect of the entire class of objects or phenomena and the other utterance asserts the same in respect of a part of the objects and phenomena relating to the same class. Both utterances cannot be true at the same time. If somebody in the beginning of a dispute will refuse something in respect of the entire class of objects and then all of a sudden he will recognize the contrary thing to be true in respect of a part of the objects relating to this class, he will for sure lose, since he will be caught at a logic contradiction. (See an example with the sobering-up station). Let us show one more classical example – a dispute between Rudin and Pegasov in Turgenev's novel "Rudin" concerning the existence of convictions:

– *Wonderful,* – said Rudin, – *So you think that there are no convictions?*
– *No, there is none of them.*
– *Is it your conviction?*
– *Yes, it is.*
– *So, how can you say that they do not exist? This is the one, – for the first case.*

The following statements as *there are no convictions* and *the one conviction exists* exclude each other. If the second is true, thereby the first becomes false.

The law of the excluded middle formulates a very significant requirement of our opinions and theoretical investigations: every time when between the assertion and refusal of this or that notion there is no middle, one ought to remove the uncertainty and discover which of them is false and which is true. If it is determined that the given opinion is false, thereby it naturally follows that the contrary opinion is necessarily true.

The law of the excluded middle, as any other law of the logics, alone cannot solve the problem of the verity or falsity of contradictory utterances. For that one ought to examine the phenomena and the mechanism of their development. The law asserts only one thing: two contradictory statements cannot be false at the same time.

The knowledge of the law of the excluded middle is necessary to come to the true conclusion upon the reasoning. Let us examine the above example with two thoughts about one and the same object: *This Russian noun is of feminine gender* and *This Russian noun is not of feminine gender*. If the first thought is true, them by analogy to the case with the contrary thoughts one may say that the second thought is false. Now let us see what will happen if we suppose that the first thought is false. In the case with the contrary thoughts, as it was shown, one cannot assert either the verity or falsity of the thought on the assumption of the falsity of one contrary thought. This example demonstrates another situation. If the thought *This Russian noun is of feminine gender* is false, then the thought *This Russian noun is not of feminine gender* is surely true, since there is no other possibility as the contrary thoughts have. In addition to the nouns of feminine gender there are nouns of masculine gender and of medium gender. However, in this case all nouns are divided into two excluding groups: "of feminine gender" and "of not feminine gender". If it is false that the given noun is of feminine gender, then one can say only one thing: the given noun is not of feminine gender, since both nouns of masculine gender and nouns of medium gender are equally included into the group of nouns of non-feminine gender.

In order to express a proof in a better way one ought to know the relations between contradictory opinions, especially between a generally affirmative opinion and private negative opinion.

A general opinion represents an opinion, which asserts or denies something in respect of every subject of any class. In a general opinion a noted feature applies to all members of the given class. For instance: *All people breathe with lungs* or *None of the people in the world breathe with gills*.

The structure of general opinions is expressed by the following formulas:

All S is P.
None of S is P.

A private opinion represents an opinion, which asserts or denies something in respect of a part of the objects relating to a certain class. For instance: *Some people are bald-headed.*

A private opinion is expressed by the following formula:
Some S is (is not) P.

Private opinions are divided into two types:

1. A definite private opinion represents a private opinion, which asserts or denies something in respect of a certain definite part of the objects relating to a certain class. For instance: *Only some people weigh more 100 kilograms.* A definite private opinion is expressed by the following formula:
Only some S is P.

2. An indefinite private opinion represents a private opinion, which asserts or denies something in respect of a certain part of the objects relating to a certain class, and at the same time it dos not assert or deny anything in respect of other objects relating to this class. For instance: *Meeting ten pupils of this class I can say that some of the pupils of this class know the Russian literature badly.* An indefinite private opinion is expressed by the following formula:
At least some S (and may be all S) is P.

An affirmative opinion represents an opinion, which reflects the relation of an object and its feature. For instance: *All worms are able to crawl.*

A negative opinion represents an opinion, which reflects the fact that the given object lacks for a certain feature. For instance: *People do not have tails.*

A generally affirmative opinion represents an opinion, which at the same time appears as general and affirmative. For instance: *All mothers are women.* A generally affirmative opinion is expressed by the following formula:
All S is P.

A generally negative opinion represents an opinion, which at the same time appears as general and negative. For instance: *None of dogs is a bird.* A generally negative opinion is expressed by the following formula:
None of S is P.

A private affirmative opinion represents an opinion, which at the same time appears as private and affirmative. For instance: *Bears are found in some forests.* A private affirmative opinion is expressed by the following formula:
Some S is P.

A private negative opinion represents an opinion, which at the same time appears as private and negative. For instance: *Some children do not know their relatives*. A private negative opinion is expressed by the following formula:

Some S is not P.

Returning to the realization of the law of the excluded middle, one ought to pay his attention to one feature. It seems that it is easier to disprove a false generally affirmative opinion with the use of a generally negative opinion. In fact, it is not. When it is necessary to prove that, for instance, the statement like: *All graduates of this gymnasium received excellent school-leaving certificates* is false, then it is quite enough to substantiate the verity of a privately negative opinion. In fact, if it is proved that even one case (in the given example – one graduate) is not right for the general rule, it is quite enough to prove the falsity of the general opinion.

It is important to understand that the law of the excluded middle applies only to the contradictory meanings, to those, for which there is no average meaning; consequently it cannot be applied to the categories of good/evil, high/low, hot/cold, many/few and so on. In addition, it cannot be applied in those cases, when the subject by volume appears in a wider meaning, then the predicate. Thus, for instance, can be a person called in general as a woman? In this case both positive and negative answers will be erroneous. In general, a person can be and also cannot be a woman.

Obviously, there are theses, which in principal cannot be proven; for instance, it is impossible to argue the following thesis: *It will be good to go for a rest, as well as it will be good to stay home*. It is impossible to prove this thesis, since its inner structure appears as follows: *to go* or *not to go* (since *to stay home* is equal to *not to go*). It is an internally discrepant structure. From the logical point of view, generally, as it was shown, an internally discrepant structure cannot be proved at all. So, if you are asked to prove or explain something, which is internally discrepant, you ought to declare this discrepancy and refuse from argumentations. In such situation one can express only some thoughts of the problem, at the most. Unfortunately, not every man and not in every situation is able to estimate a text from the standpoint of the presence of internal discrepancy in the text. It requires both training and special intellectual abilities, since the internal discrepancy does not always look like an opposition of *yes* and *no*. It may be a complicated text, the internal discrepancy of which is discovered after a special intellectual analysis. It is a frequent case, for instance, in the science. It requires a special logical analysis.

So, an internally discrepant thesis cannot be proved. Let us discuss in this connection a few examples of texts, which are with no doubt internally discrepant, but nevertheless seem to be quite intelligent.

1. *One Cretan said that all Cretans were liars.*

2.

> An erroneous statement is written in this square

In the first example, if the Cretan said the truth, he lied, and if he lied, he said the truth. In the second example, if the statement is erroneous, it is true, and if it is true, it is erroneous. The next text is expressed by analogy:

3. *When a crocodile kidnapped a child of one mother she began asking him to give the kidnapped child back to her and the crocodile promised to do it if she said the truth*

– But you won't give me the child back, – responded the mother.

– It means that I should not give your child back to you, – in its turn replied the crocodile, – despite the fact that you said the truth or not. If you said the truth, then, according to your words, I should not return the child back: otherwise you would say the untruth. If you lied, then I also should not give the child back to you, since in this case, i.e. saying the untruth you did not meet the condition.

The analyzed texts represent classical examples of the so-called logic paradoxes (in Greek *parádoxos* means sudden, strange), known from the ancient times. Under a paradox one can understand a sudden, unusual and strange statement, which evidently or actually differs from the common view or even the common sense, though it is correct from the standpoint of the formal logic. Let us discuss one more famous paradox of an ancient Greek philosopher Zeno from Elea "Achilles and a throttle": "Swift-footed Achilles is never able to come up with the smallest animal, a throttle, since provided that they start simultaneously by the moment of Achilles coming to the place of the throttle, the throttle will crawl to 1/10 of the distance, and when Achilles will go through this 1/10 of the distance, the throttle will move forward to 1/100 of the distance and so on in all other points of the distance. Since the process of the distance division is endless, so Achilles will never come up with the throttle." So we have a sudden statement that abruptly differs from the common opinion and practice, since in reality Achilles will for sure come up with the throttle. This paradox is a part of the so-called aporias (in Greek *aporía* means hopelessness) – intractable logical difficulties.

In the logic, paradoxes are included into the wider class of argumentations leading to alternative results, which are equally demonstrable and cannot be related to either true, or false. Such argumentations are said to be antinomians (in Latin *anti* means against, *nomos* means law). Aporias are also included into the class of antinomians.

Kant, who developed the teaching of antinomians, called by the name of antinomians those discrepancies into which the mind falls in a try to give an answer to metaphysical questions about the world as a whole, since in this case the mind tries to exceed the bounds of a first-hand sensible experience and to learn "things in themselves". In this case the following antinomians come to existence:

1). The world begins with time and is limited with space – the world has no beginning and no limits with space;

2). Everything in the world consists of elementary (indivisible) hings – there is nothing elementary in the world, everything is complicated;

3). There are free reasons in the world – there is no freedom in the world, i.e. everything is necessary;

4). There is a necessary creature among the world reasons – there is nothing necessary among the world reasons, every thing is accidental.

By the teaching of antinomians Kant revealed the most significant fact that discrepancies are inherent in the human thinking. For instance, the first antinomian reflects a dialectic discrepancy of the finite and infinite; the second antinomian reflects the discontinuous and continuous and so on.

It is known that antinomians (and paradoxes, in particular) gave a lot of trouble to ancient and modern mathematicians, logicians and philosophers trying to overcome discrepancies with the use of that or this methods. However, in the course of centuries they could not be explained from the logical point of view. Only in the 20-th century a notable English philosopher and logician Bertrand Russell outlined how to explain such cases.

Russell noticed that one can say about 1) the multitude (class) of objects (for instance, multitude of stars or people), but also he can refer to the multitude (class) of the multitude of objects. As to the first multitude, it is not a member of itself, since a multitude of stars is not a star and multitude of people is not a man. Russell wrote: "No one will assert that the class of people represents a man. In front of us there is a class, which does not belong to itself. I say that something belongs to a certain class, when <it> is right for the meaning, which represents the class as a whole." It directly relates to Eubulides' paradox – "Heap": "One seed does not compose a heap; by adding one more seed one cannot make a heap; how can one make a heap by adding every time one by one seed provided that none of the seeds compose a heap?"

Such a multitude, which is not a member of itself, is said to be a proper multitude. As it refers to the second multitude, it is a member of itself (for instance, the multitude of the multitude of lists is a list). Such multitude is referred to as an improper multitude. Let us assume that we shall compose a multitude of the entire proper multitudes (M). This raises the question: what kind is this multitude – proper or improper? If M is a proper multitude, i.e. it is not an element of itself, we shall include it into M (by definition of the proper multitude). But its inclusion into M changes it into the improper multitude, so it shall be excluded from M. Let us assume now that M is an improper multitude. Then it shall be excluded from M, i.e. it shall belong to the number of those multitudes, which do not include itself as a member, i.e. it will turn out to be a proper multitude. However, as a proper multitude it shall be included into M. Both discrepant assumptions lead to the discrepancy.

Russell's paradox can be illustrated by the most different examples. Let us show one of them:

Each municipality in Holland may have a mayor and two different municipalities cannot have one and same mayor. Sometimes it occurs that a mayor does not live in his municipality. Let us assume that they adopted a law under which a certain territory S is singled out exclusively for such mayors, who do not live in their municipalities, provided that the law authorizes all those mayors to live in the said territory. Let us further on assume that the number of those mayors is enough for S to establish a municipality. Where shall the mayor of this municipality live? It turns out that the mayor of the municipality of S cannot live either in his municipality, or somewhere else. In fact, if he wants to live in his municipality, the law will remove him from the municipality, since only those mayors are authorized to live in this municipality, who do not live in their municipalities. But the law demands: if the mayor of S does not live in the municipality of S, he shall live in the municipality of S. It turns out that it is an insoluble discrepancy.

Russell's paradoxes amazed philosophers and mathematicians, as long as they touched upon the basis of not only the theory of a multitude, but also the formal logic, since they prejudiced the law of the excluded middle allowing the possibility of the verity of A and non-A. The crisis was met through the recognition of the linguistic method to be incorrect. Russell wrote: "The language cannot be so universal as to allow the statements about the entire elements of a certain multitude, if the aggregate of the multitude was not preliminary defined and completed correctly. It means that the statement about the entire elements of the multitude cannot be one of the elements of this multitude; the statement about "the whole" can be valid only "from without" of this whole." The statement made upon non-observance of this veto will be not false, but merely meaningless. Exactly such meaningless statements underlie the so-called logic circle in the reasoning, which leads to paradoxes. In order to avoid the danger of such vicious circles, Russell proposed to use a division into the following "types" (*universe due discourse*): individuals, multitudes of individuals, relations between individuals, relations between the multitudes of individuals and so on. "Types" are coded in a proper manner that enables one to distinguish them and in this way restricts the possibility of their improper use leading to paradoxes. Upon an improper substitution of an argument, the function becomes nonsense; it means that some substitutions based on the linguistic bans of the theory of types make no sense. The theory of types is a result of learning the language of logic statements and establishing on this base a certain hierarchy composed of objects and the names of these objects.

The statement in the second paradox ("Square") says itself about itself, i.e. it is an element of the multitude (in this case – one-element multitude), which it says about. So, it turns out to be a proper multitude (that, naturally, leads to a global discrepancy).

One ought to distinguish both an object language and a description language, which is named as a metalanguage (in Greek *meta* means after). A **metalanguage** represents a language on the basis of which any other language (object language) and its structure are investigated.

In the course of the Russian language written for English people one can find Russian and English texts. Russian texts appears as examples and English texts represent the description of these examples. A Russian text in this course represents an object language and English text in this course appears as a metalanguage used to describe the initial object language, in this case the Russian language. One and the same course can combine both an object language and a metalanguage (description language). A course of the Russian language for Russian people may serve as an example of such a course, wherein examples (object language) are printed in, say, one type, and explanations of such examples (metalanguage) are printed in another type, or the examples are printed in inverted commas, and the explanations, naturally, without commas:

Janet loves Peter (object language).

Loves (object language) is a verb (the present tense, the third person singular) (metalanguage).

Both the "Square" paradox and the "Cretan" paradox are based on the mixture of the language and the metalanguage in one text.

The analogical situation underlies the paradoxes of the following type: A word "*Heterologisch*" (in German) means heterological. The word *heterological* designates a certain feature, which this word does not have. If this word by itself is heterological, then it is not heterological and vice versa. The word "long" (in English) means long, but it does not have such a feature, since it is a short word. This example demonstrates the mixture of the language (designation of a length of a something) and the metalanguage (the length of the word).

In the speech at the level of a single text the mixture of the language and the metalanguage are not acceptable: they are the structures that lay in different levels. Their mixture leads to the appearance of theses – paradoxes, which both the language and the science shall work off.

However, one ought to understand that the distinguishing of the object language and the metalanguage in the speech often turns out to be difficult and requires special intellectual efforts of the speaker, since both the object language and the metalanguage are usually based on the same elements, i.e. they have an unified (identical) substance.

In real texts the elements of a language and metalanguage are mixed up in an arbitrary way, and in order to investigate, analyze or describe a language *L1* we need a language *L2* to formulate the results of our investigation or the rules of use of the language *L1*. It is all the more important for the theory of translation, which at least deals with two languages. Now let us assume that we have not two, but three languages (Russian, German and French) and at first we translate a German expression into Russian and then the Russian expression into French. Thus, one of the languages may serve as an intermediate language or as they say in the theory of translation an intermediary language.

An intermediary language can optionally not be a language in the common sense of the word, i.e. a natural language. It can appear in the way of any symbolic system, i.e. any system of symbols provided that these symbols correspond with the words of the translated text.

One can single out four types of intermediary languages:
1. One of the natural languages (but it is not advantageous, since the natural languages are characterized with a high degree of polycemy);
2. A standardized and simplified natural language;
3. An artificial international language (like Esperanto or Interlingua);
4. A language, which is specially made for this purpose.

Upon the construction of such a language one may suggest two approaches:
a) This language is to be constructed exactly as a language, with its vocabulary and grammar, i.e. it appears as one more artificial language;

b). An abstract mesh of correspondences between elementary sense units ("semantic factors") and a set of universal syntactic relations applicable for all languages are taken as an intermediary language.

In any reasoning about the translation, the facts of two languages are compared either evidently or not with a certain third system, both the thoughts, expressed in the text, on the one hand, and an abstract mesh of correspondences between the units of both languages, as it is constructed upon a machinery translation, on the other hand. Thereby, a certain intermediary language is always present, so it is very hard to make a theory, which would not use this concept.

Chapter 13. **Argumentation**

> All that exists has a sufficient reason for its existence.
>
> *Leibniz*

An *argument* (in Latin *argumentum* means a logical reason, ground, proof) is referred to a thought or a clause used to prove the verity or falsity of a thesis. An argument shall meet some definite requirements.

The first requirement coincides with the thesis requirement: an argument shall be true. The verity, like in case with a thesis, is not absolute; it is of a relative character. The matter concerns the speaker's trust in the argument's verity. In this case unlike the thesis, the listener shall share the trust too. Both interlocutors ought to recognize the argument's verity. It is important to understand that if one of the speech communicants, in this case the listener, does not agree with argument, this argument cannot be used to prove the thesis; it is an often case.

If in order to prove a thought the speaker provides a clause that seems evident to him, but the listener does not agree with it, this clause (argument) changes into a thesis, so first of all it is necessary to prove its verity as an intermediate thesis and only after that to proceed to prove the initial thesis. The speaker often does not do it that is why the proof fails. It is quite a frequent situation and nobody pays direct attention to it. When one begins proving a thesis, while presenting a new argument he ought to ask the interlocutor: "Do you agree with it? In the course of argumentation it is wise to ask your interlocutor this question at every new logical stage to get his confirmation of the intermediary level of the consent. This trick is more successfully applied in polemics, when some evident clauses are presented to the speech opponent (one who has an opposite opinion) in the way of arguments, which he cannot disagree with; and when he agrees with them one ought to take one powerful logical step (demonstration) – transition to the thesis, and the man will have no choice but to recognize his intellectual defeat.

A logical and speech error in a proof, connected with the fact that in the capacity of an argument confirming the thesis, one uses such a clause, which although is not deliberately false, but it requires to be proved, is said to be "an anticipation of the grounds" (in Latin *Petitio Principii*). Even ancient Indian logicians knew this logical and speech error "Siddha-sadhya", when a proof requires to be proved. Mikhail Lomonosov gives an example of this error in the reasoning of physicists, who are proving a theorem, that "a quantity of a substance shall be determined by weight". All force of this proof according to Lomonosov was based on the experiments with the collision of bodies, which make pendulums. For the experiments they took either homogeneous or heterogeneous bodies. Mikhail Lomonosov agrees with the fact that for the first case the theorem is veritable and the proof looks conclusive. As to the second case, when they used different bodies in the capacity of pendulums, Lomonosov wrote the following: "In the second case it will turn out that he (Isaac Newton) determined the quantity of a substance in heterogeneous bodies, which he used for the experiments by their weight and he took for gospel the fact that required to be proved." If upon the argumentation in the speech it turns out that the listeners refer to one of the arguments as to an intermediate thesis, the speaker's behavior shall vary depending on the communicative situation. If the speech is homiletic, i.e. continuing (See above), one ought to spend some time to prove this intermediate thesis and only after that to proceed to prove the target thesis. When the speech is oratoric (a derivative word of *oratorios*), i.e. momentary, restricted with time, one may: 1) ask the listeners to take his words on trust – it is possible when in the given auditorium the speaker gained his private authority before the speech (for instance, he is a popular man deserving the public's high reputation); 2) to call to witness an authoritative (for the auditorium) person who believes into the verity of this argument (See bellow "appellation to a person). If none of these conditions can be met, most likely that the speech will be lost. So, upon preparing arguments the speaker ought to consider it important to analyze how much the arguments will be accepted as true exactly by those persons (considering their erudition, social orientation, professional membership and so on) who will listen to him.

It is well to repeat that the verity of an argument is conditional, not absolute. Let us demonstrate an ancient syllogism as the simplest example of a speech proof: "All human beings are mortal. Socrates is a human being. Consequently, Socrates is mortal."

The first argument is general: "All human beings are mortal". At first glance it does not evoke any doubts. Nevertheless, it is evident that there is no one who can say for sure that this thesis is true. First, no one has observed individual fates of all people. Second, no one has observed a fate of an unborn man. No one knows for sure how his life will be arranged in the universe or on the Earth. Third, according to quite numerous philosophical and religious theories (for instance, buddhist) a human sole moves to another body and exists on the Earth a lot more time then we assume. Why not forever? Under a man we shall understand his spirituality, which is put into the body. If the spirit leaves the body, the man is said to be "a corpse" or "a body"; it is not a man yet and our consciousness reflects it very well. If the spirituality, or a sole, or a spirit after the physical diminishing of the body moves to another body, then, from this point of view, the man does not die. It may happen forever: the person lives many different lives in various bodies. There are special investigations, which explain to people whom they were in their previous lives (however, they do not say whom you will be in the next life). Today's science has no arguments to disprove this concept. So, the thought about the fact that all people are mortal is not evident, however many people share it. Only in respect of the latter this reference can be used as an argument in the proof of the above thesis: "Socrates is mortal". The second reference (second argument) sounds in the following way: "Socrates is a human being". In respect of this reference one can suggest to express doubts. Who does prohibit some one to say that a man with such a protruding mind is actually not a man? May be he is half a man and half an Olympic god? It is not an easy work to disprove this thought. Thus, from the standpoint of the absolute verity none of the arguments seems to be a total-lot. It is good, since if there were absolutely true arguments, the human mind would be deprived of creativity; it would develop at an extremely slow pace, if it would develop at all. Most likely the consciousness would change into a system of absolute verities, i.e. it would become dogmatic (See bellow). We can only say that a dogmatic consciousness leads to an intellectual decay. From the social standpoint this phenomenon could be observed in this country in the second half of the Soviet period, when many long years of living in the conditions of a dogmatic thinking resulted in a massive intellectual degradation. A dogmatic consciousness is extremely harmful for the human intellect, which is dialectic by its nature. The intellect is organized in such a way that it has an internal incentive for self-development. Everything that restricts the self-development affects badly the human intellect. What kind of progression can one say about under the condition of an absolute verity?

About no one, since the endpoint in the reasoning is reached. It is important for one to understand before he proceeds to argumentation.

Paradoxical as it is, the entire referred about the argument also applies to such a phenomenon as the fact. A fact is said to be an actual, i.e. an established event. (4)

An established event appears as an element of the outer world, which is interpreted by a man with a certain error measure. It means that if even you have witnessed a fact, if it happened before your very eyes, it does not signify that you are able to interpret it correctly and adequately. This scientific thesis is hardly understandable at the every-day life level, however it is long considered, say, in jurisprudence. Every process, every investigation within the course of the centuries faces one and the same problem: several people observed one and the same event, they are asked to testify, they have no inner reasons, no motivation to give false testimonies, so from their standpoint they give true testimonies, but the testimonies are absolutely *different*. After that how can one use these testimonies? Which of them is to be taken as true and which is not? It is incomprehensible; such testimonies can only mislead the investigation. Let us suppose that five persons witnessed a man
thrust a knife into another man. These five persons give different testimonies of what they saw, sometimes opposite. One saw a deliberate precise thrust; another man saw a threat with a knife with the following incident due to an improper movement of the victim; the third one saw the exceeding of the limits of self-defense by the criminal; the fourth man saw that the victim drove the criminal to the state of temporary insanity and irresponsibility; the fifth person saw a suicide attempt made by the victim. What does it mean? It once more confirms that the analyzers perceive the reality with a significant error measure, more over that the angle of vision, i.e. the point of vision in the said situation usually differs. Then the mind decodes that visual or sound pattern, which was fixed by the analyzers (the decoding goes on with significant errors), and then the memory errors together with individual associations connected not with the said event, but with something being in an associative relation with the private life of the person, are superimposed on the decoded pattern, thus generating the different descriptions of the event.

---

(4) That which by the definition appears as a fact or an actual event, signifies, in particular, that the following expressions: "an established fact" and "a doubtful fact" are stylistically erroneous, since the expression "an established fact" is equal to the expression "an established actual event", i.e. it is a tautology. So, "a doubtful fact" is internally contradictory statement, since it signifies "a doubtful actual event". Unfortunately, these errors are diffused in the press.

For instance, if the criminal demonstrated a certain type that was physiologically unpleasant for the witness, it will surely cause more strict testimonies. As an example we can take an internal negative relation of people based on an ethnic difference, which evokes a serious problem in multinational states. Let us assume that the witnesses of a criminal act happened between a white and a black man are the people of different colors. As a rule, they give different testimonies, even if they have no relation to the incident and they have no reason for disinformation. A person can do nothing with it, he actually saw the event in this way: his perception, in particular, connected with an ethnic displeasure, determines the evaluation of the event at the unconscious level. It is one of the reasons of the diffused common opinion that a certain nationality is guilty of this or that country's misfortunes. The matter concerns the private opinion of people, which is based upon the same phenomenon: a man evaluating something negative that happened with another man or with the whole society, sincerely believes in the fact that he found the source of this misfortune. How does he look it for? He does it according to the unconscious negative relation to the people of a certain nationality, aversion of something of foreign matter in the religious, ethnical and culturological relation, in the system of habits, in the manner of behavior and even in the appearance. It is well to understand that one may accuse people in the hostility to another nation and racism; this accusation is quite justified from the social point of view, but from the psychological point of view the said accusation cannot be justified, since the people do not wield power over the unconsciousness. It is a fact of the man's inner feeling of guilt and a sense of his own depravity. In principle, who can accuse another man of his love for blonde people and dislike for dark-haired people? No one can do it. It is another matter that such kind of emotions cannot underlie the social and political program of the society, which in another case can lead to a crime called Nazism. An individual's reaction to another man shall not be liable to an outer evaluation, since it shall be subject only to the inner self-evaluation.

So, the testimonies given by a seemingly unprejudiced man, turn out to be biased. Since, both testimonies and facts are often used in argumentation in general, then upon the analysis of argumentation one ought to remember the possible informational error. Nevertheless, if a person witnessed an incident, usually it is worthy to listen to his opinion, but with a certain measure of inner caution and distrust.

In some cases the testimonies of the witnesses cannot be evaluated as adequate in general, like, for instance, in those cases when they sighted a UFO. Fourteen people at the same time observed an unusual phenomenon. They gave testimonies, which as usual varied significantly. Bellow there are the fixed impressions:

1. A small, flying towards the ground and rapidly rising ball; the sky became somewhat black; the ball revolved on its axis as a globe; one could even distinguish the contours of continents and oceans.

2. There was a light in the sky and a bright blue object; the object allegedly exploded and turned out to be half fiery, then it spread t h r e e flaming tails that reached the ground surface. The object was moving in the Western direction and it disappeared in a while.

3. A huge flash highlighted the whole sky. Just in front of the eyes the soup plate-shaped object began dividing into two parts, one of which remained to be blue, the other – fiery. When the distance between the halves increased they turned out to be connected with a few meters thick strip. In a few moments the object blew up.

4. Two luminescent approaching circles. When the circles closed in they switched on two searchlights with which they lighted up each other and then they directed the light to the ground. In two-three minutes the searchlights were switched off, the luminescent circles in full silence dispersed and disappeared.

5. A suddenly originated bright orange ball that was ten times bigger then the Moon, slowly flew from the North to the South and disappeared there, like it was switched off.

6. A red orange lentil slowly flew in the sky with a low boom. It flew from the horizon to the horizon in 15 minutes.

7. A clearly outlined black square originated in the sky. The square was seen in the clouds illuminated from beneathwith a rose light. Its dimensions were approximately equal to two moon disks. The square was preserved stable notwithstanding the fact that the clouds around it were moving and reaching the borders of the square they were disappearing.

Approximately in ten minutes the square collapsed and the rose light diminished.

8. I saw nothing unusual.

9. A vertical palatial fusiform line of rose and orange color. The line height was approximately equal to 5-8 diameters of the Moon. The phenomenon lasted 15 minutes.

10. At the distance of six up to ten kilometers the clouds illminated with a bright light. The light circle became more and more bright. It was evident that there was something behind the clouds appearing towards the ground. Breaking away in high gear from the clouds the object immediately stopped. The brightly illuminated object had a form of a hemisphere.

A huge shaft of light that resembled the light of a powerful searchlight followed it. The luminescence was of a yellowish color. The apparatus buzzed for ten – fifteen seconds and then began moving down on the angle peaking up speed. It did it with an unusual easiness and literally melted before my eyes.

11. An object in the form of a dark cigar with a row of lights at the ends. Many of other lights were seen on its background, they were placed with no visible order. Three bodies of flame resembling a rocket exhaust followed "the cigar".

12. A luminescent body flew from the Southwest to the Northeast. It was followed like on a lead by a fiery star. A quantity of light-green small lights flew at a distance.

13. A rising luminescent spot, which in a while divided into three luminescent bodies, at that, the medium body was a few times bigger then the other two. Slowly it changed into a long elongated line shining so brightly that it could co pare with an electric welding.

14. It seemed like two stars extended to each other something looking like light threads, which connected the objects. In seven – ten seconds a multitude of luminescent balls appeared from the horizon and came closer enlarging their visible forms. The stars and bolls flew synchronously.

It is seen from the testimonies that some of them differ in principal. One person asserts that being at the same place he noticed nothing unusual.

There is an interesting biblical interpretation of the phenomenon known as "Ezekiel's chariot":

"…When I was among the captives by the Hebar river the sky opened wide and I saw the Lord… and the whirlwind came from the North, a huge cloud, and a whirling fire and the brightness surrounded it… Four creatures resembling the human beings came out from the midst of it. And they looked like the resemblances of the human being. Each of them had four faces and four wings. They had legs also, upright legs and the feet like the bull's feet; they glared like a pure copper. And they had hands beneath the wings in all four sides. Their wings touched each other and they did not turn when they moved straight forward… two wings of each of them touched each other and two wings covered their bodies…"

Of course, when the matter concerns ufological phenomena one may assume (and reasonably) that at this moment there is a certain influence on the human brain, so the people have hallucinations, at that they have naturally different hallucinations. In other words, the object can exist, but it does not mean that the analyzers perceive it adequately and the consciousness interprets it correctly. Certainly, if we meet another, more developed civilization, an immediate partial affection of the mind of the people living on the Earth is quite accountable: it enables the Supreme Reason to keep a lot from us. It is comprehensible from the general point of view, but nevertheless, two persons stood nearby and gazed in one and the same direction: one of them saw something unusual and can describe it in detail, the other saw nothing…

The error measure in the testimonies of witnesses of even the mostly common event is so huge that the possibility of their application in argumentation may become doubtful.

It is well to understand that the fact description is none of the best arguments, since it is just an interpretation and the measure of its adequacy may be always called in question. If the argumentation is expressed by the words of a witness, the situation deteriorates, since one appeals to the other man's interpretation, not even to his own interpretation.

If you need to adduce facts for the argumentation where can you take their description if you did not witness them? What sources can you take the needed information from? Which of them are trust worthier? The answer to these questions is of great significance. At first you ought to designate the sources of information from which you cannot take actual material for the argumentation. First of all it pertains to the mass media. Such a conclusion may seem to be paradoxical, since it is very common method of argumentation: a person tells something and when he is asked about the sources from which he knew about this he answers: "I heard by radio. I saw it on TV. All papers inform about this." Why should not one take actual information from the press? In order to answer this question one ought to look for the scheme, proposed in Chapter 10. "Classification of Speech Goals", which presents the genres of oral and speech literature in accordance with the main problems that a certain genre solves in the speech communication. The scheme shows that such a genre, as mass media, including radio, TV and press, has no task to propagate knowledge, i.e. it has no task adequate to the information transmission. The purpose of the mass media existence is to form such a standpoint, the availability of which, in its turn, forms the intentions and stimulates the acts. The mass media in its basis appears as an ideologies genre. It is important to understand that the mass media is ideologies in the entire countries of the world. So, the ideologization of the mass media is typical not only to a totalitarian state. It is a universal feature of the mass media. A totalitarian state differs from a democratic one only with the fact that in the first the mass media as a whole forms one and the same point of view, and in a democratic state each newspaper, TV channel or radio program form the readers, audience and listeners' point of view in accordance with their own point of view. The editors' point of view represents the interpretation of established facts, which is trusted on the public. The point of view of another editorial staff represents another interpretation of the same established facts and it also thrusted on the public and so on.

In any democratic country each person has a right, if he does not go beyond the framework of the laws, to present his own interpretation of any event to the attention of all those, who want to become familiar with it. The so-called independent journalists do this professionally.

Sometimes, journalists undertake to form a certain point of view not in order to declare their own convictions or the position of their editors, but because they were financed by a certain person or organization.

At that, sometimes it is very hard to determine whose point of view a concrete reporter propagates. In any case the public turns out to be misled.

It sounds like nonsense that the mass media reflects an actual fact adequately. When analyzing any fact one can find out its different interpretation, if he takes as more as possible newspapers of different political direction or if he listens to the reports about this fact on all channels of the local and foreign TV. The interpretations will differ from each other in principal.

Who said that the interpretation of your favorite newspaper or program (and usually we choose such a press that is closer to us ideologically and at that we become a voluntary victim of more outer pressure put upon our consciousness) is the only true, i.e. it is adequate to the real event (fact)? Of course, it is not, at least that other people (sometimes they are not more foolish, but objectively more clever) choose another press, in the same way they join other movements and parties. Who is right? The formation of a concrete man ideology is, first, a unique and, second, an infinite process that goes through his entire life.

Several years ago oil-mains in Siberia broke through. The evaluations of the occurrence differed from a small incident to a global ecocatastrophe. Having read all that is written about the war in Chechnya in Moscow press, in Azerbaijan, Armenian, French, as well as in American, South African and Iraqi press one can find out not only a polar interpretation of the events, but also such information messages, which in principal cannot be coordinated with each other. If you did not witness the events yourself, you have no possibility to estimate the level of the interpretation reliability.

What texts, what genres can be used to select facts? There is such a genre: it is scientific and reference literature (monographs, dictionaries, encyclopedias, etc.), which is specially designed for the knowledge propagation and adequate information transmission. Of course, not every such a book and not in respect of every fact provides correct and adequate information, however the genre by itself corresponds to the given task. So one can and shall take actual information from scientific and reference books. It is usually suggested to use for this purpose popular scientific literature as well, however this suggestion is debatable. A popular scientific text makes an attempt to explain a complicated theoretical problem by a clear and understandable language, since this text is designed for professionally unprepared reader. None of the experts – professionals reads popular scientific literature. To explain a scientific problem to an amateur, it requires making a text devoid of scientific terms, which in their turn are needed to understand the scientific problems; it turns out to be an exclusive circle. It is impossible to explain at a dilettante level, for instance, a process of splitting of an atomic nucleus that is why the popular scientific articles give no explanations on this theme and propose some informal reasoning about the problem. It leads to such a significant information distortion that one can prejudice the possibility of the authenticity. If the authenticity of information in popular scientific texts looks somewhat relative, such texts are hardly applicable in the capacity of the argumentation source. Thus, one can freely use scientific and reference literature for the tasks of actual argumentation and he shall be careful in the use of popular scientific literature. If one of the group of people is an expert in a certain field and others are dilettantes and they debate about a scientific problem of this field, the dilettantes, as a rule, use arguments taken from popular scientific books and the expert keeps silence being an ironical witness of this somewhat enthusiastic, but at the same time quite pitiful polemics.

It is a typical situation: the less I know, the more I want to debate, since the more intelligent is a person, the more he understands about the boundlessness of his ignorance. Every time when he makes a new step of knowledge up, he sees new vistas of knowledge, which lie beyond the boundaries of his comprehension. A person who plums himself on his erudition, as a rule, is a primitive man, who does not see the boundlessness of the intellectual horizon that opens more as far as the man goes up, in the same way like a traveler sees more when he climbs the mountain and only on the top he feels the infinity. A famous phrase: "I know only the fact that I know nothing, others even do not know this." (Socrates) can pertain to the wisest man among the people, who reached the top of the mental development accessible to the human mind.

The second requirement made to the argument appeals to the sufficiency of a thesis argumentation. The argumentation shall be sufficient for the people to whom it is directed. It is important to understand that the measure of sufficiency is unequal for different people. It means that when a speaker undertakes to convince, say, ten people at the same time of the verity of a certain thesis, a part of the people will be convinced after presentation of one – two arguments, another part will resist intellectually a bit longer, some of them will oppose much more longer and so on. Thus, the sufficiency appears as a function, which changes depending on the argument, wherein under the argument one understands the mentality of the listener. There are some people who are more compliant to the argumentation, and some people who inwardly agrees with the speaker's thesis, but do not perfectly realize their consent to it, and some people who have forcible counterarguments, and some people who merely dislike the speaker and due to this dislike everything that the speaker says faces a counter rejection; all this represents various communicative situations. The level of the argumentation sufficiency is always individual. The sufficiency is not a constant, it appears as a variable and its value depends on the multitude of factors connected with the listener's concrete personality.

A disregard of the argumentation sufficiency breeds the following logical error in the speech: "should not" (in Latin *non sequitur*), the essence of which lies in the fact that a clause, which requires a proof, does not originate from the given arguments, i.e. the presented proofs are true, but they do not represent a sufficient argument for the given thesis and therefore they do not prove it.

In this way to prove that the thesis about the Earth sphericity is veritable they give the following obvious reasons: 1) when a ship approaches the coast one can see first the tops of the masts appearing from the horizon and only after that the ship's body; 2) after the sunset the sun rays keep lighting up the roofs of high buildings, tops of the mountains and clouds, and in a while – only clouds. However it does not follow from these arguments that the Earth is spherical. These arguments do not substantiate the thesis. They only prove the curvature of the Earth surface, shape insularity and isolation of our planet in the space. Other arguments has a proof for the verity of the Earth sphericity, namely: 1) in any place of the earth the horizon appears like a sphere and the horizontal range keeps always the same; 2) upon a lunar eclipse the Earth's shadow falling on the Moon, always has a spherical shape; only a ball casts a spherical shadow; 3) evidences of cosmonauts. In fact these arguments substantiate the verity of the thesis about the Earth sphericity.

Another logical error in the speech connected with the disregard of the argumentation sufficiency is referred to the following saying: "from the said in a relative sense to the said in an irrelative way" (in Latin *a dicto sekundum quid ad dictum simpliciter*). The essence of this error is as follows: a clause appearing to be true upon certain conditions is given in the capacity of an argument applicable under all terms and conditions. For instance, it is true that bromine is a remedy for the treatment of various diseases. However this opinion cannot be used as an argument without taking into account certain conditions. It is known that if one takes a large doze of bromine it will cause serious negative after-effects. So, the opinion like: "Bromine is a remedy for the treatment of various diseases" is true only under certain conditions.

Sometimes a logical error of another kind occurs by the same reason: they try to deduce from a true thesis the consequences that do not follow from it. For instance, it does not follow from the social and legal equality between men and women in the modern civilized society that a woman does not need a man's protective, well-mannered treatment, i.e. she has no need in indulgence.

The requirements of the verity and sufficiency follow from the fundamental law of the formal logic – the law of a sufficient reason (in Latin *lex rationis detrerminantis sive sufficientis*), saying that every true thought shall be substantiated by other thoughts, which verity is proved.

In symbols the law of a sufficient reason is expressed by the following formula:

If there is B, there is A as its reason.

The discovery of the law of a sufficient reason is ascribed to Leibniz, a German philosopher, who expressed it in the way of the following principle: "All that exists has a sufficient reason for its existence". It means that no phenomenon can be true or actual; no assertion can be fair without a sufficient reason. Why does the matter stand in this way, not in another? Leibniz considered the law of a sufficient reason to be a principle of all experimental truths in contrast to the law of contradiction, which he interpreted as the principle of all truths of the mind.

However, one can find the first formulation of the law of a sufficient reason in the works of Leucippus and Democritus: "No thing appears without a reason, everything originates on a certain basis and by virtue of necessity."

The requirement for the validity of thinking reflects one of the global features of the outer world, wherein the preceding facts, objects and phenomena do prepare every fact, every object and every phenomenon. None of the phenomena can appear if it is not prepared, if it does not originate in predecessors. It represents the law of the objective reality. The river freezes due to the open air temperature lowering; the smoke goes upright, as it is lighter that the surrounding atmosphere, and so on. One of the main axioms of Mikhail Lomonosov was as follows: "Nothing happens without a sufficient reason".

Nothing happens in the world without a certain reason. So, if every object, every phenomenon in the nature and society has its own reason, terms and conditions, which originated its appearance, then our thinking about objects and phenomena as well cannot assert or disprove something about an object or phenomenon, if the assertion or disproval is not founded. The entire practice of the human thinking shows that the only knowledge is said to be true, which is followed by the comprehension of this knowledge argumentation. In such a way to know the law of dialectics about the transition of gradual, imperceptible qualitative changes into the quantitative ones means to be able to demonstrate that the given feature originates itself in the outer world and in the thinking as well.

Of course, as it was above referred, such a proof of that or this thought verity in the experimental knowledge is considered to be the most accurate and reliable, when upon the argumentation the given thought is substantiated with a first-hand object or fact reflected by this thought. However, sometimes it is not possible to do. In such a way, to prove the verity of the thought about the Earth origin one is even not able to present the fact of its origin that occurred a few billions years ago, but it is very hard also to reconstruct the details of this origin. Besides, it is not necessary to present every time a first-hand fact as a proof of the thought verity. Generalized formulations are typical to the human thinking and they are often applied for the further comprehension of single objects and for logical substantiation of the thoughts about these single objects.

The law of a sufficient reason requires that our thoughts in any reasoning should be internally connected with each other, originate one from another, and substantiate each other. To be consistent means to adduce that or this true argument, as well as to explain and substantiate it, draw all necessary conclusions that follow from it.

The law of a sufficient reason appears as a universal law; it expresses the requirement for the thought substantiation in the most common way. The matter of a concrete reason is a subject of discussion in every single case.

Let us discuss the third requirement, which is made for the argument. Under the first requirement an argument in a proof shall be considered true; it means that earlier it was proved as a thesis. The said proof was expressed irrespective of the initial thesis, i.e. independently of it. It is the essence of the third requirement for the argument: it shall be a thought, which verity is proved independently, irrespective of the proven clause. One should not express an argument for a proof of a thesis, which follows by itself from the thesis. Otherwise there will be a logic error in the speech called "vicious circle" (in Latin *circulus vitiosus*), which by definition resides in the fact that the thesis is deduced from the arguments that in their turn are deduced from the same thesis.

In Bentham's works one can find the description of the following speech situation, connected with the error of the "vicious circle": in church cases, when the council discusses the necessity to condemn a noted teaching, one must not prove that this teaching shall be condemned because it represents a heresy; but to speak in this way means to act without proofs, since under the heresy the church understands exactly such a teaching, which is liable to condemnation.

Jean Batiste Moliere so neatly derided this kind of error in the following example: *The father of a null girl wanted to know why she is null and he asked a doctor for explanation. Doctor Inharel replied to his question: "It is the easiest work to do; it depends on the fact that she lost the capacity of speaking". "Of course, of course, – said the father, – but tell me please, by what reason did she lose the capacity of speaking?" "All our best authors will tell you that it depends on the impossibility to move the tongue" – answered the doctor.*

The "vicious circle" is based on the tautology (in Greek *tautó* means the same and *lógos* means a word) or an expression that repeats the previously said thing in other words, sometimes even in similar words. In may breed the texts that sound like as follows: "The workers achieved great successes in their work, since they worked successfully." This logical error is quite common especially in the mass media. Of course, the error in the referred above text is evident, as they used single rooted words in the text: a work – to work, success – successfully. But in synonymic texts the error is not so evident, especially if it refers to a capacious text (like an article). The mass media very often uses a thought as an argument, and then it is cleared up that this thought by itself originates from the thesis, which the author tried to argue in the beginning of the article. It evidences a logical and intellectual failure: the man does not understand where is the reason, where is the consequence. If something was once set as a reason, can it be then used as a consequence?

It is interesting that more often one can find such articles in the press, which resemble a pasquinade on the theme of the speeches that delivered in public by our fellow countrymen. It is absolutely evident that these speeches cannot be referred stylistically as texts on the whole: they have more logical and speech errors, as well as stylistically defects, then the sense, which sometimes even cannot be caught. The speeches quite often evidence the authors' mental defects. Practically, the logical error of the "vicious circle" turned out to be a standard for them. Unfortunately, it is a standard not only for those who is "on the top", but also for those who laugh at them. It turns out that the so-called "articles-derisions", as a rule, have the same errors, i.e. journalists by themselves moved up a short distance on the path of the speech culture as compared with those whom they laugh at in their articles. It would be really funny, "if it was not so sad".

As to the argumentation one ought to examine one more fundamental clause: psychological transfer of an argument, which is connected with the fourth requirement made to the system of arguments – a requirement for an individual treatment of argumentation that has a fundamental importance. The human consciousness responds to the convictions individually. So, in ideal there shall be as many methods of conviction, as there are people subjected to the argumentation. The procedure of a conviction looks like as follows: first the man proves the thesis to himself (sometimes during the whole life, sometimes within a short period of time). Until the man does not prove the thesis to himself he has no rhetorical right to prove it to somebody else. One can speak about, debate, ask other people about the thesis, but it is too early to prove it; the speaker is still not ready to do it. One cannot prove something to oneself and the listeners at the moment of a public argumentation; it is a common error.

In order to prove something to oneself one shall choose those arguments that seem convincing to himself. At that, the most convincing argument is said to be the main (or leading) one. It is considered to be a rough error of argumentation when a person proved something to himself and starts proving the same thing to another person, presenting the same arguments and, as a rule, in the same order of their significance, beginning with the main argument. As usual such argumentation fails, since upon the argumentation those arguments are chosen that have priority for the speaker. When a person undertakes to convince another man, he ought to choose those arguments, which are priority-driven for the interlocutor's consciousness; it might be absolutely different arguments. This process is referred to as a psychological transfer of argumentation. To pursue such a transfer successfully one shall every time gain an understanding of the listener's mentality before undertaking to argue in public, otherwise the listener may find out the arguments to be unconvincing. Let us show en example of a frequent communicative situation.

> A young girl decided to marry. First she took such a decision by herself. One shall refer to the decision-making as to a thesis, which he/she proved to himself/herself. Our girl had proved the thesis about the necessity to marry a certain B to her. She had her own arguments. As a rule, the main arguments are as follows: "B loves me." (1), "I love B." (2). However there are a few addi-

tional arguments: "B is a young man of pleasing appearance." (3), "B is clever." (4), "B is rich." (5), "B is going to make a beneficial contract for a work in a foreign country" (6) and so on. The decision to marry is rarely taken by intuition (unlike a diffused opinion); it is a result of a laborious inner argumentation. Let us imagine that further on the girl, who decided to marry B, begins convincing her mother of the taken decision expedience. The mother is absolutely against it; she has her own counter argumentation: " You are only 18 years old." (1), "Who is that B? I do not know absolutely anything about him." (2), "There is P, who is much better; he is a son of my lady-friend." (3), "You need to become a student and to find a position." (4), and so on. The girl needs to make the mother change her mind and prove the rationality of her decision to the mother.

What shall the girl do in this situation? First of all to prove the following thesis: "Mother, your counter arguments sound unconvincing". In other words she ought to execute the procedure of supplanting (See above) (it is quite easy to express the proof, so we do not produce it), and to proceed to the proof of the target thesis (substitution): "I ought to marry B." This common situation always has one and the same error: the girl begins presenting the same arguments to the mother, who may find them unconvincing and in the same order of significance, beginning from the leading argument. Thereby the proof always fails, since the mother is a different person.

How shall the girl convince her mother? She shall analyze her personality (that is not difficult, as she knows her for ages) and influence on that part of her consciousness, which is more vulnerable. Say, the mother is a greedy woman. In this case the girl shall say the only thing: "B is very rich» developing this aspect further on. Thus, she shall raise the riches as a leading argument, i.e. to execute a psychological transfer of argumentation: the reason (5) shall be transferred to the position (1). In the capacity of the leading argument the girl shall raise such an argument, which is well understandable to a concrete listener, therefore the listener may find it convincing. I the mother got tired with the life in Russia and she wants to change the place of residence, the girl shall say that B is going to make a beneficial contract for a work in a foreign country and they both can leave with him. She shall repeat it several times; other arguments are not worth saying about: argument (6) ⟶ (1). If the mother is a clever, intelligent and sensible person, the girl shall say about what a powerful intellect he has, what a kind of a refined person he is, what kind of a wonderful interlocutor and a spiritual ally the mother may find in B and how she will be pleased to talk with him: argument (4) ⟶ (1). If the mother is a coquettish woman, if she did not forget what it means to be a coquette, the girl shall say how B is attractive (it is significant for the internal emotional tone, which absolutely unconsciously appears in a growing older woman in the presence of a young man): argument (3) → (1). Sometimes it is very hard to convince somebody of something without psychological transfer of the leading argument. The biggest error is that the girl says: "Mother, he loves me and I love him", since it is her leading arguments (if she really takes a decision to marry for love). She must not say these words to her mother, at least, she shall not accentuate attention on it, as this emotion does not concern the mother and more over evokes a natural sense of jealousy. Only at the end of the argumentation the girl may very decently and as it were absolutely incidentally say to the mother: "I and B, we love each other." This love does not appear as a fact of the mother's private life and psychologically in this situation it looks like she must quit the play; therefore the girl shall not lay the emphasis on it in any case. So, in the course of argumentation directed at another person, one ought to transfer the leading argument considering his/her personality and never raise his leading argument in the course of argumentation (except those cases, when the listener has the similar values with you). In addition one can raise one more special argument, which, probably, every mother will find convincing: "B is such a man who will take care of you in your old age."

The failure to meet the above requirements for argumentation leads to the impossibility to prove a thesis. As a rule, it is connected with the breach of the verity that is customary to be called "a false reason" or "a fundamental error" (in Latin *error fundamentalis*) An error called "a false reason" implies that a thesis is substantiated with false arguments, i.e. a proof is expressed on the basis of a false opinion. However, the analysis shows that different communicative situations posed by the category of truth, originate unequal reasons of the speech failure in a proof, and thus under "a false reason" one ought to understand not one, but the whole class of errors.

Form the standpoint of the speech verity we can single out four possibilities:
1) A true thesis; the speaker believes in it;
2) A true thesis, but the speaker does not believe in it;
3) A false thesis, but the speaker believes in it;
4) A false thesis; the speaker does not believe in it.

Earlier we have specified that under the speech verity one shall understand the speaker's trust into his words. Raising a requirement for the argument verity thereby we execute a certain substitution, since the lack of correspondence between the reality and our perception exists forever. Probably a certain situation is possible: some arguments are false, they do not correspond to the reality, but the speaker believes in them: mythlogicality appears as one of the consciousness features. Nevertheless the division into the real verity and the perception verity is possible and may be wholesome, as in the different situation from among the four above possibilities the argumentation turns out to be unsuccessful by different reasons. Let us discuss each of these situations:

1. A true thesis; the speaker believes in it (coincidence of the verity and trust), but the argumentation fails for some reason. What are the reasons?

A. Insufficiency of the argumentation, i.e. the argmentation can be quite successful, but it is insufficient to express a convincing proof.

B. A psychological aspect. The argumentation is correct and sufficient, but the speaker chose a wrong leading argument; its influence turns out to be ineffective: the interlocutor is not interested in the speaker's main argument.

C. Thesis loss. The speaker presents a convincing argumention, but it demonstrates a biased thesis.

D. The argumentation instead of a false argument presents an argument exaggerated in its sense. In his strive to make the argumentation more effective the speaker either fantasizes about or exaggerates the event and among the listeners there is one who can catch him in a lie.

2. A thesis is true, but the speaker does not believe in it (however by virtue of certain reasons he must prove it). Bellow it is an example of such a situation: Imagine, please, that you are going to enter a post-graduate course and you choose a particular scientific problem as a theme of the future dissertation. A famous scientist previously examined this problem, but you are not satisfied with his point of view and the proposed description, therefore you are going to provide another description. After that you became an aspirant and it turned out that the said famous scientist becomes your scientific adviser (he is the only one who can be at the head of the work on this particular theme). What shall you do to be taken to the post-graduate course? You ought to repeat in your impressive report the same argumentation as was proposed by the future scientific adviser, notwithstanding the fact that it seems to you unconvincing (we examine the situation wherein your opinion is not true). No polemics are possible at the entrance examinations of the post-graduate course, since, first, you are, as a rule, not quite ready for well-founded polemics with an expert who devoted many years to the investigation of this problem and, second, the examination does not suit for debates. First one shall enter the courses and then propose any alternative interpretations.

So, you are the speaker, the thesis is true, but you do not believe in it. What is the reason of the failure of your argumentation?

A. Availability of a logical error. If a person does not believe in something that he proves at a certain stage of argumention he will for sure have a logical failure (it is the law that practically does not know any exclusions). Therefore if you came home and want to tell untruth about where you were, you would better not try to explain anything: the more you speak about this theme, the more there is a possibility that you will make a logical error and be caught in a lie – it is a notorious fact. If a person does not believe in a thesis (even a true one) he can face a logical failure.

B. Insufficiency of argumentation. Very often a person does not believe in the verity of a thesis, as he does not have a full volume of argumentation due to the insufficiency of information. As the person widens his knowledge, becomes more and more competent in a certain matter, it changes his conception of the verity of the thesis, which formulation implies the said matter. The longer we live, the wiser we become, the more our views transform. More knowledge – more accuracy, and more accuracy usually involves the transformation of the previous views on the world. So they say that the youth sees everything to be easy, its truths are absolute, but in older age everything seems more complcated: all thoughts seem relative in their verity.

C. A nervous failure. Of course, before going for the examination to your future scientific adviser you will analyze his personality and choose as a leading argument the one, which he may find convincing. But the problem lies in the fact that at the moment of your speech you may have a ner ous failure, since it is very hard for a person to argue in favor of something that he does not believe in. Certainly that in such a situation he will find himself in the state of a significant emotional discomfort.

D. Availability of the so-called slip of the tongue. It is well known that there is no accidental slip of the tongue. If a person feels a nervous stress, he hardly can control over the situation and naturally it may cause significant slips of the tongue. Such is the psychological state of the person.

E. Availability of a false argument. Feeling the insufficiency of his argumentation a person may make up an argument even if he understands that it is a lie, however it looks co vincing for a proof of the target thesis, but somebody catches him in a lie.

All the referred above reasons or any of them may lead to the situation wherein your argumentation fails.

3. A thesis is false, but the speaker believes in it. And he undertakes

to prove it. As a typical example we can consider the situation in the former Soviet Union, where actually great number of people believed that they lived better than all other people in the world (ten years longer then in other countries, had more freedom and so on). "I do not know any other country where the man breathes so freely" – it is an absurd thesis but many people believed in its verity. Now imagine, please, that the person who believed in this thesis had to prove its verity (let say, at the examination of politology), but his argumentation failed. What lies in the basis of the argumentation viciousness in this case?

A. False arguments, i.e. "a false reason" by itself. The person says that according to the statistics a Soviet woman lives, say, 85 years and a Soviet man – 78 years. This data is taken from the press and we won't say anything about its verity. One can select quite enough of such kind of false arguments (at that the speaker, as a rule, believes in their verity and in the thesis too). In accordance with the logics of argumentation false arguments imply a false thesis.

B. Insufficiency of argumentation. Insufficiency of arguments can be found upon the polemics connected, for instance, with the following question: "Where do you know from how people in other countries live? To understand where it is better to live, it would not be too bad first to see how it is there and then to compare." It is a simple logical conclusion. Without an experience of private observations it is very hard to answer this question and naturally it leads to the insufficiency of argumentation.

C. Thesis loss. By selecting questionable arguments one may suppose that they hardly will be convincing for a proof of a target thesis, however sometimes they help to argue an adjacent thesis. For instance, instead of arguing that a Soviet man lives much better than all other people, the speaker could prove that he lives quite well. But it is no the same thing. When proving the second thought the peaker makes a logic error in the speech called "a thesis loss". In the given communicative situation the opponent for sure will demolish the false arguments and compensate by his counter arguments the insufficiency of the speaker's argumentation, thus the argumentation will be demolished. There is a noted historical example when Leonid Brezhnev changed by himself the proposed thesis into the opposite one, i.e. he accepted another thesis. When making a formal visit to Sweden and apparently having a weakened control over himself and not understanding that his words might become popular, he said: "You don't say so. I thought that we are constructing the socialism. But in fact it is constructed long ago, in Sweden."

We shall repeat one more time that the following terms as "verity" and "falsity" of a thesis are relative. Only our feelings are absolute. Each of us believes in something and does not believe in another. The common situation is when a man does not form a certain opinion about a certain matter (it is a situation when he is not ready for argumentation). No one can be forced to have a definite opinion about a certain matter.

4. A false thesis; the speaker does not believe in it. However there are such reasons that make a person undertake to furnish proofs even in this case.

We can analyze the following situations:

White lie. You are a doctor, you have a patient who is hopelessly sick and the medicine cannot help him. You do not reveal the dreadful secret and try to cheer him up saying that in a while he will fell much better.

A self-profit connected, for instance, with a need to avoid being caught in something compromising. Unfortunately, there are quite many cases of a conscious calumny on other people with selfish ends.

A sense of fear that sometimes forces a man to prove such thoughts that looks absurd to his point of view. It is well known, for instance, that a Russian commander, marshal V. Blyukher when he was arrested, on pain of death he substantiated in writing a detailed plan of surrendering the Far East to Japan, which he allegedly elaborated in the beginning of the thirties (of course, there was no such a plan, but Stalin demanded such a plan from him in exchange for life). Why does the argumentation fail to be convincing in the above-referred cases?

A. False argument.

B. Logical failure.

C. Insufficiency of argumentation. At that not only insufficiency, but the little convincingness as well. Even the intonation in speech will be unconvincing.

D. Thesis loss.

E. Nervous failure.

One ought to pay attention to the fact that the aggregate of reasons, which entail the failure of argumentation, turns out to be different in the discussed communicative situations. As to the psychological aspect, most probably the speaker will look for such a leading argument, which is convincing for the listener at most, since he has a clearly comprehended goal – to prove a false thesis. The necessity of a psychological influence on the person in such a situation is evident. As a rule, the leading argument turns out to be successful, the speaker counts on it striving to compensate the insufficiency of the argumentation and false arguments.

F. Passing over in silence of true arguments. Usually the passing over in silence of a great number of true reasons is added to the availability of false arguments. In such a case he doctor tells the patient that today he looks better, but at the same time he conceals from him the thermometer which shows a higher temperature as it was yesterday.

If the opponent will cite as an example one of the arguments, which the speaker tried to conceal, the latter has no choice but to say: "I did not know this", – thus to recognize his defeat in argumentation.

Chapter 14. **Deductive Demonstration**

> Dictum de omni et de nullo.
> (Everything is said or nothing)

Demonstration presents the third level of the speech proof.

Demonstration (in Latin *demonstratio* means demonstration) appears as a logical connection between an argument and a thesis, i.e. a logical reasoning in the process of which one derives the verity or falsity from the arguments. Under the demonstration one ought to understand an aggregate of logical rules used in the argumentation. The application of these rules ensures a logical relation of thoughts, which shall convince the opponent of the fact that a thesis is necessarily substantiated with arguments; therefore it is true. An accidental combination of arguments never brings to successful argumentation.

A logical connection between an argument and a thesis is represented in various types. Depending on the type of the logical connection there are various demonstrations (or various proofs). Let us examine the main types of demonstration. One of them appears as a deductive demonstration.

Deduction (in Latin *deductio* means conclusion) in the broader sense of the word is said to be such a form of thinking, when every new thought is derived by a clearly logical way (i.e. in accordance to the logic rules) from the preceding thought. Such a sequence of thoughts is said to be an inference, and each component of this inference appears as either a previously proved thought, or an axiom, or a hypothesis. The latest thought of this inference is said to be a conclusion. An example of an inference, for instance, in presented by the following logicality:

$$\begin{aligned} A &\to B \\ B &\to C \\ C &= D \quad \text{premises} \\ B &\to D \\ D &\to E \end{aligned}$$

$$\overline{A \to E \quad \text{conclusion}}$$

In the above formula the letters substitute certain concrete thoughts and the line signifies the word "consequently".

In the restricted sense of the word, accepted in the traditional logics, under the term of *deduction* one ought to understand a deductive reasoning, i.e. such a reasoning that entails a new knowledge about an object or a group of objects on the basis of some existing knowledge about the investigated objects and the application of a certain rule of the logics to them.

A deductive reasoning as an object of the traditional logics is applied every time when it is required to examine a certain phenomenon on the basis of the known general point and to make a necessary conclusion in respect of this phenomenon. We are aware, for instance, of the following concrete fact – "the given plane crosses a sphere", as well as, of the general rule in respect of all planes crossing a sphere, – "every section of a sphere with a plane is a circle". Applying this general rule to the concrete fact every thinking person will necessarily come to one and the same inference: "it means that this plane is a circle". At that the course of the reasoning will be as follows: if the given plane crosses a sphere, and every section of a sphere is a circle, then, consequently, the given plane is a circle. This reasoning resulted in a new knowledge about the given plane, which does not appear directly either in the first thought ("the given plane crosses a sphere"), or in the second ("every section of a sphere with a plane is a circle"), taken apart from each other. The inference that "the given plane is a circle" is made as a result of combination of these thoughts in a deductive reasoning.

The structure of a deductive reasoning and the compulsory character of its rules necessarily forcing one to make a conclusion that logically results from the premises; reflected the most common relations between objects of the material world: the relations of type, class and individual, i.e. general, particular and singular. The essence of these relations lies in the following: that which is inherent in all classes of the given type, is inherent in any other class; that which is inherent in all individuals of that class, is inherent in every individual. For instance, that which is inherent in all nervous cells (like the ability to transmit information), is inherent in every cell, if it is not dead. Exactly the same fact was reflected in the deductive reasoning: singular and particular are placed under the general. In the process of his activity the human being, having observed billions times the relations between the type, class and individual in the objective reality, elaborated a corresponding logical figure that later on received a statute of the deductive reasoning rule.

The deduction plays a significant role in our thinking. In all cases, when we place a concrete fact under the general rule and then derive from the general rule a certain conclusion in respect of this concrete fact, we are reasoning in the deduction form. If the premises are true, the correctness of the inference will depend on how strictly we observed the deductive rules. The deduction plays an obvious role in all cases, wherein it is required to check the correctness of our argumentation. The application of deduction on the basis of the formalized reasoning facilitates the search for logical errors and helps to express thoughts more precisely.

For the first time the theory of deduction was elaborated in detail by Aristotle, who clarified the requirements for particular thoughts that belong to the composition of the deductive reasoning, determined the meaning of the terms and disclosed the rules of a certain kinds of deductive reasoning.

Descartes estimated the deduction and its role in the process of the comprehension. He considered that a person comprehends objects in two ways: through the experience and deduction. However, the experience often misleads us, whereas the deduction or, as Descartes said, a clear inference from one object by means of another is released from this shortage. Up to Descartes the initial points for deduction are finally given by the intuition or the ability of internal contemplation, which helps the human being to comprehend the truth without any logical activity of the consciousness. So, the initial points of the deduction appear as evident truths owing to the fact that the component ideas are inherent in our mind.

The classical Aristotelian logics began formalizing a deductive inference. This tendency was continued by the mathematical logics.

Under the term of *deduction* in the restricted sense of the word one shall understand the following:

1. A method of investigation upon which to obtain a new knowledge about an object or a group of homogeneous objects, one shall, first, to find out the closest class that includes all these objects, second, to apply to them a corresponding rule typical to the entire class of objects; the transition from the knowledge of more general points to the knowledge of less general points. The deductive method plays a tremendous role in mathematics. It is well known that all demonstrable propositions, i.e. theorems are derived logically with the use of deduction from a small net amount of the initial principles that cannot be proved within the framework of the given system; they are said to be axioms.

2. The form of the facts statement in a book, lecture, report and conversation, wherein one goes from general points, rules, laws to less general points, rules and laws.

A deductive demonstration (in the traditional logics) represents one of the forms of a proof, wherein a thesis appearing as a single or particular opinion is placed under the general rule. The essence of such a proof is included in the following: one ought to get the interlocutor's consent to the fact that the general rule to which the given particular or single fact applies, is true. When the consent is reached the general rule extends to the arguable thesis. Bellow there is an example of a deductive proof (demonstration):

Thesis: *a chicken has wings;*

General rule: *birds have wings;*

Reasoning: *if all birds have wings and the chicken is a bird, consequently, the chicken has wings.*

A deductive proof proposes a leading, main idea, which the speaker and the listener recognize to be true and from which the arguable thesis follows as a consequence. A particular case follows from the general point. This particular case actually appears as a thesis, which shall be proved.

It is obvious that every thesis, every point is far from being proved by the deductive method. Why are there so many different types of demonstration? The reason is that usually a certain type of a proof can be used in every concrete case; rarely one can use two types of a proof simultaneously. Every time one ought to choose that type of a proof, which is at maximum natural in a concrete speech situation and is easy to be realized. In order to prove that the chicken has wings, actually it is convenient to use a deductive proof, since a bird appears as an animal with certain features, in particular, it surely has wings. One can find the definition of a bird in the dictionary or encyclopedia: "A bird is a feathery and fluffy vertebrate with wings, two extremities and a beak". A natural consequence that a chicken has wings follows from this definition as from a true one (exactly by the reason that it is a dictionary's definition and dictionaries represent a source of true information, See above). It is very easy to prove this thesis by a deductive method. However, it is impossible to use the deductive method in the proof of the thought that " there is no one bald man in the combined football team of the Russian Federation". It is impossible to propose any general point from which the thesis follows as a consequence. Because even if propose a wide conclusion like: "sportsmen shall be healthy", it won't help in a proof, since the growing bald not always appears as a disease that prevents somebody to be a professional sportsman and sometimes it is not caused by a disease at all.

The most common type of a deductive proof is said to be a syllogism.

Syllogisms (in Greek *syllogismós* means calculation) means a reasoning in which two categorical opinions connected with a general medium term originate a third opinion called an inference; at that the medium term is not consisted in the conclusion.

A categorical opinion is said to be an opinion, which reflects the knowledge about the belonging and non-belonging of a feature to an object irrespective of any conditions, for instance: *Fungus is a spore plant; whales do not relate to fishes.*

The medium term of syllogism (in Latin *terminus medius*) means a term of syllogism that appears as a general term for both premises and which, reflecting the relations of objects belonging to the objective world, serves as a mediate element between two other terms. For instance, let us discuss the following syllogism:

Every manual shall be written in a plain language;
"Drawing manual" is a manual;
___
"Drawing manual" shall be written in a plain language.

The term *manual* represents a medium term.

The medium term is used in those cases, wherein there is no possibility to compare two things directly and one ought to have recourse to their comparison by means of a third thing. Therefore Mikhail Lomonosov called the medium term as "a mediate term". Thus, we are not able to measure the size of two fields by placing one into another, but we can measure each of them by a meter measure ruler and after calculations check out the comparative sizes of the fields.

In the Middle Ages the search for the medium term of syllogism considered to be a certain kind of art. A philosopher Jean Buridan is noted for the expression about the so-called Asses' bridge (*pons asinorum*), which was assigned to teach everybody, including "the Asses" to find a medium term in syllogism.

Aristotle determined the syllogism as an expression, in which "upon the assertion of something, something different from the asserted thing necessarily follows from it owing to this something".

Syllogism means such an inference owing to which and having recognized the verity of the premises, one cannot but agree with the verity of the conclusion, which follows from the premises.

For instance:

All citizens of the Russian Federation have the right to labor;
Fyodorov is a citizen of the Russian Federation;
___
Fyodorov has the right to labor.

If the initial opinions of the syllogism are true, then provided that the corresponding rules are met, a true inference originates from the conclusion, as it happens in the above-referred example.

Syllogism consists of three opinions. It is a mediate inference (a mediate inference is said to be an inference in which the conclusion is derived on the basis of several premises). The first opinion includes a general rule (*All citizens of the Russian Federation have the right to labor*). The second presents a concrete case (*Fyodorov is a citizen of the Russian Federation*). And, at last, the third opinion makes the conclusion (*Fyodorov has the right to labor*).

Each of these opinions has its name. The opinion that includes a general rule is said to be a **major premise**; the opinion that presents a particular case is called a **minor premise**; and the third opinion, which represents the inference from the premises, is referred to be a **conclusion of syllogism**. To facilitate the comprehension of syllogism it is conventional to place all three opinions one under another in the form of a column. At that the conclusion is separated from the premises with a horizontal line.

The minor premise of the given syllogism has a single opinion. It says about a single man. However, the minor premise often can present a general opinion also. We can see it in the presented bellow syllogism:

All human beings make mistakes;
Scientists are the human beings;

Scientists make mistakes.

The opinion like *Scientists are the human beings* appears as the minor premise. It is a general opinion, as it expresses a thought about not a single object, but all scientists. However, this general opinion at least represents a particular case in respect to the opinion, which the major premise contains: *All human beings make mistakes*.

It is clear that the major premise represents a certain general knowledge, which the conclusion originates from in this or that way. It pertains to the category of "big" truths like: "All human beings are mortal", "The Earth rotates around the Sun", "Our planet consists of the main land and water" and so on – these are general conclusions. The second premise is more concrete, the conclusion is also concrete; it follows from these two premises as the consequence. If syllogism begins from the minor premise, then it is said to be an ascending syllogism (in Latin *ascendens*). For instance:

Mica is a mineral;
Minerals are the products of physical and chemical processes, that take place in the Earth crust;

Mica is a product of physical and chemical processes, that take place in the Earth crust.

Let us discuss the structure of an ordinary syllogism: the major premise is usually begins with the word that has the following meaning: all, every, each and so on, i.e. the joining meaning, otherwise the major premise would not be of the general character. The universal quantifier sets this meaning. So, the major premise begins from the universal quantifier. The text of the major premise is divided into two logical groups. Our text is divided easily: *the human being* and *make mistake*. However, it is absolutely unnecessary for each of these groups to consist of one word. For instance, the text may be as follows: "All people that were borne and reside in Moscow have a residence permit." We also have two logical groups: "all people that were borne and reside in Moscow" and "have a residence permit". It may be a more long text: "The people, who were borne and reside in Moscow and reached the full age, have a residence permit, which they receive in the nearest to their place of residence militia department". Now, let us examine the second premise. It also consists of two logical groups: "scientists" (the first logical group) and "the human beings" (the second logical group). It also may appear as a full-scale text, for instance, the first group may be as follows: "The scientists, who are the university graduates" – in other words each logical group can have a considerable wordy extension.

The first premise consists of one mediate (medium) and one extreme terms, the second premise has another extreme and, consequently, the same mediate terms, the conclusion consists of two extreme terms. Such is the logical structure of a classical trinomial Greek syllogism.

As it is known, each opinion consists of a subject and predicate, which in the logics are used to call *terms*. At the first glance it seems that if syllogism has three opinions, then it might have at least six terms. However, let us see, is it true or not. Let us discuss the next syllogism:

All planets move around the Sun;
The Mercury is a planet;

The Mercury moves around the Sun.

In the major premise of this syllogism the term *planets* appears as the subject and *move around the Sun* – as the predicate. In the minor premise *The Mercury* appears as the subject and *a planet* – as the predicate. Even these premises demonstrate that they have not four terms, but only three, since the both premises have one common term – *a planet*. As to the syllogism's conclusion it does not have any new terms. Both terms of the conclusion repeat those ones, which we met in the premises, namely: *The Mercury*, which is present in the minor premise and *moves around the Sun*, which is present in the major premise.

Thus, all three opinions have only three terms.

Each of the syllogism terms has its name: the medium term, which is common for both premises and it does not go to the syllogism conclusion. In the above example the term that we meet in the major premise (instead of the medium) and which appears as the conclusion predicate is said to be the major term (terminus major). The term that we meet in the minor premise (instead of the medium term) and which appears as the conclusion subject is said to be the minor term (terminus minor). The major and minor terms are also called the extreme terms. As it was said, they both go to the conclusion.

What is the position of each term in the opinions and how do they correlate in the process of the syllogistic inference?

The opinion like *All planets move around the Sun* determines the relation between the medium term (*planets*) and the major term (*move around the Sun*); the opinion like *The Mercury is a plane*t determines the relation between the medium term (*is a planet*) and the minor term (*The Mercury*). Thus, the premises consider the relation of the medium term to the minor and major terms. Since the premises cleared up the relation of the extreme terms to the common medium term, it becomes possible to make up the conclusion about the fact that such a relation exists between the extreme terms.

It clears up the significance of syllogism in the thinking process. None of the opinions of the separately taken syllogism demonstrates that the Mercury moves around the Sun. In the premises the major and minor terms are not directly connected between each other. However, the major and minor terms are connected with the medium term that enabled to connect the minor and major terms with each other. Having connected the extreme terms in the conclusion, we have received a new opinion, which demonstrates a new knowledge.

So, having compared two true premises we have come to the true inference as a result of the reasoning. What does it make possible in the conclusion to get the true inference from two true premises with the help of syllogism? Syllogism reflects the simplest relations of different things.

The human being have many times observed the relations between classes and types, general and singular in the world, which, as it was said, is expressed in the following: that which is inherent in the class, is inherent in the type; that which is inherent in the general, is inherent in the singular. For instance, that which is inherent in the class of animals (the ability to feel), is inherent in every animal.

As times goes by this objective relation between the general and singular was reflected in the thinking in the form of the following point: "All that is asserted (or disproved) in relation to all objects of the class, is asserted (or disproved) in relation to every single object and any part of objects of this class", – that is called an axiom of syllogism and appears as the truth, which was many times approved and therefore it does not need to be proved.

The axiom of syllogism is frequently marked with a short Latin formula *dictum de omni et de nullo*. The syllogistic reasoning is formulated in accordance with the axiom of syllogism. It can be demonstrated in the following example:

All adjectives vary with genders, cases and numbers;
The word "fearless" is an adjective;
___
The word "fearless" varies with genders, cases and numbers.

The above syllogistic reasoning yields to the following rule: if a certain thing has a certain feature and in its turn this feature has another feature, then the second feature also appears as the feature of the thing. This point is also called the axiom of syllogism. It is formulated in the following way: the feature of the feature of a certain thing is the feature of the thing; that, which contradicts the feature of a certain thing, contradicts the thing.

The axiom of syllogism may also be designated with the following Latin formula: *nota notae est nota rei ipsius*.

The axiom of syllogism shows that not every two opinions can be the premises of syllogism and make up a correct conclusion in the inference. One ought to meet seven rules of syllogism.

Rule 1. Syllogism can have only three terms – not more, not less. If there is a fourth term, it won't be a true inference.

The substance is eternal;
The broadcloth is the substance;
___
The broadcloth is eternal.

The above error in syllogism is said to be the quadrupling of the terms. It means that the medium term, which connects the extreme terms, shall be one and the same in both premises of syllogism.

Rule 2. The medium term shall be at least allotted to one of the premises. For instance, in the bellow reasoning that in outward appearance looks like syllogism, the inference is false, since it violated this rule:

Some workers of the car factory are the inventors;
Ivanov is a worker of the car factory;

Ivanov is the inventor.

Rule 3. The terms that are not allotted to the premises cannot be allotted to the conclusion. For instance, there are two such premises: *All pressmen ought to be literate.* And *Fyodorov is not a pressman*. Can one make the following conclusion from these premises: *Consequently, Fyodorov ought not to be literate*? Of course, the answer is negative.

Rule 4. One cannot get any inference from two negative premises. As an example let as consider two following premises: *None of the planets shines with its light* and *A comet is not a planet*.

The medium term does not connect the extreme terms, as it by itself is connected with none of the extreme terms. One cannot get an inference from such premises.

Rule 5. If one of the premises is negative, then the inference will be also negative; it cannot be positive. In fact, it is seen, for instance, in the following reasoning:

All mushrooms propagate with spores;
The given plant does not propagate with spores;

The given plant is not a mushroom.

The inference in the conclusion is negative. It is expected, since the medium term in the premises separates the extreme terms.

Rule 6. One cannot get any inference from two particular premises with the help of syllogism. In fact, let us take the following reasoning as an example:

Some A-students graduate with gold medals;
Some of our school's students are A-students;

Some of our school's students graduated with gold medals.

The conclusion is made in the wrong way. Not all of A-students are awarded with gold medals. Long ago even Aristotle knew this rule of syllogism. In his "The first analytics" he wrote about the fact that there would be no syllogism, if the premises were particular.

Rule 7. If one of the premises is particular, then the inference, if it is possible at all, can be only particular. The following reasoning demonstrates this perfectly:

All fishes are vertebrate;
Some aquatic animals are fishes;

Some aquatic animals are vertebrate.

It would be a mistake to tell that; "All aquatic animals are vertebrate".

The analysis of different syllogism shows that the medium term can occupy a different place in syllogism, as it reflects the various objective relations between the objects and phenomena of the surrounding world.

One can distinguish four figures of syllogism depending on the medium term position:

1. Medium term (m) appears as the subject (S) in the major premise and as the predicate (P) in the minor premise:

All human beings (M) have a genetic father and a genetic mother (P);
Newton (S) is the human being (M);

Newton (S) has a genetic father and a genetic mother (P).

2. The medium term appears as the predicate in both premises:

All sciences (P) study the regularities of the objective reality (M);
None of the religions (S) studies the regularities of the objective reality (M);

None of the religions (S) is a science (P).

3. The medium term appears as the subject in both premises:

Mercury (M) is not solid (P);
Mercury (M) is a metal (S);

Some metals (S) are not solid (P).

4. The medium term appears as the predicate in the major premise and as the subject in the minor premise:

All whales (P) are mammals (M);
None of the mammals (M) is a fish (S);

None of the fishes (S) is a whale (P).

The ability to distinguish the syllogism figures has a practical significance. The question is that each figure reflects various tricks of the premises use. Thus, if it is required to prove the verity of a single or particular opinion, one ought to use the first figure of syllogism: wherein the single or particular case is placed under the general rule. If it is required to disprove a single affirmative opinion, one ought to use the second figure of syllogism. To disprove general opinions one ought to use the third figure of syllogism.

At that each figure has several modi; the latter differ from each other by the quality and quantity of those opinions, which compose the premises of syllogism.

The mode of syllogism are used to be written with three capital letters, which are marked as generally affirmative (A), generally negative (E), particularly affirmative (I) and particularly negative (O) opinions. For instance, the first modus of the first figure of syllogism has three generally affirmative opinions:

All mammals have a constant body temperature (A);
All rodents are mammals (A);

All rodents have a constant body temperature (A).

Since each syllogism has three opinions and each of three parts of syllogism (two premises and conclusion) can have one of the four types of opinions, so, as it was shown by calculations, it is possible to have 64 various combinations of opinions that compose the premises and conclusion of syllogism.

However, not every of three opinions can be a modus of syllogism. If, for instance, one takes two generally negative premises, then in accordance with the fourth rule of syllogism one cannot make um any inference, so, consequently, syllogism is not possible. If one examine all 64 possible combinations of opinions in syllogism from the standpoint of their correspondence with the rules of syllogism, which reflects the relations of things, then one can determine that 45 combinations of opinions cannot appear as modi of syllogism, as they contradict these rules.

Thus, modus AEA would infringe the fifth rule, which says that upon one negative premise the conclusion shall be also negative; it cannot be positive; modi EEA, EEI, EEE violate the fourth rule, which prohibits to derive any single conclusion from two negative premises; modi AIA and EIE violate the seventh rule in accordance to which the conclusion shall be particular if one of the premises is particular. Some modi are not possible, as they simultaneously contradict several rules. Thus, modus OOO has particular and negative premises at the same time. The remnant 19 combinations appear as the modi of syllogism and are distributed in the figures in the following way:

First figure	Second figure	Third figure	Fourth figure
AAA	EAE	AAI	AAI
EAE	AEE	IAI	AEE
AII	EIO	AII	IAI
EIO	AOO	EAO	EAO
		OAO	EIO
		EIO	

Only the above-referred combinations give correct syllogisms.

Each modi is given a name, in which the vowel letters designate the quality and quantity of the premises and conclusion:

First figure: *Barbara, Celarent, Darii, Ferio*;
Second figure: *Cesare, Camestres, Festino. Baroko*;
Third figure: *Darapti, Disamis, Datisi, Felapton, Bocardo*;
Fourth figure: *Bramantip, Camenes, Dimaris, Fesapo, Fresison*.

Thus, in the name of the first modus of the first figure *Barbara* we see three *a*, i.e. it has three generally affirmative opinions; the name of the first modus of the second figure *Cesare* has *e,a* and *e*, i.e. one generally negative, one generally affirmative and one more generally negative opinions.

The mathematical logics exclude two modi of the third figure (*Darapti* and *Felapton*) and two modi of the fourth figure (*Bramantip* and *Fesapo*) from the number of actual modi. The question is that the mathematical logics operate with not only informal, but also empty classes and if one put an empty class into the Aristotelian syllogistics, which Aristotle did not investigate, and then the given four modi will turn out to be wrong, as no conclusion will follow from their premises.

It may seem that some modi of the reasonings cannot be applied in the thinking practice. It is wrong. The great significance of the figures and modi of the human thought, including the figures and modi of syllogism, can be very helpful, for instance, in the expanding practice of the machinery translation. One ought to clearly understand that in addition the knowledge of the syllogism modi and search for own speech examples represent a perfect method of training in thinking.

All syllogisms are divided into three large groups: categorical syllogism, portitive syllogism and conditional syllogism.

The categorical syllogism represents a syllogism, in which the inference is derived from two premises that appear as categorical opinions. For instance:

All monoecious plants have on one and the same
sample both staminal and pistil late flowers;
Birch is a monoecious plant;

Birch on one and the same sample has
both staminal and pistil late flowers.

The partitive syllogism represents a syllogism, in which both premises and the conclusion appear as partitive opinions. For instance:

Every opinion appears as either a single opinion
or a general opinion, or a particular one;
Every particular opinion appears as either a definite
particular opinion or an indefinite particular opinion;

Every opinion appears as either a single opinion, or a general
opinion, or a definite particular opinion, or an indefinite pa
ticular one.

The formula of the purely partitive syllogism is as follows:
A is either B, or M, or H;
H is either C or D;

A is either B, or M, or C, or D.

The conditional syllogism represents a syllogism, in which at least one of the premises appears as a conditional opinion. The conditional opinion is said to be an opinion, which reflects the dependence of that or this phenomenon on certain terms and conditions and in which the reason and the consequence are connected through the logical conjunction *if... then.*

The conditional opinion is false, when the reason is true and the consequence is false; it is true, when both the reason and the consequence are true. There are three types of conditional opinions:

1) The opinions that reflect the causations, for instance: *If the Earth falls into the Moon's shadow, then it originates the solar eclipse*;

2) The opinions, in which the knowledge about one fact appears as a logic reason for the assertion of our knowledge about another fact, for instance: *If mercury goes up in the thermometer, it means that it became warmer in the room*;

3) The opinions, in which the fact is expressed as a reason for the existence of another fact, for instance: *If the weather is good tomorrow, we will go to the forest*.

The conditional opinions are very frequently used both in the every day life speech and in the science – in all cases, when we assert or refuse something not in the unconditional form, but depending on a certain circumstance.

The conditional syllogism can be set in either a positive or a negative forms. In the positive form the minor premise appears as an affirmative opinion and the conclusion – as an affirmative opinion too. For instance:

If white color penetrates through a certain absorbent medium, then the specter shows dark stripes;
The given specter showed dark stripes;
___
White color penetrated through the absorbent medium.

The formula of such a conditional syllogism is as follows:
If A is B, then C is D;
A is B;
___
C is D.

In the negative form (in Latin *modus tollens*) the minor premise and the conclusion appear as negative opinions. For instance:

If white color penetrates through a certain absorbent medium, then the specter shows dark stripes;
The given specter does not show dark stripes;
___
White color did not penetrate through the absorbent medium.

The formula of such a conditional syllogism is as follows:
If A is B, then C is D;
C is not D;

A is not B.

The conditional syllogism is applied in the cases, when the matter concerns the consequence that follows from the known conditions with a necessity. If the necessary connection between the reason and the consequence is known, one can make up a conclusion about the consequence occurrence.

The syllogism can be simplified due to the absence of the second premise not from the logical point of view, but at the speech level. One can possibly say that it can be done without detriment to the comprehension: *All human beings make mistakes, so the scientists make mistakes.* It means that without changing the logical scheme of the assertion (as the speaker considers that the scientists are the human beings, though he does not say it due to the obviousness of the premise), the syllogism can be changed into the *enthymeme*.

Enthymeme (as translated from Greek it means *in mind*) represents a shortened syllogism, in which one of the implied three parts is omitted. Syllogisms are quite rarely applied in their full form. In our every day life speech we more often use shortened syllogisms. Sometimes they say in the following way: *Moscow is a city; consequently, it has its mayor.* In this case the general opinion was omitted: *all cities have mayors.* Such is the first type of the shortened syllogism, wherein the major premise is omitted.

The syllogism, in which the minor premise is omitted, is applied less often. As an example of such a shortened syllogism we can present the following reasoning: *Every craft is useful, consequently, the bench work is useful.* This example omits and implies the minor premise: *the bench work is a craft.*

One can omit not only one of the premises, but the conclusion too. An ancient Indian logician Dharmakirty demonstrated such a syllogism, which did not express the conclusion in words.

Wherein there is no fire, there is no smoke;
And there is a smoke at that place.

The above syllogism omits and implies the conclusion: *consequently, there is a fire at that place.*

Such shortened syllogisms are applied in all cases, wherein it is not required to express for one more time the entire known reasons. Aristotle called the enthymeme a tested trick of the logical assertion in the rhetoric. It is explained by the fact that the audience not always can scrupulously follow the thread of the orator's argumentation, so the orator uses the enthymeme. Aristotle said that the speeches full of examples were convincing, however "the speeches full of enthymemes produce more impressions."

As an English logician rightfully noticed it, if sometimes you meet a full syllogism, it looks like dandyism due to its logical exactness and correctness. In the Middle Ages such public debates took place in English universities, wherein one part of the students proved their points with the use of formal strict syllogism, and the other part disproved them with the same syllogisms.

In fact, what for in the process of proving such a point that "*the chemistry is useful, as the chemistry is a science*" shall one reconstruct another point that "*all sciences are useful*"? It is well known to every sensible person. Therefore the major premise can be easily omitted. The expression without losing its clearness becomes more laconic. As a result the major premise is omitted more often, since, as a rule, it contains the general opinion, which usually expresses a notorious truth.

The first figure of a simple categorical syllogism can omit both the first and the second premises. The major premise in this figure is omitted in those cases, wherein the general point is clear to everybody. Thus, we say: "*A comet is a heavenly body, consequently, it yields to the law of gravity.*" The major premise is omitted in this enthymeme of the first figure: *All heavenly bodies yield to the law of gravity*.

However, one can omit the minor premise too. Thus, we say: "*All heavenly bodies yield to the law of gravity, consequently, the comet also yields to the law of gravity.*" This enthymeme omits the minor premise that is clear without any special mentioning: *a comet is a heavenly body*.

The second figure of a simple categorical syllogism also can omit both major and minor premises. Thus, we say: "*The religion is based on the trust, consequently, it is not a science.*" This enthymeme omits the major premise: *the science cannot be based on the trust*. However, one can omit the minor premise too. Thus we say: "*All sciences are based on the knowledge of the regularities of the surrounding world, consequently, the religion is not a science.*" The minor premise is omitted in this example: *The religion is not based on the knowledge of the regularities of the surrounding world*.

We shall say that the abridgement of the second figure is more difficult than of the first. The interlocutor does not always understand the omitted premise. Therefore the shortening of the second figure syllogism shall be made more deliberately. Since if the interlocutor does not catch the omitted premise, he won't understand the conclusion.

One ought to be more attentive upon the abridgement of a simple categorical syllogism in the third figure. This operation can be executed only upon the exclusive circumstances. The question is that the interlocutor is required to be more quick-witted to reconstruct in his mind the omitted premise. Let us show the following example: *Democritus lived in the fifth century B.C., consequently, some people, who lived in the fifth century B.C., were materialists.* However, as it is seen from this reasoning, one can feel the lack of the omitted premise: *Democritus was a materialist.*

The fourth figure of a simple categorical syllogism makes no possibilities of the premises abridgement.

One can shorten both the conditional and partitive syllogisms. However, in this case unlike the categorical syllogism, there are fewer possibilities, as one can omit only the major premise. For instance: *The given triangle is neither right-angled, nor obtuse-angled; consequently, it is acute-angled.* The major premise is omitted in this example. *Triangles can be either acute-angled, or right-angled, or obtuse-angled.* It is an enthymeme of a partitive syllogism. One more example: *Cuprum is subjected to friction; consequently, it warms up.* The example omits the major premise: *If Cuprum is subjected to friction it warms up.* It is an enthymeme of a conditional and categorical syllogism.

The syllogism, in which every of the premises represent an enthymeme, is said to be **epicheireme** (Translated from Greek it means *an assault, imposition of hands*).

For instance:

The lie arouses the distrust, since it appears as an assertion that does not correspond to the truth;
The flattery is the lie, since it appears as a deliberate misinterpretation of the truth;

─────────────────────────────

The flattery arouses the distrust.

Each of the premises of the above syllogism represents a shortened syllogism. The first premise, for instance, can be expanded into the following full syllogism (an example of Professor V. Asmus):

Every assertion that does not correspond to the truth arouses the dis trust;
The lie appears as an assertion that does not correspond to the truth;

The lie arouses the distrust.

The scheme of the epicheireme is as follows:
M is P, since it appears as N;
S is M, since it appears as O;

S is P.

The second premise could be expressed in the following way:
All O are M;
All S are O;

All S are M.

The epicheireme is usually applied in debates, but not always; it is often used in other reasonings too. It is explained with the fact that in the form of the epicheireme a complicated reasoning keeps the form of a simple one, therefore it is easy to single out the composite parts of the syllogism in it: the major and minor premises, and the conclusion. The epicheireme is especially useful in the orator's speech, as it makes it possible to distribute the reasoning in its composite parts with greater comfort. As an example we can refer to Cicero's speech in defense of Milo: "It is permissible to kill the one, who threatens our life (the major premise is approved with the right and examples); Cloudy threatened the life of another person, namely, Milo (the minor premise is approved with the examination of the circumstances that followed the Cloudy's death); consequently, it was permissible to kill Cloudy."

When applying a shortened syllogism one ought to bear in his mind that it is harder to notice an error in such reasoning, than in a full syllogism. Not in vain an English logician Mintho said that for the purposes of "a proof", enthymemes are better than full and divided syllogisms, since they fit better to hide any inconsistency in a proof. A full syllogism shows clearly both premises and the conclusion. As it concerns an enthymeme it may happen that if there is an error in the expressed opinion, it is harder to be noticed, or the opinion in this case cannot be expressed, but it is implied.

In addition to the above-referred classical trinomial Greek syllogism, there are complicated syllogisms, which are called *sorites*.

The Sorites (in Greek *sōrós* means a heap) represent a kind of a complicated syllogism, which adduces only the last conclusion that is taken through a number of premises; the intermediate conclusions are not expressed, but implied.

The structure of sorites is expressed in the following formula:

All A is B;
All B is C;
All C is D;
All D is E;
———————
All A is D.

The sorites, which omit the minor premises of syllogism, are called Aristotelian, and the sorites, which omit the minor premises, are called hoclenes.

Let us present an example of Aristotelian sorites:

Bucephalus is a horse;
A horse is a quadruped;
A quadruped is an animal;
An animal is a substance;
———————
Bucephalus is a substance.

The above sorites combined three following syllogisms:

1. *A horse is a quadruped;*
   Bucephalus is a horse;
   ———————
   Bucephalus is a quadruped.

2. *A quadruped is an animal;*
   Bucephalus is a quadruped;
   ———————
   Bucephalus is an animal.

3. *An animal is a substance;*
   Bucephalus is an animal;
   ———————
Bucephalus is a substance.

Much reasoning in all fields of the knowledge is expressed in this form of a complicated syllogism.

Lomonosov referred to the sorites or a heap, constrained by an argument, as to the combination of many premises in such a way, wherein the consequence of one becomes the premise for another. As an example he presented the following sorites:

That, which is good, shall be wished for;
That, which is wished for, shall be approved;
That, which shall be approved, is praiseworthy;

Consequently, that, which is good, is praiseworthy.

The combination of syllogisms, upon which the conclusion of one syllogism appears as a premise for another (at that the reasoning goes from the more general to the less general), is said to be a progressive polysyllogism. For instance:

All vertebrates have red blood;
All mammals are vertebrates;
All mammals have red blood;
All mammals have red blood;
All Carnivora are mammals;
All Carnivora have red blood;
All Carnivora have red blood;
Tigers are Carnivora;

Tigers have red blood.

The pentamerous Indian syllogism has been known since the fourth century B.C. For instance:
1) *There is a fire on the hill (thesis);*
2) *As there is a smoke on the hill (reason);*
3) *Wherein there is a smoke, there is a fire, as like in the kitchen, but in a pond, for instance, there is no fire (example);*
4) *There is a smoke on that hill (application);*
5) *Consequently, there is a fire on that hill (conclusion).*

In the Indian syllogism the third term (example) correspond to the major premise of the Aristotelian syllogism, the second (reason) and the fourth (application) terms correspond to the minor premise of the Aristotelian syllogism, the first (thesis) and the fifth (conclusion) terms correspond to the conclusion of the Aristotelian syllogism. However, the Indian syllogism contains three main terms as in the Aristotelian: 1) subject (in this case it pertains to the hill), which is contained in the thesis and in the conclusion; 2) causal feature (availability of smoke) and 3) demonstrable feature (availability of fire).

However, the third term (example) of the Indian syllogism is not absolutely adequate to the major term of the Aristotelian syllogism. The matter concerns the fact that Aristotle did not use single terms in syllogism; he usually put a general opinion to the major premise, but Indian logicians did not include general opinions into the syllogism, therefore the third term of their syllogism is represented by a single opinion.

As in the Indian syllogism the reason proves that thing, which shall be proved, by means of an indication to the similarity with or to the distinction from the example, since many investigators of the Indian logics identify the Indian syllogism with the reasoning by analogy.

A Buddhist logician Gautama introduced the pentamerous syllogism into the Indian logics.

The origin character of the Indian logicians' teaching about the pentamerous syllogism lies in the requirement for a support of the general point with understandable concrete examples. This theory has a true thought about the fact that every general point is based on separate facts, which we observe. This dialectic point about the unity of the deduction and induction is expressed in the Indian logics in a naive form.

However, one can meet in the Indian logical teachings not only the pentamerous syllogism that is inherent in the Nyaya School. Thus, in the early Buddhist logics the syllogism included seven and even ten terms. But at the end of the second – in the beginning of the third century there was recommended to reduce the number of the syllogism terms up to five and even up to three terms (Logician Nagardjuna).

In the European science the syllogistics in the first place is connected with the name of Aristotle, who for the first time not only analyzed the methods of reasoning from the formal point of view, but also systematized them, thus discovering the objective rules, which apply to particular cases and do not depend on particular concrete objects. Another notable contribution of Aristotle into the science of thinking was that he introduced literal symbols to designate variables, thus laid the foundation for the formal structure of the logics.

As any other types of demonstration, the deduction has its positive and negative characteristics. The positive characteristic is the one that makes the deductive proof be considered absolute. In fact, if a certain leading idea, which you use in the capacity of an argument, appears as a notorious truth, then any consequence that follows from it shall be considered true, so the proof looks very simple and convincing. In such a case you operate with a universal category, i.e. something that is beyond any exclusions. However, the deductive proof exactly owing to the absolutism has a considerable shortage, as it often turns out to be dogmatic.

Dogma (in Greek *dógma* means an opinion, a teaching) is a point that shall be accepted without any critical examination as an oracle, blindly, on trust; it is a permanent formula, which is applied with no consideration of concrete circumstances.

The proof of a huge quantity of the points in the society, constructed on the principles of totalitarianism, is of a dogmatic deductive character. If one analyzes the local texts of the Soviet period, he will easily notice a great number of deductive conclusions. We were said that the communism was a radiant future of the entire mankind. It is one of the dogmatic ideas, which originated many others. With no doubt, it appears as an abstract hypothetical idea and no one can verify its truth. It is an unsubstantial and mystical idea. Nevertheless it represented a deductive premise that substantiated the validity of various antihuman acts. If the communism is a radiant future of the entire mankind, then we won't spare forces, labor and human lives for the sake of its attainment. It is one of the dogmatic, which resulted in the death of many people, bloodshed and multiple bones buried in the earth.

The texts of those years are characterized by a considerable rigidity of any sort of conclusion, in which the inner logical unity ("all, always") almost does not have any exclusion. Therefore some of the points sound quite ridiculous. Thus, from the point that: "Every cook in this country can rule over the state", as a natural consequence, one can make up the conclusion that if a certain Ivanov is a graduate of a culinary secondary school, then he can rule over the state.

Unfortunately, a dogmatic deductive proof appears as a phenomenon of not only a totalitarian society (wherein it is natural), but it can found, say, in theological texts, wherein many points cannot be either disproved or proved directly and therefore they should be accepted on trust. However, theological texts in this respect cannot be subjected to criticism, since they are based on the category of trust, on its priorities in the people's spiritual life: a man either believes in the fact that the Creator is primordial, or does not believe; however, in this case they say that the theological text is written not for him. The trust belongs to the inner psychological categories that are taken out of the argumentation threshold. You are facing a malefactor, but you have your inner belief that his evil deed will never apply personally to you (and may be you are right, however no other person will agree with you). It is a factor of the trust. How can one prove the existence or absence of the Creator? The deductive proof is based exactly on the category of trust. As to prove to a person that it is possible to sacrifice many things to the radiant future of the mankind, it is necessary that this person should believe in the possibility of the radiant future. In fact, a certain type of people was formed in the USSR, who by analogy to the trust in the Creator, piously believed in the communist ideals.

One shall use the deductive proof with a great care, i.e. to use only that general point, which actually does not cause everybody's irritation and doubts, i.e. they shall in fact appear as universal. Definitely speaking, the people by themselves cannot formulate any universal and absolute truths that concern everything connected with the people, therefore the thesis about the human being yield badly to the deductive proof (See Chapter 13. "Argumentation" Analysis of the following syllogism: "All human beings are mortal; Socrates is a human being; Socrates is mortal."). The point that all human beings are mortal cannot be disproved by anybody, since no one can prove it also. The problem by itself gains the character of a philosophic interpretation.

The same happens with any global idea common to all mankind: it is not absolute.

The biblical precept "Do not love your neighbor's wife" is interpreted as a strict limitation of not only behavioral, but also emotional type (since the verb to love is polysemic), that contradict the psychobiological feature of the unconsciousness to seek for the satisfaction beyond the rational choice. The human being has no power over his feelings – such is his nature. It is unlikely that the biblical postulate can be considered to be universally true.

When the human being demonstrates his intellect in his speech when communicating with other people, he also shall show his intellectual mobility, the dialectic character of his thinking. To do this one ought to get rid of absolute postulates. Everything that is connected with the deductive proof appears as dogmatic by its nature; therefore it is in a certain way unnaturally for the vivid human thinking. Though if you exactly the same person, who believes in an absolute idea, expressed in the premise, then the deductive inference will be absolute for you and it will be an easy work to convince you.

The deductive proof often turns out to be very effective in the Russian language communication, as the thinking of the people is still close to the dogmatic and it easily perceives a direct inference from the general to the particular. However, one ought to avoid appealing to an Englishman with a deductive proof. Most likely he will raise doubts in the absolute verity of the main idea and will try to argue his doubts. The critical, used to irony conscious of an Englishman cannot stand any dogmatic points: it is typical to an Englishman to scoff at everything in the world and he does it extremely wittily and successfully.

If you have a task to demolish and disprove a deductive proof, you can do it only finding fault with the verity of the leading premise and with the fact that is of an absolute character; since in the deduction the course of the proof is logically irreproachable.

Chapter 15. **Inductive Demonstration**

> The general in particular case is perceived by means of comparison.
> *Socrates*

The inductive demonstration along with the deductive appears as the main type of a speech proof. The concept of induction (in Latin *inductio* means induction) underlies the inductive demonstration. In a broader sense of the word it represents a form of thinking by means of which a thought is aimed on a certain general rule or general point inherent in all single objects of a certain class.

The inductive reasoning was formed in a process of the people's centuries-old practice. Within dozens of thousands of years the human being many times noticed and fixed such phenomena, for instance, like upon making a stone axe the man who grinded one stone over another at a great pace felt that both stones got warmer; upon making a boat, the wood was scraped off by means of a knife, in the process both the knife and the wood got warmer; upon making a hut, when trailing a big dry log over other dry logs, the rubbing parts got warmer; if one quickly rotated a stick in the hollow of a wooden bar, the heat produced as a result of the friction might kindle a dry twig; in winter time when hands became frozen, as soon as he rubbed them of each other they warmed up, and so on.

Thus, investigating the natural phenomena, observing and studding separate objects, facts and events, the people came to a general rule. This process of comprehension went on inductively: the human being went on from single opinions to general conclusions, which reflected the knowledge of a general rule, general regularity.

No theoretical thinking would be possible at all, if a man in an inductive way did not come to the ascertainment of these or those general points. Until the human being studied practically different metals, he did not know the general rule upon which it is possible to determine the aptitude of this or that metal, for instance, to make a drill or a knife. Until the human being acquainted with different liquids, he was not able to know that "all liquids are resinous". Until the human being in the process of work began investigating separate gases, he had no idea about the general law of the uniform pressure of gases on the walls of vessels.

The human being begins studding of any fields of the outer world with the investigation of single objects, not with the study of the general rules and general regularities. It does not mean, of course, that it is not possible to derive logically one general rule from another. It also does not mean that one cannot obtain this or that general rule from a book or from a conversation with another person. At that one thing seems clear: any new general rules, derived in a logical way, could not appear, if there was no those general rules that underlined them. The initial general points are elaborated in the process of the human experience.

Socrates was the first who began investigating the inductive methods of thinking. He said that the knowledge represents the points about the general, and the general in particular cases is comprehended by means of comparing this cases between each other, i.e. one ought to go from the particular to the general. Socrates invented a popular method of maieutika (in Greek it means obstetrics, midwifery), which represents one of the methods of the truth ascertainment. The method of Socrates consists in the following: to lead the interlocutor to the true knowledge by means of the skillful questioning and answering. Like a midwife helps in the delivery of a child, Socrates helped in the "delivery" of a thought. Maieutika was related to the elementary inductive tricks. Socrates looked for the general in particular cases by means of comparing these cases between each other.

Maieutika always appeared in the conjunction with other methods of the Socratic method: 1) irony that implies the exposure of the interlocutor's contradiction and, consequently, ignorance; 2) induction that requires to ascend from ordinary views and single examples of the homeliness to the general points; 3) definition that means climbing to the righteous definition of a concept in the result of the initial definitions.

The debates by the methods of maieutika shall be conducted in the following way: the interlocutor is asked to provide the definition of the debated matter; if the answer turns out to be superficial, the interlocutors apply to the examples of every day life and specify the initial definition; as a result they take a more correct definition, which once again is specified by the use of new examples, and it goes on till the true thought is "borne".

Thus, the method of maieutika included elementary inductive methods. Indicating this fact Socrates tried to make up logical reasonings. Aristotle wrote: "In all fairness two things shall be attributed to Socrates – inductive reasonings and formation of general definitions..." Aristotle devoted a lot of his time to the problems of the induction theory. He singled out such types of induction as an induction through a simple enumeration and an incomplete induction. The induction was very popular in the seventeenth – eighteenth centuries, when the natural sciences began developing fast.

In restricted sense of the word the term *induction* has three meanings.

The first meaning – an inductive reasoning – is such a reasoning, which entails a general conclusion that has certain knowledge about the entire objects of the class on the basis of the knowledge about separate objects of the given class. Let us discuss, for instance, two following reasonings:

The first reasoning:
Sodium nitrate is water-soluble;
Potassium nitrate is water-soluble;
Ammonium nitrate is water-soluble;
Calcium nitrate is water-soluble;
There are no other known nitrates;

All nitrates are water-soluble.

The second reasoning:
A straight line crosses the circle in two points;
A straight line crosses the ellipse in two points;
A straight line crosses the parabola in two points;
A straight line crosses the hyperbola in two points;
The circle, ellipse, parabola and hyperbola represent the types of conic sections;

A straight line crosses all conic sections in two points.

The above reasonings differ by their content. The form of the thoughts connection is one and the same. In both cases the reasoning develops inductively, i.e. from the knowledge about separate objects to the knowledge about the class, from the knowledge about one degree of the commonality to the new knowledge about the greater degree of the commonality. An inductive reasoning makes it possible to direct the course of thinking not only from separate objects to the common, but from subclasses to the common.

The inductive reasoning appears in two types: complete and incomplete inductions. The complete induction is said to be such type of the inductive reasoning, which entails the general conclusion about the entire class of certain objects on the basis of the knowledge about all objects of this class without exception.

For instance:
Last week it was raining on Monday;
It was raining on Tuesday;
It was raining on Wednesday;
It was raining on Thursday;
It was raining on Friday;
It was raining on Saturday;
It was raining on Sunday;

Last week it was raining all days.

Knowing that a week has no other days, except the above referred in the premises, it is quite rightful to make up the conclusion: last week it was raining all days.

As a result of the complete induction the first two discussed examples gave the knowledge about the fact that all nitrates are water-soluble, as well as that a straight line crosses all conic sections in two points. The complete induction is characterized with the fact that the general conclusion is derived from a set of opinions, the sum of which exhausts in full all cases of the given class. That which is asserted in every opinion about every separate object of the given class, relates in the conclusion to all objects of the class.

The formula of the complete induction is as follows:
S_1 is P;
S_2 is P;
S_3 is P;
But S_1, S_2, S_3 exhaust the entire class;

All S are P.

Aristotle called the complete induction "the syllogism by induction". Some logicians, when presenting the following example:

The Mercury, the Venus, the Earth and others move around the Sun from the West to the East;
The Mercury, the Venus, the Earth and others appear as all known planets;

All known planets move around the Sun from the West to the East.

consider, actually following Aristotle, that the complete induction is similar in form to the syllogism of the third figure, namely, *Darapti* (See above), in which the medium term in the given example consists of a group of the known planets.

Other logicians saw in the complete induction the partitive syllogism (See above). They presented the above-referred example in the following form:

Either the Mercury, or the Venus, or the Earth, or any other is the planet;
But the Mercury moves around the Sun from the West to the East;
the Venus moves around the Sun from the West to the east and any other;

All known planets move around the Sun from the West to the East.

By means of the complete induction one can achieve the so-called a connective proof. For instance, in order to prove the following theorem "every inscribed angle is equal to the half of the central angle that leans on the same arch", they present three cases: 1) when the inscribed angle is composed from the diameter and the span; 2) when the angle is composed from two spans with the center of the circle lying between them; 3) when the angle is composed from two spans, when there is no center of the circle between them. The theorem is correct in all these cases. One cannot imagine any other cases. Consequently, upon all possible positions the theorem is correct, i.e. the inscribed angle is equal to the half of the central angle that leans on the same arch.

One ought to know that sometimes the complete induction permits a logical error. It consists in the following: Having discussed a number of opinions about separate cases of the given class or separate types of the given kind, we can formulate a general conclusion without checking the fact whether all cases of the given class are exhausted or not. Meanwhile the conclusion in the complete induction is correct only in the case, wherein the particular premises provide the full list of the objects pertaining to the given class.

The knowledge taken as a result of the complete induction that based on the true premises is quite trustworthy. However the complete induction does not give the knowledge about other objects, which are not present in the premises. In fact, the general conclusion relates only to those objects that we have observed. The significance of the complete induction consists in the fact that without empowering us with the knowledge about new objects, it exposes the discussed objects in a certain new respect. In the conclusion we consider the same objects, but taken in the capacity of the class, meanwhile in every particular premise we considered only one object at all.

A Russian logician M. Karinsky studied the regularities of the reasonings by the complete induction. He wrote about the fact that the conclusion of the complete induction seemed to appear as a simply reduced expression of the earlier existing knowledge; it was not a new truth, since it did not extend farther those objects that were mentioned in the premises. However it is not so: "The new character of a thought depends not only on the fact that the definition extends over a new real object; a thought will be new, if the definition was given to the object that earlier was characterized differently and so it appeared as a different object. In our opinion about the logic group we attribute the definition not only to the objects characterized by the known features, but to all objects that were characterized in this way; when expressing our opinion about such a group, we assert that the existence of the group features in the object is enough for the object to be related to the definition attributed to the whole group. However the opinions, which attribute this definition to particular objects do not have such a trace of the thought".

Of course, as Karinsky concludes, the science values more the opinions about such logical groups, which include innumerable number of copies. Naturally, the inferences based on the complete induction, in which the particular opinions appear as the opinions about the copies, cannot have any considerable application in the sciences. However, on shall not forget that the complete induction can operate not only with the copies, but with the species too, and it immeasurably increases the number of the applied objects. Such inferences made up on the basis of the complete induction from types to the class are applicable in the sciences.

The incomplete induction is said to be such a type of the inductive reasoning, which results in a certain general conclusion about the whole class of objects based on the knowledge about only some homogenous objects of the given class. For instance:

Helium has the valence equal to zero;
Neon has the same;
Argon has the same;
But Helium, Neon and Argon are rare gases;
___
All rare gases have the valence equal to zero.

In the above-referred example the conclusion is made up about the whole class of rare gases on the basis of the knowledge about certain types, i.e. a part of this class. Therefore, the incomplete induction sometimes is referred to an expanding induction, as in its conclusion it has more information than consisted in the premises. The scheme of the reasoning by the incomplete induction is as follows:

A1 has the characteristic of B;
A2 has the characteristic of B;
A3 has the characteristic of B;

Consequently, both A4 and, in general, all A have the characteristic of B.

Based on the observation of a certain number of the known facts the incomplete induction leads to a conclusion, which also extends to other unknown facts or objects of the given field.

The incomplete induction appears in two types:
1. An incomplete induction based on the knowledge about the necessary characteristics and causations of objects and phenomena is referred to such a type of the inductive reasoning that results in a certain general conclusion about the entire class of objects made up on the basis of the knowledge about the necessary characteristics and causations of only some objects of the given class.
2. An incomplete induction through the simple enumeration, in which there are no contradictory cases, is referred to such a type of the inductive reasoning that results in a certain general conclusion about the entire class of objects made up on the basis of the knowledge about only some objects of the given class, provided that there were no contradictory cases. The incomplete induction through the simple enumeration gives us a possibility to move from the known facts to the unknown and in such a way it helps us to expand our knowledge about the world.

However, such induction instead of true inferences in the conclusion and the general rule, gives only approximate and probable, as the inferences in this case are based on the observance not of all objects pertaining to the given class. It might happen that we could occasionally omit a contradictory example. It often happens in this way, since we still know badly the investigated area of the phenomena.

Iron is a solid body;
Cuprum is a solid body;
Zinc is a solid body;
Gold is a solid body;
Aluminum is a solid body;
Iron, cuprum, zinc and aluminum are metals;

All metals are solid bodies.

The inference is made up by the method of induction through the simple enumeration, in which there are no contradictory cases. A number of metals were investigated and the inference was made up in respect of all metals. As a result we have an erroneous inference, since, for instance, mercury is a metal, but it a liquid body. The induction through the simple enumeration, while giving a certain benefit in our every day life practice, can be applied only at the initial stage of investigation, when it pertains to the process of the actual facts accumulation and the first selection of necessary data. It is called a popular induction. At all times the popular induction is considered to be the mostly unreliable type of the incomplete induction. The probability of its conclusion is poorly grounded, as the only reason for its inference consists in the ignorance of the cases that could contradict its conclusion.

The conclusion resulted from such an induction always remains under a threat of its verity disproof as soon as somebody reveals the contradictory case, as it was with Australian black swans that overturned by their discovery the one-century old assertion that all swans are white. In a speech communication one shall use only the complete induction, as the incomplete induction, in fact, often leads to the proof of false theses. Let us discuss an example. Many universities has a rule under which strong groups of students have better teaches, who, in their turn, teach the most talented. It is a defensible pedagogical reference, since the efforts of an expert directed to a person who might not need it, won't bear any fruit. It is not expedient: the matter concerns the fact that who it will be and what he will take from the education. It is better when an outstanding expert in a certain field will teach only three students, but it will be those, who will become his true followers. In this connection the great importance is paid to the analysis of every student's progress in the studies and the evaluation of the school groups by the results of the session. Let us suppose that the council of the English language department examines the progress of the students from the first English group that consists of nine people. The curator of the course gives them the following testimonials:

Afanasyev – very backward student, badly trained;

M. Bronevoy – has very satisfactory abilities;

T. Klimova – assiduous student with undeveloped thinking;

K. Ezhov – sluggish, fails to attend many studies;

B. Klimov – extremely middling student, hardly took the session examination with "satisfactory" marks;

S. Mikhenkova – light-headed student, has no gift for intellectual work;

A. Orlov – hardly copes with the material, failed all examinations.

After that the curator says: "I think that it is enough. The group is very weak."

Now imagine, please, that two remained students of the group (S. Shevtsov and T. Yudin were not discussed, as they were at the end of the list according to the alphabetical order) represent the best students of the course.

The department's officials do not ask the curator any additional questions and the council decides to assign a young inexperienced pedagogue to teach the first group. What will happen in this situation? S. Shevtsov and T. Yudin won't take full value education, as they know the English language better than their new teacher. In addition, in their presence, other students psychologically become "null" at the lessons, since they do not want to lose their authority (by this reason in the institutions of higher educations they try to complete homogenous groups, if possible). With now doubt the above administrative decision was wrong, since the incomplete induction resulted in a proof of a false thesis: "The first English group is very weak". Meanwhile the true thesis is as follows: "The first English group in not homogenous, seven students are weak, two students are strong." This thesis would be proved upon the use of the complete induction. In the same way it would result in another administrative decision: "The first English group shall be broken up; S. Shevtsov and T. Yudin shall be shifted to another strong group and the best teacher of the department shall be assigned to teach this group."

The second meaning of the term "induction" is referred to a method of investigation that is concluded in the following: in order to take a common knowledge about a certain class of objects, it is necessary to examine separate characteristics of the given class, which will serve as the basis for the knowledge about the commonality inherent in the given class of objects. The inductive method of investigations also consists in the following: the investigator moves from the knowledge about less common matters to the knowledge about more common matters.

The third meaning of the term "induction" represents a form of the facts expression in a book, lecture, report and a conversation, wherein one moves from single and less common matters to general conclusions, inferences and provisions.

As we have above said the problems of the inductive logics aroused interest especially in the seventeenth – eighteens centuries. An English philosopher materialist Frances Bacon in his treatise "New Organon" expressed a new view on the induction. Having recognized the induction through a simple enumeration to be unreliable, he set a form finding task, i.e. to find out something stable in the phenomena as the basis of their outer relations.

Bacon assumed to find out the forms by means of a number of methods that he called as "assistance" to the mind. All found facts were required to be distributed in the tables of "presence", "absence" and "degrees". Up to Bacon it might result in the finding out of a necessary relation between phenomena. The Bacon's scheme reduced the entire multiformity of the world phenomena to a small amount of forms. Bacon called upon to study facts and carry out scientific experiments.

An English logician and philosopher – positivist John Stuart Mille developed the ideas of Bacon, as well of an English naturalist John F. Herschel. He proposed the simplest logic methods to determine the causations between the phenomena and their consequences. These methods were aimed at clearing up the question about the fact whether it is possible to consider the preceding phenomena to be the reason of the posterior one, or not. The reason is said to be such a phenomenon A, which availability causes the appearance of another phenomenon B, that is called the action of reason A, and upon the absence of phenomenon A, phenomenon B is also absent.

There are five logical methods used to examine causations, which are expressed in the form of the following rules:

1 Method of similarity" "If two or more cases of the examinable phenomenon have only one common condition, which coordinates all these cases, then it appears as the reason or the consequence of the given phenomenon".

2. Method of difference: "If the case in which the examinable phenomena occurs, and the case, in which it does not occur, are similar in all conditions, except one that appears only in the first case, then this condition, which is the solely one wherein these two cases differ, is referred to be the consquence or the reason, or the necessary part of the phenomenon reason".

3. Connective method of similarity and difference: "If two or more cases of the phenomenon occurrence have only one common condition, and two or more cases of this or that phenomenon occurrence as the com-

mon have only the absence of the same condition, then this condition, which is the solely one wherein both sets of cases differ, is referred to be the consequence or the reason, or the necessary part of the examinable phenomenon reason".

4. Method of the contiguous changes: "Every phenomenon, which changes in a definite way every time, when another phenomenon changes in a certain special way, appears as either the reason, or the consequence of this phenomenon, or it has a certain causal relationship with it.

5. Method of remainders: "If one subtracts from a phenomena that part, which, as it is known from the other inductions, appears as the consequence of some certain previous ones, then the remainder of the given phenomenon shall be the consequence of the other previous ones".

Mille asserts the possibility of treating the examinable phenomenon and the discussed circumstances as separate isolated events. He said that it is possible to speak about the connection of a separate reason and a separate action, i.e. to digress from the mutual influence of this phenomenon circumstances, from the reverse influence of consequences on reasons, meanwhile this phenomenon can be borne, as it often happens, not by a certain single reason, but due to the joined action of a number of reasons that have complicated relationship. This simplification stipulates for the fact that the given methods, as any other methods of an inductive investigation, give a probable knowledge in the conclusion. Thus, the number of the investigated cases determines the probability degree of the inferences made up by the method of similarity. However, even if such a number is great, it is still hard to decide, whether this phenomenon results from a sole condition, which turned out to be similar in all cases, or from the joined action of this sole condition and all other conditions. The method of difference gives a more probable knowledge. It is explained by the combination of this method with the experiment. However, the phenomenon put into the experiment may turn out to be complicated, therefore it will be still unaware, whether the whole phenomenon or a certain part of it appears as the reason. Other methods also have such a probable character.

Mille separated the induction and deduction that resulted in his so-called "All-inductivism". Long ago Aristotle said about the unity of the induction and deduction: "The commonality cannot be analyzed without the use of the induction".

Due to all means of perception, which the investigator is empowered with, like the deduction, analogy, hypothesis and others, the methods of investigation of the traditional logics causal relationship are widely used as auxiliary means of finding the causal dependence.

The casual relations for long have exited the people's minds. Even the works of an ancient Greek philosopher of the fifth century B.C. Aristippus forestalled the inductive methods of finding causations.

The mathematical logic as well studies the logical mechanism of inductive reasonings, applying to the methods of the mathematical logic and the theory of probability.

Many scientists assume that at present the task of the inductive logics is not to invent the rules of finding scientific truths, but to find out the objective criteria of proving hypotheses by their empirical premises and, if possible, to determine to what degree this premises confirm the hypothesis. The form of the inductive logics shall change correspondingly, as it turns out to be a probabilistic logic, and the classical inductive logic appears as a particular case of the probabilistic logic. The task of the probabilistic logic is to estimate the probability of generalization, as it is possible to determine the verity only in the absolutely simple cases.

The correctness of the inference in an inductive reasoning above all depends on the verity of the premises, which underlie the conclusion. If the inference is bases on false premises, it turns out to be false too. The errors in inductive reasonings are very often explained by the fact that the premises do not consider all the circumstances, which cause the investigated phenomenon.

However the errors may get into the inductive inferences even at that time, when the premises are true. It happens in the cases wherein we do not observe the rules of reasoning, which reflect the relationship between the singular and the common inherent in the objects and phenomena of the surrounding world. The first error, connected with a departure from the rules of the course of the inductive reasoning due to a certain misunderstanding of the law of the sufficient reason, is well known for long under the name of "hasty generalization" (in Latin *Fallacia fictae universalitatis*). The essence of the error consists in the following: the premises do not consider all the circumstances, which cause the investigated phenomenon.

There is a more vulgar error in the inductive inferences connected with the violation of the law of the sufficient reason. It is referred to the error of the conclusion by formula: "after this, therefore by the reason of this" (in Latin "*Post hoc, ergo propter hoc*"). The essence of this error lies in the mixture of the causation with the simple consistency in time. Sometimes it seems that if one phenomenon foregoes another, it appears as its reason. But it is not always so. Every twenty-four hours the people observe that the day follows the night, and the night follows the day. If one asserted on this basis that the night is the reason of the day and the day is the reason of the night, he would reason by the formula: "after this, therefore by the reason of this". In fact, neither the night is the reason of the day, not the day is the reason of the night. The changing of days and nights is a result of the diurnal rotation of the Earth around its axes. Consequently, it is not righteous to conclude about the causation of two phenomena only on the basis that one phenomenon precedes another.

All sciences apply the inductive proof, wherein the thesis appears as a general opinion. There is an example bellow of an inductive proof of a thesis that the sum of all internal angles of a triangle is equal to two straight lines.

Arguments: "The sum of the internal angles in acute-angled triangles is equal to two straight lines", "the sum of the internal angles in right-angled triangles is equal to two straight lines", "and the sum of the internal angles in obtuse-angled triangles is equal to two straight lines".

Reasoning: "since, in addition to acute-angled, right-angled and obtuse-angled triangles there are no other triangles, and in all acute-angled, right-angled and obtuse-angled triangles the sum of the internal angles is equal to two straight lines, so, consequently, the sum of the internal angles in all triangles is equal to two straight lines".

The essence of such a proof consists in the following: one ought to take the consent of his interlocutor to the fact that each separate object, which belongs to a certain class of objects, reflected in the general opinion, has a fixed characteristic. When the consent to this fact is reached, then the verity of the following thesis arises with the necessity: since every separate object has this characteristic, then, it is naturally, that all the given objects have the same characteristic.

Summing up all the above said, we should notify that the inductive proof concludes that a multitude M, which consists of a certain number n of elements, has a certain characteristic S, provided that every of these elements have the above characteristic S. If we want to make up the conclusion about the whole multitude of objects (people, things and so on), we should examine every element of this multitude. So we can make up a natural and simple inference: only those multitudes can be exposed to the inductive proof, which include a small amount of elements. If the multitude has an infinite number of elements, it will be impossible to furnish a strictly inductive proof. If the number of the elements is huge, then, of course, it is possible to furnish a strictly inductive proof, but it is very laborious and usually inexpedient activity, as one shall estimate every element separately from the standpoint of the target characteristic availability. Therefore, the strictly inductive proof extends only to the so-called low-powered multitudes (under the power of the multitude one ought to understand the number of the included elements). The multitude with power 4 is easily exposed to the inductive proof; the multitude with power 100 is hardly exposed to the inductive proof; and the multitude with power 10 000 almost cannot be exposed to such a proof. The inductive method is useless when you intend to prove a thesis about the fact that, say, all Muscovites can speak Russian. However, it is very easy to prove a thesis about the fact that in a certain room there is no broken glasses, if this room, say, has two windows, wherein each window has four glasses (so, there are eight glasses at all). One can examine the first glass – there are no cracks; to check the second glass – there is also no cracks and so on. Making sure that every glass is intact, one can make up the general conclusion: there is no broken glasses in this room, which is important, for instance, in the condition of the coming winter to decide to change glasses in the premises.

The observations demonstrate that the inductive proof often arouses difficulties. Let us provide two examples.

1. *An indoor plant has twenty leaves. Let us analyze the first leaf: it is alive. Let us check the second leaf: is alive and so on. Let us examine the twentieth leaf: it is alive. So we can make up the conclusion that the plant is alive.* It is a wrong inference. Since if the plant had even one alive leaf it would mean that the plant is alive (there is a superfluous proof). In the logics such an error sounds in the following way: "who excessively proves, he proves nothing" (in Latin *qui nimium probat, nihil probat*) – when it is too much proved, the given reasons brings not only the thesis, but a certain another (sometimes contrary or false) point.

2. Let us examine the following thesis: *The Petrov family is good. The father is an academician. The mother is a professor. The daughter is a very talented girl, a post-graduate student. The sun is a perspective young physicist.* The proof is not possible, as a good family is a family that keeps friendly human relations. To prove the target thesis by the inductive method one ought to set the following pares: mother – daughter, mother – sun, father – daughter, and sun – daughter, father – mother. After that one ought to analyze the relations in each pare and to recognize these relations to be friendly, and then to make up the conclusion that this is a good family (and still it won't be convincing enough). It is quite easier to prove the next thesis: *All members of the Petrov family have higher education.* Since the criterion *to be good* is not formal (it is the matter of interpretation), more over, the word *good* is polysemic. One person, when observing the family, will call the family relations to be wonderful, the other will consider that they are unhappy. The family relations are extremely complicated: even a fight may appear as an evidence of love. One better leave such theses without a proof. The life will prove their verity and falsity.

Chapter 16. **Analogical Demonstration**

> Assimilations do not prove,
> they just explain the proven.
> *Mikhail Lomonosov*

Analogical demonstration appears as one of the diffused types of proofs (in Greek *analogía* means correspondence, similarity). The analogical demonstration substantiates the similarity of two objects in a certain characteristic, bases on the fact that these objects have a number of other similar characteristics.

For instance, in order to prove an idea about the possibility of an organic life on a certain other planet the scientists reason in the following way: the given planet has an atmosphere with the presence of oxygen, there is water, the temperature is adequate to give rise to the life; the Earth has such an atmosphere, water and the required temperature and the organic life. Since the given planet and the Earth are similar in a number of essential characteristics, therefore, probably, they are similar in one more characteristic – the availability of an organic life.

The scheme of a proof by analogy looks as follows: let a certain object A have the consistency of characteristics $a_1, a_2, ..., a_{n+1}$ –

$A: a_1, a_2, a_3, ..., a_n, a_{n+1}$.

The second object B has a number of characteristics that coincide with the characteristics of object A, excluding a_{n+1}, which is absolutely unknown, –

$B: a_1, a_2, a_3, ..., a_n$.

Then from these two observations one can make up the inference that the second object B also has the characteristic a_{n+1} (formula 1).

The proof by analogy is based on the fact that objects can appear as similar in certain characteristics; features or relations, provided such objects differ in general. The reasoning by analogy is said to be a logical inference, which results in the knowledge about the characteristics of one object based on the knowledge that this object has a similarity with other objects.

It is obvious that the proof by analogy is not absolute; it is a hypothetic. You can only assume that the second object has some additional features. In certain cases the proof by analogy, though it is not absolute, can be extremely convincing. Let us present a historical example of the proof by analogy, which turned out to be so convincing that a very big amount of money was allotted under this proof. A person whose name was Gargreve went to Australia, to the area, which is called New Southern Wells, wherein he found out mountain rocks that too much resembled the rocks of the famous Californian mountains in the USA. He knew the Californian mountains very well, as he was and worked there many times. The mountains in California are rich of minerals.

Let us assume that in our definition A means the mountains in California, B – the mountains in New Southern Wells. Gargreve noticed a striking similarity: tin is available here and there (a_1), zinc is available here and there (a_2), lead is available here and there (a_3), iron is available here and there (a_4) and so on.

Evaluating the characteristics, which turn out to be similar for these two mountain ranges, he comes up to the main characteristic that is still not revealed, but he suspects of its availability. This characteristic is a_{n+1} – the availability of gold. There are plenty of gold in the mountains of California. He assumes that Australia should also have gold. He returns home and writes a report, providing the proof by analogy and argues the availability of gold in Australia. The report is finished by a request to allot a very big amount of money to organize an expedition for the gold exploration. The proof was considered convincing. The money was allotted. The expedition went to Australia and in fact they found gold.

A founder of the cybernetics N. Wiener when proceeding to the investigation in the field of the logic machinery construction was inspired by an analogy that seemed to be very effective. He wrote: "From the beginning I was amazed by the similarity between the principles of work of the nervous system and digital computer. I do not want to assert that this analogy is full and we will exhaust all the characteristics of the nervous system, assimilating it to the digital computer. I would like to underline that in certain relations the behavior of the nervous system is very close to that, which we observe in the computers".

A French scientist L. Couffignal testifies to the tremendous role that analogy plays in the cybernetics. He says that being convinced in the similarity of two mechanisms one can assume that the known functions of one mechanism are inherent in another mechanism, the availability of which are not established in respect of the said mechanism. For instance, how do they determine the dosage of new medicine for a man? It is done by analogy with the functions of people and animals' organisms. Upon investigation of a drug effect, at first they experiment on animals and then assume that upon the prescription of the given drug to a man the results will be analogical to the ones, which were taken upon the experiments on animals.

The reasoning by analogy as any other reasoning appears as a reflection of the common relationship of things in our consciousness. The human being in practice has observed many times the consistency and stability of the relationship between the characteristics of objects and phenomena of the outer world. With time these relationship of the characteristics inherent in things were fixed in the consciousness of the human being in a form of a certain logical figure, which gained an axiomatic character. Thus, the human being long ago noticed that if two objects or phenomena have some common essential characteristics, then, in spite of a number of peculiarities inherent in these objects, it is quite possible to assume that these objects have also other similar characteristics. If there are a root, trunk and branches, then, as a rule, there are leaves; if the body is liquid, then in any communicating vessels it will reach the similar level, though these vessels differ by form; if a body conducts heat well, one may suppose that it carries current as well, and so on.

This assurance also has another reason in the surrounding world: the common regularity, expressed in the essential characteristics of an object or phenomenon, is found in connection with one and the same stable characteristics, though the conditions in which the common regularity is found, may vary.

Our mind is so strongly accustomed to the analogy that sometimes it starts acting as if mechanically. As we saw, the analogy is based on the fact that the things looking similar in one respect are similar in all others. The people accustomed to such state of affairs wonders at the fact that woolen blankets are used to keep ice from melting; meanwhile usually the woolen blankets are used to keep warmth.

Such kind of analogy is often found in the practice of various scientists and experts. In such a way, a botanist noticing by some characteristics the similarity of a certain plant with the known members of this species, attributes the plant to this species, assuming that the obtained plant has all, including uninvestigated, specific characteristics. As we say about the analogy, we can quote a number of examples from the history of sciences: Newton's analogy between the fall of an apple and the movement of heavenly bodies, Franklin's analogy between an electric spark and lightning, the analogy between the propagation of waves on the water surface and sound through the air.

Lomonosov in one of his earlier works made up a conclusion on the basis of analogy that the light appears as the substance. He wrote: "One light darkens another, for instance, the sun darkens the light of a candle; it is similar to the fact wherein a stronger voice dampens another weak sound. It follows that the light appears as the substance." An English logician W. Jevons says that even animals "make up conclusions" to a certain extent by analogy. Thus, the bitten dog fears every stick, and there are quite a few dogs, which won't run away if you affect to pick up a stone, though there is no stone at that place. James C. Maxwell says that the recognition of a normal analogy between two systems of ideas "leads to a deeper knowledge of both, instead of the knowledge that could be received upon studying every single system individually".

The analogy is widely used in mathematics owing to its obviousness and simplicity: a) the analogy of decimal fractions with natural numbers; b) the similarity of algebraic fractions characteristics to the characteristics of arithmetical (vulgar) fractions; c) the similarity of the generation methods of the second-degree equation task solution to the generation methods of a simple equation task solution; d) the similarity of the characteristics of the geometric series members in many respects to the characteristics of the arithmetical progression members and so on.

The trace of the reasoning by this type of analogies can be written in the following formula:

A has characteristics a_1, a_2, a_3, x;
B has characteristics a_1, a_2, a_3;

Probably, B has also characteristic x.

Let us take the following example: an aircraft model (*A*) has the same form (a_1), the same connection of the weight to the planes of wings (a_2), the same correlation between the weight of the forward fuselage and the other part of the fuselage (a_3) as of the constructed aircraft. Upon testing the model in the wind tunnel it turned out that the model is unstable (*x*). On the basis of the analogy (the similarity of the model and the aircraft in three characteristics) the constructor will for sure make up the conclusion that the aircraft will be also unstable.

The reasoning by analogy is applied in the physics, dam construction, linguistics, cybernetics, history and so on. In particular, it is explained by the fact that the modeling takes root in all fields of the sciences; it helps to investigate a possible behavior of the interesting objects on the models, which are similar to the investigated object.

Under a **model** (in Latin *modulus* means a measure, in French *modèle* means a sample) the sciences understand an artificially made object in the form of a scheme, draft, logical and mathematical sign formulas, physical construction and so on, which is similar to the investigated object (aircraft, human consciousness, cell and so on) and which reflects and reproduces, in a simpler reduced form, a structure, characteristics, correlations and relations between the elements of the investigated object that cannot be investigated directly due to impossibility, inaccessibility or considerable difficulties, as well as large expenses of means and energy, and thereby it facilitates to obtain information about the interesting object.

The investigated object, in respect of which the model is constructed, is said to be *a black box*, which represents an original, sample, prototype that sometimes is far from our observation.

All existing models are usually divided into three types: physical, real mathematical and logical-mathematical. **Physical models** has the nature similar to the nature of the investigated object and differs only by their sizes, flow rate of the investigated phenomena and sometimes material. **Real mathematical models** have a different physical nature as compared with their prototypes, but they permit the similar mathematical account. **Logical-mathematical models** are constructed from signs. They appear as abstract models, which are constructed as calculations (in Latin *calculus* means calculation). Under the calculation one ought to understand a system of studying the objects of the outer world, in which material signs designate the objects of a certain area (numbers, letters and so on). These signs are used in operations, needed to achieve the target goal, according to the strict rules applicable in the system. The calculation can be also determined as a formal arrangement, which enables to obtain some consecutions of symbols from others by inference. The calculations have a finite alphabet and a rule of inference (S. Kleny). The mathematics that appeared six thousand of years ago in the Ancient Egypt and Babylon above all was constructed as a calculation. Only in the third century B. C. Euclid for the first time constructed the mathematics in the form of an axiomatic theory, i.e. a theory, which was constructed from the finite number of axioms (in Greek *axioma* means essential, worthy of respect, accepted, doubtless) – or true opinions that are accepted without proofs in the framework of the closed theory as an initial thesis and that are assumed as a basis of the proofs of all other theses of this theory. Owing to the prescribed rules of inference one can deductively derive from axioms some conceptual true clauses (theorems), formulated in the language of this theory.

However, the modern school still begins the study of mathematics from the numbering and four acts of arithmetic, i.e. from the operation with signs (numbers), which by itself appears as the calculation.

The mathematical logic has several interrelated calculations:

1) Calculation of propositions that studies logical operations with simple propositions, which combine into complicated propositions with the use of logical connectives that similar to the conjunctions used in ordinary speech: *and* (conjunction, in the mathematical logic is designated by symbol &), *or* (disjunction, symbol V), *if... then* (implication, symbol ➤), *then and only then, when* (equivalence, symbol ~), as well as with the negative, designated by a particle *no* (symbol ➤);

2) Calculation of classes that studies the Aristotelian symbolism;

3) Calculation of predicates that studies operations with propositions, divided into a subject and predicate;

4) Calculations of relations that studies the logical characteristics and operations on two-place, tree–place and etc. relations.

A model (or theory) of transformational generative grammars (TTGG), proposed by an outstanding American linguist Noam Chomsky, can serve as a model, which is constructed as the calculation. TTGG is based on the fact that every native speaker is able to understand the overwhelming majority of sentences, which he never heard. Consequently, the human mind has an inner arrangement, which helps him to understand and reproduce correct phrases of the known language(s) and to refuse wrong ones. As it was said, this arrangement is called *competence* and it is an object of the linguistic comprehension, as this object cannot be learned by modern means of the natural sciences, so it requires modeling. Under the language TTGG understands a multitude of chains from the finite number of elements. Some chains appear as the sentences, the other not. The main task of the linguistics is determined as an ability to distinguish grammatically correct sentences from wrong ones and to investigate the structure of correct sentences. The grammar appears as a model of the arrangement, which generates all correct phrases of the given language and only them. The generation does not mean the construction of a correct phrase in the mind, but the enumeration of correct phrases. At that one shall not confuse the grammaticality with the sensibility and probability of occurrence. Thus, the sentences like as follows are considered wrong:

1) Furiously sleep ideas green colorless;

2) Read you a book on modern music;

3) Je n`ai vu rien (Fr);

5) Je n`ai personne vu (Fr).

The sentence *Green colorless ideas sleep furiously* is considered to be correct. Those sentences are considered to be grammatical, wherein one can construct a correct phrase upon the change of some members of the sentence by others with the same grammatical characteristics. Every person heard in his life not so much sentences, however he is always able to distinguish the correct phrase from the wrong one. The linguist models a structure of such a type on the basis of the finite number of the known (observed) correct and wrong sentences. As an example we can analyze the following generating specifications, proposed in TTGG:

I) $S \rightarrow NP + VP$ (S – a sentence, NP – a noun group, VP – a verb group)
II) $NP \rightarrow Det + N$
III) $VP \rightarrow V + NP$
IV) $Det \rightarrow the$
V) $N \rightarrow man, ball$ ...
VI) $V \rightarrow hit, took$ ...

With the use of these specifications one can construct a correct English phrase: *the man hit the ball.*

S
$NP + VP$ (I)
$Det + N + VP$ (II)
$Det + N + V + NP$ (III)
$The + N + V + NP$ (IV)
$The + man + V + NP$ (V)
$The + man + hit + NP$ (VI)
$The + man + hit + Det + N$ (II)
$The + man + hit + the + N$ (IV)
$The + man + hit + the + ball$ (V)

The sentences like *The man hit the ball* are called kernel, since they appear as a consequence of the direct inference. One can get passive, interrogative phrases and so on from kernel sentences using the special rules.

All rules are divided into *P*-rules (rules of the components structure) and *T*-rules (transformational rules).

$A \rightarrow B$ (*P*-rules: to change A into B, or $A \equiv B$, or "A" is "B");
$A \Rightarrow B$ (*T*-rules: i.e. B is derived from A).

P-rules can be of two types: context-free and context-restricted. The rule is called context-restricted, if it stipulates that symbol A can be changed by symbol B, only if it placed in the surrounding of $X - Y$, i.e. X precedes A, and Y directly follows A:

$A \rightarrow B / X - Y.$

All other rules are context-free. The action of P-rules is determined by the following requirements:

1) Every rule shall develop one symbol;
2) Every developing symbol (excluding the initial) shall be

included into the right part of a certain rule;
3) Non of the symbols can be changed into an empty symbol (i.e. to be omitted);
4) The resultant chain shall differ from the initial, i.e.
$$A \quad X+A+Y;$$
5) The grammar cannot contain a pair of rules for any pair of symbols: $A \rightarrow B; B \rightarrow A$.

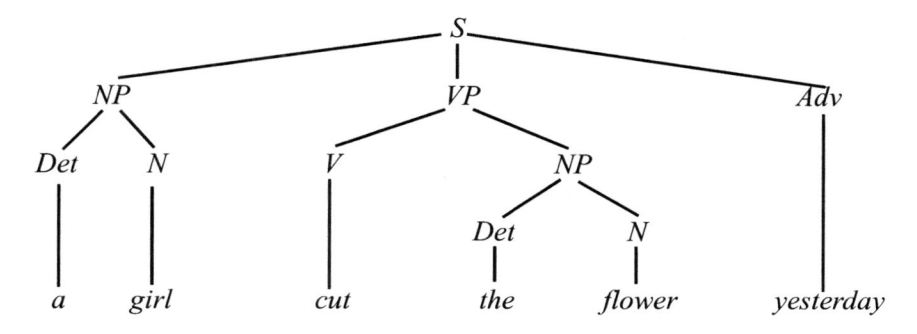

```
                         S
         ┌───────────────┼───────────────┐
         NP              VP              Adv
        ╱ ╲         ┌────┴────┐           │
      Det   N       V         NP          │
       │    │       │       ╱   ╲         │
       │    │       │      Det    N       │
       │    │       │       │     │       │
       a   girl    cut     the  flower  yesterday
```

The inference by *P*-rules can be conceived in the form of a tree. For instance:

T-rules represent the rules of substitution $A => B$. If *P*-rules convert some chains into other chains, then *T*-rules convert some trees into other trees. *T*-rules are divided into obligatory (*Tob*) and optional (*Topt*).

For instance, *Topt* : $NP + VP + Adv => Adv + NP + VP$ (optionally the adverb from the end of the sentence can be transferred to the beginning).

The left side of the transformation (*T*-rules) is said to be a structural description, the right – a structural change, and the substitution is called an operation. The operations can be elementary or represent a combination of elementary operations. Elementary operations include: 1) addition; 2) omission; 3) permutation; 4) substitution.

Examples:
1) $X + Y => X + Y + Z$ (addition)
2) $X + Y => Y$ (omission)
3) $X + Y + Z => X + Z + Y$ (permutation)
4) $X + B + C => X + D + C$, wherein D can be only terminal, i.e. a finite symbol.

The rules can combine. For instance:
$B + C + D => D + C$ (permutation and omission).

An example of the transformational rule application (optional transfer of the adverb to the beginning of the sentence) is as follows:

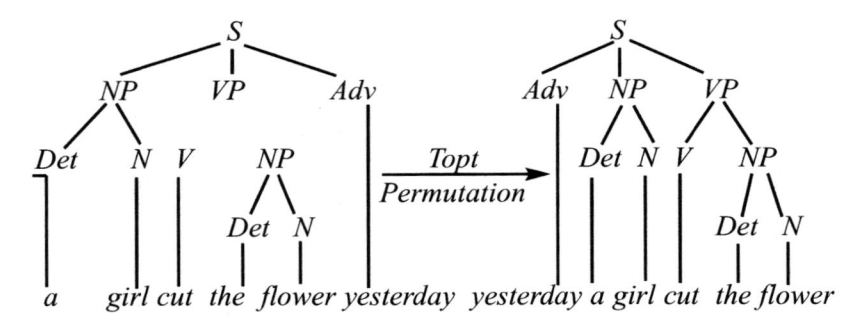

```
         S                              S
       / | \                          / | \
     NP  VP  Adv                    Adv  NP  VP
    / \  |   |          Topt        |   / \  |
  Det  N V   NP     ─────────────▶  |  Det N V   NP
   |   | |  / \      Permutation    |   |  | |  / \
   |   | | Det N                    |   |  | | Det N
   |   | |  |  |                    |   |  | |  |  |
   a  girl cut the flower yesterday  yesterday a girl cut the flower
```

The rules operate with symbols, changing them into chains and trees.

All symbols are divided into main (dictionary) and auxiliary. The dictionary symbols consist of the class symbols, which represent the high rank components – *NP, VP* and so on, morpheme symbols, which represent the low rank components – man, hit and so on. The initial symbol *S* (sentence), which relates to the main, is set till the application of the first rule; it determines the boundaries of the generative grammar. Morpheme symbols include grammatical morpheme symbols (morphemes *Pres, Past* and etc.) and lexical morpheme symbols. The morpheme symbols are considered to be finite, they are called terminal (in Latin *termino* means to restrict). A chain means a combination of one or several dictionary symbols. Auxiliary symbols are divided into flexible symbols; each has the given area of application (*W, Y, Z* and etc.), operators (→, + and etc.) and symbols of abbreviations, i.e. brackets. *P*-rules establish the structures that underlie the language and *T*-rules change the structures. A sentence, taken as a result of *T*-rules application, is called a derivation or a derived sentence. Terminal chains have an abstract look; obligatory transformations (*Tob*) change them into the language sentences prepared to the phonetic interpretation. Sentences, taken as a result of *P*-rules and obligatory *T*-rules application (and only them) are called kernel sentences. If two sentences are derived through *T*-rules from one deep sentence, they are called related sentences. For instance, the following four sentences are related:

1. Mary hit the boy.
2. The boy was hit by Mary.
3. Whom did Mary hit?
4. Who hit the boy?

The common deep structure of these sentences is as follows:

```
           S
        /     \
      NP       VP
      |       /   \
      N      V     NP
      |      |    /   \
      |      |  Det    N
      |      |   |     |
     Mary   hit the   boy
```

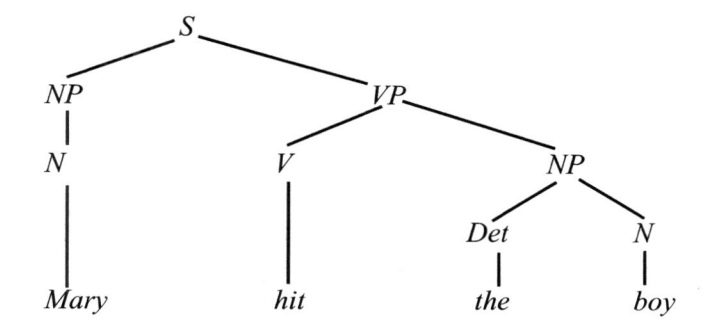

P-rules always precede T-rules. Both types of the rules are strictly ordered: after application of i-rule it is prohibited to apply j-rule, if $i < j$. One and the same rule can be applied one after another as much as possible times, if the conditions of its application are kept. P-rules require an obligatory development of non-terminal symbols of lower ranks; the development of non-terminal symbols shall precede the development of terminal symbols. These consequences shall be grouped at the end.

T-rules are bound to the observance of the following requirement: more common rules shall follow less common, provided the output of one shall appear as the input of another.

TTGG for its construction requires a frame that includes: a) a list of various maximum grammatical sentences of the target language; b) a list of various maximum non-grammatical sentences of the language. (A probate grammar can be constructed even according to the first list).

The key moments of TTGG construction procedure are as follows:

1. To determine the morpheme significance and to compile a dictionary of the kind: morpheme – its significance – affilition with a certain class (for instance, with the class of the noun suffixes).

2. To determine what classes can establish a subject and so on, i.e. to determine the functions of the classes, received in the first point, and to single out those types of sentences that are unified by the similar order of the similar functions, for instance:

Subject – verb – object (first class),
Subject – verb (second class) and so on.

3. To determine, beginning from the longest sentence, and record in the form of a table the occurrence of classes and the positions of this occurrence.

4. To determine what elements always occur, what elements do not always occur, what elements occur together and so on, and to minimize the number of possible combinations and types.

5. To determine syntactic relations between the members in various sentences.

6. To compare the types of sentences and study their similarities and differences.

7. To write down the conclusion according to the recommended order of the rules application.

8. To check the conclusion and make corrections.

TTGG pretends to have a statute of a common theory, which explains all the existing facts and prognosticates all possible new ones. The obligatory theories are considered to be the highest stage of the scientific description.

Any modeling theory shall meet the requirements of the outer adequacy (in our case – to enumerate only the correct sentences) and commonality (in TTGG common definitions are formulated irrespective of the concrete language).

The language science goes in its development through the stages connected with three different procedures:

1. Procedure of the grammar discovery:

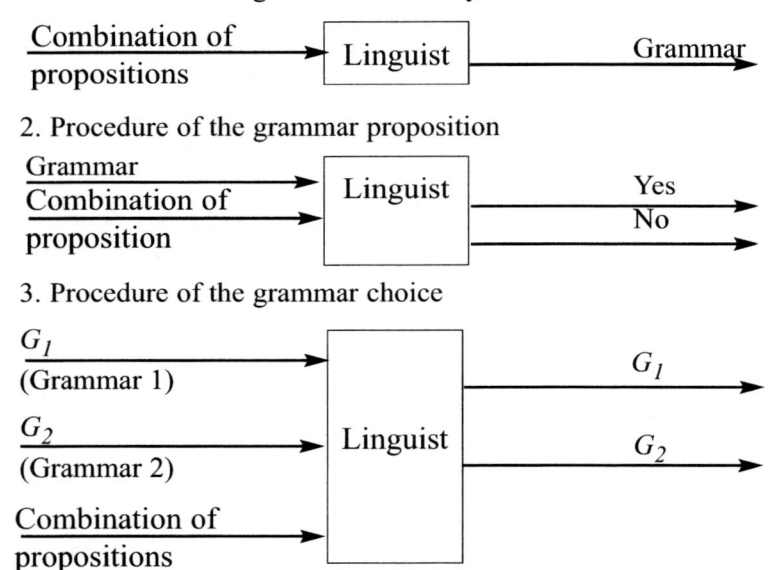

$$\frac{\text{Combination of}}{\text{propositions}} \rightarrow \boxed{\text{Linguist}} \rightarrow \text{Grammar}$$

2. Procedure of the grammar proposition

$$\begin{array}{c}\text{Grammar} \\ \frac{\text{Combination of}}{\text{proposition}}\end{array} \rightarrow \boxed{\text{Linguist}} \rightarrow \frac{\text{Yes}}{\text{No}}$$

3. Procedure of the grammar choice

$$\begin{array}{c}\frac{G_1}{\text{(Grammar 1)}} \\ \frac{G_2}{\text{(Grammar 2)}} \\ \frac{\text{Combination of}}{\text{propositions}}\end{array} \rightarrow \boxed{\text{Linguist}} \rightarrow \begin{array}{c} G_1 \\ G_2 \end{array}$$

The third procedure falls to the linguistic theory's lot. At that the modern level of the language science development makes it clear that different grammars (i.e. different models, different descriptions) can be recognized as satisfactory simultaneously; their choice correlates with a concrete goal, which underlied the given model, i.e. it is determined pragmatically (for instance, G_1 appears as a grammar assigned to teach the given natural language to foreigners, and G_2 represents a grammar used in the automatic translation programs).

The following characteristics are inherent in every grammar that appears as a model:

1. Formality, an appellation to the material side of the sign, not to its definition, i.e. no use of intuition as a basis;

2) Explicitness, an independent interpretation of all forms;

3) Completeness, the covering of all factors of the language;

4) Simplicity, the use of as less as possible numbers of symbols and possession of as much as possible generalized rules.

If the first three characteristics are available, the fourth characteristic enables one to compare various grammars between each other.

By N. Chomsky the transformational generating grammar of language L appears as an arrangement placed in the framework of a definite general-linguistic theory that meets the requirements for the outer adequacy and commonality, and has the characteristics of the formality, explicitness, completeness and simplicity, which generates (i.e. enumerates) all correct sentences of language L, attributes their structural descriptions to them and does not generate wrong sentences (not-sentences).

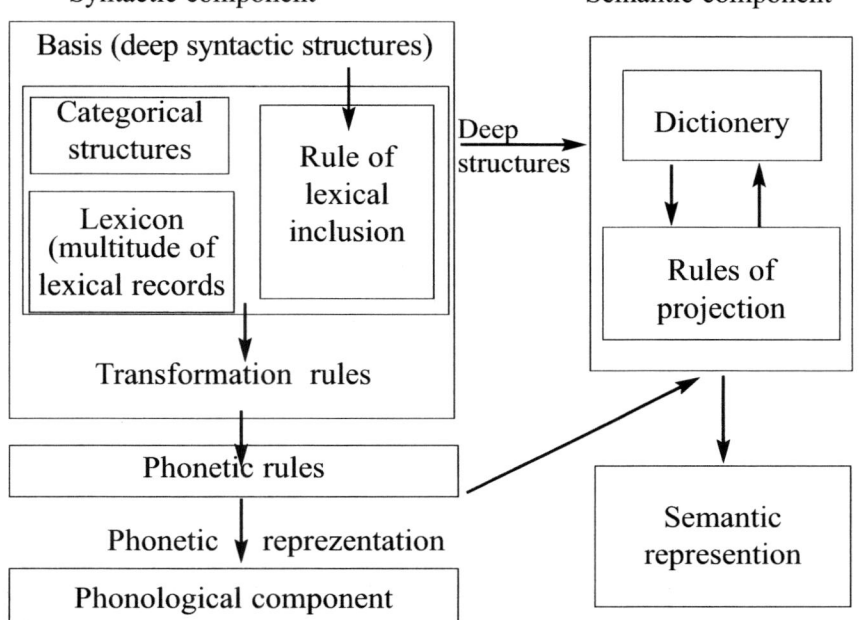

Scheme of the transformational generating grammar

Syntactic component	Semantic component
Basis (deep syntactic structures): Categorical structures, Lexicon (multitude of lexical records), Rule of lexical inclusion → Deep structures →	Dictionary ↔ Rules of projection
Transformation rules	
Phonetic rules	
Phonetic reprezentation → Phonological component	Semantic representation

The transformational generating grammar, as it is shown in the scheme, consists of three components: syntactic, phonological and semantic.

The imperishable significance of the transformational generating grammar theory lies in the fact that actually it is a single full-value effort to construct a consistent model of the human linguistic capacity, which is localized in the brain, but appears as one of the most difficult scientific secret – the secret of the human verbal thinking!

The following three types of the models: physical, real-mathematical and logical mathematical are not absolutely autonomous. Thus, the logical mathematical models can be implemented in real-mathematical and even physical, and vice versa.

The models can be constructed from the material that is homogenous with the original (for instance, a model of the wooden church in Kizhy was also made of wood), they also can use the material that differs from the original (for instance, a logician draws the model of a thinking operation in the form of a tracing or a deductive construction).

The dummy represents the simplest form of a physical model. Thus, the dam constructors, as a rule, in the beginning make a dam dummy (model) reduced in size and they use it for taking all necessary measurements, studying the water flow, the bed form, the bottom characteristics, water constructions and etc.; the architects make the house model; air-constructors – the aircraft model and so on.

The formal logics use models for a long time. Thus, for instance, the model of the first figure of the simple categorical syllogism, namely, *Barbara* (See above) is represented by the following scheme:

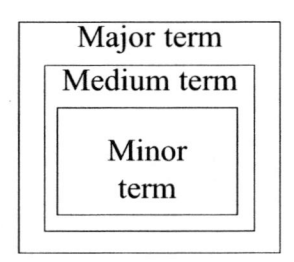

Major term
Medium term
Minor term

In the logics, the model additionally appears as a means of a concrete definition, pictorial presentation of the abstract. In some way it blends together the sensible and logical.

The logical modeling developed in the Middle Ages too. A Spanish philosopher and theologian R. Lullius tried to model logical operations with the use of a logical circle (the first "logical machine"), invented by him. In the eighteenth century C. Stanhope elaborated a "demonstrator", which he used to check, in particular, a syllogism with the quantitatively determined sentences. In the nineteenth century an English philosopher W. S. Jevons constructed a logical machine that enabled him to mechanize a number of procedures in the logics of classes and syllogistics. In principle, today we have the possibility to model many mental processes, though there are still no memorizing devices, which can be compared by the capacity and effectiveness with the billions of the brain core neurons. However, we can assume that the elaborations in the sphere of an artificial intellect are restricted a priory by a certain barrier (See above). The modern investigations go along the path of modeling separate processes of the brain activity and separate types of the mental labor and they apply to the huge possibilities of flash computers. The modeling is more and more applied in the course of the formulation and checking of hypotheses (in Greek *hypóthesis* means a reason, assumption) – probable assumptions about the reason of certain phenomena, the verity of which cannot be checked and proved upon the modern state of production and sciences, but which explain the given phenomena that otherwise cannot be explained. A hypothesis represents a method of the human mental activity.

Let us examine this problem in detail. In addition to the given interpretation of the term *hypóthesis*, as a problematic and probable knowledge, the logical literature singles out two more definitions of this term: 1) hypothesis in a broader sense of the word means a guess about anything, as a descriptive hypothesis, which, as a rule, appears as a short resume of the investigated phenomenon that describes the forms of their relation; 2) hypothesis in a narrow sense of the word means a scientific hypothesis, which always goes beyond the limits of the investigated circle of facts, explains them and prognosticates the appearance of new ones; while systemizing the knowledge, the scientific hypothesis enables one to unify a certain obtained aggregate of information into a system of knowledge, and generates a theory, if the assumption is proved practically.

In what cases the hypothesis is used? It is considered to be necessary:

1) When the known facts are not sufficient to explain the causal dependence of the phenomenon, and there is a nee in its explanation;

2) When the facts are complicated and the hypothesis can be beneficial at the given moment as a generalization of the knowledge, as the first step to their explanation;

3) When the reasons, which caused or cause the facts, are inaccessible to the experience, meanwhile their influences or consequences can be studied.

Hypotheses have tremendous significance in the comprehension of the surrounding world. No development of the modern scientific knowledge is possible without hypotheses. In the process of material welfare production, in the course of scientific investigations the people every day discover dozens and hundreds of new facts and phenomena in the surrounding world. The overwhelming majority of these new facts and phenomena are explained with the use of the modern scientific theories.

However it often happens that this or that phenomenon defies the interpretation with the use of the existing scientific theories, methods and means of the scientific investigation. In such cases first they put forward a scientific assumption on the probable reasons of the newly discovered fact or natural phenomenon existence. For instance, long ago it was noticed that upon the deepening into the Earth core every 30 –33 meters the temperature in the mine rises one degree. This fact and some other known phenomena (lava-flow upon the convulsions of nature, availability of hot springs and etc.) underlied the assumption about the fact that inside the globe the temperature rises up to many thousands degrees. Upon the modern level of the scientific knowledge and engineering the given assumption cannot be proved by direct observation. However, notwithstanding this fact, such an assumption is valuable, as it explains a number of natural phenomena (rising of the Earth temperature upon the increase of the mine depth, high temperature of lava, eruptions of volcanoes and so on).

All outstanding philosophers rated highly the significance of hypotheses in the science. M. Lomonosov saw in hypotheses a main path on which the greatest brains discovered the most important truths. Dmitry Mendeleev said that hypotheses facilitate the scientific work in the same way as the farmer's plow facilitates the breeding of useful plants. Scientific hypotheses underlie the following investigations of the natural and social regularities. As a rule, scientific theories are borne in the form of hypotheses.

A scientific assumption helps the production development and the related science. Foreseeing the course of the scientific knowledge development, the hypothesis gives a push to the production and science.

Any hypothesis remains to be an assumption until it underwent the stages of testing. So, naturally, an unsupported hypothesis is not a scientific assumption. In order that the proposed assumption takes on the significance of a scientific hypothesis, it shall be checked, i.e. one ought to compare the consequences that follow from the assumption with the observed data and the experience.

If the comparison results in the fact that the observed data and the experience conflict with the consequences that follow from the hypothesis, then in this case the only one decision will be solely right that the given hypothesis with no doubt is false and shall be discarded. At that, the hypothesis is to be prejudiced in that very case, when it conflicts with only one fact. As a rule, every newly appearing hypothesis does not discard in full the content of the previous hypotheses, but it uses all rational that was in the previous scientific assumptions in respect of the given matter.

Leibniz saw the hypothesis value in its ability to explain as more as possible data, determined by observation, by as less as possible number of the presuppositions.

A checked and proved hypothesis moves from the rank of the probable assumptions to the rank of the veritable truths; it turns out to be a scientific theory. Such transformation of a hypothesis into a theory can be demonstrated by the example of a scientific assumptions made by Copernicus about the structure of the solar system. His theory of the solar system structure remained to be a hypothesis within three hundreds of years. The Copernican system was proven only when astronomer Le Verrier on the basis of this system proved that there shall be one more unknown planet and by calculation he determined the place, which it might occupy in the space, and then in the year of 1846 Galle actually found the planet (named Neptune).

Hypothesis may be general and particular. A particular hypothesis represents a hypothesis, wherein the assumption is made in respect of a separate, particular fact or phenomenon, unlike the scientific hypothesis, which gives an explanation in respect of the law inherent in the whole class of objects. So, a particular hypothesis says about a proposed reason of a single particular fact or phenomenon. One can say for sure that, as a rule, every model is connected with this or that hypothesis or analogy.

The modeling is impossible without applying to the method of thinking by analogy. When modeling one shall always remember that in spite of the fact that the model is very good, it only approximately reflects the investigated object and simplifies it. If a scientist was able to reconstruct the true structure of an object in his model, it evidences an outstanding scientific insight. Such cases are quite rare, however they happen. An American (former Soviet) linguist S. Shaumyan many years ago elaborated an applicative syntactic model of the language, the structure of the elements dependence of which turned out to be very close to the structure of one of the brain areas that was a subject of a neurological investigation in a scientific laboratory of the USA. The coincidence was found just accidentally many years later and it caused a real sensation in the scientific world.

The model and the original are rarely found to be similar (more over, identical), since the model is required not to repeat the object structure, but to imitate the functioning. It seems that the models of thinking first of all will demonstrate the absence of the similarity with the original. Anyway, the analogy is valuable, since it brings into guesses – and this is one of the modeling goals.

All inferences by analogy have one general feature that the direct investigation is aimed at one object and the inference is made about another. Thus, the inference by analogy in the most common sense of the word is said to be an information transfer from one object to another. As it was said, the object, which is a subject of the direct investigation, is called a model, and the object, onto which the investigated information is transferred, is called a sample, original or prototype; the analogy appears as an inference from the model to the original.

It shows that the modeling appears as a wide definition, which includes the inferences by analogy as an inherent part. The analogy in the interpretation of the traditional logics means the correlation between the given model and the original, provided that in this case the result of the model investigation is assumed as the known. The meaning of the modeling method includes the process of modeling or its finding in the nature. The investigation of the constructed model, obtaining of necessary information with the use of it, and, finally, practical application in the functions of the model objects and the original, all these are considered to be an important stage of the modeling method application. However, the knowledge of all different types of inferences by analogy, known to the formal logics, is important to achieve a deeper comprehension of the modeling method.

The analogy and other forms of reasoning – deduction and induction – are part and parcel of the unified thinking process. They are interconnected and cannot exist without continuous mutual supplement and interaction.

The analogy has a certain cognitive value. In the process of such reasoning one can get a probable knowledge, but it does not brings anything new that helps to come to know the particulars of the surroundings and to foresee the direction of the given phenomenon or event development.

There are a few types of analogy:

Unconditional analogy represents an analogy, which is applied when a definite connection is determined between the common characteristics inherent in both compared objects and that characteristic, which is attributed to the investigated object by analogy with the known object. Thus, in the following scheme by analogy:

A has characteristics a + b + c;
B has characteristics a + b + x;

Probably, x = c

characteristics *a* and *b* will be common, and *c* will represent the characteristic, which is attributed by analogy to the investigated object. For instance, the investigated mammals have warm blood. The connection between the mammals' organization and warm blood is so familiar that one can say the following: the warmth of the blood is a consequence of the animal organization. If after that a whale is noticed to have some characteristics, which demonstrate that it belongs to the class of mammals, than by the unconditional analogy one can conclude that whales have warm blood.

Conditional analogy represents an analogy, when the connection between the common characteristics of both compared objects and that characteristic, which is attributed to the investigated object by analogy with the known object, is indefinite.

Simple analogy represents an analogy, in which by the similarity of two objects in some characteristics, it is concluded that these objects are similar in other characteristics. Thus, noticing that object *A* in some characteristics is similar to another object, it is concluded that it has other similar characteristics with this object.

Such inference is based on the assumption that objects and phenomena are not accidentally similar in certain characteristics, but it happens due to the fact that they belong to one kind or type, and, consequently, having some similar characteristics, they have others.

This method of analogy gains an importance upon bring objects to the known kind or type, i.e. upon classification; a zoologist, noticing by some characteristics the similarity of the given animal with the known representatives of the kind or type, attributes it to the latter, assuming that this animal has all, including uninvestigated, generic or specific characteristics.

Strict analogy represents an analogy, based on the knowledge about the fact that the characteristics of the compared objects are dependent. The course of the reasoning goes from the similarity of two objects in one characteristic to the similarity of them in another characteristic, which depends on the first. For instance, a student *A* quite often makes up his inferences on the basis of hasty generalizations, therefore his reasonings often turn out to be false. Knowing that a student *B* also quite frequently makes up hasty generalizations, one can conclude that his reasonings are resulted in erroneous inferences very often. In this case the analogy is strict, as we come to the conclusion going from the similarity of both persons in one characteristic (hasty generalization) to the similarity of them in another characteristic (false inferences), which depends on the first one (the false inferences appear as a result of the hasty generalization).

Nonstrict analogy represents an analogy as a result of which one comes to the conclusion going from the similarity of two objects in the known characteristics to their similarity in such a new characteristic, which is unaware whether it depends on the first ones or not? For instance, we know that cuprum is malleable, electro-conductive and heat conducting. When studying beryllium, we determine that beryllium is malleable and electro-conductive. On this basis we can assume that beryllium is also heat conducting. In contrast to the strict analogy, the proposed characteristic of beryllium does not depend directly on the first known characteristics (malleability and electro-conductivity).

Incomplete analogy represents an analogy, wherein the course of reasoning goes in the following way: objects similar to C in certain, indefinite characteristics, shall cause phenomenon B, but based on the knowledge about the object (or objects), due to the greatest similarity of them with C, we have the greatest reason to assume that the object (or objects) will suite the underlined group, consequently, we have more rights to hope to find the phenomenon B in this object (or objects).

The significance of the incomplete analogy lies in the fact that the given inference shows the path to the observer or experimentalist upon the investigation of the phenomenon, noticed in the known object. Even if it is impossible to check the inference experimentally, it still remains to be a credible guess, which induces to look for some substituted confirmations or disproof of it, i.e. it appears as a starting point for new investigations and reasonings, which is always fruitful for the knowledge. As an example of such a guess one can express an idea about the existence of plant life on the Mars on the basis of a considerable similarity of this planet with the Earth, which has the conditions for such life.

The inference by the incomplete analogy demonstrates the inference from a group to a particular object, but from such a group, which is not characterized with abstract conceptions, but with an indication to the sample, therefore the minor premise can be only problematic.

Despite the significance of the found similarity of the characteristics inherent in two objects, all the inferences in the reasonings by analogy are always probable. The inferences by analogy can and shall be used, but they shall not appear as an only source of our knowledge about the world. At that the data of any, even the most true analogy shall be checked practically.

When evaluating the probability degree of the conclusion by analogy one ought to take into account a number of the following conditions:

1) The more common characteristics $(P_1, ..., P_n)$ of the compared objects are known, the higher is the probability degree of the inference by analogy;

2) The more essential the found common characteristics of the compared objects are considered to be, the higher is the probability degree;

3) The deeper is the knowledge of the mutual regular relationship of the similar characteristics, the more probable is the inference, and the closer is the inference to the authenticity;

4) If a subject, in which respect we draw the conclusion by analogy, has one more characteristic that is not compatible with the characteristic, on the availability of which we draw the conclusion, then the common similarity has no significance.

The above list can be completed with the following rules:

– The common characteristics shall appear as any characteristics of the compared objects, i.e. be chosen "without prejudice" against the characteristics of any kind;

– Characteristic P_{n+1}, i.e. a feature found in the model, shall appear as the same type as the common characteristics $(P_1, ..., P_n)$;

– The common characteristics $(P_1, ..., P_n)$ shall be as more specific as possible for the compared objects, i.e. belong to as minor as possible circle of the objects;

– Characteristic P_{n+1}, quite the contrary, shall be as less specific as possible, i.e. belong to as major as possible circle of objects.

A Russian logician L. Rutkovcky warned that one should use the analogy with great care. "The best means against the errors of an analogical conclusion consists in the proof of the underlied basis. Therefore one should observe whether the similar characteristics are essential or not, and in what amount do they appear among the objects, which we bring together by means of an analogical conclusion. The more common essential characteristics are shared by the compared objects, the more possible is similarity in other respects; the more we know about the special arrangement of these objects, the more essential and trustworthy are our inferences by analogy."

M. Lomonosov in one of his earlier works wrote: "assimilations do not prove, they just explain the proven".

What is the main shortage and what is the main advantage of the proof by analogy? The main shortage, as it was previously underlined, consists in the fact that such a proof is not strict, it is of a hypothetic character. The main advantage of this proof is that the listeners perceive it easily and naturally. Why is it so? Since the perception of the world by analogy is a genetic and inherent capacity of every human being. From the first days of our life we perceive the world by analogy with our experience and the experience of those people, who lived longer then we did, in particular, with the experience of our parents.

How does a person understand that he should not touch the boiling pot? First, he was told not to do it by his mom and dad, and second, because once he touched the pot and was hurt. We do not touch the pot by analogy with those feelings that we previously had or told about. Why do we take on a fur coat in winter? Since our personal experience demonstrates that if we go out in a jacket, we will get cold, and, naturally, we will feel ourselves comfortable, if we go out in a fur coat. We can provide such examples forever, as the huge number of our deeds appears as the deeds made by analogy. The analogy is natural for the human intellect and human nature. Therefore, appealing to this characteristic of the human intellect, we find out a very attentive listener, satisfied with our reasons. Imagine, please, a situation, when you have a need to ask for a subsidy for the film production. You come to a sponsor and say: "I want to order this film to producer X, who has made four films by this time. See, the first film brought two millions US dollars profit, the second film brought one and a half million US dollars, the third film was in some way less commercial, nevertheless it was repaid with half a million dollars profit, as to the fourth film, it is just bestseller, it repaid itself five fold times and the show of the film still goes on." It is a convincing proof, isn't it? Yes, it is. If all of the films were beneficial from the commercial point of view, there is quite a considerable possibility that the money invested into the fifth film will bring profit. The inductive proof sometimes seems superfluously scrupulous; the deductive proof looks very dogmatic. But the proof by analogy is so natural for a man that sometimes he does not understand that they prove something to him.

The conclusions by analogy may have errors. The main source of an error consists in the fact that the one who concludes may fail to pay attention to those characteristics of the compared objects, which they differ from. In such cases the analogy leads to erroneous conclusions.

A false analogy may also appear in those cases, when the common characteristics are not connected with the one, which is subjected for the proof. Let us analyze an example. Imagine, please, that in formula 1 (See the beginning of the chapter) under A one ought to understand not a mountain range in California, but a bear, called Mishka, and under *B* one ought to understand another bear, called Grishka. These bears turned out to have a great number of similar characteristics: the first bear is male and the second is male also (characteristic a_1). The first bear is big and the second is big too (a_2), the first bear is aggressive and the second too (a_3), the first bear is physically healthy and the second bear is physically healthy too (an). The first bear has an additional characteristic a_{n+1}: it is brown. Can one assert for sure that the second bear, Grishka, is also brown? Why the assertion by analogy is possible in the situation with gold and is not possible in the situation with the bear? The scheme is the same. What is it not enough? Why the proof is not possible? Why is natural to assume the availability of gold, if tin, zinc, lead and iron are available? So why do not sex, size, aggressiveness and the state of health provide the reason to assume that the second bear is also brown? If they have common parents, i.e. they are brothers, and then it is possible to assume that they both are brown, if one of them is brown. If we include the common parents or such a characteristic as a biotope into the list of the homogenous characteristics, then from the fact that the first bear is brown will obviously follow that the second bear is brown too. It means that characteristics $a_1 - a_{n+1}$ shall be interconnected. The sex and color appear as the unrelated characteristics, size and color appear as the unrelated characteristics and so on. In fact, all characteristics that were listed in respect of these two bears are unrelated with the color. At the same time the biotope or the availability of common parents is related with the color, therefore the inclusion of the given characteristics makes the proof adequate.

The scientific conception development knows many examples of the false analogy. Thus, the erroneous analogy resulted in the opinion of ancient astronomers about the fact that dark spaces on the Moon surface represent seas and oceans. They reasoned in the following way: The Moon like the Earth should have seas and oceans. When powerful telescopes helped to determine that the dark spots on the Moon represent long shadows of the mountains, then the previous analogy was discarded as erroneous.

Every teacher by his experience knows that a considerable number of logical errors in the speech of his pupils results from erroneous conclusions by analogy. Thus, the availability of some similar characteristics in the operations of addition and subtraction is known from the first classes of the primary school. Both the addition and subtraction yields to the commutative and associative laws. Knowing this, the pupils sometimes come to an erroneous analogy that the arithmetical operations are similar in other characteristics.

The erroneous analogy often brings to sad results. Thus, sometimes children collect and eat poisonous berries, erroneously concluding that they are eatable, since other berries, which looked similar to them, were delicious.

So, the proof by analogy is successful only in the case, wherein the common characteristics of objects and the target characteristic (i.e. the one, which is looked for in the proof) turn out to be interconnected.

The analogy is mostly important upon the study and explanation of the correlation between the reasons and actions. Let us show two cases. First, when one has to conclude about the similarity of the reasons on the basis of the resulted phenomena. Second, when one has to conclude about the similarity of the actions on the basis of the underlying reasons.   Such an analogy is called diffused.

In other words any cases of the **diffused** analogy can be divided into those, which relate to the past, and those, which relate to the future. The analogy related to the future represents an effort to reconstruct the reason according to the available result. The model is as follows: it is known that a certain consequence B usually is a derivative of a certain reason A; it originates a phenomenon B, which the man observes, and after that he reconstructs the reason of this phenomenon in the form of A. If they observe the phenomena, provided that the reason of their origin is known, they reconstruct the reason. The medical diagnosis is constructed on the principle of the analogy related to the past. How does the doctor behave? He observes the patient's symptoms: his claims, results of analyses and etc. Some time ago the doctor was taught that the symptoms of that kind result from a certain disease K. In addition, his medical professional experience let him assume that the teaching was correct. In fact, every time such symptoms turn out to result from disease K. Observing the same symptoms, the doctor concludes that his patient has the said disease K. Unfortunately; it happens quite often that the diagnosis turns out to be wrong, i.e. the reconstruction of the reason fails. Why do they make wrong diagnoses? Do they have an unsuccessful life experience? No, they do not. Merely, the human being and his psychic are constructed in such a complicated way, that one and the same symptoms may result from different diseases. For instance, if a man is physically weak, i.e. his entire organism is weakened, in particular, the nervous system, quite serious symptoms can result from a minor disease. If a person is strong and enduring, then even a serious disease may result in weak symptoms. What are the errors in the diagnosis adequacy, i.e. the errors connected with the argumentation by analogy? A diagnosis may turn out to be wrong in the determination of the disease stage, then the analogy turns out to partially wrong. However, the diagnosis may be absolutely wrong. For instance, an unhealthy state of the human organism may relate to the rupture of the energetic field, an aura around the human body, which protects us and sometimes can be breached. A beam of a negative energy falls into the breach, perniciously affecting the organ, which is located near the breach. The organ is not sick; merely a beam of a negative energy squeezes it. It is a phenomenon that is now much spoken about. Thus, the first reason of a false diagnosis: the symptoms are determined not by the fact that it is a sick organ, but because it is a "luckless" organ, which lays in the way of a negative energy beam that penetrated into the organism and it "took the blow upon itself". Another reason is also possible: the disease may relate not to the organ, which is sick. The disease is available, but it is localized in another place. For instance, in the sick person's brain. The symptoms of any organ disease very often can appear as the symptoms of a psychic disease. Let us present a trustworthy example, which makes one think not so much about the wonders of the medicine and diagnostics, as generally about the relativity of the observed things interpretation.

>One girl many years suffered from a liver disease: she suffered from frequent paroxysms; she felt a severe pain in the right side, fever and other symptoms. Her parents were very well provided for (the father was a famous solicitor) and they did not spare either themselves, or assets to cure the daughter; they went to Truskavets, Karlovy Vary and Pyatigorsk. Whatever waters the girl drank, what ever doctors tried to cure her. There was even a doctor from Switzerland. Such a long-term treatment gave rather negative result, as year by year she felt herself worse and worse. She was diagnosed: cholecystitis and constipation of bile ducts. One day just by an occasion a psychiatrist came to the house of the solicitor and his girl. The psychiatrist hired the solicitor, the girl's father, to plead his personal case. They were sitting in a drawing room and discussed their judicial problems, meanwhile the girl, who was sitting in the same room, accidentally felt herself bad, then worse and worse and she broke into a paroxysm. The father got very anxious; he rushed for the drugs and decided to call for an ambulance. At this moment the psychiatrist, who observed the development of the paroxysm, told the solicitor: "Still, I am a doctor, do not call for an ambulance. I will try to remove the girl's paroxysm." The solicitor objected to his words: "But you are not a gastroenterologist!" "It does not matter. I am a doctor. I will try

and, please, do not interfere me, leave the room, please, for a while" – answered the doctor. The father went out. The psychiatrist spoke with the girl in several minutes and her paroxysm began calming down and absolutely diminished in a while. Taken aback and rejoiced, the father did not know how to please the doctor, but the psychiatrist upset him very much saying that the girl was with no doubt sick, however her liver was absolutely healthy, she had schizophrenia. "If you want to cure her liver, you have to put her into my clinic" – said the psychiatrist. So, the girl was put into the psychiatric clinic, she was treated by psychotro-pic drugs for a long time and for the last twenty years her liver has been healthy. So, what happened? For many years she was diagnosed by the best gastroenterologists, they found the dieases, proved by analyses and roentgenoscopy, which she actually did not have. In fact, she had the so-called phantom pains and phantom symptoms. She really felt a pain in her liver, she felt feverish and sick.

However it was not real, she felt fear of the pain and an internal sureness that there was no way out of the pain; in fact it is a symptom of a serious psychic disease, which, fortunately, was cured.

This example proves the relativity of the medical diagnostics based on the principle of analogy.

Everybody, who will try to establish the reason of phenomena according to the observed characteristics, ought to remember that if he/she will do it by a stereotype or by analogy, he/she may turn out to be as so "successful", as those doctors, who for many years treated the girl of the disease, which she never had. Two different persons can behave absolutely equally (symptomatic of behavior) by the reasons, which can be absolutely different. As an example we can use the interpretation of an unruly and incorrect behavior, which is, alas, typical to many contemporary young people. It is used to consider such a behavior to be the consequence of an internal dissipation and superfluous self-reliance. Nevertheless it turns out that this view is absolutely wrong in more the fifty percent cases. The unruly behavior can reflect the young man's inferiority complex, considerable dissatisfaction of himself, significant exposure and efforts to thoroughly conceal this dissatisfaction and exposure. The young man takes on the mask to protect himself even in this way. If one draws straightforward conclusions, most likely they will bring to the proof of a false thesis, which happens quite frequently. We draw wrong conclusions about the people mostly by the fact that we do it by analogy with other people. It is customary to the secondary school to stick labels on the pupils and their behavior is interpreted by analogy with those pupils, who have the same labels. Unfortunately, sometimes in schools the distinguishing of the personalities is substituted by the distinguishing of the groups that have the common label.

The analogy related to the future represents another type of the diffused analogy. This analogy is based on the fact that the identity of events or actions enables one to prognosticate the identity of the result. In the same way, as the analogy related to the past appears as the basis of the medical diagnostics, the analogy related to the future underlies the pedagogy. The pedagogical principle is based on the fact that when breeding a child by a unified scheme, we suppose to achieve a prognosticated result: to form a socially stable, law-abiding and full-value person, who is able to realize all his internal personal potential. It is considered that in order to achieve such a person in the future, today one ought to put into him these or those bases: to teach him the behavioral rules, sciences, laws of community; to inculcate moral values in him and to present the belief. These efforts shall bring to the prognosticated result. In the same way as in the sphere of diagnostics and medicine, one is able to set and determine the errors in the framework of the pedagogic. The fact that thirty children stay in one and the same class, they are exposed to the pedagogical influence of the same teachers, but as a result we can observe thirty absolutely different characters and fates of thirty absolutely different people – even does not worth speaking about. As a more demonstrable example we can use the cases of breeding several children in one family, wherein brothers and sisters (especially upon the minor difference in the age) were exposed to one and the same pedagogical influence, but later on they had different fates – one of them became a law-abiding and respected person, another became a social outcast and even a criminal. The wonderful novel of Irwin Show "The rich, the poor…" represents a family chronics that relate to the fate of three persons: two brothers and a sister. All of them rose in the parents' house, in a family of the German origin; they went to the same gymnasium and were bred in the same atmosphere. Nevertheless, the difference between their fates was considerable: one brother becomes an American senator; the other becomes a criminal, who spent several years in jail. It is another case that the novel at another deeper psychological level shows their common genotype and finally it becomes clear that in spite of the difference in their fates all three of them internally resemble each other too much. However, at the social level one of them is a senator, another is a criminal. It is a convincing example. It proves the fact that, with no doubt, the prognostication in the sphere of the human "self" is quite conditional. Therefore, when a person breeds his children, assuming that they will become so, so and so, he shall not be very upset if they will turn out to be absolutely different. The efforts aimed at the reference to breed a certain type personality, usually lead to the result, which can be evaluated only in the probabilistic categories. When applying such efforts (sometimes, very considerable) one should not hope for a successful result, in order to avoid a severe frustration in future.

Why is there a gap between parents and children? It often results from the parents' prognostication a genius formation; they imagined that their child is a wunderkind; they prognosticated a super personality, but instead they received a normal man, who is even displeased with their request to demonstrate extraordinary capacities. The parents cannot forgive their child that he/she does not correspond to the result, which was programmed by the moment of, if you wish, conception or a bit later. All of us do not meet the prognoses of our parents. It is absolutely obvious that we cannot be that etalon, which our moms and dads dreamt for. Just in rare cases the dreams are realized or even the result may surpass all expectations. However, these results are rare and they do not disprove the general rule. Thus, the analogy, connected with the proscopic and perspective conclusions, seems especially doubtful.

We ought to draw the following general conclusion: the analogy relating to the human personality, as a rule, turns out to be false. As to the projection of one man's behavior to another one, first, it is not expedient; second, it is restricted in its verity. Nevertheless, it is very popular. We are all the judges; we like to judge each other. When we begin judging, as a rule, we do it by analogy with the people, whom we know. It is a classical example when the father's characteristics are transferred to the characteristics of the existing or potential sexual partners. All psychoanalytical theory of Sigmund Freud is constructed on the position of an internal torture, suffer and dissatisfaction of a person, and first of all, a woman, aroused by the fact that every her new darling is far from being her idol. That man forms a cult of the male origin in the consciousness of a little child, a little girl, in particular, whom this girl often sees in her early childhood (usually it is her father, but also it can be the grand father, older brother and etc., i.e. under the father one ought to understand the first big male figure, which is idolized in the unconsciousness of the little child and is perceived as inaccessible and so especially desirable). The entire private life of a woman represents a constant search for a man, who will resemble an ideal pattern of the father; it is a futile and senseless search. The human path on the Earth is a path of suffering, since it appears as a chain of empty and fruitless efforts. What kind of search is it? It is a search by analogy. When a woman begins choosing a partner in her life, then at the unconsciousness level she looks for a man, who corresponds to her inner etalon and she compares every new person with this etalon. The comparative activity begins from the height and color of eyes, it expands to the minor and major habits and finally covers the personality. By Sigmund Freud it is the same path of suffering: you may look or not look for – you won't find anything, since the human being is a closed-loop system and it is assigned as the one, which has no analogues. The people are still the people, as they are absolutely unique, the personality of one man never copies the personality of another (unless some physiognomic coincidences are possible). Sometimes, there is a search for the father's pattern by contrast, when the circumstances caused a considerable estrangement from the father or a fear of him, or some other complexes, and then the woman looks for a pattern, which is quite contrary to the father's. It is still an analogy, as in the beginning the father's characteristic is taken as a reference point and the search is aimed at the characteristic, which is the same, but in the opposite side. It happens at the unconsciousness level. So much the painful is the search. At that in ninety percent cases the woman does not realize who she is actually looking for. Along this path she can find phantom things, but they bring only a temporary satisfaction. No attempts to draw an analogy between one man and another seem responsible. The projection of one personality to another appears as a mistake, a very consistent mistake, which, first of all, shall be called a false analogy. Let us show an every day life example:

> A woman was married and this marriage ended dramatically: her husband was unfaithful to her and he left her. The breakup was preceded with the following peculiarities of his behavior: in the morning he began watching closely his toilet and appearance before leaving the house for a work (characteristic a_1); he began coming home later (a_2); sometimes she could feel a smell of an expensive cognac (a_3); he turned out to be inattentive (a_4); and sometimes he began to be rude (a_5). It was ended by his unfaithfulness and divorce. A certain time has passed and our woman married for the second time and quite suddenly she begins noticing that in the morning her new husband fishily began watching closely his appearance before going out (a_1); he began coming home later (a_2); sometimes she could feel a smell of an expensive cognac (a_3); he turned out to be less attentive (a_4); and sometimes he began to be rude (a_5). The woman immediately, by analogy with her own experience (and this experience was very dramatic) draws the conclusion: "That is all. He found another woman. He is the same as the first one." May be there is no quarrels, but, there is

no doubt, that after this conclusion she looks for something, pays attention to the phone calls, in general, changes her life into torture.

The symptoms are similar. Let us analyze the reason. The husband felt that he has a possibility to make himself a carrier (*de facto* – not *de jure* for the first time) and he began doing his best: he tried to come to work elegantly dressed, spent more time on his place of work, sometimes had a drink with the chief. His self-consciousness raised, therefore he turned out to be less attentive to his wife; his internal self-esteem also raised and sometimes he allowed himself to be rude, more over, especially when he was drunk. There is nothing common with the first case; it had no relation to any other woman, though the symptoms look similar. It is hard to find a woman, who, having analyzed everything in the second marriage, would not come the same conclusion. She will draw the same conclusion by analogy, especially if the coincidence happens in details (the same toilet water, the same brand of cognac, and etc.).

Any conclusions by analogy in respect of the human behavior are senseless. Every new person, whom we meet in our course of life, we ought to welcome as Adam, as the first man on the Earth, as an extraterrestrial; we shall have no associations, which can influence on us at the moment, when we begin entering into the communication with this person. Of course, it is not possible. Since, as it was said, such is the nature of the human consciousness. We are the children of the analogy: we dress by analogy; we behave and speak by analogy; we enter into the human relations by analogy and so on. However, the knowledge about the fact that the analogy, which we draw between the people, is false helps us to increase the level of the perception adequacy in the human communication. We will judge every person, whom we meet in our life, by analogy in any way; however, at least, we will know that we should not do it. The inner sensation of the fact that by doing something inevitable we make senseless efforts appears as a pledge of a dialectic collision and as a result the truth grows ripe. When one part of our consciousness painfully rejects the other, something that comes to the light as a result of this wrestling, can pretend to the verity in the evaluation of people. A person on this path opens a door to the inner intellectual resources.

There is one more example of a false analogy. There is a rule (which is observed strictly in the local prestigious higher educational institutions): if a student fails to pass one exam in two weeks after the beginning of the new term, he will be sent down. Why so? Since it is considered that the informational volume for the term in a course is so huge, that if a student fails to take it in time, he won't do it in respect to the new knowledge, which will be studied in the next term. It is a very strict directive, the students are sent down with no indulgence, based on the perception by analogy of all human intellects as if they are equal by capacity. Yes, it is true, the informational volume is huge; however there are some people, who are so talented that it worth nothing for them to fill such an informational gap, at the same time for another person it will take several months and even years of hard labor to do the same. There are some students, for whom such an anecdote: "Do you know Chinese? – Well, when do we have the exams – tomorrow morning or may be the day after tomorrow?" – is not an anecdote. Young people, staying in the language environment, learn a foreign language at the level that seems enough to pass the entrance exams in a higher educational institute, i.e. to enter into the speech communication with the members of the entrance examinations. Such a communication requires quite a proper level of the language knowledge. However, for some people the lifetime is not enough to learn and speak in a foreign language. Therefore, when somebody says that if a student won't pass the exams, say, by the twentieth of February, he should be sent down, as he will be not able to take the other information due to the gap in the knowledge, it is not right. It is only one of the administrative directives by analogy and this analogy is false, since the conclusion is drawn in respect of the people.

Chapter 17. **Additional Kinds of Demonstration**

> The myth is a developed magic name.
> *A. F. Losev*

The speech proof represents the central part of the rhetoric as a discipline, since only a substantial, effective and expedient speech appears as a derivative of the human mental activity. No one can arrange a successful text, if he fails to logically express the idea and concept; in such a situation the speech turns out to be unsubstantial, embroidered and appearing just foolish. In other words, any attempts to work with the text irrespective of the content are senseless and fruitless. First of all, one ought to train the consciousness, and then, as a derivative, he shall train the speech. In this respect the people, who did not study the logics of the human thinking, find themselves in a hard situation; such situation is typical for Russia. The absence of a course of logics in the educational programs of the medium and higher educational institutions looks absurd; such a state of affair is "motivated" only by the ideology of totalitarian systems and should be rejected in a civilized society (as antihuman) from the standpoint of the common sense. The saddest situation occurs in those cases, when some gymnasiums introduce a course of logics, but they engage those people to read the course, who are not specially educated, like teachers of informatics or physic (there is a hope that it is not so in higher educational institutions): it brings a dilettantish pedagogical chaos and as a result the children not only fail to learn how to think logically, but they can break their innate logical thinking. The Soviet ideologist made everything to breed obedient and controllable people, who cannot withstand intellectually. The totalitarian society set and executed the goal aimed at the creation of a new kind of the human being. Three generations – it is quite a long term; moreover the school does not teach the logics, children are raised in such a linguistic environment, wherein nobody knows the logics. Where can they learn the bases of the logic thinking?

The modern situation in Russia resulted in an intellectual paradox: there is no politician, who is able to prove the relevancy of his point of view, and almost no voters, who understand whom and what they shall vote for. When there is no substantial reason to vote for something positive and new, it arouses a desire to vote against everything and everybody. In such a situation the vote against everything and everybody means the vote for the past, for the customary mentality. It does not matter whether it is good or bad, since there is no other things that look convincing. An orthodox and underdeveloped thinking inclines to reject all intellectual activity and thus to vote for something known and customary.

In this context it is wise to provide those additional kinds of demonstration, which reflect the specifics of the local thinking.

The first additional kind of demonstration represents an appellation to a person (in Latin *ad hominem*) – it is such a means of convincing, wherein instead of substantiating the verity or falsity of the concerned thesis with the use of objective arguments, they turn into a positive or negative characteristic of the man's personality, whose assertion is either supported or contested. This method of convincing is designed to concern the feelings of the opponent or listeners instead of relying on the objective data. Therefore it is considered that this method can be applied as an addition to a proof, namely, "to get the truth", however, to use it as an independent proof is considered to be a logic error.

What is the basis on which the logic connection in the "appellation to a person" is constructed? Instead of arguing a thesis directly, i.e. to furnish reasonable and sensible arguments for his point of view, the speaker adduces only one argument: a certain person shares this point of view, thus he transfers the trust of the argumentation to the opinion of a famous and authoritative person. Sometimes, such an approach turns out to be absolutely enough in certain situations. For instance, a person suffers from the stomach ulcer and he began treating himself of this disease, choosing a certain method of treatment. He is asked why he chose this very method of treatment. Of course, there is a direct argumentation for the relevance of the chosen method of treatment.

1. The medicine, which I take, splits the enzymes, heals inner ulcers of the stomach walls or duodenum and so on (he describes the medicine action).

2. Special water procedures regulate the blood exchange, which, in its turn, leads to the improvement of metabolism; the metabolism, when renewed, lessens adipose fractures in the tissue structure, as a result it brings to complete recovery;

3. A special regimen normalizes the state of the nervous system; the nervous system is directly correlated with the activity of the brain core. The brain appears as a commanding center of the organism and its accurate order is a pledge of accurate work of all organs and so on.

In such a situation the above direct argumentation is quite rare. Usually, the person acts in an opposite way; he says: I had an appointment of Doctor K. (he calls the name of a famous and authoritative doctor) and the doctor said that I should be treated in this way. So, I treat myself in this way." It is an argument, isn't it? Yes, it is. This speech represents an appellation to a person, to an authoritative man. At that, the more authoritative is the person the better is the argumentation. The meaning of authority is not binominal or double contraposition (authoritative – not authoritative), it provides a scale, on which every person in our consciousness occupies his own place. The authority can be great and minor. There are two extreme points: absolute absence of authority and deification. Let us cite a trustworthy example (however, it is not up-to-date):

> In Moscow there is a State Scientific and Investigation Institute of Gastroenterology. An academician of the Academy of Medical Science V. Vasilenko was for many years the director of this Institute. In the sixties-seventies his professional capacities aroused many legends. He had a huge office room and when at one side of the office the door opened and a patient came in, whom the academician saw for the first time, V. Vasilenko at a distance diagnosed the disease, and till the patient approached to his table, he wrote out a prescription. Vasilenko did not need to ask for symptoms, he was able to describe them by himself. Practically he never made a mistake and very often by his diagnoses he contradicted the complete medical checkup, which the patient was exposed to before he came to the academician's office room. It was considered that academician V. Vasilenko was a diagnostician of genius and a great doctor. It looks that it was

231

like that. He was a legendary personality in those years. Many people, who suffered from a certain gastrointestinal disease, knew this name, and his opinion was considered to be absolutely incontestable. If V. Vasilenko told do nothing, it meant that the patient did not need any treatment, and if he gave the prescription, the patient strictly followed it.

It is obvious that there are some people, whose opinion one can appeal to. If you need to make a contract and you are asked, why you put into the contract the following points, you can explain in detail on the basis of what law and by-law you did this, but you can also tell that you hired a professional lawyer from a noted consulting company and the lawyer made this contract. If the company has a stainless reputation, then the contract, made by the officer of the company, is not discussed from the standpoint of its judicial adequacy and correctness.

There is no doubt that the appellation to a person follows from such an internal state of the listeners' psychic, upon which the sensation of an idol seems natural. If you face a person, who has no idol in any sphere, the appellation to such a person, as a method, will turn out to be senseless. The essence of such a communicative situation does not consist in the fact that the speaker considers somebody's opinion as authoritative, since he convinces not himself, but the listeners of the fact that they consider this person to be authoritative. If a person decides, say, to be treated according to the doctor's prescription, he convinces himself. However, it is typical to the speeches directed to other people. In this case an appellation to a person is possible only then, when the authority in respect to anybody is natural for the listeners.

The people in Russia are suited well for the argumentation of this kind, as the consciousness of an average Russian appears as a *mythological* consciousness. Let us discuss it in detail.

A **myth** (in Greek *mýthos* means a narration and legend) represents the creature of the collective national fantasy that generally reflects the reality in the form of sensible and concrete personifications, which are thought by the consciousness as quite real. Though the myth in the exact meaning of the word appears as a narration, such a combination of "stories" about the world, it is not a genre of philology; it is a definite concept about the world. A mythological disposition is expressed not only in narrations, but also in other forms: ceremonies and rituals.

A **ritual** represents traditional forms of conduct that follow the most important moments of the collective activity at all social levels: family, community, state (See above, in particular, about ritual speeches).

A mythological thinking is characterized by a number of special characteristics. It is based on the fact of a "non-evolution yet" of the man from the nature, undifferentiating of the logical thought from the emotional sphere, inability to disengage from the concrete and so on.

First of all, the peculiarity of the myth is closely tied up with the personality on that very basis that the personality has and overpasses an antithesis of "self" and "other", i.e. of the subject and object relations. The myth usually singles out the alternatives (binominal opposition): mine – other's, life – death, male – female, nature – culture, which are considered as universal. The personality assumes the availability of a body and consciousness. It appears as an expression and symbol. The personality does not only exist, it is understandable as such. Every object bears a layer of the personal being, i.e. a myth; at that, the infinitely different forms depending on the corporeal, space and time existence can represent every «personality».

The static image of the mythical era has certain features of a syncretism association about the time as a sphere of causality, as an area of elementary contraposition of "earlier" and "now", the past and the present. The myth concept as a means of the conscious struggle against the historical time is concordant with a definite anti-historical philosophic position in the 20-th century.

The secondary sensible characteristics by the contiguity with space can also be transformed into a causal effect; and the origin – in a sense – can substitute the essence. The last line (typical to the childish thinking too) is extremely essential, as it leads to the myth specificity.

The myth is compared with the religion; the mythology leads many things to dogmata and mysteries, to the substantial assertion of the personality in the eternity.

The religion requires the trust in the extra sensible world and the life according to this trust. The most important prerequisite of the mythological thinking is the non-evolution of the man from the nature, which arouses, in particular, the general animation and personalization. The non-evolution of a man from the tribal community leads to the fact that the man everywhere sees the tribal relations; the kindred relations unify all objects and phenomena.

The myth belongs to the history as a marvelous historic formation of the personality in the ideal synthesis of this formation and primeval integrity of the personality ('holly history"), which constitutes the truth of a "miracle". Only through the historical marvelous existence the "personality" reaches the self-knowledge that is realized in "the word". The personality, history, word and miracle represent the basic components of the myth.

4. So, "the myth appears as the given marvelous personal history in

words", but with the consideration of personality's dialectic synthesis, its self-expression and wordy comprehension in the name; "the myth is a developed magic name" (A. Losev).

5. *First of all the mythological thought is concentrated on such "metaphysical" problems, as a secret of birth and death and so on, which in a sense are considered to be peripheral for the science and their purely logical explanations do not always satisfy the people of the modern society. It partly explains the noted vitality of the mythology, and, consequently, the title to its viewing in a synchronistical respect. However, the matter concerns not the interesting objects, but the mythological reference to the exclusion of unexplainable events and indissoluble collisions that go beyond the framework of the stable social and cosmic order. It constantly transmits the less understandable through the more understandable, incomprehensible through comprehensible, and especially, the more intractable through the less intractable (that requires the appearance of mythological mediators – heroes and objects).*

The mythology is not intended only for the satisfaction of primitive curiosity, but its cognitive pathos yields to the harmonizing and regulating purposefulness; it is aimed at such an integral approach to the world, which does not allow even the slightest elements of the chaotic state and disarray. The main sense of the mythology lies in the transformation of chaos into cosmos, provided the cosmos from the beginning includes a value ethic aspect.

"The mythological symbols function in such a way, which enables the personal and social behavior of the human being and his ideology (axiological oriented model of the world) to support each other within the framework of the unified system. The myth explains and sanctions the existing social and cosmic order in such its meaning, which is inherent in the given social culture, and by doing this it explains the human being to himself" (E. Meletinsky).

Carnivals represent one of the characteristic elements of the myth. However, the cyclic recurrence of carnivals in no way includes a modernist idea of the eternal rotation and historical making-no-headway. In the humanistic cultivation, the carnival character contributes to the historical transformation of the world. The festive and convivial moods that generated the appearance of so many fantastical patterns of Francois Rabelais, analyzed by M. Bakhtin, directly point at the ritual genesis, which is comprehended, however, in a very broad sense due to the people's disposition. The matter concerns not the genesis of the ritual plot, but the genesis of specific characters from a special folk form of the ritual disposition.

M. Bakhtin's analysis of the carnival and carnival "ideological" traditions finds an interesting affirmation in the latest work of W. Turner about the temporal breakage of the social hierarchic structure and the appearance of an amorphous "communality" in the period of the probationers' isolation in a ritual of initiation and other transitional rituals down to the termination of the ritual and obtaining of a new social statute. Turner sees something similar in the correspondence of the historical periods of the strict social hierarchy and their breakage, inspired by "communal" equalitarian ideas.

The mythological thinking goes aside from the evolutionism, the theory of "remains" and other different kinds of enlighteners' traditions. It is not by occasion the myth apologetics was picked up by the Nazism, which demagogically tried to "regenerate" the German paganism and its ecstatic heroism. This experience helped to identify the myth with the social demagogy resulted in the aspiration for the unmasking of various ideological myths. The unmasking of myth little by little extended to the sphere of the every day life, which turned out to be an action field of the multitude of minor myths and rituals.

Among all theoreticians of the myth only Levi-Straus most clearly points to the barrier, which separates the mythogenic archaic "cold" cultures with a high measure of the semioticity, and the total cross-linkage from the "hot" historical societies. However, another structuralist R. Barth, quite to the contrary, considers the present as the most "mythological".

With no doubt, the myth played a considerable role in the genesis of various ideologies in the capacity of the primitive syncretism realization, and in this, exactly this, sense it appears as a prototype of ideological forms. In addition, some peculiarities of the primitive thinking (as a concrete, perceptible thinking with a strong emotional nerve-strain, with the unconscious automatic usage of symbolic cliché, sacralized historical remembrances and so on) are fractionally recalled in certain social spheres, especially, say, within the framework of the modern western "mass culture". Finally, a certain conduct reutilization persists in any society both in the social and private respects, down to the weakened or substituted "transitional rituals".

All around the myth breaks the laws of the formal logics, in particular, the law of the excluded middle, united characteristic of the logic division and so on. The myth logics use a false reason when the premise, required for the conclusion, is accepted in advance as a silent admission. The myth presents the conditioned as the unconditioned, hypothetic as categorical, absoluteness as conventionality. The creative freedom of desires and esthetic plays, prevailing in the myth, entails the "marvelous" with the inherent absolutization of characteristics and capacities, creatures and objects, their complete transformability, openness of the entire secret and secrecy of the entire open and so on.

However, the esthetics of the myth is somewhat objective and ontological. The mythological thinking represents a creative and cognitive activity with its reason and logics. In some way it forestalls theoretic arrangements in modern sciences (the primacy of imagination over the experience in the mythology and the primacy of a theory over the experience in the quantum mechanics), when it convinces the reader of the fact that the image is not a performance, it is a sense, as a concrete object in the myth turns out to be a symbol.

The availability of a "cultured hero", who "manages to obtain" both cultural welfare and natural objects: fire and the sun, health-giving cereals and other plants, means of labor and so on, represents one of the most important characteristics on the myth.

The heroes, who lived and acted in the mythical time in the archaic mythologies, and whom we can call our forefathers – demiurges, correspond to the acts of Creation. The ideas about these categories are mixed up, or rather syncreticly undivided. A primogenitor – generic, tribal – appears as a basis beginning in this complex. Sometimes he can be considered as the common to all mankind, since the tribal borders in the consciousness of primitive community members coincide with the common to all mankind. The primogenitor – demiurge (a cultured hero) models the primitive community, which as a whole is identified with "the real people". The tribes of the Central Australia and Palaeoafrican nations (bushmen), in particular, Papuans and some groups of American Indians regard the mythical heroes as totem ancestors, i.e. primogenitors or creators at the same times of both a certain group of animals (rarely, plants) and the human generic group, which considers the given breed of the animals as their "flash", i.e. their own relatives and totem.

"Thus, the united substance of a social group and a breed of animals are derived from their common genesis in accordance with the mythological logics of the essence and origin identification. The totemic with its classical forms given by Australian aborigines represents a specific ideological superstructure in the early tribal society and, on one hand, it transfers the concepts about the tribal social organization to the surrounding nature, and, on the other hand, it presents a specific natural code for the classification of various phenomena, first of all, of social character, including "the language of the ontological system". The totemism serves as a special mediator between the "time of dreams" and modern people" (E. Meletinsky).

The specifics of the mythological thinking are often underestimated.

Sometimes, one can hear a strictly negative position in respect of the myth as a product of an irrational thought, which roughly deforms the reality (C. Jung).

Jung brought together the myth with the other forms of imagination and derived it from the collective unconscious psychological symbols – archetypes. He discovered the commonality in various types of the human fantasy (including myth, poetics and absolutely unconscious imaginations in dreams) and expressed an assumption about the availability of a primary image-bearing symbolic language of the human imagination. In some respects C. Jung made a step forward as compared with his teacher S. Freud, moving from the individual psychology to the "collective" and from an allegoric interpretation of the myth (as a direct expression of the suppressed infantile sexual attractions and so on) to symbolic. By his deep understanding of the metaphoric nature of the myth (it cannot be absolutely rationalized; it can be only translated into other image-bearing languages), as well as by the hypotheses of the "psychic" energy dialectics and the multitude of the unconsciousness senses, Jung foresaw some points of the informatics and semiotics. He put forward a hypothesis about the inherited character of the archetypes.

As the myth is not possible without the availability of a cultured hero, then the mythological consciousness foresees a life with an idol ("I need someone to pray to"), the holly trust in this idol and, according to this trust, a desire to do the same things as the idol suggests to do, and has the same opinion as the idol suggests to have. The mythological consciousness, which turned out to be a popular theme of multiple scientific conferences, both local and international, is a fact that is not surely formed in a totalitarian society (for instance, in the former Soviet Union). The mythological consciousness represents a national factor. More over, the possibility of the cult of personality (for instance, the cult of Stalin's personality lasted for many years in the Soviet Union) – appears as a projection of the mythological consciousness historically inherent in the Russian people. The Russian tsar was considered to be the God's anointed sovereign. The mythological consciousness is formed on the basis of a certain kind religion. As a rule, it is formed by Islam, and in the Christianity – by the Orthodoxy. If one analyzes the Catholic or Protestant branches of the Christianity, he will notice that the vicar usually interprets the biblical text, otherwise the Orthodox priest imposes the biblical text as a dogma that is the truth by definition, which shall be not discussed, but accepted at the level of one's trust. Islam is based on the similar principle. Therefore, the dogmatic thinking pertains to the Asiatic consciousness and Russia, in this respect, is an Asian country.

In Russia the mythological thinking was so strong in the beginning of the 20-th century that upon the coming of the totalitarian power it was natural to transfer the idolization of the Christ image to the image of a concrete man: Lenin, then Stalin and so on. The mythological consciousness of Russian people easily transferred their trust from one substance (extra human, supreme) to another substance (human), raising it to the godlike level resulted in the tabooing of any critical analysis of this personality's deeds and thoughts. As a fact of the consciousness, this phenomenon shall not be evaluated by the scale good/bad; it requires the examination. Nowadays we face a tragic process for the mythological consciousness – dethronement of the idol. Russia is not used to it, Russia lived with idols for many centuries, and however for quite a long time the country exists without any ideological, spiritual and intellectual idol. After the occurrence of the economical necessity of the Soviet power break-up, there was an attempt to reconstruct the church position. It is a purely psychological trick. They should find a substitution to the trust in the communist ideal, which many people share and which was abruptly and quite roughly revoked with the use of the mass media. If the Bolsheviks were managed to substitute the trust in the communism for the God, it seemed possible to substitute the God for the trust in the communism. However, those attempts failed: the communist ideals crashed (except the ability to live among and to adapt to them), but the God did not come back, since the real trust in the God cannot occur as a result of a propaganda, i.e. under a suggestion.

However, some one shall fill the vacuum (the psychologist write a lot about it), and the people look for this one. It is a natural and very dangerous process: one ought to remember that all fascist regimes in the world were established by super personalities, who were clever, of an extremist character, and wonderful orators. When analyzing the history of the mankind, starting, say, with Neuron, it is easy to understand what kind of personality won the brains of the average people. The human history is profoundly dramatic. Only the following devise: "Do not make an idol" can protect one from the blunders, which are usually made by the victims of the cult of personality.

Such people consider the appeal of the idol, chief and father of the nations and etc. to be the natural reason for their decision-making in respect of a certain deed. A certain personality is perceived euphorically; all declarations of this personality are accepted as the truth at first instance. In principle, every real orator and preacher appears as such a figure, which suppresses the surrounding people's intellect and psychic and turns out to be a godlike. Hitler's speeches inspired Germans to monstrous crimes, which they make in the euphoria of the authority buttress. Not forever the Germans thought that it was the order and they should obey. No totalitarian regime uses it as a basis. The totalitarian regime is based on the image of a psychological idol, which simultaneously is shared by the majority of people. When in the USSR in the thirties they put forward a slogan: "The son is not responsible for the father" (that turned out to be an appeal to denunciation as a norm of life), a great number of people began denouncing to each other. There should be a reason, which can explain such a collective dimness of the consciousness and the moral failure. Pavlik Morosov (a son, who betrayed his father) is not a myth; it is a norm, which lasted for many years in this country. It is a denunciation, led to the apogee, the denunciation of his father. The utmost point is to denounce against himself.

Thus, the mass appellation to the opinion of the personality, which turned out to be an idol, looks very dangerous for the mankind.

In our intimate life many of us become a victim of a strong, authoritative and attractive personality. An inner desire to leave the soul to somebody, to choose such a man as a guru, appears as that psychological sensation, which many people (especially woman) perceive as the love. Women often choose not so much a man, as an idol. This choice, as a rule, is unsuccessful, as it leads to the suppression of the personality, which is not compatible with, say, sex. Especially it concerns young women, if they choose an older man, who has a social position, or, vice versa, a man with an evident anti-position (a leader of the underground – "no one here understands me") – frequently such a character attracts due to some psychological reasons. You ought to analyze your surroundings to understand whether there is such a man, who suppresses you, the one to whom you constantly appeal, when making a certain deed, and about whom you constantly think (though nobody forces you to do it): Will she/he like it? Do you need it? Of course, there are such people, who can be exemplary. However, every person represents a separate world, to be exact, every person has something, which can be considered exemplary.

One can rule over the people with the mythological consciousness only if he becomes an idol of these people.

The Greek term *democracy* consists of two roots: *démos* – people, and *krátos* – power. The distribution of the roots inside the word is as follows: *demós* – argument, and *krátos* – function. Depending on the arguments' meaning, the function's meaning changes. The meaning of *democracy* is not similar in the application to different nations. Therefore, the democracy in such a country as the Great Britain is not the same as the democracy in French, more over, in Russia, Cyprus or China. The same function appears under different meanings upon different arguments. The people are not universal on this planet. (Therefore, the word people has a plural form.) Every nation has its historical traditions and culturological preconditions for the formation of a certain kind thinking. Thus, the democracy is not a static value, it's a variable; in particular, it means that there cannot be an American type democracy in Russia (the reproach of the Americanization is fair); it requires the Russian people to become Americans. After many centuries it is impossible to transform the consciousness of the Russian people under one's desire and suggest them to apply the democracy under the model of the USA or any other country. The meaning of the *democracy* function shall be absolutely different. The absence of the supreme personality idolization entails a pledge of political failure. For the last several years the mass media unmasks any cult, which is absolutely impossible for the Russian mentality, as it brings the people to the chaos. In Russia the nostalgia for the past is used to realize an inner desire to have the God, or an idol. The Soviet power lasted so long for one more reason that both Lenin and Stalin understood the necessity in the idolization; this understanding determined the public behavior of both leaders. At the funerals of Lenin and then Stalin the people died of despair, grief and horror – they lost their God! Whether you like it or not, it is a psychological and historical phenomenon, which should be considered. One can arrange a democracy model only considering the peculiar properties of the people, to whom the leader offers its realization as a norm of the social life.

As an average Russian man due to many-centuries traditions appears as a creature with an inclination to the mythological consciousness and idolization, the appellation to a person is natural for any Russian native speaker, therefore, this method of argumentation, as a rule, turns out to be very convincing. Almost all Russians have their intellectual, ideological or spiritual idol and the appellation to the opinion of this idol looks like a very effective and convincing procedure. Let us imagine a scientific dispute, say, in a post-graduates' sphere. In the course of a dispute you all of a sudden memorize a convincing citation from a scientific work of a scientist, who is a theoretical chief of your opponent. It is a very serious argument in the dispute (See above). That is why the majority of reports and information letters, especially connected with certain know-how and offering an independent point of view, begins from the developed fundamental citation quoted from the works of a person, who won the respect of the public. It is a good style. The matter concerns not so much the etiquette, as the fact that from the beginning it arouses a trust to those intellectual sources, which underlie your report. On the background of the direct argumentation it is expedient to additionally appeal to a person, whose point of view is extremely authoritative among those, to whom you direct your report.

At the level of every day life we use an appellation to a person quite frequently. Let us suppose that you have a girlfriend, who has a wonderful sense of style and who knows well what is worthy or not to see in a theater. She is an authority in this sphere. Before taking a decision to see a new performance, surely ask her advice. If a man has no such advisor, this place, as a rule, is occupied by advertising: one ought to see something that is more spoken about. The number of texts on the target theme (connected with the meaning of quality) substitutes for an authoritative position. It results in an important rule of the advertising: it shall be many times repeated, as its task is to make the potential consumers accustomed to a certain name (of bank, firm, goods).

All people at that or this degree suffer from the advertising obtrusiveness, even if they internally try to struggle against its influence, as a successful advertising is based on the scrupulous study of the human psychology. It is another matter of fact that sometimes we can see less attractive advertising in this country. However, we shall wait for a progress in this direction: the advertising brings big money and it is a significant stimulus to the perfection.

So, in practice a large number of repetitions frequently substitutes for the authority of an opinion, however such a substitution is less effective upon the making of a complex mental decision. In this case the appellation to a person turns out to be more effective. Since the Russian people easily give in under the press of argumentation *ad hominem*, this fact shall be considered upon choosing the method of argumentation. However, it is wise to avoid using the appellation to a person upon the communication with foreigners, as the mythological consciousness does not pertain to the consciousness of the modern Europe (more over, the USA), wherein they apply to the concept about the availability of many etalons, i.e. exemplars (See above). The availability of many exemplars leads, on the one hand, to the real respect for every personality and, on the other hand, to the impossibility for one personality to turn out to be an idol in the consciousness of another personality. Therefore, by appealing to a person and singling him out you most likely will arouse a perplexity of a western speech communicant, who does not understand the category of the cult of personality as alien to him (you may apply only to the law). In his consciousness his personality is not less significant as any other's.

Having observed the layers of American and European societies one can resume that the appellation to a person is less effective, except two exclusions: when your interlocutor is a victim of the mass culture imposed on average people, or if he is a student of a prestigious university: Harvard, Oxford, Cambridge, Massachusetts technological institute, Sorbonne and others, wherein the prestige and authority of the professors is very high. The western system of education considerably differs from the local, since it is customary there not to attend the courses, but a certain professor, whom the student chooses by himself, having the right to an alternative. As soon as the choice is individual, the respect for the chosen professor is evident. The applicable democratic manner of the professor's communication with the students does not hamper his authority. The student's consciousness regards the professor's point of view as almost true (with the rare exceptions). If there is an inner contradiction, misunderstanding or disagreement, the professor allows this. The student does not look for an expert aside; he waits for a seminar in order to solve his intellectual problems. Therefore, the "truancies" are extremely rare, though the auditorium's doors are always open. The professor is raised to the rank of a supreme arbiter; so, if you try to prove a certain thesis, say, to a student of the Harvard University and say that his professor shares this thesis, it will be a very convincing argument.

It is extremely important before the beginning of the proof *ad hominem* to analyze the level of the concrete person authority in the given auditorium, i.e. the public, which you are addressing to. It is not always obvious and sometimes requires a preliminary analysis.

One and same physical person, a man, whose opinion you are appealing to, can be perceived by various people and collectives absolutely in a different way, therefore, in some cases the argumentation *ad hominem* turns out to be convincing, in other cases it does not give the desired result, and in third cases it can prove an opposite thesis. Let us cite an example.

Let us imagine a physics congress, wherein somebody is making a report, which presents (as it usually happens) a basic formula that underlies the following reasonings. The speaker writes down the formula and some one of the attendants asks: "Dear colleague, First of all we would like to hear the substantiation of the verity of your formula. Thank you!" There are two methods of behavior as a reaction to this request. The speaker asks the chairman to give him additional fifteen minutes to argue the formula (as a rule, his request is rejected), or he says: "Gentlemen, this formula is not mine; it belongs to Einstein. I found it in his drafts." After his words the necessity of the proof becomes absurd, since there is no physicists, who does not assume that Einstein's brain is more powerful than his own. Einstein is the supreme authority in the scientific world; he is a criterion of the verity in the 20-th century. The modern physicians regard the appellation to the intellectual property of Einstein as an absolute appellation and it is perceived as a more than convincing proof.

Now let us imagine a man, who came to the North to Chukchi people with a purpose to tell them that their many centuries idea about the rightfulness of their living in tents of skins is relative (he wants to convince them of the need to move to the blocks of houses with the light, heating system and water). As an argument he quotes the points of Einstein's theory of relativity, in particular, the relativity of historical world outlook. Do you think that this argument is able to convince the Chukchi people, who hardly ever heard the name of Einstein?

Let us analyze the third case. Let us imagine a person, addressing the members of the partnership called "Memory", who propagate anti-Semitism. In the argumentation of his thesis he appeals to the opinion of Einstein, who, as we know, was a Jew. What is the reaction? They immediately perceive the thesis as false and thus they prove the verity of the anti-thesis, i.e. an opposite thesis.

A skillful orator can use this trick, if the true goal of his speech is to prove the anti-thesis. The model is quite simple: he argues thesis *A* through the appellation to *X*, the declaration of his name is prognosticated as provoking the listeners' negative reaction, which automatically leads to the proof of the *anti-A* thesis. It is obvious, that such a speech conduct requires special rhetoric know-how.

One more kind of demonstration is represented by **an appellation to the public** (in Latin *ad populum*). It is such a means of convincing, wherein instead of substantiating the thesis verity or falsity with the use of objective arguments, there is a task to influence on the people's feelings and in such a way to prevent the listeners from making an objective and unbiased opinion about the disputable object.

This method of conviction has more psychological than logical nature, as its action is always aimed at the mental and emotional state of the listeners. This method is suited more to set the will in a motion, than to influence on the mind.

This means in conjunction with the reasonable arguments shall be used in every addressing. Since every orator deals with the people, who have certain emotions and every thought turns out to be more clear, when it is perceived not only by the mind, but also if it goes through the heart. The demagogues of all kinds, who lacking reasonable arguments try to play only on the listeners' feelings, often adopt this method. In such cases the appellation to the listeners' feelings is usually constructed on the choice of externally effective examples. A variety of this approach is represented by a popular propagandist trick, when the orator "in confidence" appeals to the public and swears to it that he understands their needs and desires. It looks like he says to the auditorium: "Look, I am so close to you, how well I understand you, I share all your needs, all your intentions, I am like you, trust in me."

As a rule, the appellation to the public substitutes the argument "it is beneficial to you" for the direct proof.

Let us imagine another situation. The teacher suggests writing down a report about his discipline a month before the end of the school year, for that he promises an "excellent" mark at the examination in advance. There is no doubt that for many students the further explanations about the necessity of writing down the report will be superfluous. This is an example of the direct appellation to the public.

Every one of us in his life was many times subjected to the application of the discussed kind of proof; we were caught at this trick, and we made deeds not due to the reasonability (as nobody convinced us of the reasonability), but under the influence of the internal sensation of a profit, which is inherent in every person.

The appellation to the public as a method turns out to be very effective upon the influence on American and European listeners, as it is based on the important feature of the western disposition – "the cult of usefulness", which is connected with the total propagation of the pragmatism, as a philosophy (See above). An appellation to the profit, to the pragmatics appears as an appellation to that, which is natural for the modern western consciousness. The child is taught from the childhood: the useful is true. If the argumentation supposes the usefulness of a thesis, it is automatically perceived as a veritable due to law of transitivity: $A = B$ and $B = C => A = C$ (the thesis is useful, the usefulness is equal to the verity, consequently, the thesis is veritable). The world community is open to the appellation to the public.

One ought to say that not a few bloody crimes in the history of the mankind were "implicated" in the appellation to the public. For instance, Hitler's argumentation aimed at the proof of the concept about the necessity to win the Soviet Union, was constructed exactly on principle of the appellation to the public: everybody, who takes on a uniform and crosses over the border of the Soviet Union, will be granted an estate in the territory of this huge country. It was one of the main Hitler's slogans. Thus, Germans fought for the lands for their families.

Consequently, the appellation to the public can have both positive and negative by-effects, depending on the fact of what kind of thesis is proved. Only an internal moral barrier can prevent the orator from calling upon to the evil, if the evil is beneficial. In this case everybody should judge himself.

We would like to underline once again that the western consciousness is open to the appellation to the public at the same extent as the Russian consciousness is open to the appellation to a person – it depends on the peculiar properties of the culturological development of different nations. The misunderstanding of this fact leads to the speech failure. In Russia we can see attempts to appeal to the public in the western manner ("do it in the way as you find it profitable"), which do not find an understanding among the people.

The appellation to the public underlies every advertising text: "Buy the given goods, it is profitable for you". The inner structure of goods advertising is as follows:

Goal: to do something to sell goods A.

Thesis: it is profitable to buy goods A.

Direct argumentation: goods A have a number of advantages – comfort, esthetics, cheapness and so on.

Argumentation of contraries: the absence of goods A arouses a discomfort.

Imperative influence: to buy goods $A1$ of the competitors is a) unprofitable ($A1$ is more expensive, less comfortable, less durable and so on than A) – an influence on the customers' self-interest; b) dangerous ($A1$ does not guaranty the quality unlike A) – influence on the fear.

Every man can be subjected to the appellation to the public (in particular, a victim of a skillful advertising), therefore, one ought to analyze every time the measure balance of the advantage and disadvantage of that, which you are appealed to; that which looks advantageous today, may turn out to be disadvantageous tomorrow. Imagine, please, the schoolboys, who today have a test on the mathematics. All of us were the pupils and dreamt "to escape the test". In every class there is a dashing boy, who calls upon to do it, appealing to the public: "All of us right now will run away. If all of us go, none of us will be sent away, but right now we will escape the test." Everybody leaves and due to the age, nobody think what it will be tomorrow. First of all, it will be a scandal; second, they will have to write the test. They cannot avoid it; they can only postpone it for a while. When you are called upon to do something and they appeal to your understanding about the advantage, you always ought to understand: this advantage is either prolonged or momentary.

There is one more method of argumentation, based on the psychological influence; it is called a **riposte**, upon which the remark or argument is directed against the one, who expressed them.

Every orator shall skillfully use the method of riposte, including such its acute polemical variety as the picking-up of a remark, since it is a diffused trick in the polemics. The method of riposte is based on the following: you are asked to argue a certain thesis (as a rule, in the form of a question), which you find difficult to do it or which discredits you in some way. Instead of arguing this thesis you direct the "sting" of your tongue to the personality of the questioner. For instance, you are addressing a public and some one from the public is asking you: "Tell me, please, how did you manage to become so rich?" You can argue the following thesis: "I became rich in a legal way" (however, as a rule, you do not want to do it!). You may say: "I do not answer swindlers' questions of such a kind". Of course, it is a blunt answer. However the riposte, in principle, appears as a blunt form of the speech conduct (one ought to say that the thesis "You are a swindler by yourself" can be proved, and when it is done in extremely polite expressions it makes more strong impression).

The method of riposte is based on the substitution for the direct argumentation in the same way, as the appellations to a person and to the public, however it is the substitution of a specific kind: the transfer of the text sense to the personality of the speaker. The essence of the method is included in the words of Aristotle: The said against us we will direct against the speaker". This method requires the people with great intellect, quick reaction and sharp tongue. Having caught the word (idea), like a ball, thrown by the opponent, the person turns it to advantage and parodies it. If you are blamed for the swindling (at the semantic level), you ought to transfer the characteristic of "being a swindler" to the personality of the one, who is addressing to you. If they try to force you to explain a certain little-comprehended or unsuccessful decision of yours (who does not make mistakes), you say in public that the questioner is short of brains by himself and inclined to make mistakes, therefore it is not up to him to ask questions.

The method of riposte represents a public speech conduct in the presence of witnesses, who actually appear as the speech addressees, since the prime goal of the given speech act is to win the public's authority.

Let us cite some more examples.

    1. A. – Academician Sakharov told me about that...

        B. – Of course, he told only you about, and nobody else, but it is not published anywhere.

C. – If he did not tell you about this, it does not mean that he did not tell somebody else about.

In this polemics one and the same remark is passed over from one disputant to another, necessarily with the elements of irony and aggression.

2. Let us see how two notable polemists mutually used this method in a dispute in the year of 1925.

Metropolitan Vvedensky: "I actually do not insist on such a point of view that not all of us were originated from monkeys. You, as the materialists, know better your relatives".

A. Lunacharsky: "However, I do not know, who is better – the one, who was originated from the lower classes, from the animals, and developed by the efforts of his genius to the present man, or the one, who was created by the Supreme God in his own image and who sank down to the level, that, as Mr. Vvedensky says, it is pity for the animals, when the people are compared with them".

The method of riposte is especially effective, when the opponent has a shady reputation, arouses distrust and in the polemics shows the lack of respect to the opponents.

3. Polemics of the accused with the chairman of the court.

The accused: "On page 72 of the bill of indictment it is said that though the accused was not present at the locus delicti by the moment of the crime commitment, it does not change anything and does not exempt him from…"

The chairman: "You should not read here the whole bill of indictment: we know it quite well".

The accused: "I should say that three fourth of the whole things, which were said at the court by the prosecutor and the defenders, has been known to everybody for long, however, they repeated this here once again".

4. A popular historical anecdote. There were debates in the British parliament. Churchill, leader of the conservatives, was the speaker. As usual, he scoffed at his eternal opponents – the Laborites. Finally, failed to stand it, an old and ugly woman sprang to her feet and shouted to the whole auditorium: "Mister Churchill, you are intolerable! If I was your wife, I would add some poison to you coffee!" A snicker was heard in the air. However, the imperturbable descendant of Dukes Marlboro, sustaining a pause and casting a commiserative glance at the enraged lady, said: "If you were my wife, I would drink this poison with great pleasure…"

5. In June of the year of 1979 at the Vienna Summit the general secretary of the Soviet Union L. Brezhnev, as a matter of fact, was not able to walk on his own. He was carried skillfully, almost imperceptibly for the outsiders; he was carried, exactly, not supported by his brave bodyguards. The atmosphere was filled with the questions about the general secretary's state of health. The Soviet diplomats felt themselves very vulnerable. In an attempt to "reconstruct the destroyed parity", one of them, Melor Sturua, dared to ask the question: "How do matters stand with the political health of President Carter?" There was a burst of laughter in the auditorium. The sense of the question was clear for the devoted and only devoted people attended at the Summit. The political future of President Carter looked very obscure... An American diplomat kept his head: "The political health of Carter is the same as the health of Brezhnev"– answered the diplomat with a slight smile: it is up to you how to interpret.

The method of riposte was very popular in the discussions at the literary meetings in the beginning of the 20-th century, especially among futurists, where V. Mayakovsky and D. Burlyuk read poetry. The speaker surely came out having such an appearance, which was to provoke the public (for instance, dressed in a yellow shirt). The public was provoked to express their critical remarks (the speakers discussed any possible remarks and prepared the replies in advance). It was a striking performance, in which the most refined orator turned out to be a hero (as a rule, Mayakovsky won Burlyuk). The young people gathered for an occasion to take part in the speech contest and the people were rarely mistaken in their expectations – the performance was worthy of it.

When summing up one ought to repeat that the method of riposte is designed to precipitate the authority of the opponent and to raise the one's own authority. At the speech level the method of riposte requires not only a special rhetoric skills and responsiveness, but a sense on humor as well.

Chapter 18. **The Art of Public speech and Discussion**

> Many people argue against the truth only for the reason that they will disappear if they recognize it as such.
>
> *J. W. Goethe*

A dispute appears as a special kind of the speech communication, which realizes all kinds of demonstration.

A dispute is said to be an argumentation of something, in the course of which each of the parties asserts its understanding of the disputable matter and disproves the opponent's opinion. One of the diffused kinds of the dispute is represented by **polemics** (in Greek polemikós means belligerent, hostile) – a dispute at a meeting, in the press, etc, on a certain matter upon the discussion of a certain problem. Sometimes under this term they use the term "discussion", which is polysemic. Under the **discussion** one ought to understand the discussion of a disputable matter, based on the ability to reason and express one's thoughts according to the laws of the mind, as well as the form of a scientific communication and obtaining of a new knowledge, i.e. the logics of a scientific search.

Let us cite Aristotle's opinion about the discussion: "As to the dialectic conversations, in which they reason not for the sake of the dispute, but for the obtaining of skills or investigation of the truth; however nobody have managed yet to gain an understanding of what the respondent shall strive for, what he should what he should not agree with in order to prove the thesis properly or improperly; though, it turns out that we have no rules, left by our ancestors, to be given to them, exactly to those, who converse with each other for the sake of the truth investigation, so we have to try to tell something by ourselves."

It is clear that the discussion is based on a dispute. The thinkers were always interested in the art of disputing. The art of disputing or the art of polemics that uses all of the tricks intended only to win a victory over the opponent, so called **eristic** (in Greek eristikós means disputant) was formed in its most classical type by the philosophers of the fifth century B.C. The following work on this theme "The Art of Disputing" is attributed to an ancient Greek philosopher, the leader of ancient sophists, Protagoras from Abdera. Ancient philosophers – sophists put forward the teaching about the general relativity; about the fact that one can express two opposite opinions in respect of every phenomenon; about the fact that the human being is the measure of all things (See above).

Aristotle considered the matters of polemics in connection with rhetoric, logic, esthetic and dialectic.

The followers of a Chinese philosopher Mo-zi distinguished seven methods of disputing: 1) analogy (confrontation of things), 2) comparison of opinions in parts, 3) use of contradictions in the opponent's arguments, 4) imitation of the opponent and so on.

Even ancient Indian logicians praised highly such features of a disputant as a knack for finding out an error in the opponent's reasoning, the ability to understand quickly what the opponents say, to penetrate into their thoughts and find out the answers, to conceal any depression upon the dispute, to remain calm and collected, to hide tiredness, to avoid irritation, anger, rudeness, and causticity in respect of the opponent: "One should not lose his temper, even if he is right".

After the Middle Ages with their scholastic logomachies, the Renaissance once again gave birth to the sanguineous art of disputing, which was directly connected with the acute life problems. In new times there were attempts to generalize theoretic bases and practical methods of the polemics. A. Schopenhauer's book "Eristic, or the Art of Disputing" was published in the year of 1820. The philosopher's reasonings and recommendations were based on the thought that all means are useful in the struggle. Schopenhauer enlists about forty tricks, which, for instance, include such ones as bewildering with a senseless mere verbiage, provoking anger by knocks and so on.

Scientific disputes have great significance for finding out the truth. It is said not in vein that the truth is borne in a dispute, in the struggle of opinions. However, one cannot give devices for all cases of disputes as how to dispute, what shall a dispute start and finish with. There is no specially elaborated procedure of a dispute. A dispute requires a mental activity and creative efforts; it is impossible to find out such a means, which could automatically teach someone to be original; as such a means first of all would exclude the originality. However, Socrates was the first who applied a number of the disputing methods. There are quite many indications to the technical methods of disputing in the "dialogs" of Galileo, Berkeley, Hume and other authors. A German logician and mathematician P. Lorenz elaborated a "disputing logic", which by its character resembles so called tables of a Dutch logician E. Beth. However, no one has made a generalized and systematic work about the methods of disputes yet.

Also there is no a common classification of disputes. In the beginning of the 20-th century a work of a Russian professor S. Povarnin became popular. In his work the author distinguishes two kinds of a dispute: 1) over the verity of a thought, when the dispute entails the determination of the verity or falsity of the disputable thesis, 2) over the argumentation, when the dispute entails the determination of the fact that the opponent's thesis is not proved and the disputant's own thesis is not disproved. In addition to these two main kinds of a dispute, the author analyzes many other (fixed and formless, simple and complicated, written and oral and etc.). The second part of the book is devoted to clearing out various tricks in a dispute. The author calls a trick in a dispute by every trick, which is used to help the disputant and hamper the opponent to dispute. The trick can be permissible ("postponement of objections", revelation of weak points in the argumentation and others) and not permissible ("breakdown of a dispute by shouting", threatening with something, etc.). There are also some psychological tricks (irritation of the opponent, abstraction of the opponent's attention from a certain thought, which shall be expressed without any critics and so on).

The author considers sophisms or deliberate errors in the argumentation to be the most common and pet tricks. He divided all sophisms into several large groups.

1. Digression from the task of a dispute. The author includes in this definition first of all the sophism of a deliberate uncertainty or complexity (of a thesis, arguments or the entire argumentation), when the speaker says in the way, when it is hard to gain an immediate understanding about what exactly he wanted to tell. These kinds of sophisms also include "substitution of the dispute over the argumentation for the dispute over the thesis", wherein instead of the thesis one disproves the course of the argumentation, but it is feigned that the thesis is disproved. Such a trick is also considered to be a sophistic digression from the task of a dispute, when instead of the thesis essence one disproves its less important parts, but it is feigned that the thesis is disproved.

2. Digression from the thesis. The author includes into the number of such tricks first of all a trick known under the name of "to make a diversion", when the disputant from the beginning gives up an argument or a thesis and catches at another one. The author also includes "the descending to personalities" to the same number of tricks. He distinguishes the "digression from the thesis" from the diversion (See above), wherein the disputant does not give up the thesis, but quite the contrary, he feigns that he holds to it, however, in fact, he proves another thesis. The author relates the thesis contraction or expansion to the kinds of such a substitution. For instance, the disputant sees that he fails to prove his thesis "All people are rabbits", and then he tries to contract it and declares that he meant not all of the people, but the majority. As one of the most frequent substitution for a thesis the author considers to be such a substitution, wherein the thought, which is expressed with a certain stipulation making this thought true, is substituted for the same thought, which is expressed generally, without any stipulation.

3. False arguments. First of all this group includes the "multiplication of an argument", wherein one and the same argument is repeated in different forms and words and is posed as a few arguments. However, it happens that the disputant adduces a merely false argument. It also includes awkward arguments and random arguments.

4. Imaginary proofs. They relate to the tricks of a random argument. It leaves room for several tricks: a) the use of identical words, wherein *the*

same thesis, but expressed in other words, is presented for a proof; b) the use of a reciprocal proof, wherein a true thought is transferred into a thesis, and a probable thought is transferred into an argument; c) the use of "a circle in the argumentation", wherein thought A is proved with the use of thought B, and then thought B is proved with the use of thought A (See above).

5. The methods of inconsistency that the author calls as the sophisms of a wrong reasoning in which the thesis does not "follow from"the arguments.

As the experience shows, the use of words in different senses results in many disputes. Therefore, before starting a dispute, you ought to specify the definitions (See above).

It is especially important to avoid changing of a dispute into an end in itself, when the attention is concentrated not on the finding of a truth, but only on the goal to win, to become right at any price. Such disputes descend down to wrangles, scandalmongers and squabbles. As a rule, "farcical" disputes descend down to the personalities, wherein instead of the substitution of the thesis verity everything descends down to the negative description of the opponent; the use of sophistic tricks, psychological methods (irritation of the opponent, abstraction of the opponent's attention from the main thought, etc.), false arguments, abusive epithets, invectives and other unworthy tricks. However, such "methods" usually do not succeed.

When the dispute descends to the personalities, one ought to be able to overrule the attempts to digress from the discussion of a thesis and to square personal accounts, as well as to disclose sophistic and psychological tricks, however, before doing this, one shall know them well.

In a public speech, if it appears as an element of an oratoric speech, i.e. a momentary speech act, it is especially important to gain the auditorium's attention, as, actually, the orator has no time either to repeat or to specify anything. The gaining of the auditorium's attention represents the realized oratory. All the proposed rules can be discussed only as recommended, wherein a concrete communicative situation dictates the possibility of their application.

As Plutarch advised one should speak "either as short as possible or as pleasant as possible". One can start from either the objective of the speech, or the remainder of a notable fact, or unknown statistic data. However, every time one ought to look for the tricks capable to arouse the interest, which, of course, will be different in every single case.

For the first it is advisable to polarize the auditorium's attention, arouse the interest, dynamically increase the emotional tone, and only then one can develop the main thought of the speech.

Let the listeners catch the main thought right in the opening. It can be reached by a clear arrangement of the thesis, wise aphorism, quotation of an authoritative person or a document. The speech goal should also be clear for everybody, and then the people start following the thought development and the course of its argumentation.

Certain "surprises" stand in good stead not only in the opening; a certain case, some pleasant surprise, a humoristic remark, compliments and other "triggers", as A. Koni called them, all they are necessary in the course of the whole speech. Try to gain the auditorium's attention and favor.

The speech composition consists in eight forms, arranged in a definite order, however, they can be composed in a different way, depending on the speech disposition, i.e. depending on the speech volume and inferences by content. Ancient Greek rhetoricians called them as the parts of the speech (speech parts).

The speech composition is arranged as a consecution of the speech parts in that or this configuration, wherein one form, repeated, changes another and combines with others in a different way. The skillful usage of the speech parts constitutes the basis of its disposition.

The speech parts appear as major rhetorical arguments and means of a rhetoric argumentation. Let us present their classical consecution: address, theme denomination, narration, description, proof, disproof, appeal and conclusion.

The first speech part is called the **address**. This is an argument of the speaker's personality. The orator's image serves as a convincing argument. However, the orator's image acts through the speech addressed to the auditorium. Therefore, the address' content requests of the auditorium in this or that way to hear everything that follows it.

The address acts as a separate rhetoric argument only in a consultative speech. If the orator is well known to the public and the public holds the orator in respect and gives credence to him, in such a case his address to the auditorium is quite enough to accomplish the task. It is true especially for the cases, wherein the discussion requires the transition to actions. In other cases the address is used surely with the other parts of the speech.

The direct task of the orator's address is to win the auditorium's favor. Therefore, in his speech the orator poses as a man of a certain mental character and social position. He directly or indirectly calls upon to listen to his speech, demonstrating his awareness of the auditorium's needs, moods and way of thinking. It looks like he says: "You need me *now*".

The strength of an address lies in the fact that under the rules of speaking every speaker should be listened to. Every one ought to stop doing everything and listen to the one, who is addressing to him. The rule of the listening in preference to any acts is learned in the childhood and it becomes automatic. Therefore, such an address provokes the concentration of the auditorium's attention. Lectors often use the address in the course of their lecture, when the auditorium's attention starts loosing.

The address makes and develops the actual function of the speech. It is directly connected with the emotion of love. Therefore, in the address the orator ought to be plentiful of words, he should be able to praise the auditorium, both directly and indirectly; any digressions are admissible. The address should not be boring, make the public angry or demonstrate any kind of neglect, except exclusive cases.

Sometimes, when the auditorium is well disposed toward the listening, the address can be omitted.

The second part of the speech is called the **denomination** or designation of a theme. It is also an important rhetorical argument. The name of a theme and its explanation constitute the semantic center of the argumentation. It happens that having heard the name, the public does not want to listen to anything else or, quite the contrary, the public has already agreed with the orator. The auditorium understands that the theme is the center of the speech content and supposes all possible arguments.

The name of a theme should, first, correspond to the speech subject, second, be clear for the auditorium, and, third, it should be stylistically arranged in such a way as to rouse the listeners' interest. It means that from different by style utterances one ought to choose something striking and modern, which will suit the auditorium's taste and subscribe the lecture's subject.

The name of a theme represents a necessary part of the composition of any lecture. After the address or its meaningful omission this part is used to open the public speech. One cannot omit the name of a theme in a homiletic public lecture. On the contrary, the oratoric usually permits the name omission.

If the theme is formulated with the use of expressions, which contain a secret, or if its name has a descriptive character, as a rule, the orator develops its content, comments or makes the words of the comment to serve as the names of various parts of his speech, using them as the table of contents in the following arrangement of his speech.

The following part of the speech is called the **narration**. In the narration the lecture's subject is developed in its historical formation. The history of the subject formation (either as a thing or a thought) is usually simple for the comprehension of the auditorium. However, every narration is admittedly incomplete. The events, which constitute the narration, are arranged in such a way as to lead the listeners to certain conclusions. The striking composition of the parts of a historical narration represents the subject of an oratory. Owing to the fact that the narration is comprehensible, as a rule, the auditorium willingly follows the consistency and composition of the events.

However, the principal impossibility to present the complete composition of the events makes the narration vulnerable to the criticism. Some one from the attendants in the auditorium can remember the events, omitted in the narration, and in such a way disprove the course and semantic content of this part of the speech, or the speech as a whole. Therefore, in the narration the lector shall not merely omit some episodes that seem useless for him (as court orators like to do it), but substantiate well the choice of events. The narration also includes the discussion of the lecture subject, as a part of a wider problem.

The fourth part of the speech is called the **description**, which presents a systematic pattern of the subject. The subject is analyzed either in parts in their correlation and as a whole. It always represents a systems analysis of a subject.

The description usually introduces the methods that contain a mental experiment. In such a case the description directly precedes the proof.

The fifth part of the speech is called the **proof**. It contains a logic argumentation, which applies different kinds of arguments, examples and other forms of argumentation, for instance, nonverbal, like material evidences. The choice of the proof form depends on the auditorium character and the direction of the argumentation, as well as on the convictions and moods of the listeners.

In the times of antiquity it was said: "The arguments should not be enlisted, but weighed". In fact, not the quantity of the proofs is important, but their ponder ability and appropriateness. One ought to immediately discard the arguments that are not to the point of the matter.

The proof is the central part of the speech. As the speech can be of different size, the proof can be omitted up to any concrete conditions. However, the omission of the proof does not mean its absence. The orator shall keep the proof in mind after thinking over it in details.

The sixth part of the speech is called the **disproof**. It follows the proof. The disproof in the rhetoric theory about the speech parts appears as the rule of contraries. The orator puts forward possible objections against the proof and then disproves them. Owing to this method the proof is strengthened through the fundamental discussion of the theme.

In a concrete oratoric practice the disproof can become not only abstract, but real too. It happens when the lector receives answers and objections that start the dispute. In such a case the disproof depending on the character can be made in the form of dialectics, polemics or eristic.

Under the dialectics in this (antique) sense of the word one ought to understand a logic argumentation with the use of examples and enthymemes, not only syllogisms; in the dialectics both the speaker and the listeners mutually look for the truth.

In the oratoric, i.e. court, advisory and demonstrable speeches, they always pursue their own ends, instead of looking for the truth. Since the interests differ, it arouses polemics or a dispute.

In the written speech the dialectic position is possible in a literary text and it is not possible in letters, documents and the mass media information.

The dialectic relations to the speech subject shall be specified expressly. It is done through an appeal to the auditorium: one ought to call it upon to regard the subject in a dialectic way, i.e. not to strive for the self-assertion, but to start looking for the truth together.

Under the condition of a public lecture the dispute can be made either with an abstract opponent, when the lector and auditorium appear as they were together against the opponent, or with one of the listeners or with the auditorium as a whole.

Sometimes (and quite often) it happens that the auditorium as a whole or some one of the attendants intends to "fight with the lector", i.e. is in the mood for polemics. Then the lector chooses the polemic disproof.

The objective of the **polemic disproof** is to demonstrate the verity of one's point of view to the opponent and incline him to accept it. The success of the polemics is determined by the fact that the opponent becomes convinced and accepts the verity and rightfulness of the arguments.

The polemics is favorable for the lector. It helps to develop and consolidate his point of view. Usually the polemics takes the shape of the auditorium's questions and the lector's answers.

Under the eristic dispute the meaning of the correctness and verity of arguments practically does not change; in this case the disputants pursue their own ends (the ability to bargain on price at the market represents the simplest example of the eristic). An eristic dispute should result in an agreement, which to a certain degree suits both parties.

The seventh part of the speech is called the **appeal**. It is an appeal to the listeners' hearts and their emotions.

The eighth part of the speech is called the **conclusion**, which usually sums up the lecture and gives some perspectives for the future.

Let us examine some specifics of the public speech in detail.

Thus, the first major stage in the composition of the orator's speech – making a contact with the auditorium – is of great importance. The best beginning looks like an appeal to reflection; it is an attractive appeal, which one hardly can stand.

You were able by the first phrases to attract the auditorium attention and even make them interested in the speech perspective. However, the listener will follow you, if he understands what it is for. The listener shall feel the personal need in the information. It is possible that he thinks about the hunger in Ethiopia, but automatically he asks himself a question how this problem relates personally to him. The lector shall help the listener to realize his complicity to the theme. Thus, the "laying a bridge" from the general interests and needs (state, group and etc.) to the personal, individual ones represents the second stage of the auditorium submission to the orator's will.

Until the orator inclines the auditorium to the speech listening and reveals the motivation, there will be no need in the comprehension of the delivered information. The main part of the speech ought to be devoted to the substantiation of the main thought – one ought to start from the general purpose-oriented assertion of the thesis.

You ought to express your position openly. The failure to mention something will arouse the opposition reviving. Try to demonstrate more sincerity; do not skimp in your feelings. Show your personal conviction. "The secrecy arouses the distrust". Demonstrate the fruitfulness of your suggestions not generally, but in a concrete way, down to the details. The less is the educational level of the auditorium, the more you have to concern about the examples, to use visual aids as often as possible and to add also an inner vision. What does it mean? K. Stanislavsky wrote: "To listen in our language means to see what it is spoken about, and to speak means to draw visual patterns. The nature is arranged in such a way that upon the oral communication with other people, first, we see by our inner vision that which is spoken about and only then we say about the seen. If we listen to other people, first, we perceive by the ear that which they say to us and then we see by our eyes the heard." Sometimes, the people remember what it was spoken about only owing to the examples. They see an object, imagine and fix it in the memory (the image bearing thinking is realized in this way).

Seneca said: "Preaches make the path long, the examples – short and easy". The examples are divided into short or detailed illustrations (reference to the case, known to the auditorium, or a story, or an event), actual stories or anecdotic incidents, comic narrations or a strict ascertaining of facts and so on.

1. Examples in the form of stories.

Let us assume that you put a question before the public whether one can win or not if he sentenced to death. The following story is quite appropriate here. According to the legend in Ancient Greece judges sentenced a beautiful woman called Phrine to death for the fact that she admired her own naked body too much. In order to save the beauty her advocate tore her clothes off at the court. The judges, saw her nakedness and amazed by the beauty of her body, revoked the sentence.

2. Examples from the life of the people known to the listeners.

3. Examples, which use new statistic data.

"For the last few years in Sweden the range of goods for pets has increased considerably – now it includes about two hundreds positions. Dogs' and cats' cans, crackers, giblets, bones... What else? The fantasy is not enough."

4. Examples, based on contrast or colorful comparisons.

The most effective comparison is based on analogies, fixed in the individual life experience.

5. Examples, which are visually arranged.

If the orator does not try to reach imagery, using such words that agitate the imagination, if he fails to reconstruct the scenes from the listeners' personal experience, his speech will remain abstract and it won't impress the public. A striking, i.e. stimulating the imagination, emotional, i.e. appealing to the feelings, sincere, i.e. demonstrating the speaker's conviction, – only such a speech represents the oratory. In this connection the oratory appears as a special form of influence on not only the mind of the listener, but on his feelings and imagination as well. One ancient Chinese philosopher not in vein concluded: "A sincere person, who practices a false teaching, makes it true, an insincere person, who practices a true teaching, makes it false".

Try to speak clearly. All great orators held to the rule, formulated by Aristotle long ago: lucidity of mind – clearness of speech – clarity of public interest.

Inconsistency is a typical defect of a non-logic thinking, wherein the orator, reporter, author of disputant expresses a certain opinion and then immediately refuses it. The inconsistency always breaks the requirements of the formal and logical rule of the contrary. The inconsistency is such a position, wherein the premises do not result in the inference, which inevitably follows from them.

Your reasoning shall surely include the reasons of the doubting opponents in such a perspective, which might be advantageous to you. To do this you ought to determine the opponents' weak points in advance. It is quite possible that you will be able to arouse a prejudice against the opponent's speech, if you are sure that the polemics will be inevitable.

If you suppose an obvious counteraction of the disinterested persons, you ought to fundamentally substantiate your views, stagger the listeners by an original theoretic proof and amaze them by the logicality of the substantiation.

Avoid making your own evaluations and using superlative degrees of congruence and frequent references to authorities. It hurts the interlocutors' feelings.

Express your thought in three steps: first, deliver the determination of the definition, then compare the subject with something known (identification), and after that furnish the arguments. In such a way you will provide for the simplicity of your argumentation and the logicality of your expression.

If you speak in the first part, in the beginning prove your thesis and at the end try to cast doubt on to the antithesis and slightly criticize the opponents. In that way you will hamper their task. Since in this case they will have to start not from the persuasion, but neutralization of your premises, thus they will waste time to substantiate the alternative. In any case begin with something that rallies you. There are two noted Latin utterances: "Cum principia negante non est disputandum" and "Contra principia negantem disputari non potest", which mean that one cannot dispute against the one, who refuses the main point; one should not dispute against the one, who refuses the principals; the disputants shall recognize some common principles that underlie the settlement of their dispute. Every auditorium has some areas of the content, which are recognized as true and proven by the public experience. They are called as the common points. One ought to distinguish between the common points and the prejudices. The **common points** represent the categories of the speech content, which are proven by the people's historical experience and therefore they are considered to be true. The **prejudices** appear as the errors, which are temporarily shared by the majority of people. Thus, for instance, the common point will represent the fact that children are borne only owing to the union of a man and a woman. The prejudice will represent the fact that evil forces can meddle in this union.

The common points represent the results of the mankind's cognitive activity. They are developing together with the knowledge and speech development. Therefore the common points can be basic, i.e. independent of the literature kind, and complementary, i.e. accepted in a certain kind of the literature. First of all the basic common points appear in folklore. The folklore is the common knowledge; it includes the initial system of the knowledge, which underlies all other attainments in the following development of the public thought. The common points are formulated in the shortest folklore genre – sayings and proverbs.

The **topics**, the combination of the common points (top or topes is said to be the common point; a top and the common point are synonyms), is related by Aristotle to the logical form of the oppositions typical to sayings, which is characterized by the combination of assertions and particular objections against the asserted thing, like: Many is good, but more is better; good things come in small packages. Aristotle's "Rhetoric" includes this kind of reasonings in the description of the topics.

The basic common points were elaborated by the rationalistic rhetoric with M. Lomonosov's rhetoric taken as the exemplary: "All ideas are usually invented from the rhetoric common points, which include: 1) kind and type, 2) the whole and parts, 3) material characteristics, 4) living capacities, 5) name, 6) actions and sufferings, 7) place, 8) time, 9) origin, 10) reason, 11) the preceding and the following, 12) showings, 13) circumstances, 14) similarities, 15) contrary and dissimilar things, 16) equations."

The complementary common points are characterized by the fact that they are used in texts with a definite semantic content, for instance, in scientific texts. However, at that they look like they divide the given kind of the literature into diametrically opposite groups. Thus, the diametrically opposite kinds of the fundamental knowledge: natural historic and public historic are opposed to each other in the framework of the science.

The combination of such complementary common points in the science represents the pattern of the scientific subject. The cognitive activity results in the development of the common points. The informational classifications of knowledge are arranged with the orientation to the common points. For the first time this thought was formulated in K. Zelenetsky's work "Particular Rhetoric".

In addition to the common points and prejudices the positive cognitive process in the speech communication contains also the temporary results of the comprehension. It includes such phenomena as popular scientific hypotheses, righteous points of various ideologies, religious dogmatic, terms, standards and, finally, the stipulations of the law, administration, ideological opinions of the mass media and so on, common in the present state of the society or its certain part.

To make the expression of the speech content more convincing, one ought to hold to the common points and opinions, popular at the present time, and realize that there were and are the prejudices, which one should struggle against.

The common points in the scholastic rhetoric were understood as a mechanical means of the speech invention. The rationalistic rhetoric did not avoid the same understanding of the common points too. It understood the common points as a means of the thought invention through the combination of the common points and their logical multiplication. As it turned out this method is useful only to form a dogmatic speech, wherein the goal of the invention is the reminder or additional interpretation of truths, known to the public, i.e. the action is aimed at the invention of a new literary form for a trivial knowledge. The common points appear only as a means of establishing the speech communication, which requires the semantic comprehensibility. The orator, relying on the common and comprehensible, develops a principally new thought.

If you speak in the second place you have two options of the speech beginning.

You can immediately start arguing your point of view, without taking into account everything that was said by the opponent. It is a vantage order, if you are definite about the invulnerability of your argumentation. You have something on hand to amaze the auditorium and the atmosphere is favorable to your position.

If the forces are about to be equal, you ought to begin with the analysis and examination of the opponent's argumentation, knock loose his demonstration and hence to loose the influence exerted upon the auditorium. After that you can proceed to the argumentation of your thesis. The second case requires more time and strong counter-argumentation. At that "One ought to place strong and significant arguments in the beginning of the speech, those, which are weaker – in the middle, and the strongest – at the end of the speech, since the listeners and readers comprehend and remember more the beginning and the final" (M. Lomonosov).

As soon as you feel that the goal is achieved, ask the auditorium for definite actions. Any appeals and addresses are appropriate here. The speech shall be ended with a mighty final "accord" for all people to hear you.

You ought to consider a person, whom you know nothing about, to be a difficult interlocutor. The one, whom we know nothing about, may turn to be the strongest one. On the other hand, a person, unprepared to conversation, can quickly give rise to an active hostility up to the confrontation of a friendly and positively intended interlocutor. An "innate naughtiness" is inherent in some people: they always consider themselves to be right, and the interlocutor – to be wrong. It causes a disrespectful relation to other people's principles, opinions and views, as well as arouses biliousness and malevolence in the communication. Such a man does not conceal his unwillingness to listen to you. Stop the conversation, as it will lead to a quarrel, offensive reproaches and a psychological barrier. "Many people argue against the truth only for the reason that they will disappear if they recognize it as such" (J. W. Goethe).

A psychological barrier in the communication generates an increased egocentrism (the interlocutor tries to raise himself and concentrate all the attention on himself), lack of discipline, laziness, unwillingness to think, dishonesty, rudeness, morbid pride, vanity, conservatism in thinking, unbalanced character, unscrupulousness, lust for power, hot temper and so on. As you see, there is something to be considered. So, you ought to be able to "model" your interlocutor and prior to the conversation prognosticate the communicative situations.

Many circumstances force one to prepare oneself to the opposition and defense, and the striving for the truth is considered to be the main of them. Pysarev noted: "Clever and energetic people struggle up to the end, however, empty and grotto people yields without a slightest struggle to all minor incidents of their senseless existence."

Why is it necessary to go up to the opposition?

First, it is necessary due to the fact that the dispute involves the people, who are incompetent, shortsighted and restricted in the knowledge about the disputable matter. Also one can face the opponents' stubbornness.

Second, it is necessary due to the implacability of the disputants' positions, their "prestigious" intents, considerations of the moment and difference of opinions.

Third, it is necessary due to the disputants' aversion of views and hypotheses till their verity does not become an inevitable necessity.

Fourth, it is necessary due to the application of the public opinion to the discussion, provided such an opinion can be accidental and deliberately formulated in the wrong way.

Fifth, it is necessary due to the inability to listen to and understand the interlocutor. If your opponent is a quarrelsome person, keep quiet; do not allow him to disconcert you. Let other people criticize his position, thus you will preserve your forces and find out the opponent's weak points from the outside.

You ought to avoid encourage a positively intended interlocutor to express his approval (why do you keep silence?) and force his activity. Since he is your potential companion-in-arms, you would better let him have the possibility to sum up and express the resume.

The demagogues shall be very tactfully stopped by counter-questions and requests for more precise definitions. Your irony is quite appropriate in this case.

Try to strengthen the confidence of shy people (the public attention is always pleasant). It may arouse their willingness to speak in the favor of your idea.

As to the noted authority, you would better content yourself with a compliment to his address. If you pay attention to his opinion and ask for his advices in respect of your argumentation, the interlocutor will feel the significance of his personality and willingly support you.

Disinterested skeptics are notable for their acute self-esteem. You would better avoid wounding them, try to take no notice of their objections or gently neutralize their negative reaction.

The defense of your own position lays not so much with the protection of your idea against the interlocutors' critics or invulnerability of the argumentation, as in the successfulness of your counterblows against the weak points of the alternative. The human brain makes the final choice after the whole chain snapped into action: argumentation, opposing, and counter-argumentation. As a rule, a method of constructive critics may be conclusive. Therefore, when listening to the interlocutor, notice the weak points of his speech for your counterblow. What does it mean? Contradictions in the opinions, unfounded arguments, garbling, unsuccessful analogies, biased evaluations, speculations, demagogic evasions, sophistic tricks and errors due to the violation of the logics rules. Without the revealed weak point in the opponent's argumentation the protection will change into the defense. Usually any idea captures the people only upon the combination of the assertive offence with the pre-emptive counter offence. The symbol of the ancient rhetoric not in vain presents a muse holding a sword and a shield. Cicero asserted that the oratory is related to the military art. The discussion appears as a battle of brains.

First of all what we lack in the discussion is the ability to listen to the interlocutor carefully and catch his thoughts. If you watch two disputants you will probably understand that they both try to make the opponent to change his mind and they absolutely forget about the necessity to listen to the interlocutor. What should one undertake to successfully protect his position? Let the interlocutor express himself and do not interrupt him. Try to get his point of view and find out the contiguity of your positions; memorize the complementary arguments. Try to catch the opponent's thought, concentrate on its development and substantiation, and avoid finding faulty words. Do not try praise and criticize the opponent at the same time. When winning a victory in the dispute do not show your triumph: there is no need for you to wound his self-esteem. If you turn out to be wrong, recognize it quickly without any hesitations. Do not tell the interlocutor directly: "You are wrong". Remember, he is worry about the reputation. Before criticizing, recall the analogical case from your practice and tell it to the interlocutor. Use the signs (nodding, words and gestures) to show that you follow the development of his thought and sincerely approve it. Show your patience; do not hurry the interlocutor up, if he still is speaking, while you caught the idea. Our thoughts many times pass ahead of the words and phrases. The more intelligent is the person, the quicker he makes the conclusion. If you do not want to hurt the opponent, ask him to argue the interesting thoughts.

The psychology of business dispute and communication elaborated the recommendations of how to react to various types of the opponent's conduct (See table)

Incorrect action of the interlocutor	*Neutralizing protection of the interlocutor*
"Exaggeration" of the problem, leading of the problem out beyond the framework of the discussion.	Remind about the framework of the discussion and its objective. Ask for one more time to specify the antithesis and return the conversation to the previous course and to the determined framework of the discussion.
Snatching of particulars (facts) that do not concern the basic thesis.	Ask the orator about his goal of the discussion and the goal of his speech. Inquire about what thought the interlocutor developed and proved.
The opponent's attempt to catch the initiative in choosing the direction of the conversation: a) Substitution of the references to the details for the principal point; b) Raising a question not about the essence of the problem; c) Raising a counter-question, ignoring the delivered opinion and argumentation.	Foresee the opponents' objections, examine their motives and positions, etc.: a) Explain to the interlocutor that he digresses from the disputable matter; b) Inquire about what thought he proved; c) Ask for expressing his relation to the argumentation and the delivered opinion.
Making allusions that compromise the interlocutor, in this way prejudicing against his thought and suppositions.	Do not exclude compliments to the opponent's address, try to win by benevolence, demonstrate your objectiveness:

a) Transfer of the critics to the speaker, to the personality;	a).Notice that "a clever thought may shine up in a dark room too";
b) Attributing of odd utterances to the speaker.	b) Do not try to vindicate yourself, do not show any acute emotions, and do not yield to provocations.
Deliberate leading away to false conclusions and garbling with the aim to catch the opponent in illiteracy and dilettantism.	Stop interchanging with the opinions, praise the interlocutor's analysis for its profundity and ask him to make a presumptive conclusion.
Masking of extremely negative relation to the position or the author of the idea with the benevolence.	Wittily unmask the orator and remind the fact of the similar "benevolence", disclose his intention to the attending people.
Demonstration of the opponent's incompetence in the problem; demagogic reasoning.	Do not demonstrate superfluous delicateness; inquire about what the subject of the discussion was and what for.
Playing on the opponents' mistakes, shortcomings, imperfections; ignoring of the pro and con; tendentious delivery of the facts.	Ask for expressing any ideas of how to overcome the difficulty.
Constant changing of the position; beating about the bush; attempts to find a third course.	Do not insist on the recognition of, consent to and support for your idea. Your interlocutor is just a puppet. Cut down the conversation, which will never lead to anything good.
Rude snubbing of the interlocutor.	Do not give vent to your feelings. Hence, the interlocutor tries to disconcert you and play it. If possible, use irony, satire and parody.

One can find useful advices in the thoughts of a French poet and writer L. Vauvenargues. Bellow we would like to cite a number of them:

1. Do not count on your friends' support. Stake on the combination of people.

Usually, the people only in extreme cases give other people their due. It often happens that even those whom we call our friend do hesitate to recognize your virtues. There is an ancient saying: "The friend does not believe his friend". Why is it so? Since, the greatest people started like we. The one, who saw their first steps, remembers those people as weak and clumsy and now he does not like the breach of the previous equality (as it erroneously seemed to him). Fortunately, outsiders turn out to be fairer than friends.

2. Do not lose your courage because of revealed errors. It may be a possible escape from the failure. Errors in fact are the mind's characteristic.

Nobody made so many mistakes as great people. However, even historians do not remind their errors of youth, which were wiped out by their posthumous glory. The sages made thousand mistakes in their reasonings and guesses; they felt indignity due to the ignorance. The path to the truth is blocked at every step with prejudices, intrigues, conjectures and snares of the envious people. The rumors are insidious. However, it is no use to give way to despair. Go forward if you see the goal and know the path. Having taken a false step, return to the path and once again go forward.

In a dispute sincerely thank the opponents for their remarks and promise to elaborate your suggestion while trying to keep your wool on. Think over your conception and tactics in such a way that even a failure could provide a certain benefit.

3. Be sociable. Do not avoid conversation with clever people. The communication gives flexibility and ease to the mind, makes the person be more self-restrained and tractable, suppresses superfluous vanity and inures to the naturalness and easiness and at the same time empowers with the prudence and the reasons for conclusions based not on speculative illusions, but on the doubtless lessons of one's personal experience and the experience of other interlocutors.

4. Avoid polemics with a narcissistic and arrogant person. If you face a scapegrace, who is ready to express his opinion on any occasion, be sure that such an interlocutor is able unceasingly scoff at every thing that aspires to the recognition. It is such a person, whom no body likes. He prefers tyrannizing other people; he has a ready tongue; he speaks about everything and lays claims to everything.

As a rule, such a man does not recognize spiritual values, however he is always ready to catch the initiative, as other people emphasize it. He has an only credo to show off in any case. In a discussion with such a man, try to offense immediately with an accident joke, irony and sarcasm. General laughter will put him in his place for long.

5. Be afraid of shy people. Even if you manage to snatch out their approval either by a sudden attack or force, after leaving you they will return to their limited nature and become more hostile to you.

Questions and remarks are among the permanent attributes of the disputes, discussions and briefings mechanism. Exactly the questions and remarks express doubts, i.e. a convergence of views, as well as they demonstrate the positions, arguments and reasons. The appearance of a question emphasizes the first sign of the human thinking. However, not all the remarks and questions are of a constructive and productive character. They can be destructive, even obstructive resulting in the breach of a creative process. To make the approach to a dispute more constructive (i.e. expressed in the disputants striving towards exchanging of views, conversation and looking for an agreeable solution), the following psychological principals should rule all the participants: a) equal safety, b) decentralized direction, and c) adequacy (correspondence) of the said to the perceived.

The principal of the equal safety declares: do not cause psychological or other damage to any of the disputants; do not do things that you won't like by yourself (See above in Chapter "Morality of the speech"). The above principle relates to many psychological factors of the personality, first of all to the self-respect. It prohibits any offensive and abusive ripostes against the interlocutor's personality, regardless of any his thoughts and ideas. If some one breaks this principle it may lead to the substitution for the goal (attainment of the truth); the disputes turn out from the logical rails of the thought development and it leads to struggle of ambitions. If a man turns out to be an object of ridicule, he often blindly and mercilessly revenges himself for the humiliation.

One more principle is said to be a principle of the decentralized direction and it prescribes one to be able to analyze a situation or a problem from the point of view of another man, and to regard one self and other people due to the business concern, not one's personal objectives. Shortly, the credo looks as follows: do not cause any damage to the business.

This principle foresees the mutual assistance to each other and the solution of any problem by joined efforts, as well as the search for an option, which will suit everybody. If the dispute brings to such a direction, then the interlocutors will be able not only to raise themselves over their personal interests, but also to break through the external and internal limitations, in particular, through psychological barriers, which prevent from seeing the truth or an optimal solution.

The decentralized direction develops under the conditions of an alternative, i.e. upon the examination of several points of view. Such thinking develops in frequent communications with other people, who are able to uphold their points of view upon the constructive approach to a problem solution.

However, the direction, as the combination of persistent motives of activity, which are relatively independent of the situation, can be only egocentric. At that, the personality is governed exclusively by the motives of his prosperity; strive for prestige and victory in the dispute. The interlocutors with the egocentric character usually are engaged in their problems and they pay no interest to the problems of other people; they are in a hurry to make conclusions and assumptions; they try to impose their opinion on the surrounding people; they deprive other disputants from the sense of freedom; they do not orient themselves in the situation; they do not know when to say and when to keep silence and listen to; their behavior does not demonstrate friendliness.

The credo of an egocentric person sounds in the following way: "My point of view, my theory lies in the center of attention, not the opponent's." In a dispute he divides people into the useful, who help him to stand up for his point of view, and detrimental, who hamper his progress. Such a man is able "to put the opponent in his place", upbraid and pull him up, scold, humiliate and offend. When he cannot do anything from the above list, the egocentric person demonstrates that he is misunderstood and bitterly injured. The sincerity of his indignation can mislead the opponent. The egocentric person more often than other people inclines to a destructive approach in a dispute.

The third principle is significant too. It is the principle of adequacy of the said to the received. It says: do not dandify the thought by a deliberate or unintentional distortion of the said (heard).

For this principle to serve for the disputants, one ought to comprehend the essence of the heard adequately. One shall strive for the simplicity and accurateness of utterances. If phrases are dim, it causes declining of the attention to the interlocutor's speech (See above). When the interest is kept, the sensitivity restricts the listener's desire to specify the essence of the said and he has to complete the comprehension according to his images. It always bears the danger to reflect in the consciousness the things that differ from what the opponent intended to say. It may result in a semantic barrier – the convergence of the heard with the said.

There can be different psychological barriers lying on the path to an accurate comprehension of the orator's speech. They pertain to the personality's specifics, its psychological state or reactions that hamper the comprehension or acceptance of the adequate sense of the opponent's utterance or point of view. It can be the manifestation of the orator's superfluous surety, aplomb, ambitions, ignorance of other people's opinions, self-attraction, envy, hostility and so on.

The principle obliges the disputants to consider the opponent's ability to quite adequately comprehend the sense of the reasoning chains and to make the facts comprehensible without congestion and simplification of the statement to the prejudice of the depth of thoughts.

In addition, one ought to keep in mind the inertness of thinking inherent in many people, which can lead to dogmas (See above). New scientific thoughts are always paradoxical, if one charges them on the basis of an average consciousness; the person unwillingly discards blinders of the used and substantiated experience.

Not all the people have a systemic thinking, i.e. the ability to consider an object as a system included into the multitude of connections with other subsystems. One perceives the object like an illuminated target; the other one due to the tunnel vision sees only a spot on the object of comprehension. Partial and unsystematic attainments stipulate the doubts there, wherein other person sees everything in a clear way. This situation originates semantic barriers.

As a result it leads to the following error: "That which I saw and heard is the whole thing that can be seen and heard in this utterance".

The surety in the infallibility of one's own view in a dispute leads to a senseless squabble, which brings to the situation when the disputants put the disputable matter aside and try to uphold their own positions, considering the opponent to be wrong.

To realize the third principle one ought to learn to listen to the opponent. What does the inability to listen to the interlocutor and, consequently, his inadequate comprehension, originate in?

We are not able to hold our desire to express a precocious opinion; we are in a hurry to disprove the opponent without going into the root of his reasoning; we interrupt him, though he did not finish and then find ourselves in an awkward situation; we cling to the externals and as result get tired before reaching the main thing; we look aside at something in the orator's appearance, at the shortcomings of his speech and therefore miss the essence of his thoughts; without having heard the whole speech we prepare for parrying his hints at our ignorance; we do not consider the opponent's motives that induce him to oppose our standpoint on the problem; we are confident in the fact that our knowledge is enough to uphold our own position; we come to believe that the truth is on our side and in advance we dispose ourselves to disagree with the opponent's assertions.

All this hampers the mutual understanding and adequate comprehension of the said.

Let us cite some goals of speculative remarks and questions that arose in such a situation: to impose confrontation; insipid the value of an idea; increase the differences; compromise the initiator of a suggestion; block the discussion; lead the problem to the deadlock; prevent the opponent from solving his problems. One ought to consider that the opponent's reasons, motives and stimulus underlie the questions and remarks. Let us indicate some of them:

1. Natural motives: caution as a result of the life experience; defensive reaction due to the unexpectedness; revenge for the failure in business (rivalry), envy, personal hostility, conservative thinking.

2. Motives dictated by a certain interest: threat to the personal position; weakening of the opponent's position; desire to get an additional information; exclusion of a mistake in the decision-making; determination of the opponent's abilities; clarification of the opponent's competency; revealing of possible difficulties; determination of the degree of coincidence in the opinions; upholding of classical approaches; disclosure of arguments; playing for the time to consider the tactics.

As we see, the doubts expressed in the form of questions and remarks reflect a large spectrum of personal motives.

In addition to the constructive and destructive approaches to the discussion, there is one more, the third one: Laissez faire, laissez passer (French), wherein one tries to adhere to the position of non-interference, passing over in silence and reticence.

What kinds of questions can one meet in disputes, discussions and conversations? The following incomplete list demonstrates their variety.

1. **Trapping questions** suppose a trick. As the practice demonstrates, one ought to keep in mind that a number of skillfully selected questions can make the opponent hopping mad. When losing his temper the man will lose the self-control and the trace of his reasoning; you know that the demoralized opponent is not a rival. Do not let the opponent to involve you into the conversation, which is advantageous to him. Humor, irony, anecdote, parody and riposte represent the means of parrying any trapping questions.

2. **Counter-questions** are often used to neutralize the opinion.

3. **Blocking questions** have the function to hide the opponent's horizon and to press for such answers, which correspond to the interlocutor's concept; and if the questions are formulated quite skillfully, they push the thought in only one direction, blocking any other alternatives.

4. **Ticklish question**. As it is known, Socrates led his opponent to a full crash by his ticklish questions (See above). When Socrates was judged, he explained in details, why he constantly addressed ticklish questions to other people: he was driven by an aspiration for awakening the sense of justice of those people and deterring them from evil deeds. He compared himself with a gadfly that prevents cattle from being fat from slumbering.

If the listener feels a trickery or lie in the orator's reasoning, more often his objection is expressed in a ticklish question. A dilettantish approach, nonsense and attempts to mislead and embroider, all this arouses the opponents' ticklish questions.

5. **Compulsory questions**. The interlocutor uses compulsory questions to persuade us into the agreement with him. Usually these questions sound like: "You won't deny it, will you?" Extorting our consent, the interlocutor practically gives us only one possibility – to recognize our own defeat. Do we have any way out in this situation? Yes we have one to tell him the following: "Do not extort in this way".

6. **Rhetoric questions**. Apply to these questions if you think it appropriate or if the listeners are ready to an approval. These questions provide for the interlocutor's silent consent to our opinion, i.e. their support. Formulate these questions in such a way that the interlocutor can give only simple answers – yes or no; the answers should be short, make a rhythm and consolidate the thought. Rhetoric questions in a large auditorium join the people very much (in such a situation the silence will mean the consent to your opinion).

7. **Quickening question**. In such cases when we want to influence upon the opponent's point of view and to push him to the consent or confirmation of an earlier agreement, one ought to apply to the quickening questions. These questions force the interlocutor to speed up the argumentation of his opinion. However, it has a certain danger: the interlocutor may have an impression that he is interrogated. The center of efforts deviates to your side, the opponent is deprived of his activity and, therefore, he can "blow up" in the following way: "Do not hurry me up". Apply to these questions with great care and only in those cases, when the disputants are quite familiar with the problem.

8. **Specifying question**. Use this kind of questions only if you need any additional facts or if you want to reveal the true motives of the opponent, when he takes a neutral or positive position in your respect and is ready to transfer this information. These questions usually begin with what, who, how, why and how much. For instance: "What do you think is absent in the argumentation of this suggestion?"

What the use of such a question? The interlocutor stays in an active condition, he turns out to be a source of information, ideas, suggestions; he is capable to give information at his discretion; the attention to his opinion flatters his self-esteem, it removes the psychological barrier in the dispute.

What is the danger of the frequent use of the specifying questions? Of course, you lose the initiative and the conversation may turn to the course of the opponent's interests and problems. Do not let the opponent lead you away to a meaningless talk. He can guard himself against your critical analysis and winkle everything that he is interested in out of you. He will do it with great tact and attention.

On the one hand the questions help us to maximally activate the opponent, thus we let him consolidate himself, and on the other hand, we improve our situation and lead the opponent away from the analysis of our positions. The opponent feels satisfied in the possibility to speak his mind and we facilitate the solution of the problem.

The questions play a significant role at all stages of the discussion, consolidating the intermediate results of the exchanging of views.

How do we react to the remarks? Do they cause a problem in the conversation? Do they hamper the mutual understanding? Of course, they do. But one cannot avoid them in any dispute. We have no choice but to agree with the opinion of Leonardo da Vinci: "The enemy, who discloses your errors, is much more useful than your friend, who conceals them".

What kind of references can you meet?

1. **Ironic**. "When learning to walk, a man learns to fall, and only falling he learns to walk". Skeptic, spiteful, provocative. "A bald man flung invective at Diogenes for his neglect of the gods. – I won't swear at you, at all. I even praise your hair for the fact that they came out from your stupid head" – answered Diogenes."

2. **Compromising**. Paganini in his youth age promised his friend Kiarelli the following: "I will "coach" you and you will become the first violin in a military orchestra". Later on the envious Kiarelli became an inquisitor and by his will the dead body of Paganini dragged all over Italy for long and within forty years they did not buried him.

3. **Objective**. One of the company's officers reproved his chief: "An ancient philosopher Pliny said that "a man can be recognized by his relation to cattle and slaves." The chief answered: "Well, we do not have slaves".

4. **Threat**. "If you talk in this way, you won't be able to open the way to the sub-faculty and more over to the council" (A. Raykin).

5. **Unfriendly**. "The credo of an evil-wisher: it is not enough for a load off one's mind; it is important that the load will squeeze the neighbor at the same time" (V. Kolechitsky).

6. **Obstructionist**. (A loud shout, a hysteric cry, a stubborn repetition). "A nightingale breaks off when asses begin yelling" (Sa'adi).

7. **Flattery**. "Flattery on the tongue, revenge in the mind". Do you remember the words of Paganini: " They are envious of clever people, they harm talented people, they avenge on genius people"?

8. **Accusations**. "A dispute cannot be eliminated by another dispute,

as the fury of one person cannot be eliminated by the fury of another person. One has to persuade." (Antisphenes)

9. **Spite**. "The mind loses all its charm if it is filled with the malice" (R. Sheridan).

10. **Forestalling**. "An acute mind, not wide, rushes forward at every step, but it cannot go forward" (R. Tagore).

If one wants to uphold his position in a dispute, he ought to neutralize his interlocutor. To do this one ought to localize, i.e. to restrict the area, which the answer will extend to, and make the analysis, i.e. to specify the goal of objection or any other reaction of the interlocutor and his thought, hidden in his question or remark; to reveal the reason (basis) and value of the doubt. The choice of practice and an appropriate method of defense depend on this operation.

The tactics are divided into four kinds.

1. Not to contradict. If the interlocutor tries to impose the confrontation beside the point, disconcert you and lead the conversation away to a wrong path, you ought to keep silence and disregard all his remarks.

2. To plead. If the reality does not coincide with your opinion and the opponent forces you to recognize the impossibility to substantiate your position right away, you can avoid the direct answer. Do not always react to the provocations.

3. To vindicate. Our argumentation does not seem always ideal upon the substantiation. Some good reasons may be useful to cover its weak points, however it looks not effective.

4. To defend. One ought to act in case of the opponent's strong counteraction, critical offense with the task to discredit the author or to ruin the idea at the stage of its birth.

The answer can be given before and after the opponent's remark.

If it is known that the opponent is in mood to drive you into a corner, you ought to deliver the supposed remark as an alternative right at the stage of your argumentation and comment it before the opponent will have a chance to speak.

In all cases after the opponent's remark it is necessary to give an answer in a quiet atmosphere of the mutually interested interlocutors' conversation. An immediate answer is justified only in order to avert the further development of the conversation along the unacceptable line and to prevent the opponent's incorrect deeds.

A certain delay in answering are possible if you do not have an appropriate facts or in the case when an immediate answer will threaten the normal course of the discussion from the psychological point of view, i.e. it may cause an emotional blow-up with undesirable consequences.

Also it is possible to ignore the opponent's remarks and questions when you notice a psychological trick or if the opponent's remark is dictated by his hostility, makes a deliberate hindrance and does not concern the fact of the matter even if the interlocutor is right. In the last case you have nothing else to do.

You should not always strive for irrefragable answers and immediate reaction to the opponents' remarks, retorts and objections.

As a rule, the neutralization takes place in support of one's own thesis and it does not concern the opponent's antithesis. However, in some cases the effect of support becomes apparent in direct critics of the opponent's position. The critics mean the examination and analysis of the opponent's thesis and consist in two stages during which one destroys the wrong argumentation of the opponent's idea. By making a critical analysis, the orator realizes the second stage that includes the formulas of constructive critics, realized in such questions like: why not.

The proof of falsity or inconsistency of a certain thesis is said to be the **disproof**. The most successful and correct method of the opponent's thesis disproof is a disproof by facts. If the proof of falsity or inconsistency of a certain thesis is substantiated with actual phenomena and events that contradict the thesis, in such a case the task of the disproof often turns out to be accomplished. As they say, the facts are the stubborn things.

There are also some other methods of disproof. One can criticize the arguments, which the opponent put forward to substantiate his thesis. The task is to prove that the arguments of the refutable proof are false and inconsistent. If one manages to do it, the thesis will turn out to be not proved.

When saying about the critics of the opponent's arguments one ought to notice that it is not allowed to refuse other arguments without proving their inconsistency (falsity or uncertainty). In addition, one ought to keep in mind that the disproof of other arguments does not include the disproof of the opponent's thesis as whole and it does not prove the verity of your thesis. The question is that the opponent's thesis may have more precise arguments than the disproved. Therefore, in order to complete the disproof of the opponent's thesis one ought to prove the inconsistency of not only the proposed arguments, but the content of the thesis as a whole.

One ought to prove that the verity of the refutable thesis does not follow from the arguments that the opponent put forward to substantiate his thesis.

A new thesis, which appears as a contrary or contradictory opinion in respect to the refutable thesis, shall be proved independently. This method of disproof is quite often. It consists in the following: Let us suppose that our opponent put forward a thesis and substantiated it with the corresponding arguments. Disagreeing to this thesis, we temporarily put aside the given thesis and the arguments, which are used to prove its verity, and pay all our attention to proving the verity of a new thesis, which contrasts with or contradicts the opponent's thesis.

Let us assume that one of the members of a biological society put forward the following thesis: "None of deep-sea fauna members can be a shellfish". The thesis is false. In order to prove it we ought to substantiate the verity of the contradictory thesis. "It is known that some deep-sea fauna members are shellfishes", that is proved by some singular facts, for instance, a shrimp, as a member of the deep-sea fauna, is a shellfish. Cuttlefishes that live deep in the ocean also belong to shellfishes. So, in fact "some of deep-sea fauna members are shellfishes". If it is true, then the above thesis "None of deep-sea fauna members can be a shellfish" is not true.

The disproof often proves that the given thesis originates such a consequence that contradicts the truth. It is a diffused method of disproof and it is referred to the **reduction to an absurd** (in Latin reductio ad absurdum), which consists in the following: it is temporarily assumed that the refutable thesis is true. Then one tries to deduce consequences from it. Since the consequences that follow from it turn out to contradict the reality, one can conclude that the thesis is also false. According to the logics rules the truth can be deduced only from the truth. As the consequences are actually false, one makes the conclusion that the thesis is false (See above).

The expression reductio ad absurdum is used in those cases wherein the opponent is so confused that he comes to absurd inferences.

Sometimes one can use an indirect method of disproof – the method that consists in the contradiction to the consequence deduced from the refutable thesis, which is such a thesis that is true and at the same time contrary to this consequence.

In general the disproof can be divided into two stages. The first stage: criticism of inconsistent arguments. It is a destruction of arguments from which one deduces a conclusion that pretends to be the truth. One can use the following methods: determination of the information source; exposure of doubtful authorities; appellation to facts; contrast comparison; indication to the failure to mention; adducing of counterarguments.

The second stage: criticism of the demonstration, i.e. the destruction of incorrect relation between the arguments and the thesis in the process of reasoning. It is a certain severance of sources from the thesis, deprivation of the thesis from the supporting force of reasons. At that, one uses more complicated logical methods: concrete historical analysis; the author's comments of utterances; analysis of an evident (actually inconsistent) analogy; examination of inductions (a mental operation of inductions); disclosure of falsifications and substitution for a concept; demonstration of supposed consequences constructed on conjectures and estimates.

When a blow is struck against the reasons and the arguments, which underlined the idea, are destroyed, then the entire argumentation seems to be unconvincing, the thesis looks unsubstantiated and, naturally, it cannot be considered as proved. The one, who tried to prove it, has to prepare a new argumentation that will be more consistent and convincing.

It is not advisable to apply to acute critics in a discussion. If the argumentation is reliable, a clever opponent will hardly provoke an active defense. As a French writer A. Maurois noticed, "The most difficult is not to defend the opinion, but to have it".

Actually, we do not like any sort of friendly critics, either objective or quiet. Remember, please, that every person can be wrong (however he does not think so). The examination of arguments, their analysis, whether we want it or not, represent the interlocutor in an unfavorable light. Since all of us strive for prestige, recognition and respect to this or that extent. The opponent always apprehends an incorrect, malice and exultant protection as a humiliation. So, La Rochefoucauld may be right when he advises: "If you want to have enemies, try to surpass your friends. But if want to have friends, let your friends to surpass you".

There are three kinds of disputes: apodictic, eristic and sophistic. The kind of a dispute depends on the goal that determines the method and means of its achievement. If the interlocutor's goal is to look for the truth, he focuses on an apodictic dispute (a trustworthy one, based on the formal laws of thinking and the rules of inference). If the opponent's goal is to persuade and incline to his opinion, he focuses on an eristic dispute (or, as it is called, dialectic, i.e. based on the entire laws of the dialectics). If the opponent's goal is to win in every way, then he focuses on a sophistic dispute (based on verbal tricks that mislead the interlocutor, See above).

At the least two parties are involved in a dispute. Their joined conduct can vary. There are some options that follow:

The first one strives for the truth (an apodictic dispute); the second party does the same (an apodictic dispute). The first party strives for the truth (an apodictic dispute); the second one tries to persuade (an eristic dispute). The first party strives for the truth (an apodictic dispute); the second party strives for the victory (a sophistic dispute). The first party tries to persuade (an eristic dispute); the second party strives for the victory (a sophistic dispute). Both of them try to persuade each other (an eristic dispute). Both of them strive for the victory (a sophistic dispute) and so on.

A dispute can be symbolically expressed as the movements of chessmen on the chessboard. The knight moves in its way, the queen moves in its way and the bishop – in its way. The game of chess enlists thousands of accurately calculated sets, each having its name and possible outcomes. However, if we imagine that the chessmen are living people that have souls and all human passions, and then any game would be unpredictable. The chessmen have strong restrictions; the people do not.

In a dispute one ought to be disposed to any unforeseen expressions of the interlocutors' mind and feelings. A person, who is prepared for a dispute, should be able to play his own game, improvising in the circumstances of the other people's improvisation, without any bewilderment, but picking up the thought, joining the opponent's melody, feeling the rhythm and holding to the common theme. In other words, in a dispute, like in the Dixieland, the disputants have mental parts: a dialectician leads the part to the truth, an orator inclines everybody to the like-mindedness, and a sophist sees his goal only in a victory, however the theme is heard.

Let us discuss the main kinds of disputes.

Apodictic dispute. It assumes a precise formulation of a thesis, the availability of a basic argument (a trustworthy assertion – major premise, which begins the chain of conclusions), the absence of disagreements in conclusions, reliability and adequacy of arguments. At that, the conclusions will be constructed according to the figures of syllogism.

Upon the formal observation of the laws of thinking and the rules of inference the mind will bring us to the truth by means of conclusions that are called apodictic. In this case the credo of a disputant is as follows: "Plato is my friend, but the truth is dearer". This kind of a dispute requires precise (scientific) definitions of concepts, proven scientific theses in the capacity of major premises, established facts, clearly formulated problems, reliable arguments and comprehension of the crux of disagreements (a matter of argument).

K. Zelensky noted that in syllogisms "the motion of a thought on the path (rails) of the logics demonstrates such a forced character of the inference that fascinates every scientist and paralyzes the imagination… It is a railway transport of a thought, which delivers you to the truth as a terminal station of destination".

What does the psychological aspect of an apodictic dispute lie in, when both disputants are focused on it and they pursue the one goal – to find the truth or at least to approach it? The opponents prove themselves to be psychologically symmetrical, i.e. they both check the verity of the thesis (of the proponent) and the antithesis (of the opponent). At that, holding each other in high respect, they highly evaluate the interlocutor's conclusions and mutually induce each other to specify and correct their formulations, interpretations and definitions; they show patience, strive for clearing up the opponent's views, look for and notice that things in which the opponent is right. Speaking figuratively, they behave like two persons that cut up a tree trunk by a two-handled saw.

An apodictic dispute requires such personal characteristics as competence (knowing of the common points and details of the discussion), concernment, optimism (including the sense of humor), responsibility, constructive approach (preparedness to defend the position and views, to develop and continue the conversation), profoundness of opinions (philosophic level of thinking), argumentation of inferences (solidity of facts, ability to use options of argumentation as the truth requires not a declaration, but a logical proof), concentration on the problem (singling out of the most essential, clear delivery of a disputable point, short and clear formulation of theses), trade-off approach (preparedness to yield, take a risk, change the position), sociability (ability to renew the psychological contact), intelligence (intellectual tolerance, sincerity in the expression of joy and restraint in anger).

Eristic dispute. As it was said an eristic dispute arouses when it is necessary to convince the partner in something, win him over and make him be a like-minded person.

This kind of dispute includes an initiator and an opposing partner. In groups, the position and opposition present them. Therefore, such a dispute is called as parliamentary. Its theoretic base includes the following conceptions: reasoning, validity and persuasiveness. The reasoning appears as a chain of conclusions (not always apodictic) expressed in a logical order. The validity represents a logical forced character of the thesis inference (the reasoning may seem convincing). The persuasiveness is a psychological concept, which is based on the trust in the truth of the expressed ideas connected with the listener's certain emotions. The validity provides for the coincidence of views and the persuasiveness ensures the coincidence of feelings. In a dilettantish dispute one can see the prevalence of passions and emotions. Without excitement and agitation of the people's nervous system one cannot even merely gather them and send to extinguish a fire. More over one should avoid inclining without agitation. The validity is understood as the substantiation of assertions, confirmation of a thesis by sources, facts, observations and so on. As soon as the arguments gain a psychological character, their persuasiveness increases immediately and they start working for the speaker's goal realization. In other words, the influence on the mind and reason shall be necessarily supported by an irrational influence on the feelings, and then the argumentation will be well reasoned and convincing.

The disputants' argumentations can be evaluated in the next way: a) well-reasoned, but not convincing, b) convincing, but not fully reasoned, c) well reasoned and convincing.

An ideally well-reasoned argumentation is said to be conclusive. Its characteristics are as follows: distinctness of conceptions, consistency of opinions, and adequacy of reasons for the thesis approval (See above). However, having a logical ideal character, such an argumentation can turn out to be unconvincing, i.e. not affecting the emotional state of a man.

One out to understand that the non-deductive conclusions very often have the greater convincing force, especially for those, who is used to rely on the opinion of the majority, authorities, leaders, respectful persons or own experience.

To imagine the psychological characteristic of an eristic dispute we will compare the motives of a person, who inclines the auditorium to his opinion, with the motives of a person, who opposes this influence.

Why does the initiator argue?	*What is the opposition caused by?*
To achieve his goal;	Strive for avoiding the influence of another man;
To warn about an unreasoned decision;	Realization of the principal incompatibility of the initiator's and the opponent's points of view;
To stimulate the availability for service;	
To win over;	The initiator's utterance com prehended in a wrong way;
To win the consent;	
To make the partner be an associate.	Prejudice in favor of his personality;
To find the truth or an optimal solution.	Relation to the dispute as to the sport; *(Who will win?)*.

As we can see, the range of an eristic dispute motives is quite wide. All this forces the disputants to bear a heavy burden in the communication in addition to the personal characteristics, which presuppose the interlocutor's approach to the dispute: constructive (creative) and destructive (destroying). Both of them can show a defensive reaction. Let us assume that the initiator puts forward a proposal and argues it, however, the partner, under the influence of his own motives, personal problems and failure at work or due to the fear to be involved into the situation, which does not bode well, does not promise a quiet life or seems unpredictable, defends himself by offering an alternative.

The happened collision of the alternatives also generates a defensive reaction, which can appear as a counter argumentation or an obstruction (barrier, hindrance) in respect to the interlocutor. In this case the disputant demonstrates an increased sensitivity to even minor attempts of the interlocutor to have an influence on him.

Having his doubts as to the sincerity and benevolence of the initiator's first position, the partner objects by either offering an alternative, or constructing a psychological defense; he manifests watchfulness and doubts; he bombards the interlocutor with many questions and remarks; he strictly controls his utterances and pick holes.

If the proponent in such a situation still tries to continue the conversation, the opponent may drop the dispute. In the worse case he starts from a counterattack with obstruction, killing critics, discredit and exposure of the assaulter, giving a start to any arguments. The squabble begins with two – three words. The dispute finishes with the parties' direct or indirect disagreement.

What are the frequent errors in an eristic dispute?

The first error is the overestimation of the interlocutor's knowledge. The breach of the principle of the decentralized direction causes the following situation: that which is known and clear to the initiator is considered to be known and clear to the partner. As the consequence the arguments fail to be well reasoned.

The second error: our opinion should arouse the same emotions of another person as we have. It is a frequent error. Emotions and feelings are interconnected and depend first of all on the motives, which are hardly to be revealed and comprehended.

The third error: the ignorance of the principle of adequacy leads to the overvaluation of one's own possibilities and capacities and underestimation of the opponent's.

The fourth error: non-existent motives of conduct are attributed to the interlocutor and the initiator spends time and efforts in a wrong way.

The fifth error: a superfluous appellation to the partner's mind to the prejudice of the persuasiveness of an emotional influence. Cicero made the following conclusion: "The orator should possess two basic merits: first, the ability to convince with precise arguments, second, the ability to agitate the listeners' feelings by an impressive and effective speech."

However, one cannot guarantee a positive outcome of the dispute even if he follows good advices and knows the common errors. As it was said, an emotional communication arouses psychological barriers connected with the peculiarities of the personality, psychological states, situational relations, which hamper the mutual understanding or prevent form comprehending the essence of an utterance.

The psychological barriers are divided into semantic and communicative. The semantic barriers occur due to the breach of the laws of logics (See above). The communicative barriers arouse due to the incomprehension of the nature and psychology of the people's communication, essence of the processes of their comprehension and interaction, and finally, due to the reality aversion.

There are two the most significant communicative rules that underlie every dispute, especially, an eristic one.

The first rule: the agreements should be observed. Ancient Romans formulated this rule long ago when the state relations between the people began forming. The laws begin with it. Any agreements, wills, promises and assurances shall be concluded by certain deeds and concrete actions. The failure to observe this rule considerably damages both business and personal interrelations. It is quite easy to imagine what would happen if this norm lost its sense everywhere: the people's conduct will become unpredictable. We could not orient ourselves in the simplest human relations.

The second rule: the human being is the measure of all things. The recognition of the human being to be the supreme value represents the general norm of communication. If in a dispute two opponents struggle for an idea, they should not kill each other due to dissent or destroy themselves as the bearer of the idea.

Politeness is a great art. It was said not in vain that nothing is gained so easily and nothing is valued so dearly as the politeness, which originates from the reference to the respect of the partner's virtues, the desire to comprehend his strives and the fear to wound his self-esteem. "The mind loses all its charm if it is filled with the malice" (R. Sheridan).

Upon any polemic nerve-strained dispute the man should not lose his charm and tactfulness, the ability to proportion the assaulting force to the object of this "assault": it is funny to break a butterfly on the wheel. Sometimes it is useful to look at the dispute like from aside in order to suppress an unjustified irritation, which threatens such living values as respect, inclination and friendship; it is better to live with other people in such a way that "your friends won't turn out to be enemies, and the enemies will turn out to become friends" (Pythagoras).

V. Levy suggests four rules that help preventing the interlocutor from holding an egocentric position. One egoist can use these rules to psychologically neutralize another egoist with the most pleasant emotions for each other.

First: go into the heart of the matter of the interlocutors' utterances. It means to suppress your emotions and look at the one with whom you are dealing. Try to understand his point of view, his circumstances, put yourself on his place for your sake. Take all needed information about the interlocutor in advance; remember the dates, tastes and interests.

Second: make a favorable atmosphere. It means to smile as wide as you can, begin with "yes" and consent to. If the opponent blames you, disarm him by a phrase like: "Yes, I am wrong". Express your sympathy and do it as more sincere as possible. Speak with him about something that he likes or about him, begin only with it, never begin with "I". Apply to the motives of his personal interest. And bestow a smile, do a favor and make gifts...

Third: do not humiliate another person. Do not wound one's self-esteem. Do not hurt it carelessly. Do not blame, threaten and order; do not show your distrust; do not interrupt the interlocutor, do not boast, do not demonstrate that he is nasty or not attractive; thank and make excuses when you refuse...

Fourth: Ennoble the interlocutor. Pay an increased interest to him; demonstrate your confidence; listen to him attentively, praise, praise and praise; give him the possibility to feel himself a significant person... Let him boast and feel his superiority, ask for his advice as of a senior person. If you have an idea, suggest it to him gradually in such a way that it will seem to him like his own idea ...

Of course, these rules are not doubtless; one cannot enter into an argument without considering one's individual characteristics, as well as his national, social and age-specific peculiarities. For instance, Aristotle recommended to head for such characteristics as up to him are inherent in the youth and old age.

Young people:	Old people:
Inclined to desires, passionate, hot-tempered, do not endure any kind of disregard, like victory, are absolutely not wicked, good-natured, credulous, live with a hope, , extremely courageous, generous, like friends, like extreme things, do everything enough and to spare, consider themselves to be omniscient, available to compassion, like laughter and say witty remarks.	Do not assert anything positive, "assume", but "know" nothing, ill-natured, suspicious, distrustful, likes and dislikes are not strong, poor-spirited, do not strive, are not lavish coward, afraid of everything, selfish, lives by remembrances, their anger is fiery, but effortless, governed by benefits, unfair, malicious, grumbling, not alert and not risible.

Having read these characteristics of a young and old men, one can tell for sure that any dispute between them won't come to any result. However, the people still argue and make themselves angry.

An ancient Greek philosopher, Antisphenes noted: "A dispute cannot be eliminated by another dispute, as the fury of one person cannot be eliminated by the fury of another person."

What is the reason of other people's anger? Ancient orators determined the following reasons: if the orator demonstrates his neglect in our respect, i.e. contempt (wounding one's self-esteem), petty tyranny (preventing from our desires), mockery (inappropriate unpleasant joke); if the orator is proud of his appearance and philosophy and demonstrates his superiority; if the orator speaks well about the opponents; if the orator speaks badly about those whom we admire; if the orator speaks badly about us in the presence of that one whom we admire or whom we are ashamed of or one who is ashamed of us; if the orator does not thank us forgetting our names.

The psychological barriers may also be originated by the following psychic states like stress, and frustration that appear in the form of anxiety, tension, fury, aggression or loss of interest in life and apathy. Such peculiarities of a personality as diffidence, absent-mindedness and fear of reciprocal measures can also bring to the communication barriers. A dispute cannot help getting rid of psychological barriers, but it may help reducing their influence.

Sophistic dispute. Sophos – a sage of Ancient Greece – thought out certain training methods for his pupils' mind. By solving sophistic tricks (See above), the pupils developed their abilities to withstand the opponents' unfair tricks. They organized sophistic disputes to demonstrate the virtuosity of oratory. The goals of such disputes were to win a victory over the opponent; the disputants were not interested in the search for truth. The goal justified the means of its achievement. It originated the sophistic – an oral virtuosity, evident obviousness of conclusions, substitution of one conception for another, art of misleading by means of abusing the "flexibility" of conceptions and impermissible psychological methods.

The main characteristic of the methods applied in sophistic disputes includes the digression from the principles of disputes, namely: substitution of dependence on views for handling of trustworthy facts, egocentric direction for decentralized, destructive approach for constructive, neglect for respectful relation to the personality.

Disputes represent the most inappropriate form for communication. As a rule, it appears as an expressive collision of two parties, wherein each of them strives for the triumph of its opinion. In nine cases from ten the dispute is concluded by the fact that each of the interlocutors becomes more certain of his truth.

The means, used by the speaker to defend his point of view, are conditionally divided into logical, parrying, speculative and incorrect. All of them come to disproof, neutralization and defense. Discrediting utterances shall be disproved; errors and incorrect inferences shall be neutralized and attacks shall be repulsed by one's defense. The methods complement each other. One and the same method in different situations plays different roles.

Let us examine some means of the oral resistance.

Effective comparison. It is a very easy logical operation (See above). The method turns out to be effective owing to the force of trust. If a person trusted into the verity or falsity of something on the basis of a certain fact and after that he faced the fact that contradicts the first one, his trust diminishes to the value of the persuasive force of this new knowledge. This has now been demonstrated with the following:

> A French bacteriologist Louis Pasteur investigated a culture of smallpox bacteria in his laboratory. Suddenly a stranger came to his place and introduced himself as a second of one grandee, to whom it seemed that the scientist insulted him. Pasteur listened to the messenger and said: "Well if I am called out, I have the right to choose a weapon. Here, I hold two retorts: in one – smallpox bacteria, in another – pure water. If the man, who sent you, agrees to swallow the content of one of them, I will drink another". The duel did not happen.

In this case you can see the action of an indirect critics. From his part, Pasteur did not analyze the grandee's accusation, but immediately neutralized it.

One ought to consider that the persuasive force of new information, compared with the existent information (persuasion), is not similar. That which disproves one, may have no effect on another. The method power impresses by the contrast in evaluations of one and the same phenomenon (fact). Opposite opinions represent the event in volume. As a result it highlights that side, which was not seen before.

The method called "a killing argument" represents an option of the effective comparison. An ominous at first glance name of this method corresponds to the destructive force of its action. The killing argument refers to such an opinion (counter argument or fact), which strikes a smashing blow to the opponent's thesis. After the application of this method the further assertion of one's opinion turns out to be senseless and effortless. This method is applied when other, "softer" methods are ineffective. The killing argument is especially destructive when it corresponds to the opinion of an authoritative person. It is frequently used in this option to put an end to a dispute.

When in the year of 1957 there was an attempt to dismiss N. Khrushchev from the post of the first secretary of the Central Committee of the CPSU, marshal G. Zhukov, who had the great power and popularity in that time, said: "The Army is against this decision and no single tank will move from its place without my order".

Author's comment. The point of the method is to expose garbling, falsifications, false analogies, sophisms and other tricks and misuses of the opponent. By destroying the "camouflaged" argumentation this method enables one to divest the thesis of its supporting arguments. The thought becomes doubtful; it does not follow with necessity from those premises, which the interlocutor put forward, and consequently, it cannot pretend to the verity.

After destruction of the argumentation, which has to shake the trust in the inference, the author, as the source, is subjected to an attack. One uses discrediting facts to demonstrate the dishonorableness of the personality that adduced the thesis. In this way one tries to prejudice the sincerity of the other side's intentions and undermine the opponent's authority. This step serves for indirect critics.

The disproof is completed by humor, irony and sarcasm in order to gain an emotional support of the executed analysis.

Counter question. It is an effective method of neutralization, ducking away from speaking to the point. As a result we do not answer either "yes", or "no", just "think what you want". In another case the counter questions enable one to reveal weak points in the interlocutor's position or to expose nonsense. The method does not concern to either thesis, or antithesis; however, it prevents from any further discussion, expansion of a conversation in an unpleasant direction and excludes the possibility of critics.

To take somebody at somebody's word. The point of the method is to demonstrate to the interlocutor that he does not accept the thought, which he proposes by himself.

Analysis of an inference. The method represents the analysis of the interlocutor's argumentation, which leads to an error. It helps to destroy the logical consequence, adduced by induction, deduction and analogy (See above).

The logical methods of disproof are based on the disclosure of paralogisms in the interlocutor's argumentation.

A group of parrying methods is applied to repulse accusations and incorrect remarks that compromise the orator's intention. They serve for the defense of the orator's personality and indirectly his position. These means of a dispute do not lead to a constructive result, however they are necessary to continue the discussion. The main function of the parrying methods is to cool down violent disputants and in some cases to demoralize the opponent. The parrying methods include: riposte (boomerang) (See above), wrathful rebuff, counter example, irony (See bellow) and others.

Wrathful rebuff. It is such a method, which is aimed at the neutralization of the interlocutor's thesis, but the personality also suffers at the same time. Essentially, it is an objection made in an acute, sometimes an aggressive form against the assertions concealed in a benevolent opinion. An example of such parrying we can find in a political practice of Ekaterina Dashkova.

"Prime minister, prince V. A. Kaunitz, an Austrian state chancellor, in his conversation with Dashkova about the role of Peter the First in the history of Russia expressed the following thought:

– Princess, do you think little of the fact that he brought together Russia with Europe and that Russia became known only from the time of Peter the First, don't you?

– Prince, the great empire that has such inexhaustible sources of wealth and power, as Russia, does not have a need in closing in with anybody. Such a menacing mass, as Russia, governed in a correct way, attracts everybody, which it wants. If Russia had been unknown till that time, which you say about, Your Grace, it proves – forgive me, prince, only the ignorance or light-mindedness of European countries that ignored such a powerful state."

Counter example. One ought not always answer the question asked by the interlocutor. Of course, he has the right to ask about everything, however, the opponent has the right not to answer, more over, if he notices the opponent's attempt to provoke the transfer of information, which can be used against him. One has to do only one thing – to counter the question tactfully.

However, one ought to be able to duck away from the answer without hurting the interlocutor. In such a case the counter question will be quite appropriate. You can conditionally approve the question, even to agree with the opponent's thought without repeating it, and to cite an analogical example or a case, which is well known to the disputants. The associations will do their job.

In a conversation with cosmonaut A. Leonov at the meeting in the USA one of the reporters noticed as it were casually: "The investigation of the space is a very dear thing, isn't it?" Leonov agreed: "Of course, it is expensive,"– and then parried: "Probably, the Spanish queen grudged spending money to the expedition of Columbus. But she gave the money. And who knows when America would be discovered if she was greedy."

With no doubt, the knowledge of the methods of critics imparts confidence to the polemist, however it does not guarantee the success. The matter concerns the skills, the sense of the communicative situation, and the tactics of balancing on the verge of the permissible and illicit. The dispute dialectically merges positive and critically negative elements of utterances; the birth and search for the truth takes place in an emotionally strained form. Here one ought to orient himself straight off: at what moment to loosen the opposition and to yield and compromise; where to impose greater demands on the opponent's argumentation, trustworthiness of the adduced facts; what shall one do in case of a psychological barrier, antipathy; and the most important, when to stop, break the monolog and give other person the possibility to express himself and to comprehend his point of view. All this forces one to learn self-regulation. One needs a good practice and regular training.

The table bellow demonstrates the means of verbal opposition in different kinds of dispute.

Kind of dispute	Goal	Argumentation (Proof)	Counter argumentation (Critics)
Apodictic	Truth	Appellation to a fact Conclusions Effective comparison Question – answer step Picking up of an idea Example Deductive conclusion Inductive conclusion Conclusion by analogy Illustration	Revealing of failure to mention Contrast opposition Demonstration of an apparent consequence Skeptic remark Attack by a question Author's comment Reduction to an absurd
Eristic	Consent	Deductive conclusion Inductive conclusion Conclusion by analogy	Raising an alternative Obstruction Reduction to an absurd Critical remarks

		Appellation to facts	Riposte
		Appellation to a person	Psychological
		Appellation to public	aversion
Sophictic	Victory	Sophism Falsification Demagogy Appellation to an interest Misleading Inconsistency Flattery Bluff Substitution for a conception Substitution for a thesis Primitive analogy Speculation in an authority	Taking smb. at smb.'s word Riposte Counter example Anecdote Irony Counter question Killing argument Revealing of weak points Compromise Wrathful rebuff

Speculation in an authority Taking smb. at smb.'s word Riposte Counter example Anecdote Irony Counter question Killing argument Revealing of weak points Compromise Wrathful rebuff

It is very important to emphasize once again that all the above rules of conduct in a discussion have a conditional character, not absolute. Any of them may turn out to be ineffective or just wrong in a concrete situation. Only the communicative environment including the interlocutors' internal world, their system of values and psychological state determine the tactics of a speech conduct.

PART IV

THE TEXT

Chapter 19. **The Text as Sequence of Symbols**

> Eloquence belongs to those arts that make everything and achieve everything by words... Since it collected and holds, as one could say, the powers of all arts.
>
> *Plato*

The text appears as the third level of the communicative four: *goal – – intention – text – reaction.*

This level has a special significance, as it is the first one of the levels given to the man in direct observation. According to the text we reconstruct the speaker's (writer's) intention and goal.

The **text** (in Latin – *textus* means textile, texture, combination) represents a sequence of symbols joined by semantic dependence, the main characteristics of which are coherence and integrity.

The science considers the text as a sensible sequence of any symbols, any form of communication, including ritual, dance and ceremony. However, the man considers the sequence of verbal (wordy) symbols to be the basic. In such a way the natural language gains a special significance among all symbolic systems.

The correctness of a verbal text combination, which can be both oral and written, is connected with the correspondence to the requirement of "textuality" that appears in external coherence, internal intelligence, possibility of modern comprehension, provision for necessary conditions of communication and so on.

The matter of the text identity is essential for both kinds of the text – written and oral. It refers to the so-called canonic form, which is investigated by a special branch of philology – *textology*. The linguistics describes specific means that ensure semantic references in speech: lexical, grammatical and syntactical, for instance, the order in a sentence, inflexional means (for oral speech), special graphical means – underlining, type accentuation, punctuation (for written speech).

The correctness of the text comprehension is ensured not only by linguistic units and their combinations, but the necessary common foundation of knowledge and the communicative background.

The minimal size of a text is a subject of discussion (for instance, is it possible to consider a single communicative remark to be a text).

The possibility of a detailed analysis of a text (belles-lettres, colloquial and etc.) is ensured by considerable scientific achievements in the field of the linguistic system analysis as a text code. The linguistic structure is described through modeling the human linguistic capacity localized in the brain. The text is investigated as "a language in action".

In different countries the text is investigated under different names (text linguistics, hermeneutics and so on), and their ontological statute enables one to say about the necessity of establishing a common theory of the text.

The text (in a linguistic sense) is said to be a sequence of verbal sounds (letters), to which native speakers attribute a certain meaning. It is important to understand that the text is such a sequence of sounds (letters), which is sensible both to the speaker and the listener under the condition of communication, i.e. it is not a casual sequence. There are many definitions of the text (it is with no doubt a polysenic term). The given definition is maximally convenient for comprehension of the communicative functions of speech. Thus, a text can be called the text only if it is comprehensible. Therefore, the classical example «глокая куздра» (it is a senseless phrase that sounds like in Russian, but means nothing, however the words are arranged under the rules of the Russian grammar) "moundness wenker" is not the text, however, if we think it over, we can assume that it is something spoken in Russian, and it may be a combination of an adverb with a noun, and if it is a noun, it may be of the feminine gender, as it agrees with, in particular, by gender with the adverb. Nevertheless, it is unclear what is it and it is not the text by definition. Of course, such a collocation has the right to exist, but it is not the text (at least, it is not the text in the metalanguage, i.e., in the language of description). However, the above-mentioned unclear phrase "Green colorless ideas furiously sleep" (See above) is the text. Though it is hard to catch the combined sense of this phrase, nevertheless, one can present its sensible interpretations, as it consists of such elements, the sense of which individually is clear to Russian native speakers.

Generally speaking, the given definition of the text means that a phrase in a natural language (L) said in a conversation with a foreigner, who does not know the L language, is not the text, however in a conversation with the L native speaker is the text. One and the same set of sounds (letters) can and cannot be the text in different situations. Thus, the definition of the text turns out to be the functional definition, not static; it depends on the speech communicants and the communication as well. The text represents a communicative structure, which is specially designed for comprehension. The language is designed to comprehend the reality and the speech – to transfer information about the results of this comprehension from one man to another. The text appears as realization of the speech function.

The level of the transferred information authenticity is not too significant, since: 1) not the real world, but only its pattern is transferred, stamped in one person's (speaker's) consciousness; 2) physical and psychological losses upon the information transfer always exceed 15 percentage barrier, however, the transferred information is adequately clear to the listener and reader (See above).

It is interesting that all natural languages elaborated a decoding mechanism that renders physical assistance to the people in the text comprehension (decoding). The matter concerns the redundancy of language as the common linguistic universals. Every typology assumes an isomorphism of classified objects, and in this sense the classification of linguistic universals gains a special significance.

Universals (in Latin *universalis* means common, general) as linguistic characteristics inherent in all or many languages appear as the object of investigators' special attention, as their investigation helps one to penetrate into the depth of phenomena that go beyond the framework of natural languages, but belong to the people by nature (See Chapter 6. "Provocative Speech"). It is known that if in a certain classification one and the same characteristic has one and the same significance for all classified elements, it means that it does not belong to the given classification and should be withdrawn from it. Absolute universals shall be withdrawn from linguistic descriptions, as they do not represent the fact of natural languages, but they belong to either the human thinking *ab ovo* or human physiology.

The theory of linguistic universals distinguishes and determines:

1. The common characteristics of all human languages in contrast to the languages of animals. For instance, in a human language the channel for any linguistic communication is audio-vocal; the human language makes it easy to synthesize and comprehend any new information; the human language uninterruptedly originates a new idiomatic and so on.

2. The combination of conceptual categories expressed in every language by these or those means. For instance, every language reflects the relations between the subject and predicate, categories of evaluation, distinctness/uncertainty, plurality; all languages are familiar with the division into the topic and comment (See above).

3. The common characteristics of the linguistic structures that relate to all linguistic levels. For instance, every language can have not less than ten and not more than eighty phonemes; the ratio of the number of vowels to the number of consonants cannot exceed two; if in a language a word is always monosyllabic, then it is isomorphic and this language has a musical stress; if in a language the subject and object go prior to the verb, the language has the case; if in a language the subject goes after the verb and the object goes after the subject, the adjective is placed after the name, and so on.

There are other universals that pertain to all linguistic levels. For instance, a marked member of the sentence distinguished for any contraposition is more infrequent than the unmarked one.

The assertions about the availability of universals can be traced back to ancient grammars. The Middle Ages were marked with the origin of a term *grammatica universalis*; with the appearance of the Port-Royal grammar this definition gains a linguistic basis. Nowadays the expansion of borders of the structural typology, acquaintance with languages (often with no written language) of Africa, Oceania and Latin America helps investigating linguistic universals. In the recent years one can see the conversion of investigators to the text universals and the order of components in syntactic structures. These universals find an explanation in the "world pattern" comprehended through the language.

Upon investigation of universals the reference to their interpretation is of paramount importance. For instance, advancing of important by sense elements to the beginning of a statement is interpreted through greater soundness (and greater perceptibility) of the initial position of the statement; the raise of intonation at the end of a general question is explained by the compression of the speaker's vocal cords, who internally did not finished the communication; the lowering of tone at the end of a statement is explained by the relaxation of the vocal cords. The outcome beyond the limits of the internal system interpretation entails new possibilities in the explanations of the universals actions: social reasons, codification, appearance of written languages and etc. The interpretation and verification of the accumulated universals can facilitate the search for new universals and make it not only empiric, but also a priori.

The universals can belong to one natural language ("for each object of the L language it is fair...") or go beyond the framework of one language.

The universals are divided into deductive and inductive (V. Uspensky). Deductive universals follow from the language assumptions in general, i.e. they relate to the human nature; for instance, the following utterance represents a deductive universal: *Every language has phonemes.*

An inductive universal characteristic assumes that if even a certain symbolic system does not have it, we still can call this system as a language. Inductive universals are postulated empirically, as they do not follow from the initial assumptions. Absolute inductive relations (i.e. such relations, which always take place, but one cannot prove their universal character) deepen the knowledge about the essence of the related phenomena. Analogically, the mathematics have an indefensible rule of four paints stipulating that the geographical map can be painted with four paints in such a way that two adjacent countries will be painted in different colors.

Inductive regularities bear more information about concrete languages than deductive, since they do not follow from anything and not predictable in anyway. Deductive universals are useful, as they are not self-evident.

Empiric (inductive) universals, widening our knowledge about a certain language, present potential facts to allocate deductive rules.

Universals can be absolute (with no exceptions) and static (with exceptions). Both of them can be elementary (a = b) and implicative, demonstrating a hierarchic dependence of the language elements (aab). The following utterance can serve as an example of an implicative universal: *In all languages the nasal phonemes are secondary, they appear only if there are voiced consonants.*

Also compare the following:
CCCV —> CCV —> CV;
VCCC —> VCC —> VC —>V.

The syllables of structures CV and V dominate the rest in the languages.

Or:
Triple —> Dual —> Plural —> Singular
Singular dominates in natural languages.

From the linguistic point of view the implications that disclose exclusive phenomena (additional distribution at the interlinguistic level) are of the paramount interest. Some universals disclose universal characteristics of a static (synchronic) state of the language, others relate to the temporal (diachronic) level of the language development. Thus, a diachronic universal represents a postulate about the constant of the basic vocabulary disintegration. The recognition of universals in the diachronic (for instance, the assertion about the fact that the latest verbal tense in the language is *Futurum*) assumes the acceptance of the idea about the uniderectionality of the language development. The theory of diachronic universals relies on the hypothesis about a system closeness of languages with archaic structures and on the latest variability of new languages. The idea of the uniderectionality of the linguistic evolution does not suppose the evaluation of languages; there is a need for investigations in respect to the compensatory and functionally synonymic phenomena in the languages of the new times. The law of formation of, at first, demonstrative, personal and interrogative pronouns and only then reflexive, possessive, indefinite and negative pronouns, relates to the more frequent diachronic universals. The search for diachronic universals is connected with communicative references of communication, i.e. the theory of universals includes both the man and his evolving standards of communication (T. Ghivon, C.N. Lee, and A. Timberlake). In such a way they assert and explain, for instance, various stages of the verbal tenses appearance (aorist frequently precedes perfect), later appearance of a grammatical subject from the initial theme and so on. Diachronic universals are connected with the change of the native speakers' "world pattern".

The knowledge of diachronic universals clarifies the data of the synchronic typology, thus enabling one to prognosticate the loss of some phenomena and the appearance of other. For instance, an implicative universal ($a \ a \ b$) in a diachronic sense means that if a language has a and it does not have b than one can predict either the loss of a or the appearance of b. The theory of diachronic universals represents a considerable basis for the reconstruction of former states of one language, even a parent language. In the last case it is important to single out the knowledge of universals that belong to ancient structures. Diachronic universals are essential for etymology too.

Only upon a negative test of an analyzed linguistic phenomenon for the statute of a universal one can say about the real similarity, genetic closeness or adoption.

The linguistics divides universals into phonologic (R. Jacobson), grammatical (D. Greenberg), semantic (U. Weinreich), and symbolic (S. Ulmann). The examination of symbolic universals is restricted by a single example: almost in all languages the designation of mother has a resonant consonant (may be it is connected with the sucking movements of a baby, as more habitual to him, and therefore easier upon the pronunciation of the first word, which usually is an appeal to mother).

Universals in a language are distinguished with the use of comparison: 1) with other languages or 2) with the systems of a closer order, for instance, with the communicative systems of animals (C. Hockett). The assertion that the redundancy of every language is approximately equal to 50 percentages, relates to the second type of universals of the general extra linguistic order. This assertion is based on the comparison of languages with other systems of information transfer.

Let us examine the following example in the Russian language: *Молодая девушка сидела на скамейке.* (A young girl was sitting on a bench.) In this phrase the meaning of the feminine gender was transmitted three times: 1) in the ending of the adjective (***молодая***) – young, 2) in the root of the noun (***девушка***) – girl, and 3) in the ending of the verb (***сидела***) – was sitting.

In particular, the redundancy is connected with the so-called obligatory grammatical categorical values, which every native speaker should include into his every statement irrespective his own will. In the Russian language it is not possible to express an adjective and a verb in the past tense without giving additional information about the sex of the subject, expressed as the noun, with which they have a semantic connection, provided this subject is animate (for inanimate subjects this value is called "gender" and appears as a purely syntactic).

In order to check the level of the text redundancy one can make the following experiment: to take any (better typed) text, for instance, an article in a newspaper, and, at first, to wipe out one letter at the end of a certain word; then to show the text with the wiped out letter to any intelligent language speaker with the request to reconstruct the wiped out letter. As a rule, it is an easy job. Then, you have to wipe out one more letter – even the last one (it is not obligatory) in another word and ask another intelligent native speaker to reconstruct the initial text without two letters. It will be also not difficult. You shall repeat this procedure till the moment when there will be so many wiped letters that it will be hard to reconstruct the text. The counting number of the letter, after which lies the misunderstanding, divided into the general number of letters and centupled, will give the percentage of this text redundancy.

In an oral communication the redundancy helps to recognize the essence of speech signals under the conditions of noise interferences, wherein a part of sounds is indiscernible. This linguistic characteristic renders a man a significant communicative assistance.

There are two tendencies working in the process of speech communication: 1) strive for a clear expression of a thought (to be better comprehended); 2) strive for economy of efforts. It is obvious, that the redundancy assumes a polycemy, which results in the availability of lesser number of symbols (as one symbol has several meanings). In this sense the redundancy of speech contributes not only to the first tendency (that is evident), but to the second also.

When recognizing the patterns in a written text, the man have a lesser need in the redundancy, however, one shall remember that the written language is secondary in respect to the oral language, and the language was "created" for the needs of the oral communication; we have only to be amazed by the expediency of its creation.

At all times the issue of the natural language origin agitated the people's brains. Socrates (a hero of Plato's dialog "Kratil") expressed a neutral position in a dispute about the fact whether the language is given to the people by nature or by agreement. The dispute aroused long before the Greeks in a Jewish community. The Bible has a contradiction in this respect: "And the God called the light a day and the darkness – a night (by nature). "And the God brought them (the people) to see how they would call them (by agreement). Stoics (Seneca, Chrysippus) considered that the language is given to the man by nature. In fact, how can one agree upon the language without having it? The evolving theory in this respect looks less convincing. Where is that historical point, before which there was no language, and after which it appeared at one stroke as a system of symbols?

The text is a linearly developed structure. It means, that every following element follows the preceding one. There is no single man, who is able to formulate simultaneously two different senses expressed by different sequences of sounds. The vocal apparatus is constructed in such a way that it can pronounce only one sound in a unit of time; thus, it arranges a sequence of sound with an assigned sense, one after another.

When looking at the text one can easily notice its division, for instance, into words (it is harder to do it in the oral speech, since there is no phonetic pause between some words). The words do not represent the minimal unit of the semantic division (the minimal unit is presented by a morpheme – a significant part of the word: root, suffix, prefix and ending), the words appear as the second from beneath level of the text division into the semantic units. When they say "an articulate speech" (See above) they mean, in particular, the level of the semantic division, i.e. the text division into separate units, each of them is assigned a certain sense. At that all units many times met in other texts.

What do the semantic units, into which the text is divided, represent? They represent symbols.

A symbol appears as a material perceived object, which symbolically and conditionally represents an object, phenomenon, action or event, characteristic, relation or connection, it signals about an object, phenomenon and characteristic, which it designates, and it refers to it.

By materializing mental patterns, the symbol gives the possibility to collect, keep and transmit information. None of the forms of the human activity (including mental) can do without symbols.

Therefore it is clear that even in Ancient Greece such thinkers as Plato, Aristotle. Chrysippus and others were interested in the place and role of symbols in cognitive and practical activity of the people. In the 20-th century all major philosophers, logicians, linguists and culturologists paid attention to the problem of symbols and symbolic systems. The symbol by its sensible obviousness facilitates logical operations. G. Leibniz said about the fact that the people use symbols not only to transfer their thoughts to other people, but also to make the thinking process be more productive. Any operations with symbols should reflect in a symbolic form all permissible conjunctions of the presented objects, at the same time revealing the impossible corresponding combinations. Up to Leibniz when creating symbols one should be governed by two following rules: "first, symbols shall be short and compressed by form and include the maximum sense in the minimum of continuation; second, in an isomorphic way they shall correspond to the designated meanings, deliver simple ideas by as more natural means as possible".

The significant characteristic of a symbol is its ability to symbolically designate not only objects, but the character of operations with these objects too. The science of symbols and symbolic systems is called semiotics (in Greek *sēmeion* means symbol, characteristic). W. Okham and T. Hobbes are considered to be the founders of the semiotics. The semiotics studies the types of symbols, regularities of their combinations in different systems.

The following three fundamental semiotic ideas were formulated in the 19-th century:

1) Absolutely conditional character of the combination between a symbol and the designated (concept, object);

2) Identity and difference of symbols, detachment of the language as a special type of symbols;

3) Communicative function as the most important function of symbols, in general.

At that time the semiotics developed within the framework of the logics and physiology. An ideologist of American pragmatism C. Piers is considered to be the founder of the science of symbolic systems. He proposed the following concept of a symbol. The logics deal with expressions, which true sense depends on the choice of appropriate symbols that represent the means of expression. C. Piers saw the main function of a symbol, with a certain thing as its object, in the quantification ("framing") of the experience. He assumed the relation between a symbol and logical operations of the investigating subject as the basis of the concept of *meaning*. The relation of symbols to objectively real objects is mediated by the consciousness. A symbol refers to its relation to the meaning, i.e. to that which exists in the consciousness as to basic. The unity of a symbol and its meaning composes a necessary condition of communication, as symbols can serve for the process of the thoughts exchange only upon the availability of the meanings that are clear and comprehensible to those, who communicate. Symbols should be perceived directly by those, whom they are assigned to. C. Piers constructed a system that includes sixty types of symbols divided into ten classes. Every expression is made on the basis of choosing this or that combination of symbols from the system. The symbols are determined irrespective to a concrete system; therefore every system includes all sixty types of symbols. "A symbol or its substitution is something that substitutes for something in somebody's favor in respect to a certain relation or characteristic" (C. Piers).

Another scientist, who laid the foundation for the semiotics, was a German philosopher and logician E. Husserl. He proposed the concept of "Expression" and "Meaning" (which was reflected in works of F. Saussure – a founder of the modern structural linguistic) – in terms *"plan of expression and plan of content"* that later on was literally perceived by L. Hjelmslev, the leader of the Copenhagen school of structuralism (glossematics).

Husserl's teaching about the expression and meaning and Piers' determination of a symbol as the relation represent two principles that underlie the theory of semiotics constructed by the philosophical and linguistic thought.

Right after Piers, an American philosopher C. Morris formulated the basic conceptions and principles of the semiotics. The meaning appears as a component of an experience designated by symbol M. It is composed from the following "modi":

1. M_f – relation of symbols in the system (syntactic);
2. M_e – relation of a symbol to an object of perception (semantic);
3. M_p – relation of a symbol to the bearer (pragmatic).

In general view: $M = M_f + M_f + M_p$.

In accordance with one of the concepts (I. Narsky) the relation of symbols to objects and processes should be necessarily mediated by the consciousness, as genetic and hormone structures and processes are interpreted as symbolic relations. Both the material and the meaning of a symbol can be either material or ideal. However, the opinion about the symbol as a material object, which the people attribute a certain meaning to is more diffused.

In such a case the symbol is understood as a product of the people's intellectual activity. There is a common conclusion that the symbol has such a characteristic as "to possess" or "to include" a meaning. At that one ought to notice the fact that the semantic criterion of the symbol is not argued. From the standpoint of the symbol's material nature and, consequently, the absolute conditional character of the symbol and its meaning, the problem of these two conceptions' interrelation appears as a principal problem of the semiotic theory.

There is such a point of view that the meaning is a non-semiotic category, in particular, non-linguistic by its nature, and it appears as one of the specific functions of thinking or one of its material processes. At that they usually adduce a counter argument that the polycemy of a word exists only in the combination of real contexts, provided each of them appears as a separate meaning of the word. Since one cannot analyze all contexts, then the description of the general meaning of a linguistic unit looks subjective.

In the framework of this concept the traditional problem of the language and thinking interrelation at the modern level can be interpreted as the problem of two material structures interrelation – the language as a system of symbols, which accomplishes a communicative function, (plan of expression) and the mental activity – a system of neurons and their relations, which accomplishes the function of the human organism control. Consequently, a linguistic symbol does not include the meaning, which appears as a factor of the consciousness and represents a common object of investigation by the linguistics, logics and psychology. The symbol is connected with the meaning historically and synchronically. It determines the linguistic aspect of the meaning, as a special, but not closed problem. The meaning can be determined as the relation of the thinking to the system of material symbols that represent the basis for the analyzing and generalizing activity of the consciousness. Functionally, the language as a system of material symbols appears only as an impulse that agitates a similar thought (meaning), which the man develops in the direct relation to his personality.

G. Frege considered that under the symbol one can understand a certain designation, which appears as a specific name, consequently, its meaning relates to a certain object, not to a certain conception or relation.

The meaning of a name is such an object (*denotatum*), which is designated (called) by this name.

The sense of a specific name can be described as such information, such facts, which are included in the name and the comprehension of the name by a man appears as the comprehension of this information.

"A specific name (symbol, combination of symbols) expresses its sense, designates or means its meaning. With the use of this symbol we express its sense and designate its meaning" (G. Frege).

In addition to specific names that designate objects (Aristotle, Morning Star, etc.) Frege singled out functional names – designations of functions and conceptual names – designations of conceptions and characteristics.

One ought to separate the meaning and sense of a symbol from the conception connected with the symbol. If the meaning of a specific name is a perceived object, then the conception of a man about this object represents an inner pattern that originated from the remembrances of the former perceptible impressions. The sense of a symbol radically differs from the conception evoked by this symbol, in the fact that it can be a common property of many people and, consequently, it is not a modus of a single sole.

The relation between the name and the designated object (in the given language) is used to call as the relation of denomination. Its essence lies in the fact that one and the same object can have different names, however, the given name shall be the name of a single object. The connection that, as a rule, exists between the symbol, its sense and meaning, appears in such a way that a certain sense corresponds to the symbol, a certain meaning corresponds to this sense, and at the same time not only one symbol corresponds to one meaning (one object – denotatum).

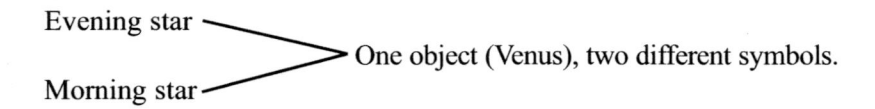

Evening star ⟶
                  ⟶ One object (Venus), two different symbols.
Morning star ⟶

The sense of a name can be considered as the expressed (assigned to it by linguistic means) information about an object that identically characterizes this object.

One ought to emphasize that the comprehension of the name's sense does not guarantee the fact that it's meaning is obvious. The analysis of the name's sense does not always enables one to determine its sense. More over, the name's sense does not determine the existence of the object. The following expression: the slowest convergent series has a certain sense; however, it was proved that this expression is senseless, as for every convergent series there is one slower convergent, but still convergent series. It follows that if we understand the sense, it does not mean that we have the meaning.

Logical and formal languages require that every expression made from the earlier deduced symbols in a grammatically correct form in the capacity of a specific name should actually designate an object, and no symbols should be introduced in the capacity of a specific name, if it does not have the ensured meaning.

In mathematics all righteously made symbols shall designate something.

The mathematical logics call the rules, which provide every righteously made name in its calculation with a certain definite meaning, semantic.

One and the same name in one and the same natural language can have different senses. Both ambiguity and polycemy are widespread in natural languages. It is all very well if a certain name used in different contexts has only one meaning (denotatum). One and the same sense can be expressed by different names. The names, which express the similar sense (in the logics – absolutely similar), i.e. synonyms, have the similar meaning (denotatum).

In natural languages personal names are divided into simple and complicative (compound). This division is kept in formalized languages too. A complicated name is such a name that consists of sensible parts; sensible parts pertain to both personal names, and designations of conceptions, logical connectives and other expressions. A name, included into the composition of another name, is called a component name. For instance, the composition of the following name: *Tutor of Alexander, the Great and Plato's pupil* (1) includes the component names *Plato* and *Alexander, the Great*. Not all complicated name has component names, as the following name: *the one who discovered an elliptic form of planets* does not have any component names.

Simple names are not composed of sensible elements. They can be included into the composition of other names, but they contain no names. The examples of similar (elementary) names are as follows: Aristotle, Venus.

An elementary name ad arbitrium designate a certain object. A person, who gives a name, has a right to attribute this or that symbol to the named object – its name. A complicated name designates an object not under the people's will, but due to the sense, which it parts have. However, one ought to remember that the breach of rules, under which a certain name is constructed, can also deprive it of its sense. For instance, if in (1) one places the AND connective to the beginning, the sense will be lost. It means that not every sequence of sensible utterances in the given language appears as a sensible utterance in another language. Every language has the rules of sensible utterances formation; these rules are included in the language grammar. In practice senseless utterances of a natural language are easily distinguished from sensible ones by means not only of grammatical rules, but also with the use of the general context of the speech and situation.

The rules of sensible utterances formation in the formalized languages shall be strictly formulated.

So, the sense of its parts and the character of those rules, under which it is constructed, determine the sense of a complicated name. If one considers that its linguistic character determines the sense of every part, and its grammatical structure fixes the rules under which the name is constructed, then it will be clear that the sense of a name is expressed by the language means and only by the language means.

The sense shall be given in a symbol – in its form, structure and the character of its parts. Since where can we get information about the denotatum?

Names can have a various structure, which, nevertheless, does not affect the sense:

2^2 and $(-2)^2$.

There is no formal method that enables one to solve the problem of the equality of any two names' senses in respect of a wide circle of languages. It can be done owing to the native speaker's intuition.

Even in a strictly formal linguistic model of I. Mel'čuk: *Sense – Text* the sense of a text is determined as a common sense of synonymic changes of this text, however, the problem whether two texts (sentences) are synonymic, or not shall be resolved intuitively.

As to the sense of elementary names like Aristotle and Venus there are different points of view.

1. These names have no sense, though they have a meaning, as they do not express any characteristics, which can belong to these objects (D. Mille)

2. An elementary name informs about the object that it is called by its name. It is its sense. The knowledge about the object's name is still certain knowledge (A. Church).

Let Z be a symbol for P. To the question of what is the objective meaning of symbol Z, the investigator should indicate what does this symbol designate (what object). The meaning (i.e. objective meaning) of symbol Z is not object P, not thoughts, which can appear in the investigator's head upon handling *Z*, but only that which it designates *P* and the investigator knows it. The meaning is not a simple naming, it is a predicate introduced as an abridgement of a certain situation description, which uses symbols.

The symbol has a meaning only if one can choose (perceptibly) or indicate with the use of other symbols at least one object from the multitude of objects that corresponds to this symbol. If it is impossible, the symbol does not have any meaning. There are known cases, wherein a certain object *Z* appears as a symbol for some objects from the standpoint of some investigators, and as a symbol for other objects from the standpoint of other investigators. In such cases they say about the polycemy of a symbol. In such cases the logics consider that they use different symbols, as every symbol has one and only one meaning.

3. A natural language can have different opinions about the sense of such names, for instance, as a sense of name *Aristotle* one can take the following: *Plato's pupil* and *tutor of Alexander, the Great*. However, every man using such a name shall relate a certain sense to it; the fact that different people will mean different senses won't lead to misunderstanding, till they assume one and the same object. Any fluctuations in sense are not admissible upon the arrangement of a science and they should not appear in a formal language.

If one substitutes the name that has the same meaning as of the substituted one for one of the component names, included in the given complicated name, then the complicated name resulted in such a substitution will have such a meaning that will coincide with the meaning of the initial complicated name. Thus, if in (1) (*tutor of Alexander. The Great and Plato's pupil*) *Plato* will be substituted for the identical name *the founder of the Academy*; the meaning of the new complicated name will coincide with the meaning (1).

As to the sense of the complicated name that we get after such a substitution, one cannot tell anything definite: it can and cannot coincide with the sense of the initial name. In our example the sense will differ. However, if we take the newly obtained example and substitute the name *the one who founded the Academy* for *the founder of the Academy*, the sense won't change.

The sense of a complicated name does not depend on the meaning of the component names. "When a component name is substituted for a name with other meaning, then the newly obtained complicated name may have the same or different meaning, however the sense of the new name will be always different" (G. Frege).

A complicated symbol represents an ordered with space and time collection of distinctly localized symbols.

Simple symbols are invariable; nevertheless what kind of combinations and relations they get into. Simple symbols are combined into the complicated ones under definite rules, and a complicated symbol has something that indicates to them: closeness and order of symbols in space and time, as well as some other additional objects that constitute a certain physical whole with the combined symbols. These additional objects can be called symbol-making operators. For instance, from symbols *a number* and *is divided into two* a symbol-making operator *that* will make a new symbol: *a number that is divided into two*.

Symbol-making operators are always exactly localized and evident in a complicated symbol.

The symbols that are made through the combination with other symbols can be divided into two groups:

1) Symbols, the meaning of which is known if the meaning of the symbols from which they are made is known;

2) Symbols, the meaning of which is not possible to determine, if one knows only the meaning of those symbols from which they are made.

In both cases the rules of the symbols combination are supposed to be known.

For instance, the following words: *kilogram-meter* and *dynamometer* are made, each of them, from different words. However, the first one designates the result of some operations of measuring and multiplication of values, and the second – a device used to measure some values. This meaning of them is hardly possible to determine, if one knows only the meaning of the component parts and the corresponding rule of formation.

Thus, one ought to distinguish:

1) The rules of symbols combination into new symbols that do not depend on the peculiarities of these or those symbols as material bodies, and which enable one to get the symbols of the first group;

2) The rules of symbol combination as special material bodies (sounds, lines on paper and so on).

The above given words are made under the rule of the second group.

Considering all the above-said one can make the following definition: symbols are called structurally-complicated (simple) if they are divided (not divided) into other symbols and symbol-making operators.

Symbols and symbol-making operators are in definite order ranked in a complicated symbol; however, usually the symbol does not reflect this. Every symbolic system has its own means used to organize simple symbols into more complicated.

It is a complicated and unelaborated matter (G. Frege has an interesting point of view, See bellow); therefore it is accepted to recognize the following assumptions:

1) To determine the meaning of a complicated symbol it is enough to know the meaning of all component simple symbols and the characteristics of all component operators (it is not true for a native language, therefore the meaning of a syntactic is introduced into the linguistic symbol);

2) If this method does not help to determine the meaning of a symbol, this symbol is recognized as simple by structure.

A complicated symbol can be identical by meaning to the component simple symbol.

For instance, let's use a special operator to construct from the following symbols: *a table* and *a writing-table* such a complicated symbol, which can designate both tables and writing-tables. This symbol will be identical by meaning to the symbol of *a writing-table*.

But, for instance, a complicate symbol constructed with the use of the same operator from the symbols of *a scientist* and *a sportsman* won't be identical by meaning to any of them.

Symbol Z_1 depends by meaning on symbol Z_2, if one ought to know the meaning of Z_2 to determine the meaning of Z_1.

The significate (or significant) X of a symbol is called the representable through the significates (or significants) of other symbols ($X^1, ..., X^n$), if X can be written as a result of the combination (of logical sum) operation applied to objects $X^1, ..., X^n$.

Symbol Z is quasi-representable through symbols $Z^1, ..., Z^n$, if: its significate is representable through the significates of these symbols, and its significant is not representable through the significants of these symbols (upon the simultaneous observation of the following conditions: a) even one of the significates of symbols $Z^1, ..., Z^n$ is regular in the given language; b) this language does not have symbol Z^p that is representable through symbols $Z^1, ..., Z^n$) or 2) its significate is not representable through the significates of these symbols, and its significant is representable through the significants of these symbols.

A symbol is called elementary if it is neither representable, nor quasi-representable through other symbols.

A morph can serve for an example of an elementary symbol.

A non-elementary symbol can be one of the next three types:

a) A symbol representable through other symbols – a free symbolic complex (multitude of symbols, on the basis of which the hierarchy of relations is given, i.e. the multitude of symbols that has a certain organization), for instance, a non-idiomatic derived basis; a word-form that consists of more than one morph;

b) A symbol that is quasi-representable under the significant through other symbols – idiomatic symbolic complex;

c) A symbol that is quasi-representable under the significate through other symbols (I. Mel'čuk).

The most diffused point of view attributes the meaning to the linguistic category that is determined as a phenomenon of the objective reality reflection by the consciousness. This concept follows from the definition of a language as a means of a thought expression, which lays a logical foundation to include the meaning into the nature of a symbol. A symbol is represented as a cover of the meaning, sense and content. The relation between a symbol and meaning is formulated as the inseparably whole.

One of the options of this concept appears as an idea about the fact that a language shall be determined as an immanent system that exists in itself and for itself; a symbol is principally separated from its material equivalent (sound, i.e. an elastic sound wave, letter, i.e. a light quantum) only by the fact that a symbol by its nature and functioning in the system appears as an objective bearer of the meaning. A symbol is characterized by its meaning, and its nature is entirely exhausted by a semiotic aspect. The semantic is determined as an independent (but linguistic) system, i.e. "a system in a system". This point of view was founded by F. Saussure, who determined the meaning as a special and pure "value" (significance) that belongs to not the material speech, but to a psychic language, in which the natural data does not have any place and which is determined by nothing, except "pure values" (significances) that are included into the language system.

Saussure found the analogy between the category of a meaning in semiotic systems and A. Smith's idea about two kinds of value. As it is known, commodities can have both *a concrete use value* that is included in the unique material quality of the given commodity and in the fact that it can be consumed (eaten, drunk, taken on and so on), and *an abstract exchange value* that is determined by the relation of this commodity to other commodities.

By analogy with the above said, one can single out two meanings in a symbol:

a) Concrete, determined by unique qualities of the given symbol as a separate phenomenon (for instance, such are the meanings of words written in explanatory dictionaries; however abstract are these meanings, they appear as concrete words-symbols, as they can be described by ordinary dictionary methods);

b) Abstract, determined relatively, i.e. by the relation of the given word to all other words of the language (practically to all words of the same linguistic group). When describing a language as a symbolic system, at first, one ought to determine " a relative meaning" of every element (calling it "meaning", "value", "significance" or "concept"), and only then determine to what phenomenon of the outer world beyond the language (denotatum) this element is attributed by our consciousness.

For instance, a Russian word *green* has the following concept: "one of the seven colors of the solar spectrum between yellow and blue"; in order to explain "denotatum" one ought to indicate a certain object of green color. It is interesting that explanatory dictionaries usually do in this way: "green pertains to the color of grass, leaves and greens" (D. Ushakov).

The problem of meaning plays a leading role in the theory of translation, as the meaning of every linguistic symbol can be also understood as its translation to another alternative symbol.

There are three types of translation:

1) Intralinguistic, i.e. the interpretation of wordy symbols with the use of the same language's symbols;

2) Interlinguistic – the translation in its true sense, i.e. interpretation of wordy symbols through wordy symbols of other language;

3) Intersemiotic, i.e. the interpretation of wordy symbols through the symbols of nonverbal symbolic systems (text a cinematography)

Is it possible to translate a text of one symbolic system into a text of another symbolic system? Will this translation be adequate, for instance, to the interpretation of a work of art to the language of cinema? There is no single-value answer to the question about the adequacy of the intersemiotic translation (See above). However, one can lay down the ways of solution in this respect, if the translation is considered as a sequence of two procedures: 1) analysis of the initial text in order to clarify the sense; 2) transfer of the sense by means of another semiotic system.

The majority of scientists considers symbol Z in an inseparable conformity of its two sides: plan of content (the significate as *signifie "X"*) and plan of expression (the significant as *significant "X"*), wherein the first designates the sense, i.e. all that is informed by the symbol, any information transmitted or interpreted; the second means an outer substance that a man can perceive by his analyzers.

Two sides of a symbol cannot be divided in the same way as we cannot divide the right and the backside of a sheet. A circle represents the symbol's scheme with a line drawn along the diameter.

$$\frac{\text{Significate}}{\text{Significant}}$$

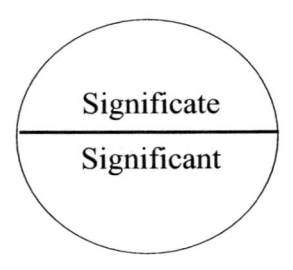

Natural languages in respect to the symbol determination differ from all other symbolic systems by the fact that they determine the symbol not as the dual: *significate – significant*, but as a well-ordered triple:
$$Z = < X, \text{``X''}, ?x >,$$
wherein under ?x one ought to understand the syntactic – the aggregate of such facts about any possible combinations of the dual *significate – significant* with all other similar duals, and about the "conduct" of the significants in these combinations, which cannot be fully derived from the significant or the significate. In other words, the syntactic describes a non-standard compatibility (I. Mel'cuk). The examples of typical components of the syntactic are as follows: part of speech, grammatical noun genders or government of verbs (in such a language as Russian), type of declension or conjugation, indication of interchanges.

There are evident correlations between the syntactic, on the one hand, and the significant and significate, on the other. Thus, in the French language, the noun gender depends on the phoneme content of the basis: the bases ended by a voiced consonant are mainly related to the feminine gender. At the same time in many languages the noun gender depends also on the sense: in particular, the names of the feminine gender nouns usually pertain to the feminine gender and so on. Nevertheless, such correlations, as a rule, have a static character, not absolute. Let us compare two commonly known German words: "das Weib" (a woman) and "das Mдdchen" (a girl), which relate to the neuter gender. Such examples do not hamper the principal delimitation of the syntactic as an aggregate of facts about the non-standard and unpredictable compatibility.

There are following examples of linguistic symbols: morphs, word-forms, and syntagmas.

There are following examples of main types of linguistic non-symbols: sounds and phonemes, as they do not have the significate; semes, as they do not have the significant. L. Hjelmslev called sounds, phonemes and semes as the figures.

Morphemes and lexemes are not symbols; they are multitudes of symbols.

Artificial formal symbolic systems – like languages of the mathematical logics or programming – practically do not have any syntactic. The rules of symbol combination in these languages, i.e. composition of correct utterances, are formulated exclusively on the basis of these symbols' semantic content. Thereby, all the compatibility in artificial formal languages appears as standard, i.e. semantically conditioned.

The semiotics as a science develops in various directions. The first direction investigates the systems based on the natural, i.e. significant for the existence of an organism, biologically relevant symbols (biosemiotics). As to the starting point, the biosemiotics investigates the systems of animals' communication. It relies on the biology in general (Hockett, Zhinkin and others). The second direction is aimed at the anthropology and ethnography, i.e. it investigates primitive and highly organized societies, social psychology, philosophy and literature (ethno semiotics; Levi-Strauss, Lotman, Foucault and others). The third direction studies the natural language and investigates other symbolic systems, since they: a) are functioning in parallel with the speech (paralinguistic, i.e. Body Language; See above); b) compensate the speech (expressive stylistic intonation, typographic types); c) modify its functions and its symbolic character (for instance, an eloquent speech). This direction also studies various families of artificial languages (informational, informational-logical, programming and others) and deals with the problems of modeling natural languages (linguasemiotics). The fourth direction studies only the most common characteristics and relations that characterize symbolic systems irrespective of their material realization. The most abstract, logical-mathematical theory of symbolic systems is created within the framework of this direction; therefore it can be called as an abstract semiotics. (Carnap, Gorsky and others).

In principle, one could also emphasize the fifth direction, which deals with the semiotics due to the relation with the cybernetics and the theory of information. This section could be called as a cybernetic semiotics; however, it is probably a section of the cybernetics.

We will generally discuss the provisions of the fourth and the third direction in the semiotics' development, i.e. the general semiotics and linguasemiotics, as the most important for the comprehension of the speech communication bases.

However, the area of the semiotics' investigation as a science includes any symbolic systems that have various material natures and affect different analyzers in the perception.

1) Sound (oral speech, music, Morse code and so on); perceiving analyzer – aural;

2) Graphics (alphabet, painting, photography, stenography, general scientific symbols, notes, topographic maps, hieroglyphs and etc.); perceiving analyzer – visual;

3) Movements (dance, BL, language of deaf-and-dumb people, positions of a traffic controller's hands and etc.); perceiving analyzer – visual;

4) Smell (perfume and etc.); perceiving analyzer – olfactory;

5) Color (white color is perceived by Moslems as a symbol of death, as to Christians the same function is performed by black color; traffic lights and etc.); perceiving analyzer – visual;

6) Shape (correlation of embossment and hollows of the blind people alphabet and etc.); perceiving analyzer – tactile;

7) Objects (a fur tree in a European house in December as a symbol of Christmas, wedding ring as a symbol of faithfulness and etc.); perceiving analyzer – visual;

8) Material (gold as a symbol of wealth, clothes of black leather with metal rivets as a symbol of a membership of a hard rock or heavy metal lovers' club and etc.); perceiving analyzer – visual;

9) Deed (a wedding ceremony as a symbol of promise to marry and etc.); there can be different perceiving analyzers, however, the main one is the visual.

Let us make some comments.

1. What is a significate of a work of arts (in particular, painting) as a symbol? When looking at a painting, made in a realistic manner, it becomes clear that the painting, as a rule, resembles the painted object, the natural life. Abstract paintings to a minimal degree resemble objects, which the painter tried to paint. However, it is obvious, that any art represents a symbolic system.

Consequently, the determination of fine arts does not include the resemblance criteria. A man, who painted an elephant, which resembles the original too much, does not make a work of art. A photo, if it reproduces the natural life and nothing else, is not an art (for instance, a passport photo). A painting's material element consists of a set of colors and lines, however they symbolize not a concrete object, but the internal world of the man, who makes a work of art, to be more precise, an image in the consciousness of this man that is associatively connected with a concrete object, event and so on. For instance, there is a house on the picture – it symbolizes an associative conception about the house; it can be a resemblance of the childhood, nostalgic feelings and so on, i.e. that state of the soul, which felt by the painter, when he worked over the painting. It becomes absolutely evident, say, in "Prado", the national museum of paintings and sculptures in Madrid, which exhibits the largest collection of paintings that belong to the greatest Spanish painter, who suffered from schizophrenia, F. Goya. The composition is well thought; at the first floor there are paintings of a court painter, a respectful, quiet, self-confident; at the basement – the paintings of a man, who suffers from schizophrenia with the "shifted" consciousness that is symbolized by the following phrase: "a dream of the consciousness gives birth to monsters". Even without looking narrowly at the subject of paintings, the spectator understands that these two expositions represent two different states of the painter's psychic, two different internal worlds, as if there were two different men – healthy and sick (F. Goya's psychic disease became apparent in his middle age, when he was a matured and famous painter). The painter, by itself, his personality, the system of his intellectual and perceptible associations, all this appears as the sense of his paintings.

Let us compare two painters, who painted from nature – I. Shishkin and van Gogh. When you look at the works of Shishkin, it is clear to you that they symbolize a forest; they appear as concrete paintings of a pine forest (associatively connected with the light, sounds and smells, which a man perceives when he walks in a forest). If you look at a bunch of flowers, painted by van Gogh, it is clear that it symbolizes not a concrete bunch of flowers, but it symbolizes a certain state, which was cast over the painter (probably by the flowers, but it is not necessarily) and which he transferred through his painting. Therefore the works of Shishkin canonically is not considered to be painting, and the author is called "a draftsman" or a photographer; but no one will risk calling the works of van Gogh inartistic (today, van Gogh is the most "dear" painter of the world: his paintings are evaluated at fabulous prices).

Any work of art's plan of content appears as a definite block of consciousness (or unconsciousness) of the author.

For instance, music expresses one's mood, i.e. the author's mood and his psychic state at that time when he wrote a musical phrase represent the meaning of this phrase. This state can be expressed in a better or worse way, i.e. to a different stage of adequacy, and, thus, the listener comprehends it in a better or worse way having a freedom to do his own interpretations. Nevertheless, there are quite a few people, who can interpret a bravura, gala music as a funeral and sad. Usually, a man, who wrote music, quite adequately expresses his psychic state.

It is important to understand that the plan of symbols content in arts is not represented by denotatums, but by consciousness and unconsciousness patterns in the brain of a concrete man as the reflection of his individual world perception, i.e. an emanation of an individual's psychic activity.

If it is so, then there is no basis to consider that arts should be realistic, i.e. addressed to that concrete (thing, man, event, etc.), which casts this mood. This concrete should not be necessarily painted to express one's inner state. The painter can paint only lines and spots; there is no difference. In this respect the works of van Gogh do not differ from absolutely abstract works of V. Kandinsky: they both express the painter's inner state. In the first case the painter as if makes like a re-addressing through the denotatum, at that van Gogh's denotatum is consciously wrong: the painter as if "misleads" his spectator; it is felt that his "real" flowers absolutely "have nothing to do with it"; other painters may have more adequate re-addressing (for instance, it pertains to O. Renoir), in this case the painter as if helps the spectator, prompts to him, therefore, the more realistic is the painting, the easier it is perceived, especially, by an untrained spectator. Kandinsky does not have such a re-addressing.

The value of a work of art depends on the profundity of the author's inner world and on the way of its expression: whether one can or cannot comprehend it.

Of course, in case of abstract arts, the spectator has a need in the knowledge about the fact, how the concrete painter interprets definite lines or colors (i.e. the painter's "vocabulary"). Sometimes, such a vocabulary constitutes a basis of the whole group of painters' memorandum (for instance, the painters that belong to a vanguard direction of suprematism headed by K. Malevitch).

It is not possible to divide a painting into elementary symbols. Thus, a picture is not a text or we can say that it is a text that consists of one symbol.

So, semiotic systems are also divided according to the possibility/impossibility of information transfer with the use of linearly well-ordered symbols in the text.

If one analyzes a single author's collected works (for instance, all paintings of a painter or all musical compositions of a composer), does he have any bases to assume that the significate of this aggregate symbol reflects the whole inner world of the author? Does the sequence of all paintings of one painter exhibited in a gallery appear as a text composed of many symbols? This question requires a thorough analysis. On the one hand, it seems that every following painting transmits something new in the painter's psychological state and his inner world and this world is fully expressed only in the aggregate of his paintings. Then the exhibition of paintings appears as a text divisible into symbols. However, there is another point of view: a painter always paints one and the same state, which is typical to him as a personality (A. Zholkovsky). Then, going from one painting to another, you do not get any new information; you can get only the same information transmitted in a more effective way. This interpretation does not consider the exhibition of paintings to be an articulate text.

2. What is the significate for the smell? There are some certain details that are not comprehended by the majority of people. For instance, a smell of perfumes. Of course, it is a symbol. What sense can a smell have, in particular, a smell of perfume? A mood, a state of soul. Hence, one can make a conclusion that the perfume exists to influence not so much on other people (as it is customary to think), as on one self: they form that state of soul, which the man wants to feel. Different perfumes form different states. One class of perfumes stimulates an erotic state. There are perfumes, which stimulate one's aggressiveness (a man scented with such perfumes starts feeling this emotion, which he needs, say, for a talk with another person). There are perfumes that stimulate one's relaxation, meditation and thoughtful mood. A large group of perfumes represents a dope for one's nervous system (a man scented with such perfumes feels "competitive spirit", he feels a special sort of energy, which enables him to function actively). This smell as if stimulates his "paddy walk" for a day.

Every man chooses perfumes in a different way:

1) He can change them depending on his state, which he wants to arouse; then he changes them within a day and perfumes slightly in order to smell the order only by himself; 2) He can disclose he main characteristic of his personality or its typical state through the perfume; from this point of view the perfumes symbolize his inner world and make a certain image. In the second case the man chooses such a perfume, which provokes his self-realization; the surrounding people perceive this smell as his personal symbol and they receive information about the kind of personality and what it wants to pretend to be. Such a perfume is more communicatively arranged. One ought to emphasize one more time that the smell appears not only as a symbol of one's psychophysical state – it puts the man into the state that it symbolizes. In this case the symbol provokes the state, not the state determines the symbol. In this sense smells remind the symbols of BL, which upon their conscious realization puts the man into a certain emotion (see bellow).

There are smells, which appear as a consequence of concrete events, for instance, a smoke – a symbol of a campfire (see bellow).

3. What is the significate of a ceremony or ritual as a culturological symbol? Partially, the answer to this question was given in Chapter 5 "Ritual Speech". The people's culture appears as a well-ordered symbol-

ic system that to a certain extent is analogical to the linguistic system.

Fixing the common in different symbolic systems the semiotics determines the common relation between the organizational principals of:
    a) Language;
    b) Material culture;
    c) Spiritual culture.

However, one ought to emphasize one specific of culturological languages. Native speakers do not identify the meaning of many of them, as the symbols were formed historically. For instance, nowadays not every girl knows that the bridal veil symbolizes the bride's virginity. Nevertheless, practically always the brides wear the veil at their wedding, even if it is not the first. It means that the people can use symbols without any understanding of their meaning.

When performing a ritual the modern people quite often do not understand it's meaning either as a whole, or partially. For instance, some religious orthodox rituals (Eucharist, anointing and etc.) performed by all the faithful in the church exemplify the fact that the absence of erudition in the theological sphere has practically an almost total character. The collocation a *sacrament of Eucharist* or *a sacrament of penitence* stops being a metaphor, it can be understood in its direct meaning. It is the character of culturological symbols; it is the semiotics of a special order connected with the necessity of the joined existence in the framework of a certain culture. The speaker can hardly use the symbols of other semiotic systems, for instance, the natural language (words), the meaning of which is not clear.

4. Another symbol can appear in the capacity of the significate symbol.

Notes – represent a graphical system that expresses sounds: it is a musical alphabet. The alphabet of blind people in the same way, as an ordinary graphical alphabet and a part of symbols pertaining to the language of deaf-and-dumb people, symbolizes the sounds of speech.

Some symbols of the deaf-and-dumb people's speech designate the whole conception, i.e. they appear as an analogy of a hieroglyph. Thus, the language of deaf-and-dumb people is combined. Such a symbol as watches is also a combined symbol. The watches designate time through changing of the arrows position: the moving picture symbolizes the time flow. It resembles the cinematograph that symbolizes the development of events or the changing of the heroes' hearts state.

Of course, different types of symbols came to existence for that only purpose as to specialize a means of communication in different various spheres of the human activity.

It follows from the symbol definition that if a certain object is considered to be a symbol (i.e. it is called a symbol), then there should be a possibility to choose another object that it designates. There is no significant without the significate, as like one man can be considered a chief only if another man can be called his subordinate.

In addition to the fact that symbols stay in correspondence with the designated objects, they also have other characteristics, however, they are taken in the capacity of symbols exclusively from the standpoint of their place in this correspondence. Not any, but only those objects that suit well this objective are chosen for the role of symbols. Everybody knows that it is quite an easy job to repeat a word and words are the cheapest thing in the world.

The designated objects can be non-existent and inaccessible to the direct comprehension. However, symbols shall represent the objects, which can be directly perceived by those people, whom they are assigned, i.e. they shall exist empirically and be accessible to the eyes, ears, tastes and smell.

The objects turn out to be symbols not due to any circumstances that are inherent in them, but under the will and desire of the investigator. At that, in order to make an object be considered a symbol, it is necessary to have consent of many people; the will of a single man is not enough. As everything in the world, symbols are not eternal. When conditions change, an accepted symbol can be eliminated or changed into a more convenient one. The people's objective need gives birth to every symbol.

Symbols differ from the objects' perceptible images: the latter appear as the investigator's state, and the first exist by themselves. The aggregate of symbols and their operating rules form a symbolic (or artificial) apparatus of reflection, however, probably, it cannot exist without a natural apparatus of reflection.

The determination of a symbol and comprehension of the correspondence entail the fact that an object cannot symbolize itself. There are some cases, wherein the difference of the designated objects and their symbols is a quite delicate work, however, in all cases such a difference can be determined.

As it was previously said, every symbolic system includes three levels: syntactic, semantic and pragmatic.

1. Syntactic level (syntactics) represents the interrelation of symbols, i.e. it is an inner structure of a symbolic system irrespective of its functions. At the syntactic level we do not know the list of symbols, but we know well what to do with them. For instance, we have the rules of construction of complicated symbols from simple ones.

2. Semantic level represents the relation of symbols to those things,

which they designate; at this level symbolic systems are considered as a means of the sense expression; and herein one makes their semantic interpretation.

3. Pragmatic level represents the relation of symbols to those, who use them. At this level one considers a symbolic system in relation to the speaker and listener; at this level the semiotics deals with the laws that depend on the observer's position; for instance, it considers modal aspects of the language that express the speaker's relation to the utterances (can, should and so on), as well as the imperative logics connected with the orders (imperative mode).

One ought to specify that a language as a system of symbols knows only two components: syntactics and semantics. The third dimension – pragmatics – adds the speech as a communicative structure.

The main problem of the linguistics is formulated as a necessity to penetrate into the structure of thinking though the comprehension of the language structure (i.e. to model it; See above). One ought to construct such a theory of language and thinking that make the provisions in respect of these two objects accessible to an experimental test. The linguistics represents an essential part of the modern psychology of perception, which tries to rely on experimental facts. G. Piaget wrote: "An intellect represents a system of operations, which result in the construction of an internal model of the outer world. This system of operation has a certain purposefulness that is dictated by the situation in the surrounding environment". In the speech this purposefulness gains its maximally explicit expression.

The development of the human thinking and language appears as the development of their operational structures. There is such a point of view that the inner model of the world, which is constructed by each of us, reflects those regularities and phenomena that a man meets in his life. Then the human mind and thought appear as a more or less complete reflection of the regularities that exist in the world.

In accordance with the opposite point of view, the ignorance of things leads to the development of logics and the development of logics leads to the cognition of things. An experience appears as just a condition for the development of thinking, which, however, develops under its own laws.

When analyzing, we shall also proceed from the speech, as the speech sequence represents the first thing that we deal with. We use only speech sequences to single out those segments, which shall be related to the language. In general, we shall relate to the language that entire common, which we find out among the multitude of concrete cases. The language is segregated from concrete linguistic tasks and a concrete situation of the speech. The procedure of singling out the common from the concrete takes place at two levels:

1. Construction of a certain abstract system. At that one can use different degrees of abstraction, therefore, there are various grammatical systems: phonetic, morphological and so on. One can consider the relations between the units or only the character of their relations, or (in an ultimate case) only the systems of abstract operations (See above the model of N. Chomsky).

2. Singling out the linguistic units. Sometimes, they say not about the system, but the aggregate of units. At that, the principles of segmentation (syntagmatics) are considered as basic – as it was previously said about in connection with the text division – and the principles of classification (paradigmatics). Various scientists perform the procedure of these principles application in different ways.

A language appears as an abstract system, constructed on a discrete principle, which is aimed at the regulation of facts that observed in the speech; it is a system, composed of different levels, which is based on a certain hierarchic principle, i.e. a system of subordinate levels. (One can consider this definition as a working one, as the language belongs to the category of undefined notions – there are more than 200 known definitions).

The segmentation goes hierarchically from top to bottom, from minor to major. The principle of hierarchy works in the majority of symbolic systems. Classes in the paradigmatics and lengths in the syntagmatics are correspondingly connected with one and the same inner relations that are concluded in three types of dependences (L. Hjelmslev):

1) Determination – constant – variable relation (—>);
2) Interdependence (interrelation) – two-constants relation (<—>);
3) Constellation – two-variables relation (>—<).

Various particular cases of linguistic relations can be brought together in one of these types.

The relations of determination, interdependence and constellation can be presented as a combination of two more common relations of the mathematical logics:

1) Transitivity:
If A aB & B aC, then A aC;
2) Symmetry:
If A aB, then B aA,

Wherein "a" appears as a symbol of any operation. The determination is equal to the transitivity and asymmetry, interdependence – to the transitivity and symmetry, constellation to the non-transitivity and symmetry.

As a rule, symbolic systems have no one-one correspondence between the significant and significate. In other words, one plan of expression can be taken to correspond to several plans of content (ambiguity), and one plan of content – to several plans of expression (synonymy) (See above the law of "asymmetrical dualism of a linguistic symbol" of S. Kartsevsky).

In the speech this law requires from the speaker to remove polycemy in the text in order to gain an adequate understanding (removal of ambiguity) through the specification or by any other means, as well as to choose from all synonymic options the most effective one in a concrete communicative act. The latter has a great significance for the comprehension of the stylistics as a science of synonymy: various means of expression of a single content, in particular, in different styles of speech.

Let us analyze in detail the problem of synonymy that plays an important role in speech. **Synonyms** can be symmetrical and unsymmetrical. Let us examine, for instance, a set of meanings of the word *number*:

1) Ordinal number of an object (*ticket's number*);
2) Label (metal plate) with the imprint of a figure (*wardrobe's number*);
3) An object, marked with a certain number (*I live in room 9*);
4) A separate part of a combined concert;
5) Freak, deed, trick. (Typical to the Russian language).

The word *number* is polysemic (five meanings!). The characteristic of polycemy is common to natural languages. The following synonyms will be symmetrical: the word *number* in the fifth meaning and the word *trick* (they are interchangeable) (In the Russian language). The following synonyms will be unsymmetrical: the word *number* in the first meaning and the word *figure*, as the word *number* in the first meaning can be changed, i.e. described by the word *figure*, but not to the contrary (the number is a figure, however the figure is not a number).

The symmetrical synonymy represents a particular case of the interdependence (*number <—> trick*).

The unsymmetrical synonymy represents a particular case of the determination (*number Я figure*). The determination is recognized to be the pivotal type of the linguistic relations.

The syntactic relations in complicated numerals of the Russian language exemplify the constellation: (one hundred and >—< twenty >—< four).

One can take an example of the determination in the so-called context synonymy that appears as the basis of the singling out of lexical functions in the language, which idiomatically joins words in lexical combinations (See the works of I. Mel'čuk, A. Zholkovsky, Y. Apresyan).

It is noted that one and the same meaning can be expressed in the language by different words (which in a classical dictionary of synonyms are never included in one synonymic series) depending on the kind of word they are combined with in the text. A set of meanings that join the lexical combinations in such cases is said to be lexical functions, which are included in a special automated dictionary of the semantic synthesis.

Let us cite the examples:

i	Figur*
Satire	Sting
Conscience	Voice
Dream	Hugs
Marriage	Ties
Mist	Shroud
Plot	Threads
Secret	Cover
Slavery	Yoke
Blockade	Circle

* Figur – means something figural, an image-bearing designation, and an accepted metaphor.

i	Magn**
Rain	Downpour
Black-haired woman	Raven-head
Fool	Perfect
Truth	Absolute
Zero	Absolute
Scientist	Of genius

** Magn – utmost.

In all analyzed examples of a full context synonymy one word (i) determines the choice of another.

The synonymy in a language yields to the law of hierarchy.

The law of hierarchy is most generally represented in the fact that every semiotic system can be compared with other two systems – one of the lower order, the other of the higher order in respect to the given. The gamma of classifications illustrates this general law. One ought to distinguish, for instance, a sonic language, determined by articulation, from a literal language that appears as a consequence of the higher level consciousness, which was able to investigate its own concepts (metalanguages are constructed on the basis of this human capacities; See above).

The law of hierarchy, in particular, becomes apparent in the fact that every class of semiotic elements (symbols), in its turn, composes an element of the supreme class. Upon the description of a symbolic system this characteristic is reflected as a characteristic of the description self-expansion: the rules of the description composition, applicable to one stage, are applicable to all other stages. Finally, the hierarchy becomes apparent in the form of the law of equivalence in absolutely another respect. In a common case the law of equivalence is formulated simply: one symbol can be equivalent to another. One can say in respect of every two symbols whether they are physically distinguished or not by their visible, heard and so on (perceptible) form. If the symbols are considered physically identical, then they represent the samples (autokey) of one and the same symbols.

The action of the law of equivalency is associated with the problem of identity: two symbols should be discernible and, at the same time, identical in this or that respect. The question is to make various lines of connections, in which it sounds reasonable to learn the equivalency of symbols from the standpoint of the semiotics. Let us examine two such lines: 1) *top-down* – under the semiotic hierarchy (in the paradigmatic respect) and 2) *in breadth* – within the limits of one stage of the hierarchy (in the syntagmatic respect).

1. Paradigmatic connections stipulate that the more abstract is the symbol and the less limits it has in the position upon the application, the more freedom of occurrence it has. Upon the movement from the top to the bottom along the stages of semiotic systems the connections of equivalency bear the character of a model: a symbol of one stage appears as a model of symbols of another stage; it models these or those characteristics of the symbols.

2. The equivalency in syntagmatic connections manifests itself in another way. In this respect several basic cases of the equivalence are possible:

A. Both elements are met in one and the same environment, in one and the same position;

a) The elements are interchangeable, at that, both of them and their environment keep identical: *between logs – among logs;*

b) The elements are interchangeable, but there is no common identity kept: to put on the table – *to lie on the table.*

B. Both elements do not meet in one position. Thus, their direct comparison is not possible: I go – we go. In this case one ought to consider the entire combination as a whole to be the element and then act in the same way as in case A.

Case B represents the greatest interest for the semiotics, as it often appears in semiotic systems like the symbolic logics, the considerable part of the rules of which is limited to the rules of equivalency determination in those cases, wherein it is not apparent at first sight, i.e. to the exposure of the hidden equivalency.

So, the language is not a mere system of symbols; it is the system of subordinated levels of symbols: everything that stays beyond the limits of these levels does not relate to the language. It is quite complicated job to determine the top and down levels of the hierarchy in the language, since the language does not have clear limits; it is open. The level character of the language belongs to the linguistic theory.

The down level is usually recognized to be the division into morphemes (minimal symbols). However, the latest phonetic investigations demonstrated that a syllable appears as the bearer of a certain rhythmical characteristic and, therefore, one can single out the syllable as a level.

The realization of the fact what structure appears as the top level of the given language represents one of the central problems of the linguistics. In this context the main attention is paid to the examination of the sentence.

The relations between the top and down levels are equal to the relations between the method and goal.

The entire hierarchy of the language is kept on the basis of the linear character. When accepting the linear character and subordination of the levels one ought to recognize one more notion: every language has its own strictly limited rules of construction of syntagmatic and paradigmatic series, which include the units of different levels of the language. Finally, these series yield to the semantic criteria. The linguistic units do not exist beyond the syntagmatic and paradigmatic connections with other units of the language. Every unit of any level appears as a point where the functions and means cross.

The subsymbolic level gives the means for the construction of a symbolic level, the elements of which, in their turn, represent the basis for the construction of the subsymbolic level. Under the language L. Hjelmslev understood a system of connections, which is superimposed on the continuum of the reality.

The scientists consider a sentence, which restricts the system of the language levels from the top, in two ways. The most popular point of view asserts that the sentence belongs to the speech, not to the language.

The famous French linguist E. Benveniste wrote: "A sentence appears as an indefinite, limitlessly varying creation, the life of the language in action. With the sentence we leave the language area as a system of symbols and we get into another world, the world of the language as a means of communication with the speech as its expression".

However, a sentence is constructed from the language material of down levels. The language units give birth to a creation that belongs to the speech, not to the language. It is interesting that one can form a sentence from any unit of the down level, even from a morpheme. An American linguist F. Boas cites the following dialogs as an example:

– He dances well!
– He danced well.

"The perfection of a though (availability of the combined subject and predicate) and the completeness of a verbal expression that "requires a special intonation" appear as the condition of a word or a lexical combination transition into the sentence" (A. Shakhmatov).

N. Chomsky relates the sentence to the language units – it is an opposite point of view.

Totally, there are more than 150 definitions of the sentence, however all of them have common references:

1) The sentence is a point in which the language phenomena transform into the speech phenomena;
2) The sentence is recognized to correspond with the reality;
3) The sentence is connected with the thought;
4) The sentence expresses the perfect thought.

The sentence has the completeness and integrity.

The sentence easily makes the syntagmatic level apparent. Is it possible to single out a sentence at the paradigmatic level as a separate linguistic unit in order to form a structure of a higher order?

Higher than the sentence one can raise the text level, connected speech (or discourse). The discourse is characterized with the unified modality and the unified stylistic character. If a higher level is singled out, one can establish paradigmatic connections at the sentence level and, thus, the sentence will become a whole unit that yields to all rules inherent in the units of the down levels.

The division of the language and speech shall be of absolute character. The speech differs from the language by the quality of the situational attachment (the speech is determined by situation). The situational character underlies the speech perception, and the direction of the speech is aimed at the comprehension.

The situational character includes:

a) Extra-linguistic context;
b) Wide linguistic circumstances;
c) Emotional and psychological context of eloquence.

Thus, it becomes clear that the speech cannot be investigated by formal linguistic methods (its investigation uses the methods of various sciences; See "Introduction"), as the number of situations cannot be calculated even in its most typical expression. Probably, one should not set a task of such enumeration. The situational character shall be understood in its abstract character, i.e. as the speech inherency, and one ought to investigate the fact of how the situational character influences on its structure. In the semiotic terms the situational character is determined exactly through the pragmatic component. The difference of the language and speech by the number of measurements (the language has two, the speech – three) is demonstrated well by the dramaturgy of absurd. (S. Beckett, E. Ionesko and others), wherein the pragmatics is displaced and the speech functions are transferred to the language. A dialog turns out to be absurd exactly by the fact that it is constructed on the pragmatic emptiness. Since the speech is not possible without the pragmatics, then it is set by means of the language. Let us examine the following dialog:

I love apples.
You can love everything.
Everybody can, everybody cannot and so on.

Every next remark "picks on" the word, i.e. an outer circumstance. Such dialogs have no situations behind.

Acting persons do not have sensible speech. The author's task requires that they should speak without any goal of communication and with no consideration of it. Such dialogs are connected in an outer way, not inner, thus reminding the wordy plays of L. Wittgenstein), at that, they can be so substantial that can be of interest of the public. Let us examine two texts:

1.He stayed home. Kate likes to dress up. If you have spare time, call for me. Tell him just a single word. You helped to rear a foal-sucker. There were mountains seen at a distance in the midst. Na zdorovie! I lost the book and I am very sorry about. Do not tease the dog!

2. Within three years Mishka, an elk-calf, turned out to be a big strong elk. He was almost tame and walked without leash along the forest. Once a story happened to him. It is a funny and instructive story. One day Dasha let a bull calf to walk on a clearing and she set under a tree to read a book. Suddenly a wolf jumped out from the bushes and rushed to the bull calf. It's a bad job! What can she do? Suddenly Mishka also jumped out from nowhere. He dashed to the wolf and with all forces stroked him by his leg. The wolf started rolling on the grass. Mishka run after. He dashed to the wolf once again and stroked one more time. The wolf kicked the bucket.

The first text does not belong to our speech activity. It is not a discourse, as there are no connections between separate sentences. A discourse without fail assumes the availability of an inner semantic connection. The sentence cannot exist beyond the boundaries of a discourse: only within the boundaries of a discourse one can single out syntagmatic and paradigmatic connections. The inner connections within the discourse are not restricted by semantic connections, though there are some species and temporal connections (all sentences in a discourse are constructed in one species and temporal clue), well ordered by modality, personal correspondence (a point of view that underlie the expression of sentences), by stylistic and expressive parameters (it is dictated by the artistic task) and so on. The types of a discourse are very multiform: monologue narration, dialog, etc.

Let us examine the peculiarities of a sentence as a member of the discourse:

1. Situational attachment. Such a speech always relates to a certain concrete circumstance. The discourse by itself indicates the situational attachment – the main theme. If we examine the sentences beyond the discourse, then they won't have any situational attachment. The situational attachment does not let any machinery cope with the language. This is the main reason of the machinery translation failure (though, it is not a single one). How can one translate the following name of Boris Pasternak's circle of poetry "My sister – life" into the Czech language, if in Czech the word "Life" is of the masculine gender? (Example of R. Jacobson).

2. Availability of sense. How can one determine the sense? One can make the following working definition: the agreement of the mental content of the sentence with the situational needs of a speech act forms the sense of a sentence. It assumes a situational attachment of the sentence, consequently, it 2) follows from 1) and appears as it's development.

3. The sense of a sentence as a member of the discourse is always completed. The integrity of the sense manifests itself in the sentence in the fact that it is able to get into the semantic connections with other units of the same order within the limits of the discourse. These connections are determined as syntagmatic.

In contrast to the units of other linguistic levels, the sentence as a separate unit, has the whole number of specifics:

1) Creative productive character, which enables one to transform any

lexical combination into a sentence; sometimes it goes against the literally understandable sense (for instance, in the poetry of V. Khlebnikov);

2) The borders of the completed senses are flexible.

The punctuation reflects the comprehension of the sense borders. One can change punctuation marks in the second text. In the first text the punctuation is dictated by purely formal rules. The change of these punctuation marks is not possible. "To comprehend some sentences (anomalous) one ought to "dip them into the discourse" (V. Zvegintsev).

It seems that there are so much definitions of the sense meaning as many there are linguists. Sometimes it is convenient to use the definition provided by I. Mel'cuk and K. Zholkovsky: the sense manifests itself as that common, which is shared by different expressions recognized as synonymic, i.e. the sense represents an invariant of synonymic transformations (See above). This definition assumes that the sense of a sentence has an autonomous character. However, many sentences do not allow rephrasing. Nevertheless, the sense of a sentence is specified and, probably, determined by the discourse. This provision is compared with the noted point of view under which the linguistic symbol gains it's meaning only in a context (Ancient Indian linguistic school).

A sentence represents a speech unit, which is able to form a discourse. A sentence withdrawn from a discourse is not the sentence in the true sense. In this case it stops being a speech unit, it turns out to be a language unit (pseudo-sentence), losing the sense that it gains in the discourse. That is why a quotation taken out of the context can be comprehended in the sense, which does not relate to the fact that the author wanted to say. Quite many people were discredited in public by such false quotation, which is equal to the slander.

It is wise to divide the conceptions of the *meaning* and *significance*. To have a meaning means to have a semantic content that is logically organized in the correct way. To be significant means to realize that designation, which is assigned by the communication. Sentences, taken out of the discourse, have a meaning, but they are not significant. They gain the same statute as the words in an explanatory dictionary (with the set of possible definitions). Their meaning is abstract; it becomes concrete only in a discourse. Pseudo-sentences are subjected to the segmentation and classification that lead to the singling out of down levels units with the use of formal and semantic rules. On the basis of these rules one can synthesize correct sentences, which will be useless, as they will perform no communicative function.

One ought to look for the word's meaning in its connection with other words, not with the denotatum. The relations between a word and a thing lie beyond the linguistic system; it is performed through the sentence. Sentences differ from pseudo-sentences by the presupposition. The concept of the presupposition had its origin in the logics philosophy (G. Frege), wherein it designates the sentence's semantic component (opinion – *P*), which should be true to make the sentence (*S*) have the truth value in the given situation, i.e. it would be either true, or false. The following sentence: *Philip knows that the capital of the USA is Washington* appears as true or false depending on the geographical knowledge of Philip, and the next sentence: *New-York is the capital of the USA* with the false presupposition cannot be either true, or false, since it is senseless.

In addition to the presupposition as a provision of the comprehensibility and availability of a true meaning (semantic presuppositions), there are also pragmatic presuppositions. Sentence *S* has pragmatic presupposition *P*, if upon any neutral (i.e. non-demagogical, non-ironical and others) application of *S* in an utterance the speaker considers *P* as obvious or merely known to the listener. The corresponding pragmatic presupposition cannot duplicate the semantic presupposition of a sentence. Pragmatic presuppositions are used upon the description of the sentence actual division semantics. The availability of a presupposition underlies the sequence of sentences in a discourse on the imperceptible basis.

Let us consider the following sentence: *Врач бегло говорила по-немецки* (A doctor fluently spoke in German). (In the Russian variant the doctor is a woman). There is no any senselessness, as this sentence meets all those rules, which are necessary for the sentence to be comprehended. The presupposition can be subjected to the calculation:

*Врач (*a doctor) – feminine gender;

*Немецкий (*German) – it is a foreign language to the doctor;

*Бегло говорила (*fluently spoke) – however, it is not known whether she speaks now, or not, and so on.

Thus, the presupposition represents the whole underlying theme of the given text.

When one makes agree the sentences in a discourse, the agreement of presuppositions is also takes place. Presuppositions connect sentences into the discourse units. Therefore, in the speech communication it is so important to understand, whether the knowledge behind the text is common to all interlocutors, or not. The phrase like: *Galina Sergeyevne has a birthday today – we have to make a gift to her* has a sense only upon the addressing to the man, who knows what it is said about. Otherwise, the phrase turns out to be senseless, and the speaker's speech becomes uninformative and even suspicious in the listener's perception.

Hereinafter we cite an example of a symbolic system construction (in an artificial language). Let us have three symbols: *a*, *b*, and *c*. We will try to construct a symbolic system of them. We divide all symbols, which we will construct, into three classes. The definition: every symbolic system represents a certain object (class of expressions), which is constructed in the following way:

1) A certain amount of initial symbols (semiotic atoms) is specified; these symbols are called as simple;

2) The rules of constructing complicated symbols from initial symbols are given; the application of the rules will result in several classes of symbols.

3) The aggregate of the constructed symbols represents the symbolic system.

We will construct three classes of symbols from the initial ones.
The rules:
Symbol *a* **E** (belongs) to the first class of symbols.

If symbol *X* **E** to the first class of symbols, then *Xb* **E** to the first class of symbols.

As a result of these two rules application one can get an infinite number of symbols like: *a, ab, abb, abbb* and so on (all of them belong to the first class).

If *X* & *Y* **E** to the first class, then *XcY* **E** to the second class.

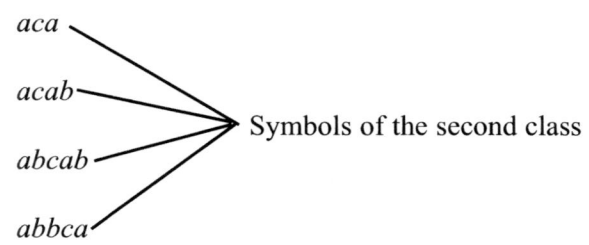

aca
acab
abcab ⟶ Symbols of the second class
abbca

4. Symbol *aca* represents a symbol of the third class. Thus, the third class appears as a subclass of the second class, since we allocated subclass *XcX* from it and named it as the third class (another definition).

If *XcY* **E** to the third class, then *XbcYb* also represents a symbol of the third class.

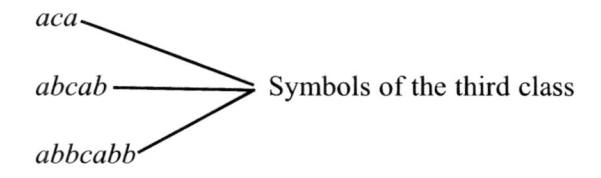

aca
abcab ⟶ Symbols of the third class
abbcabb

327

We don't know the meanings of these symbols, but we construct the expressions of a certain type (syntactic level).

Now, we have to proceed to the level of interpretation. We can give three different interpretations to our system by our request. (i.e. three types of the semantics in a broader sense):

1) Grammatical interpretation;
2) Logical interpretation;
3) Arithmetical interpretation.

1. Grammatical interpretation

The expressions of the first class can be interpreted as nouns and as definitions to nouns.

Rules: (For the Russian language)
1) a – (*дом*) (house) – noun;
2) b – (*маленький*) (small) – adjective;
  ab – *маленький дом* (a small house*)*
3) c – verb;
4) any expression of the second and third class appears as a sentence.
  abca – *маленький мальчик читает книгу* (a small boy reads a book);
  abbca – *пес большой красивый кусает хозяина* (a big beautiful dog bites the owner).

2. Logical interpretation

If the grammatical interpretation distinguishes correct and wrong sentences (for instance, *ba* is a wrong sentence, as it does not follow from our rules), then the logical interpretation distinguish true and false sentences. Let *c* be interpreted as a sign of equality. Then, the sentence *abca* will be correct, but false, and the sentence *aca* will be correct and true (as the entire third class): $a = a$ ($ab = ab$; $abb = abb$ and so on).

Thus, grammatically correct sentences can be both true and false from the logical point of view:

1) c – predicate;
2) any expression of the first class – an argument of the predicate;
3) any expression of the second and third classes – a sentence;
4) any expression of the third class – true,
5) if the expression does not belong to the third class, then it is false.

3. Arithmetical interpretation.

We will interpret this system as the class of natural numbers:
a is 0 (zero);
b is 1;
c is "=" (as in the logic interpretation).

Then *abb* – 011; *ab* – 01, *a* – 0 and so on.

The semantics includes the rules of interpretation, which, naturally, are set separately from the rules of construction. The example of a great German mathematician G. Cantor looks very interesting in the given context.

If we have a series of natural numbers, we can place to its correspondence a series of even numbers. The series will be equal, thought the second series belongs to the first series, and i.e. it turns out that a part is equal to the whole.

| 1 | 2 | 3 | 4 | 5 | 6 | 7 | ... |
| 2 | 4 | 6 | 8 | 10 | 12 | 14 | ... |

Every natural number has an even number that can be placed to its correspondence. Both classes turn out to be equal upon the condition of their infinite character.

Thus, the *truth – falsity* in the mathematics is the matter of inference, not the reality.

We can construct an algebra (for instance, the Boolean algebra), wherein $a + a = a$ (the law of idempotency).

The *truth – falsity* of an expression is determined only by the rules (interpretation), nothing else is applicable. The matter of interpretation is connected with the fact of *what* we want to get. The interpretation should be set explicitly with the use of strict rules of deduction.

The pragmatic aspect in our example resides in the choice of interpretation.

The semiotic system is needed to comprehend the reality, not as a matter of fact. The choice of interpretation depends on our objectives (this choice manifests the pragmatic level of the system).

The rules of construction (i.e. the syntactic rules) are primary. If the syntax of the semiotic system is prescribed, then the system is also prescribed. The syntax appears as the skeleton of the system.

Any symbolic system differs from the mathematical system by the fact that the first one does not have axioms, and the second has axioms.

It is very important to emphasize that a symbol is a material object. What does make the given material substance be a symbol (with no guesses about the fact that behind the perception of the given object as a symbol "there is something different except the perception)? This something different can be disclosed in the essence of the symbol on the basis of the following universal semiotic principle, proposed by N. Wiener: "The organism is opposite to chaos, destruction and death, as the symbol is opposite to noise". It is a metaphor that underlies the determination of the symbol material difference from noise and it appears as an achievement of the modern scientific thought. The symbol represents an audible result of the correct action of muscles and nerves.

The most essential in the material characteristic of a symbol is the righteous and regular relation of any symbol to other symbols, either preceding or following.

Being opposed to the noise as a specifically well-ordered element, the symbol has the repetitive and conditional characteristics.

The real existence of a verbal symbol is restricted with the time of its production and perception. A symbol exists a restricted period of time as a certain measure of energy. The noise has a tendency to increase, but the symbol's organization – to reduce! At a certain breaking point the symbol transforms into the noise or is perceived by the speaker and listener only as a noise. Therefore, every communicative act corresponds to one serious of symbols. As it was said above, the functioning of the natural language manifests itself in the repetitiveness of symbols and their sequences. A language as a communicative material object differs from a living organism exactly by the production of material elements not in the framework of the "language" as a whole, but only as separate combinations of symbols, connected with the relations of the precedence and following.

The characteristic of the symbol's repetitiveness (or reproduction) according to the terms of its material nature is the most essential to comprehend the natural language structure.

The conditional character is the "senior" in the determinant set of the language symbol characteristics and usually it is recognized as the leading and determinant one. F. Saussure determined the relation between the conception and acoustic image as arbitrary in the framework of the individual psychic or collective consciousness. According to Saussure an arbitrary relation between the significant and significate appears as a symbol. The conditional character (amotivational character) of a symbol, by definition, manifests itself in the relation between the elements of one and the same object of the consciousness. In other words, one part of the consciousness (significant) appears in a nondeterminate way in respect of the other (significate). Saussure indicated that one couldn't reveal the significate's randomness at the sight; it could be done as a result of many errors.

The discussed basic characteristics of a language symbol do not exhaust its complicated nature, however, they are quite enough to single out the symbol in general as a separate object of reality.

The symbolic system appears as a material mediator that serves for the information exchange between two other material systems. It is necessary to point at that wider material system, which includes the given symbolic system as a link-mediator. Having looked through quite a large number of such systems, we become confident that they can be placed in a certain sequence. The verification of this fact represents a semiotic law.

So, symbolic systems in aggregate constitute a continuous series of phenomena in the objective reality, the continuum. In this connection, Y. Stepanov gives the following interpretation of the conception of *information*, which is included into the definition of a symbolic system: "Information is always a minor energy than that one, which is necessary for the real existence of the specified material systems. Energetic costs of the symbolic system existence are proportionate to the energetic volume of the transmitted information. The higher is the organization of the symbolic system, the less part of the common energy is consumed by the transmitted information and the less is the energy necessary for the existence of the symbolic system". In this sense the symbol is understood as "a state of a symbolic system at every moment of time, if this state differs from the preceding and following ones. For instance, a curve of a flower pedicel caused by the influence of the sunlight represents a symbol; we distinguish it from the pedicel position before and after this".

If a symbolic system is a material mediator between two other material systems, such is the symbol in the simplest case:

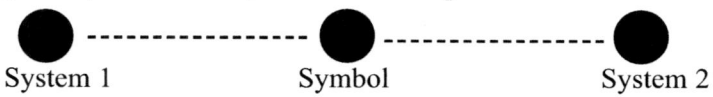

●--------------●--------------●
System 1   Symbol   System 2

However, in developed symbolic systems – languages – the symbol has a more complicated structure. The complication consists in the fact that those parts of both systems, which directly contact with the symbol, in their turn contact with each other, and all three systems form an original triunity (the famous triangle of Frege). The Frege's triangle that was further on developed in the works of Aldin, Stern, Ulmann, represents a system of the symbol, conception and denotatum (thing) contrapositions.

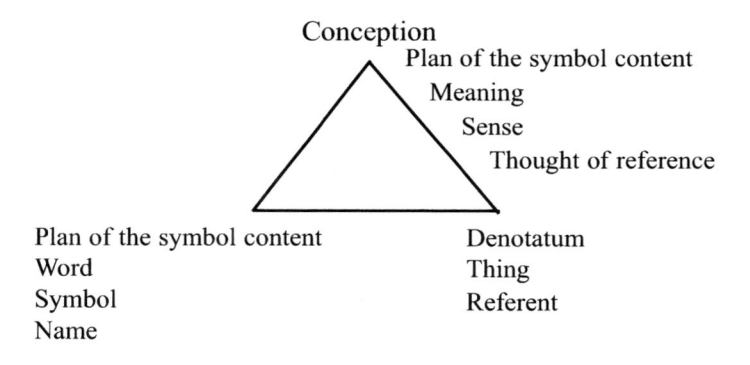

```
                    Conception
                   /\    Plan of the symbol content
                  /  \     Meaning
                 /    \    Sense
                /      \   Thought of reference
               /_____\

Plan of the symbol content      Denotatum
Word                            Thing
Symbol                          Referent
Name
```

The symbol has causal relationship with the conception; it symbolizes the conception, which relates to the thing. The symbol substitutes for the thing; however, there is no direct relationship between them. This relationship can be inexact and even false. The symbol does not truly reflect the thing, since they relate to each other not directly, but through the conception (the top of the thought of reference). In that lies the basic shortage of the natural language as a communicative system: words reflect things inexactly (the people saying the same things often think about different things; it was much spoken about).

However, not all symbolic systems have a concept as the plan of the symbol content, in some of the systems the plan of content is represented by the thing (or denotatum).

In this respect the trinomial classification of symbols into signs-symbols, symbols-images and signs-indexes, based on the different degree of the symbol randomness, seems to be very important. Actually, the word table is, probably, absolutely random (i.e. such a symbol, which has no material resemblance between the plan of content, significant, and the plan of expression, significate (Compare *a table* in English and *der Tisch* in German), and the picture of a tree in a painting often resembles a real tree (See above). It is obvious that symbols according to the degree of their randomness are not identical. Signs-symbols are absolutely conditional; they have no logical connections between a material object and denotatum. They are absolutely amotivational symbols. The natural language is considered to be the most striking example of a semiotic system consisting of the signs-symbols. F. Saussure wrote, "the language is a system of symbols assigned to express ideas, consequently, it can be compared with the military alphabet and so on, but this system is the most important one". Saussure considered the symbol to be absolutely random (See above) subjected to the competence of the people's agreement: "… and not only other figure that portrays a horse, but any object, which has nothing common with it, can be identified with the horse, since it will be given the same significance".

However, the investigations of R. Jacobson and some other linguists demonstrated that the problem of the absolute randomness of a language symbol couldn't be solved identically. First, practically all languages have imitative words (*to crow, to meow* and so on), the phonation of which resembles the sound that they symbolize. (1)

---

(1) There is such a point of view that the natural language began with the imitation. However, this theory is disproved, in particular, by the fact that the languages of native people almost do not have imitative words, but there are quite many of them, say, in the English language.

Second, the human consciousness established the correlation between certain sounds and their patterns, for instance, Hindus perceive sound [l] as soft and smooth, but [r] as a movement; they perceive the Russian sound [и] as narrow and long and sound [o] as short and circular; in this case the word *needle* cannot be considered as a fully arbitrary sound, since the object, that it symbolizes, is also narrow and long (sound symbolism). The language can fix not only actual (as in an imitation), but also a numerical similarity. For instance, it is known that a president is a more important figure than a secretary and this fact determines the following phrase structure: *The president and the secretary visited the exhibition* (a phrase like: *The secretary and the president visited the exhibition* is not likely). Consequently, this complicated linguistic symbol (phrase) has a certain numerical connection between the significate and significant. However, the basic amount of language symbols is arbitrary.

The signs-symbols (icons) appear as symbols that outwardly resemble their denotatum, for instance, pantomime or topographic symbols: blue resembles the color of water, green – color of forest, brown – color of mountains. That is why they so easily are memorized in the school (as the symbols of many minerals). Some traffic signs are iconic, for instance, a sign of prohibition ("NO ENTRY" sign) can be associated with a barrier that bans thoroughfare.

Geometrical signs are also considered to be iconic. C. Piers thought that signs – symbols are present in algebra as well, for instance sign plus ($a + b$) – a space separator. Signs – symbols has symbolic elements, but in general they include patterns. Music that consists mainly from signs – symbols, also has icons (imitation of water splash and rustling of leaves, etc.). Photography represents an ideal example of a iconic symbolic system.

Signs – symbols lay on the border of a sign and non-sign. Indexes fix cause-and-effect relations in the surrounding world. The consequence appears as a symbol of reason, for instance, smoke symbolizes a campfire; light symbolizes the fact that the earth occupied a certain place in respect of the Sun.

Some scientists (for instance, S. Shaumyan) derive signs – symbols from the composition of symbolic systems, as every symbolic system represents a public phenomenon and, consequently, generally speaking, in the nature beyond the man there is no other language. However, the people believe in omens, for instance, they determine the weather by the wind. We notice certain relations in the nature and transform it into a sign – symbol. Beyond a man (or an animal) there is no either signs-symbols, or information. *Cells bear genetic information* – it is a metaphor.

Some scientists (for instance, I. Mel'čuk) consider that a symbol represents a more superficial notion of any deeper sense, as a reason, which stipulated its appearance (in particular, in the text synthesis). From his point of view one ought to notice the "relativity of the significate/significant opposition": the significant can be significate for one deeper significate (a semantic notation or a semantic conception (the significate of an utterance) can be interpreted as the significant for a deeper sense, i.e. for that which can be called "conception", "theme", "subtext")".

Since the symbol appears as a mediator between two material systems, each of them can be considered as the significant of the other. In a particular case in the language both the phonation can be the significant (symbol) for the sense, and the sense can be the significant (symbol) for the phonation. This situation evidentially follows from this very fact that we use two types of dictionaries: on the one hand, the Russian language explanatory dictionary (or, for instance, an English – Russian dictionary), when we want to know the sense, accepting the phonation and spelling of a word as the significant of this sense, as its symbol; on the other hand, a dictionary of synonyms, as well as a thesaurus ("a dictionary of ideas"), when we want to find out a word that corresponds to our thought; in this case we accept the known sense as the form (the significant) of the looked for phonation and spelling.

For the first time the law was ascertained by L. Hjelmslev: "terms "plan of expression" and "plan of content", as well as "expression" and "content" were chosen in accordance with the established conceptions and they were absolutely arbitrary; their functional definition has no requirement to call that very, not other plan as "expression" or "content".

The law of the plan transformation (the plan of content transforms into the plan of expression, and the plan of expression transforms into the plan of content) is generally illustrated by the triangle of Frege, every top of which theoretically can be accepted as the initial point upon the establishing of directed relations. Of course, in such general formulation the law is valid for the one, who observes the symbolic system from without, and as to the participant of the symbolic system (communicant) it can be valid only in some special cases.

In conformity with the human symbolic systems a more condensed and more specified formulation can be given to this law. The transformation of plans takes place only when from the mental content and the symbol sense we go to the symbol. The law becomes apparent, consequently, upon the alertness of the though: from the cognizant (a man, subject) to the outer world, object. This law is connected with the principle of man's activity in the world.

In the same ambiguous way they try to solve the problem of the means of expression based on the symbols that are fully natural (like, for instance, pantomime): whether they relate to the competence of the semiotics as the science, or they should be excluded from the field of the semiotic investigation. A perceiving individual associates the sign – symbol with the designated object due to the connection that actually exists between them in the nature, the iconic symbol – due to the actual similarity, whereas there is no naturally stipulated connection between the sign-symbol and the object, which it refers to. A sign-symbol is defined as an object symbol "as agreed". It was previously noticed that the symbol is invariable and a single person is not entitled to alter it. The alterations are made not according to one's will, but due to certain reasons of the social order. In our everyday life the usualness and discernibility of visual symbols-indexes is higher that of the acoustical ones. On the one hand, acoustical iconic symbols, i.e. an imitation of natural noises, are hardly recognized and practically are not used. On the other hand, as to the symbols – indexes and iconic symbols, the universality of music and the fundamental role of speech in the human culture enable one to make the inference that the vision prevails over the hearing, but as to the sings – symbols the hearing prevails over the vision.

Traditional rules underlie the relations between various symbols of one and the same system. The connection between the perceived significant of a symbol and mentally comprehended (translated) significate of this symbol is based on the agreed, memorized and customary association. Thus, signs – symbols and symbols – indexes have an associative connection with objects (in the first case the association is artificial, in the second – natural), and the essence of an iconic symbol lays in the resemblance with the object. On the other hand, a symbol – index contrary to an iconic symbol and a sign – symbol with the necessity assumes the actual availability of the designated object. In the strict sense the basic difference between the symbols of the above three types most likely lays in the hierarchy of their characteristics, than in their very characteristics. The role of iconic symbols and symbols – indexes in the language is still waiting for a thorough investigation.

The main object of the semiotics' investigation is defined as an aggregate of systems, based on the randomness of a symbol, as every means of expression accepted in this society basically lies on the collective customs or (that is the same) on the conventionalities. The courtesy signs, however expressive they are (repeated nine times bows to the Chinese imperator), nevertheless are fixed by the rule: exactly this rule makes their application, not the inner significance of these symbols.

Consequently, one can say that fully arbitrary symbols better than other symbols realize the principles of the semiotic process. That is why the language, the most complicated and diffused system of expression, at the same time is the most characteristic; in this sense the linguistics can serve as a prototype of all semiotics in general, however, the language represents only one of many semiotic systems.

As a resume we can propose the following classification of symbols and symbolic systems:

1. First of all, the symbols can be *singular* (a shoe painted above the door) and *systematic*, wherein every symbol is opposed to many others. For instance, a school bell ring is not opposed to its absence, the absence of the bell ring means nothing; so the bell ring appears here as a singular symbol, which does not oppose to any other symbols and has no significance. Every symbolic system represents a communicative arrangement, however, not every communicative arrangement represents a system, for instance, an aggregate of singular symbols (signboards).

2. One can say about *conditional* and *natural* symbols. A natural symbol is close to the significant phenomenon. A natural symbol's significate and significant form a natural unity. In contrast to the significant objects, natural symbols have an appellation function. The human conduct consists of significant actions, but only after obtaining the communicative direction in the speech, these actions turn out to be symbols. Gestures and mimics represent significant objects; an observer by look of one's mimics can guess the man's state (See bellow), and when the gestures and mimics are meant for the observer they become natural symbols.

2a. conditional symbols are divided into *arbitrary* and *symbolistical*. For instance, when seeing a traffic sign "No Parking", we cannot guess its meaning, if we do not know it before hand. At the same time if we see a painted bagel above the door, we can guess that it is a bakery. The first symbol is conditional and the second –symbolistical.

3. There are *direct* and *indirect* symbols. An indirect symbol has another symbol in the capacity of the denotatum. The Morse code consists of indirect symbols that are used to transmit other symbols, language symbols. The written language also represents a system of indirect symbols, as letters are used to transmit the sonic language. On the other hand, a symbol can directly transmit the sense and does not sort with other symbols, for instance, figures 1, 2, 3 directly designate the concept of the calculation irrespective the language. The majority of the human sonic language units are defined as direct symbols; they designate the conception or name the thing; phonemes are exceptional.

4. There are *syntagmatic* and *asyntagmatic* systems. In the latter every symbol is equal to the whole statement. For instance, it is impossible to make syntagmatic connections between traffic signs. When situated nearby, two signs "No Parking" and "Straight Only" do not form any syntagmatic sequence, they are perceived separately; signals of a space station are asyntagmatic: each of them bears information about one parameter and it does not make a combined statement with a separate signal. In other symbolic systems, for instance, in the natural language, Morse code and so on, the statement is equal to the sequence of symbols. The difference between the syntagmatics and paradigmatics is possible only in respect of the syntagmatic systems.

5. Symbolic systems can be *thematic* (restricted) and *athematic*. Thus, symbolic notations of a chess game can serve for the transfer of qualitatively restricted information; topographical symbols also serve for one type information transfer in contrast to, say, the Morse code or the natural language, which transfers qualitatively-unrestricted information.

6. Symbolic systems can be *static* and *operational*. At that, the latter designate operations made over other symbols and signs, for instance, "+", "–", or "shift", "interchange" and "turn over" in proofreading.

7. Symbols can be *situational* and *asituational*. The symbols of situational systems have different designations depending on the situation. Thus, A + B in a certain situation can have denotatum 6+4, in another situation – 3 + 2 and so on. Pronouns are considered to be situational among other language symbols. The next words: *right* and *left*, *west* and *east* also belong to the situational symbols (for instance, Alaska is the outermost west in the American continent and the east in the Asian continent).

8. There are also *closed* and *open* symbolic systems. The number of symbols in closed systems is strictly determined and every newly appeared symbol changes the initial system into a new one. The appearance of a new symbol in open systems does not destroy the old system.

Thus, the number of proofreading symbols is not determined; every proofreader invents so many symbols like h, g, ;, o, ,, as many corrections should be done in the given page. It seems that the language vocabulary represents an indefinite system, if one includes into the vocabulary the words like: *understaffedness, dust-and-watertightness* and so on.

9. It is important to distinguish *simple* and *complicated* symbolic systems. In a complicated system a certain aggregate of symbols, which does not exhaust their general number, also is defined as a system different from the system as a whole by one of the enumerated above characteristics. Thus, for instance, the system of symbols, applicable in the arithmetic, includes operational (+,–) and static (1, 2, 3 and etc.) signs.

9a. Simple systems are qualitatively *homogenous*. Complicated systems can be multi – and one-deck; the first one originates an hierarchic subordination: the units of one subsystem can be brought together and simplified to the unit of another subsystem, or, in other words, a unit of one subsystem represents the utmost minimum of units of another subsystem. One-deck complicated systems form no hierarchic relations inside.

Symbolic systems are comparable according to these characteristics and they form the same types of opposition as the units.

10. In contrast to the units two systems can be *cross* in respect of each other (these two systems have one and the same symbols inside) and *distinctive* (none of the symbols of the first system is presented in the second).

10a. Cross systems can be *coordinated* or *contrasted*. In the last case the repeated groups of symbols do not appear as a subsystem in any contrasted systems. Coordinated systems hierarchically subordinate the repeated group of symbols as a subsystem inside. For instance, the vocabulary of the natural language hierarchically subordinate to itself a group of abbreviated words, which is defined as a subsystem inside the system of abbreviations, applicable in definite areas of communication, the part of which does not appear as words.

In a semiotic sense, the language can be defined as an aggregate of conditional (2), arbitrary (2a), direct (3), syntagmatic (4), athematic (5), static (6), asituational (7) symbols that form an open multi-deck system (8), coordinated with other symbolic systems (10a), but hierarchically not yielding to none of them. These systems are the subject of the linguistics' investigations.

An important principle of the general semiotics sounds as follows: the semiotic typology should be constructed more on the principle of isomorphism and the difference of symbolic systems, than separate types of symbols. While considering any symbols, the semiotics proceeds from their physical nature and the area of the human life, where they are applied. Its method is not to observe actually encountered symbols (although this observation plays a role of the reference point), but to investigate all conceivable possibilities of the symbols formation and their logically controlled characteristics by means of introduction of special operators for them. Irrespective of what kind of symbolic formations we take, we cannot reveal such kind operator, which could not be logically anticipated in the common theory of symbols.

Chapter 20. **The Communicative Expressive Force of the Trope**

> There is no existence beyond comparison,
> as the existence makes the comparison.
> *O. Mandelshtam*

One and the same thought in the language is expressed by many means (See above), and one can use the most effective due to a concrete communicative situation. In addition to the psychological and logical aspects, the purely linguistic aspect has also a conception of the information transfer performance. It is connected with the choice of the speech's style and genre and with the application of the methods of expressiveness that redouble the text perception.

A **style** (in Latin *stilus* means a pointed stick for writing, manner of writing) refers to a variety of language, set-aside by the tradition of the given society for one of the most common sphere of the social life and it partially differs from other varieties of the same language in respect of all basic parameters: vocabulary, grammar and phonetics. Modern developed languages have three largest styles: a) neutral, b) "higher", pedantic, and c) "lower", colloquial (familiar – colloquial and colloquial – vernacular).

For the communicative point of view, under the style one ought to understand a generally accepted manner, common method of a certain concrete type of speech delivery: oratory, editorial in a newspaper, scientific (not a highly tailored one) lecture, court speech, every day life dialog, a friendly letter and so on. In this sense, the style is characterized not only by a set (parameters) of linguistic means, but the speech act composition as well.

From the functional point of view, in many modern literary languages one can distinguish colloquial – literary, journalese – political, industrial – technical, official – business and scientific functional styles, however, the volume of each of them, their relationship and the place in the stylistical system in different languages vary. In all languages the central place is occupied by the colloquial – literary style that is typical to the wide everyday life non-special communication and in belles-lettres, – "a neutral" variety of the literary language, on the background of which other functional styles demonstrate their characteristics that reflect the difference of the communicative situation types. The journalese – political style is connected with the public and social sphere of life; the official and business style represents the style of business letters and a special communication in economical, legal and diplomatic spheres and so on. The scientific and industrial – technical styles attend to the science and industrial – technical sphere. The statute of the belles-lettres language arouses disputes. Some scientists consider it to be a functional style; others see in it a special phenomenon, noticing that it sorts with the whole national language, including territorial and social dialects. The point of the place of the colloquial variety in the system of the literary functional style remains disputable.

The functional style represents a category that depends on the historically changing social and cultural conditions of the language use, which was borne by the complexity and multiformity of the social and communicative practice of the people. The systems of functional styles vary in different languages and in different epochs of one language existence. Thus, many nations consider the spheres of folklore and cult to be socially significant, so it gives rise to the corresponding functional varieties of the language. In certain periods, especially those that preceded the formations of nations and literary languages, foreign languages can attend to certain spheres of communication; for instance, the Latin language is able to perform this function.

The functional style is realized in the written and oral forms and it has its specifics in the vocabulary, phraseology, word-formation, morphology, syntax, phonetics, in the use of emotional – evaluative, expressive and image-bearing means of expression, in the availability of its own system of stereotyped means.

Every speech segment (both oral and written) is set in a certain style. It is expedient to choose a style so, that it will correspond to the communicative situation. It is not advisable to use the elevated style in the communication with criminal people, in the same way one should not use a criminal slang when preaching and so on. It is absolutely evident that the choice of the functional style corresponds to one's purpose. The genre is to be chosen in the same way. For instance, if you write down a business letter, you shall not present it in the form of a dialog.

The speech expressiveness first of all is connected with the communicative function of comprehension. Definitely organized repetitiveness can improve the comprehension, however not in the cases, when it concerns a thought (i.e. the plan of content) – it leads to the desemantization (See above), but when the form is reduplicated (i.e. the plan of expression): alliteration, as well as parallelism, anaphora and epiphora.

Alliteration (in the Middle Ages, in Latin *alliterato*, in Latin *ad* – means to, by, and *litera* – letter) is defined as the repetition of consonants, primarily in the beginning of words, as an ornamental method of singling out and consolidation of the most significant words (*It is time, the pen requires rest...* – A. Pushkin).

A poetic text, as a rule, represents a symbol of the author's mental state, which he stays in during the creation of this text. With no doubt some sounds transmit definite mental states, for instance, like [sh], [s] and [p] (See above about the sound symbolism):

"And the silken, sad, uncertain rustling of each purple curtain, thrilled me – filled me with fantastic terrors never felt before…" (E. A. Poe).

All methods of expressiveness are divided into tropes and figures. **Tropes** represent the methods of expressiveness that are realized at the level of words or collocations. **Figures** represent the methods of expressiveness that are realized in a text, which is equal to a sentence or bigger than a sentence.

As a rule, tropes are connected with the re-comprehension. The linguistics also offers the comprehension of a trope as a stereotyped application of a word or an utterance in a figurative sense (metonymy, metaphor). It is an unsuccessful comparison, since, generally speaking, there is no figurative sense. Under the figurative sense usually one ought to understand a typical sense of another linguistic symbol. Every symbol has several interpretations: first, second, …, and so on. Some interpretations are very diffused, then they are called main, some of them can be met only in a single combined collocation (nevertheless, they are present in the language). When a word comes into a context, it realizes not only one of its meanings. It often turns out that a symbol has such a meaning, which is not considered to be the main one, however, the same meaning will be main for another symbol.

One can carry out an interesting computer-based experiment. An explanatory dictionary with a set numbered meanings of each lexical unit is fed into a computer, then they are automatically redistributed inside the dictionary, at that, the meaning in its wordy formulation becomes the title of a dictionary entry and all lexemes that include this meaning in the initial dictionary (it is not important under which number) turn out to be the content of a dictionary entry. This method is useful to test the real level of the lexical synonymy of a concrete language. To perform this work one ought to have quite a mass of dictionary entries fed into the computer. To do this it is necessary to formalize one of the most complete explanatory dictionaries (the formalization is necessary, since any dictionary of such type is resulted from an individual verbal world outlook of its compiler).

So, in the natural language various symbols in the set of their meanings can have intersections with other symbols. The metaphor is constructed on this principle. For instance, in the Russian language the word (*шляпа*) – *a hat* in a usual colloquial speech can be applied to designate an unpractical person – it is so-called "erased" metaphor. A common lan-

341

guage's semantic model can use the same word in the sense of "a man in a hat". These tropes side with the cases of the contrast transformation of the semantics, including the stereotyped (in the Russian language, for instance, if you call some one *Espinoza*, it means that the man is the author of not a deep thought), i.e. irony, as well as various figures of the quantity – hyperbola and litotes (compare: *I told you hundred times about!* and *it's a stone's throw!* – *he is two years old* and *with no doubts*). Periphrasis and epithet, as well as the comparison are connected with the conception of the trope. They often, but not obligatory, has a tropical meaning. Synecdoche is considered as a type of metonymy. In addition, personification, allegory and oxymoron relate to tropes.

In sophisticated medieval descriptions tropes and figures consisted of the nomenclature of 200 and more units. Many on these terms are used in the modern philology, striving to overcome the contradictions in the classification of tropes and to reveal the system in the relations between tropes and figures. The exclusive multiformity of the tropes' and figures' relationship in texts makes the difficulties on this path. The determination of their system assumes the account of formal and semantic similarities and differences, for instance, between a metaphor – comparison *ruddy fists of apples* (E. Bagritsky) and its possible transformations: *apples as ruddy fists* (comparison), *ruddy fists* (in the sense of *apples* – a common metaphor), *apples, [these] ruddy fists* (metaphoric periphrasis) and so on. Belles-lettres texts, especially the prose of the 20-th century are reputed to have such a phenomenon of the so-called "reversibility of tropes", under which one and the same object obtains various tropical designations. For instance, the eyes of a personage, *look like case-shot*, further on are designated as *canister-shot eyes* and *eyes – case-shot*, and *eyes as pieces of ice* turn out to be *blue pieces of ice*.

Tropes help to reach an esthetic effect of the expressiveness, first of all, in the artistic, oratoric and publicistic speech (as well as in the every-day life and scientific speech, and in advertising, etc.). However, the methods of expressiveness were investigated mainly in conformity with a belles-lettres text, therefore from the purely rhetorical (communicative) point of view tropes and figures are not much investigated.

Folklore abounds in tropes; they are widely presented both in lyrical and epic folk poetry, and in sayings and proverbs – in general, in various forms of mythology, typical to the phraseology of the standard language as well; let us compare, for instance, *you must reap what you have sown, this is diamond cutting diamond, good riddance,* – and *to gape, he is itching to do it, stumbling-stone* and so on. Tropes underlie many aphorisms and the so-called winged words.

The artistic effect is determined by common esthetic factors of image-bearing motivations and functional-stylistical relevancy of separate elements in the structure of the whole work, by the sense and profundity of the representation. The abundance or absence of tropes in a certain text does not manifest its artistic value. However, by representing the linguistic form of expression, tropes are always connected with the content; they form and implement it.

Therefore, the problem of tropes requires not only systematic, but the historical approach as well. In various epochs, in various genres and even in separate pieces of text, the artist's relation to tropes as facts of the poetic language varies. The investigators direct their efforts to study the evolution of tropes due to the development of the artistic speech as a whole, as it is obvious, that according to the preferences given by this or that artist to some of tropes, according to the frequency of tropes' occurrence in texts, and the full or partial refusal from tropes and so on, one can reveal typological differences of a certain ideological character.

The structural poetics tries to describe any contextual transformations of a word (or a collocation) in its phonation, meaning and syntactic position. The uniform description of the tropes' and figures' functions enables one to move from the empiric stage in their investigation to the construction of a modern theory of these methods of artistic thinking. The semiotic approach to the arts (See above), valuable for the uniform coverage of its various types, often leads to a spontaneous expansion of meanings of the whole series of the tropes definitions, which are not strict by themselves, for instance, to the transition of the following conceptions: *metaphor* and *metonymy* to the cinematograph. Thereby, "the theory of tropes and figures" in its philological aspect gains a significant role for the whole study of arts. A successful application of a method of expressiveness in the process of communication improves the text comprehension. Unsuccessful application of such a method, quite to the contrary, worsens it. A text with the unsuccessful application of the methods of expressiveness determines the speaker as a not clever man, and it is the worst by-effect of the speech.

It is interesting that reading the works of young writers, as a rule, they are stylistically not perfect, one can make a conclusion about the level of the author's mind: some of them – with no idea about the fact that they are not able to use the methods of expressiveness, nevertheless, they oversaturate the text with them making the text be hand-to-scan; others understand that they won't be able to apply tropes and figures skillfully and they make the text neutral from this point of view, using the so-called "telegraphic style". It is not always appropriate, however, the text is more comprehensible in contrast to the pilled-up methods of expressiveness unskillfully used. The neutral text, almost lacking the methods of expressiveness, looks scanty, that is absolutely evident, but, at least, it does not characterize the author as a fool man.

What does it mean to apply a method of expressiveness successfully?

Let us try to show it on the example of one of the most diffused trope – **epithet** (in Greek *epítheton* means applied) is defined as an image-bearing definition of an object (phenomenon, action) and its characteristic. In contrast to a usual logical definition, which distinguishes the given object from many others (*light peals*), the epithet either distinguishes in a thing one of its characteristic (*majestic horse*), or as a metaphoric epithet – transfers the characteristics of another object to it (*living track*). Folklore usually uses a constant epithet that is notable by its simplicity and invariability (*good brave, open country, fair maiden*). The professional literature comes to the individualized unique epithets. The system of epithets reflects the writer's style, epoch, given literary school (for instance, *fruity singer, cold ashes* are typical to sentimentalism; *yellow dawn, snowy wine* belong to the poetic system of A. Block and so on).

Epithets can be divided into those, which prescribe the characteristic of an action, and those, which prescribe the characteristic of an object. The predicate usually represents the logical and semantic center of the sentence (See above about the actual division of the sentence). Therefore, to transmit a thought in a better way, one ought to strengthen the group of the predicate (not the subject – as it is customary to think). As a rule, the predicate is expressed by a verb and the verb is determined by an adverb. Therefore, the best epithets are presented by adverbs, not adjectives and participles.

By definition, the epithet prescribes the characteristic of an object (phenomenon and so on). However, every object has a great number of characteristics. Which one shall be chosen? Let us cite an example of selecting epithets to the word *eyes* (it is meant human eyes).

EYES

We have placed into the frame not the sense of the word and not the very word, but the denotatum – an object of the outer world. Let us find out a characteristic of the given denotatum. At the first stage epithets are to be chosen not to words, the definitions are selected for the denotatums (not the word of *dawn*, but the dawn, by itself, is seen to Block in orange color in a definite perspective of illumination).

Eyes, as an object of the outer world, can be characterized from different points of view: color; shape (size); impression, which they produce on other people; health; age; reflection of inner essence of the man (character, intellectual, mental and moral characteristics of the people's heart), esthetics, psychological state, in which the man stays by the moment of eloquence, ethnic characteristics and so on.

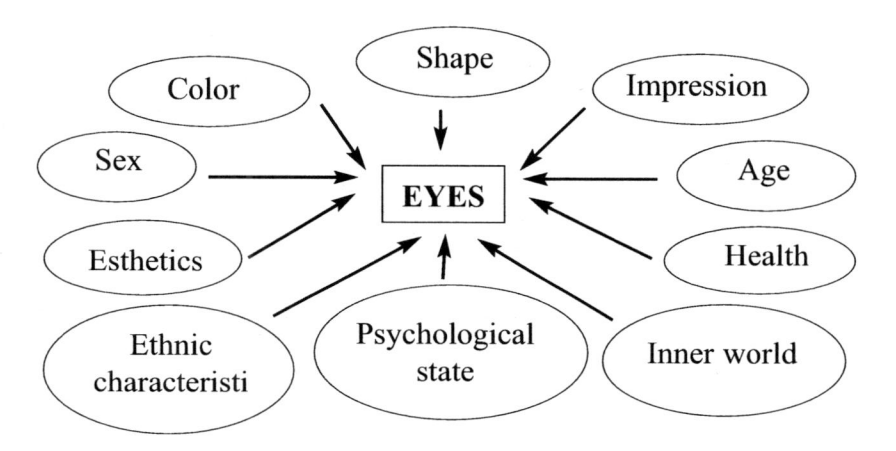

```
          Shape
 Color             Impression
 Sex    →  EYES  ←   Age
 Esthetics  ↗  ↑  ↖  Health
 Ethnic    Psychological   Inner world
 characteristi   state
```

If the eyes as an object of the outer world are characterized from the various points of view, then what does "the characteristic" in the definition of the epithet mean? Since, there are quite many such characteristics (by the number of the characteristic zones). Every such zone is directly correlated with the text genre that determines it. In other words, the characteristic zone relates to the whole text, to its stylistics, tonality, purposefulness. If the speaker evaluated the characteristic zone by the text in a wrong way, he comes into an awkward situation. For instance, if in a medical article about the eyesight problems it is said that a woman with beautiful almond-shaped eyes came to the doctor for the consultation, it is funny. In the same way we will find funny a belles-lettres text, fully connected with the impression, which are produced by eyes, that includes the transfer of the man's world outlook by the time of communication, his state and so on, if it says: "She looked at me with the dreaminess eyes, which were infected by conjunctivitis". The genre is not consisted; the stylistics of the whole text does not coincide with the characteristic zone. Or, say, a scientific article, devoted to the biological characteristics of the iris color, says: "She gazed at me with the sad Armenian eyes, in which one can read the century-old sorrow of her nation". It is utmost important to understand that before choosing an epithet, one ought to determine the characteristic zone. Everything starts from the text. First, one shall make a text and then incorporate the methods of expressiveness into it. Of course, many texts allow the intersection of some zones. Say, one can imagine a text, which at the same time discusses the ethnic characteristics and the forms of eyes; or one's psychological state, characteristics of a personality and impressions; health and age and so on. In other words the characteristics may appear in pairs and triples, and in such view correspond to one text, but never all together.

The discussed example makes it obvious that the eyes often transmit the personal characteristic of a man and at the same time, the state of his heart by this very minute. Let us examine the collocation *kind eyes* used in the following phrase: *He looked at me with the kind eyes*. The collocation represents a syntactic homonym. In the first sense this phrase is comprehended in the following way: He looked at me and he was kind", in the second sense – "He looked at me and had a kind spot for me by that time". The third sense of the phrase represents the combination of the first two. If in the speech the homonymy is not taken away, if due to the wide context of the speech the listener (reader) does not understand what kind of the senses is presented; it is an unsuccessful text.

The next difficulty in the epithet selection (as any other method of expressiveness) is directly connected with the text perception. The matter concerns the phenomenon of decemantization as the sense reduction in a frequently repeated text (See above). The more popular is a concrete example of a trope (in particular, epithet), the more it is desemantized. If there is something desemantized, what kind of expressiveness can one mention? The method of expressiveness should amaze both the reader and the listener. The effectiveness is reached in those cases, wherein the addressee of the speech is shocked by what he heard or read. It is not possible to gain such a result with the use of a stock phrase. There are more desemantized structures among epithets, than other tropes. When, say, a man hears the collocation *lilac mist* for the first time, he is impressed by the unusualness of the image. However, a few years ago a song with such a name was very popular and this fact made impossible to use the collocation further on, except as in quotations. It is quite a complicated job to invent a non-desemantized epithet, however, one cannot use any others. Thus, one can consider that epithet to be successful, which strengthen the main thought, which is consistent in the common stylistics of the text, non-homonymic and non-desemantized, which makes a striking and unexpected impression and appears in a text that is not overburdened by the methods of expressiveness, if it is possible.

Metonymy (in Greek *metonimia* means renaming) is defined as a trope, which is underlied by the principle of contiguity. The metonymy follows from the word's ability to a certain redoubling (multiplication) of a nominative (designating) function of the speech; it represents the superposition of its main sense on the untypical sense of a word. Thus, in the phrase *I ate up three plates* (I. Krylov), the word *plate* means at the same time both *a dish* and *a plate*.

The metonymy appears on the basis of internal or external connection between objects and phenomena (i.e. denotatums). This connection is projected to the plan of content of the linguistic symbols. One thing gains the name of another thing that is connected with the first one. The phenomena, which are brought to the connection by means of the metonymy and form "an object pare", can interrelate in various ways: thing and material (*I had dinner not only on the silver – on the gold. –* A. Griboyedov); (*All dressed in tulle and panne Lenochka came into the room. –* A. Galich); the significant and significate (*Stoked furnace crackles –* A. Pushkin); the support of characteristic and characteristic (*The courage conquests cities*); the creation and creator (*Muzhik... will carry Belinsky and Gogol from the bazaar. –*N. Nekrasov); the action and a means of this action (*Their cornfields and villages for the violent foray he doomed to the swords and fires.*); place and the people, who stay at that place (*The entire Moscow speaks about.*).

The following types of the metonymy are diffused:

Human being	– place of work
	– place of residence
	– epoch
	– circle of people
	– race
	– nationality
Abstract notion	– science
	– author
Object	– designation
	– appearance
	– impression
	– color
Animal	– environment of existence
	– impression
	– behavior
	– interaction with the human being
Action	– objective
	– result
	– the one who acts
	– time
	– method (means)

347

The metonymy, as the renaming, is based on the contiguity of senses, mainly spatial, temporal and casual. The main characteristic of the metonymy relates to the fact that the connection between the objects assumes that the object, which name is used, exists irrespective of the object, which this name is direct to, and both of them does not constitute a single whole.

Upon the metonymy the replaceable and replacing notions do not have a common semantic part. In other words, the metonymy acts in the field of the non-intersecting classes. This fact distinguishes the metonymy from the metaphor (See bellow). Upon the metonymy the transition from the initial notion (*I*) to the resulting notion (*R*) is performed through the intermediate notion (*IM*), which appears as comprehensive both for (I) and (R).

Let us cite the following phrase as an example: "Prenez votre César" (*Take your Cesar*), which the teacher directs to his pupils during the lesson devoted to the study of "De Bello Gallico". The spatial-temporal unity appears as an intermediate notion, including the life of the famous consul, his love adventures, literary works, his participations in wars, his city and his entire epoch. And only in this unity Cesar and his book will be connected by the contiguity.

The metonymy requires the use of connotative semes (elements of the meaning), i.e. adjacent semes that belong to the wider whole and are included into the definition of this whole.

There are two sources of connotation: comparison of one word with another (it means both the comparison of significants and the comparison of significates) and the comparison of the word's denotatum with other creatures of the real world (consequently, extra linguistic creatures). Linguistic connotations occur on the basis of the comparison between the given word and the units: a) the phonetic (sonic) structure of which coincides with the phonetic structure of the given word; b) which can be placed instead of the given word in the prescribed context; c) with which the given word can combine; d) into which the given word is included as a component part; e) the semantic structure of which partially coincides with the semantic structure of the given word; f) the graphical structure of which partially coincides with the graphical structure of the given word.

These are the virtual rows of comparisons and they cannot coincide upon the transition from one speaker to another.

As any context first of all bans a part of forms and meanings of the component lexeme, one can consider that the customary network of comparisons relate to the forms and meanings of the given word, which are not compatible with this concrete context. The secondary network can be taken by means of the *a – e* rules applied to the given word, the tertiary network – by means of the same rules applied to the result of their first application and so on.

The main types of connotation quickly turned out to be customary to us and even in our everyday life communication we come across various classes of more or less stable metonymic formations, such as, for instance, a class of "symbols" for this or that group of people: *sweetie, simpleton, lump, muff...* Probably, this very "natural predisposition" of the metonymy to stereotyping made it so unpopular in the modern literature, as it is met there far rarely than in an everyday life speech. We can cite an example of a pure "not stereotyped" metonymy, borrowed from the sports vocabulary:

Fords released the gas. [slowed down, stopped] (a reportage from a motor-cars racing)

Fords: instrument – agent; *released the gas*: cause – effect.

If a metaphor is constructed at the minimal semantic intersection (See bellow), the metonymy can cover any possible "ambient" multitude. Thus, in the utmost case, these figures coincide, though it is not substantiated by either internal, or external reasons. Such a possibility (not to say a danger) is widely used in the advertising, wherein the necessary ambient multitude, as if is constructed with the help of a text; however, as a result, we often come across the assertions that seem incorrect from the logical point of view. Let us assume, that there is a powerful sports car depicted on an advertising hoarding, which through the metonymy symbolizes a man of action. The advertising says: "SPRINT – A CIGARETTE OF A MAN OF ACTION".

If one connects sprint – powerful car – a man of action, then he will notice that it is an absolutely arbitrary connection between the sprint and the cigarette. This advertising does not use the types of the metonymic relations; it sets absolutely new connections between the objects.

Synecdoche represents a special type of the metonymy. Synecdoche (in Greek *synecdoche* means correspondence) is defined as a literary method, which is used to reveal the whole (generally, something big) through its component part (something smaller, a component part of the big one). For instance: *"Hey, the beard! How can we get to Plyushkin from here?,,,"* (N. Gogol), wherein the meanings of *"a man with a beard"* and *"the beard"* – as an addressing, are combined; "And you, the blue King's coats, and you, the people, obedient to them". (M. Lermontov) – about gendarmes.

The **synecdoché** (in Greek *synecdoché* means correspondence) differs from the metonymy by the fact that both objects compose a certain unity, correlating as a part with the whole, and they do not exist absolutely autonomously.

The synecdoche is realized by several means:

1. The singular form is used instead of the plural form: *Everything sleeps: both a man, and a beast, and a bird* (Gogol). The expressiveness in the Russian language is obtained by means of the fact that the category of form is obligatory (See above), i.e. it must be expressed. A conscious alteration of the grammatical form upon the preservation of the semantic one is perceived as a rhetorical method.

2. The plural form is used instead of the singular form: *We all dream to be Napoleon* (Pushkin).

3. A part is used instead of the whole: *Do you have a need in something? Yes, we have, in the roof for my family* (Gertzen). (2)

4. A generic conception is used instead of aspectual (generalizing synecdoche): *Well, sit down, please, the Sun* (Mayakovsky).

5. An aspectual conception is used instead of generic (narrowing synecdoche): *Most of all take care of the kopeck* (Gogol).

The author means not a kopeck, but money, i.e. it means the use of, first, an aspectual conception instead of generic and, second, the singular form instead of plural, i.e. the synecdoche is applied twice.

The next example presents a stepped metonymy: *A Zulu night behind the window*: (*black – Negro – Zulu*).

A special interest is paid to a variety of the synecdoche, which performs the transition from the particular to the general, from a part to the whole, from minor to major, from type to class. Let us point to the vagueness of all these conceptions, which in the science is used to depict in the form of "a tree" or "a pyramid", however, "trees" and "pyramids" do not always reflect the scientific concept about the world. We often feel convenient with the taxonomy at the level of the primeval conscious too. We can restrict ourselves with the criteria of ancient rhetoricians: more instead of less. In an arbitrarily chosen literary text one hardly can find out many evident characteristics of the generalizing synecdoche: *The people are called "more mortals", but these words with the same success is applicable to the animals, which are mortal as we are*. Bellow, there is more striking example, borrowed from R. Keno:

He kept going: his head was full of thoughts, legs neatly walked along the road, and he finished his route with no incidents. In the house the garden reddish and the cat, which mewed in a hope to get a sardine, and Ameli, having lawful feeling of anxiety due to slightly burned ragout, expected him. The master of the house eats a vegetable with a crunch, strokes the animal and to the question of the human class' representative, how are things going on, answers: "So – so". This example is enough to illustrate the partial reduction of semes, which leads to the widening of the word's sense. It is easy to notice that the generalizing synecdoche attaches to the speech a more abstract, "philosophical" character, which in this naturalistic parody is evidently distinguished on the background of the concrete text.

The narrowing synecdoche, with no doubts, appears as a more diffused trope, especially in novels. When R. Jacobson wrote about the predisposition of "realistic" schools to the metonymy, he meant the narrowing synecdoche, which in his concept is combined with the metonymy.

An identical and adequate comprehension of a text is provided only then, when the new replacing term retains the "specifics" of the old one, i.e. a certain enclosure of one into another takes place.

The model of "classes enclosure" initially assumes certain heterogeneity of its elements, as the criterion of division into smaller classes alters at every new level. It is unstructured classification, wherein we find out two types of classes:

>Classes that include various, but equivalent from the chosen point of view units.

>Classes that include various parts of the organized whole.

In the classifying "trees" the semes can be preserved upon the movement from the top to the bottom along the pyramid (1) or be distributed between the component parts (2).

The generalizing or narrowing synecdoche is taken to the replacement of one unit to another, at that, the second unit does not have some semes, which are necessary for the discourse, in other words, these are such semes, the elimination of which makes it unclear. In order to keep the message comprehensible, one ought to take care of the essential semes preservation.

Let us consider, for instance, the description of a murder in a novel. The instrument of the murder can be described by the following words: *dagger, weapon,* and *object* (an example of J. Dubois).

---

(2) The given example suggests an idea about two different psychological types of the people: for some people – the house means the roof (They are afraid of superior forces, which, as a rule, "fall on one's head" – a reflex of the pagan consciousness); for other people the house means the walls (they are afraid of the danger that comes from the people, i.e. communicative danger, from which they want to protect themselves).

A seme, essential for the murder theme (with no further specifications we will name it as "aggressively-murderous"), is present in the meaning of the first two words, but it is absent in the meaning of the third one. In the meaning of the first word it is surrounded with the additional "inessential" information – not superfluous, but secondary.

Thus, one ought to distinguish two stages of replacement: the change of the first stage affects only the secondary information; at that, essential semes keep safe (a *weapon* instead of the *dagger*). The alteration of the second stage destroys the essential semes (an *object* instead of the *weapon*). The alteration of the first stage usually remains unnoticed: they are revealed only in the process of a semantic analysis of the discourse. The first stage enters the "permissible zone", wherein the speaker by himself can set the level of the definitions uniformity upon the choice of vocabulary. As to the alterations of the second stage, they are identically perceived as tropes: one can use them only in the case, when the essential semes are present in the context due to the semantic superfluity of the text. For instance, the word *iron*, in principle, can be used instead of the *dagger*. The replacement of the word *iron* can be realized in three series, pair intersections of which correspond to the notions absent in the information

The transitions, performed upon such a modification: the meaning of the word dagger narrows and we get a new word: *blade*, then the *blade* is generalized to the meaning of *hard metal*, and then, one again, it narrows: the collocation *hard metal* transforms into *iron*. Neither *blade*, nor *dagger* is named in the text. However, the essential seme in the situation of murder, as we have previously said, appears as "aggressive – murderous", and this very seme is lost upon these transitions. The semantic relationship between the raw material (iron) and the product (dagger) is not enough to reconstruct the sense of the information, since in other contexts the word iron can designate the objects that are not connected with the idea of aggressiveness, like, for instance, in the following sentence: *The iron, which finds a better application, will cultivate the land*. In this example the word *iron* (owing to the expression of *a better application*) can be compared with two null stages (weapon and plough). Or in the next construction: *The gold [wheat] is splayed by the iron*, though in this example the synecdoche has a slight metaphoric color. Only the context, the possibility of semes transition to other units of the narrative sense, in other words, the semantic superfluity, enables one to take two last applications to their "agricultural" meaning.

The comparison (in Latin *comparatio*) appears as one of the most diffused methods of expression. The comparison is defined as a trope, category of the stylistics and poetics, image-bearing verbal expression, in which the represented phenomenon assimilates to another by the characteristic that they both share in order to reveal new significant characteristics in the object of comparison. For instance, the following assimilation (confrontation): *The poet's eternal madness as a fresh spring among the ruins...* (V. Soloviev) indirectly provokes an image of the continuous *beating* and "eternal" vividness of the poetical word on the foil of the "temporal" empiric reality. The comparison includes the compared object (object of comparison) and the object, which is subject to comparison (a means of comparison), and their common characteristic (basis of comparison). The value of comparison as an act of the artistic comprehension lies in the fact that the closing in of various objects helps to reveal a number of additional characteristics in the object of comparison, except the main one, which considerably enriches the artistic impression. The comparison can perform the figurative (*And their curls are white as the morning snow on the glorious top of the barrow* – A. Pushkin) and expressive (*So beautiful, as an angel of heaven* – M. Lermontov) functions or combine both of them. The usual form of comparison serves as the combination of its two members with the use of conjunctions: *as, like, as if* and so on, one can often come across the asyndetic comparison (*In iron armour samovar is noisy like a home general* – N. Zabolotsky).

The comparison appears as the confrontation of two phenomena in order to explain one through another. Such a delivery of the object description is typical to the human thinking. Sometimes it is very hard to describe a certain object directly, however, it is easy to distinguish it from other objects or to find out something common in it with other objects and in this way to determine the given object. This method of description is known for the centuries and it is very diffused. For instance, what does the esthetic component mean? What is *an attractive man*? An attractive man is the one, who by some characteristics differ from other men, and by some other characteristics coincides with them. One cannot find any other explanations. Such a man by some characteristics has a priority over other men, and by other characteristics he looks like them. And when somebody says: "He was so attractive as Marlon Brando", it means the availability of a known standard and another man is brought to this standard and characterized from its point of view. The comparison underlies too many aspects of the human communication. It is inherent in the man to compare everything with everything, and having an internal feeling of the standard and in respect to this standard determine those, who surpass this standard and those, who does not correspond to it (See above the proof by analogy). The comparison presents an accessible, easy, but not the in-depth method of description. When it is hard to describe something directly, it is easier to compare and in this way to demonstrate the shortages and advantages of the described object or to specify certain characteristics. The comparison is so inherent in the human thinking that the natural languages know special grammatical and stylistical forms of comparison. In the Russian language the following methods of comparison are realized: 1) the form of the instrumental case: *пыль столбом* (a cloud of dust); 2) comparative syntactic construction: *лучше меньше, да лучше* (better less, but better); 3) comparative turn: *Под ним Казбек, как грань алмаза, снегами вечными сиял* (Beneath him Kazbek, as a face of diamond, shined by eternal snows) (M. Lermontov); *Впрочем, это были скорее карикатуры, чем портреты* (These were rather caricatures, than portrays, though) (N. Gogol); 4) lexical method: *Ее любовь к сыну была подобна безумию.* (Her love to her son was like a madness.)

The comparative turn of speech is very common in the speech. When analyzing a spontaneous speech, one can draw his attention to the fact that there are quite a number of comparative turns in it. It is important to remember: that which is frequent is always not deep – the maximal depth is correlative with non-standard and unusual.

The example of comparison can be used as a basis for construction of not only a single collocation, but a text of any volume, as well. In the bellow example borrowed from N. Gogol's poem "Dead Souls" the comparison is realized at the level of a paragraph. If a trope is realized in the text that is bigger then a collocation, then it is called developed and it transforms into the figure.

Chichikov still stood motionlessly on the one and the same place, as a man, who joyfully went out to the street for a walk, with the eyes well disposed to look at everything, and then all of a sudden he stopped, remembering that he forgot something, and there will be no one more foolish than such a man: in a twinkling, careless look flies down from his face, he tries to remember what he forgot. May be handkerchief? No. The handkerchief is in the pocket. May be money? No. The money is also in the pocket. It seems that he has everything on him; however, at the same time a certain mysterious ghost whispers into his ears that he forgot something.

How is it possible to transmit the man's look by words? It is a very hard job. A direct description, as a rule, creates no image. You are reading about one's eyes expression and look, but visually you cannot imagine it. Of course, the imagination works, but it differs. Therefore, one and the same description makes different impressions on different people; this fact is easily proved by the choice of actors upon the filming of a novel.

How many there are producers, so many there are decisions. Some times two producers choose absolutely different dramatic types for one and the same role and both of them are absolutely sure that this is an ideal model, which exactly corresponds to the text. Everybody reads the description of the portrait of Natasha Rostova and everybody has different visual image of the hero. It is difficult to transmit by means of the natural language such information, which is transmitted by the Body Language, and it is naturally: if a man in his speech uses both systems, they should be organized in such a way as to supplement each other, i.e. to express one information by means of the first system, and another – by means of the second system: the intersection zone should not be large (See bellow). That is why it is hard to describe one's look by means of the natural language. Gogol wanted to transfer the determination of the man's look, and as a very perspicacious writer, he understood that he would not be able to describe adequately the look in the direct way. Then he used a silly trick: he gave the reader the possibility to imagine the required look. He placed the hero into a psychological situation, wherein such a look is natural. Each of us can easily imagine some one in the situation, when all of a sudden the man understood that he forgot something. The segment, constructed on the example of comparison, is very successful by this very fact that the comparison enables one to model the situation, and the visual image, which is usually transmitted by means of the Body Language, appears by itself in the reader's consciousness.

With no doubt, the comparison as a method of expressiveness can be realized not only at the level of a paragraph, but at the level of the whole text, though it should not be a literary-fiction text. The comparison is also realized in other symbolic systems, for instance, in the cinematograph. A French film "Marital life" is constructed on the principle of comparison: a married couple during their divorce suit remembers the episodes of their mutual life, the first part of the film shows the husband's perception, the second – the perception of the same events by the wife. There is no psychological intersection: the events are the same, but the perception differs. The whole film is constructed on the principle of confrontation, and, of course, there is no summing up at the end. What kind of summing up can be in the human relations? Simply, there are two opinions about the same problem: male and female.

Imagine, please, that you were asked to describe a certain person. You can start with saying that this man has a certain age and sex, he has certain mental characteristics, appearance and so on – it will be a direct description. You can compare this man with some one else, who is well known – it will be a description through comparison. And you can use a special method (for instance, M. Bulgakov frequently used it): to tell episodes from the hero's life and retell the impression, which the man produced on other people (at that you do not tell anything about what kind of the man he is). Through episodes and impressions one can provide the man's internal characteristic, which turn out to be the inference that the reader makes by himself nin this case. It is a more intelligent work, than to characterize directly that some one was scanty or kind, humane or fair, since, if the inference refers to the people, it better should not be declared. It is another case that skillfully selected episodes will bring one to such an inference, which the author desires. It is the most difficult and the strongest method of the human personality disclosure. This method does not refer to comparison; it is an **operational determination** of the description object.

The comparison is frequently used in business relations, for instance, upon the signing of a standard contract. You are addressed to that thing that you know well – it simplifies the comprehension. But when you are told that the business terms and conditions in which you are functioning resemble the terms and conditions of, say, Germany of the year of 1946, then you should treat such a comparison with a great care, since the word *resemble* is not the comparison. You ought to ask a question: "By what parameters and to what extent do they resemble?" The modern Russia is frequently compared with many countries. And each of these comparisons does not stand up to criticism, since if there is a certain analogy with some periods of the world history, it is only partial and it should be specially stipulated. The method of comparison on its own is quite superfluous, therefore, when the matter concerns something serious, important and significant, one better avoid using it. But in the case (remember Gogol), wherein the matter concerns the perception of the man's look, his motions and so on, the comparison is effective. How can one transmit the dance? It is impossible. However, one can tell: "Remember, how did you see "Giselle for the first time"; remember, who was dancing in "Giselle"; refresh the impression, which you had. The thing, which I want to tell you about, is very similar". The comparison works well when the matter concerns the perception of something that directly cannot be transmitted by the natural language, but it penetrates into the consciousness through the image-bearing structure of the thinking. Since the imagery is badly recoded to the natural language (See above), then a person needs a possibility to imagine visually, i.e. to switch on another – image-bearing channel of the information transfer and reception. Gogol's comparison is so successful due to the fact that readdressing to the visual image it transmits information in the optimal way. If you want to evoke a visual image in the consciousness of another man, compare something that you tell about with something that he saw and imagine well, then he will perform the natural logical transfer to the given object.

There are different types of comparison.

1. Synecdoche-type comparisons. Let us discuss some applicable image-bearing comparisons: poor/church mouse, clear/day, boring/rain, null/carp, beautiful/Apollo, powerful/bull, and alone/finger.

These pairs were taken from the expressions like: poor as a church mouse (absolutely poor), clear as a day (absolutely clear, absolutely evident) and so on.

It is obvious that these stereotyped comparisons, into which content the speaker often does not penetrate, in many respects differ from the "true" comparisons. Such stereotypes more often function as intensificators; they express a high degree of quality with a shade of exaggeration, i.e. they function as separate semantic units. However, one can divide each of these expressions into two parts at the level of description (as in the above-referred example), then it becomes evident that the first word correlates with the second as a resulting and initial notion of the generalizing synecdoche, or, to be more accurate, the second word plays the basic role in these expressions – it narrows the meaning of the first word by means of adding new semes to it. But there is no semantic figure, as there is no deviation from the lexical code. By the way, that is why the traditional rhetoric considers image-bearing comparisons as the varieties of the figures of thought (not as tropes or semantic figures), or to be more precise, as a variety of the figures of imagination. The image-bearing comparison appears only as a method of an object description; it "closes in various objects in order to describe one of them in a better way" or "closes in two different phenomena with the same goal" (Ts. Todorov).

2. Metalogical comparisons. As distinct from the referred-above comparisons, which could be called "true" and "real", the rhetoric tropes are always "false". For instance, the utterances, like: *He is as strong, as his father* or *She is beautiful as her sister* can be considered only as the correctly constructed sentences. But when "he" is weaking and "she" – ugly person, the trope appears once again: in this case it is an irony, which is determined as a figure that influences on the referent of information. Quite many rhetoric comparisons look similar; they often appear as hyperbolas. The transition from one type of tropes to another is traced well on the canonical examples: *as reach a Croesus* (in principle, it is a hyperbola, though the wealth of a multi-millionaire quite perfectly can be compared with the wealth of the last king of Lydia) and *He is just Croesus*, where we come back to the narrowing synecdoche.

3. Metaphoric comparisons. Some image-bearing comparisons can be considered as metaphors. Let us cite the following expressions: 1) *her cheeks are as fresh as roses*; 2) *her cheeks like roses*; 3) *roses of her cheeks*; 4) *and two roses on her face*.

The words and expressions are "normal" and compatible with each other from the standpoint of the lexical code only in the first expression. However, we come across the anomaly – the absence of the noun part of the combined noun predicate, as early as in the second expression. Since the ultimate class is not indicated here, the reader by himself ought to perform the operation of reduction. The conjunctions *as* and *like* stipulate a non-trivial relation of the equivalency between the words.

In expressions (3) and (4) we deal with the metaphor.

The metaphor differs from the metaphoric comparison. The comparison is defined as a binominal syntactic structure, which in the non-trivial way combines two semantic multitudes; at the same time the metaphor in the strict sense of the word has no connection with such a combination. In the sentence *"Put the tiger into the motor of you car"* the word *tiger* is perceived as a metaphor, as from the semantic point of view it is not compatible with the other part of the sentence. This incompatibility originates the comparison between the notion being the most possible for the given context and the notion that really exists in the information: *Tiger – petroleum of the supreme quality*.

The **metaphor** (in Greek *metaphorá* means transfer) represents a type of the trope; a transfer of one object's (phenomenon or an aspect of existence) characteristic onto another by the principle of similarity in a certain relation or by contrast. In contrast to the comparison, wherein both members of comparison are present (*Like wings misfortunes rose and separated from the earth* – B. Pasternak), the metaphor represents a hidden comparison, in which the word *as, like, as if* are omitted, but meant. *Charmed flow* (V. Zhukovsky), *a vivid chariot of the Universe* (F. Tyutchev), *the fatal fire of the life* (A. Block), *And Hamlet, thinking by timorous steps* (O. Mandelshtam) – in all enlisted metaphors the various characteristics (those which the object and its characteristics are assimilate to) are presented not in their qualitative separateness, as in a comparison, but in a new undivided unity of an artistic image.

Among other tropes the metaphor is distinguished by a special expressiveness. Having unlimited possibilities in the closing in (often in an unexpected use) of various objects and phenomena, essentially, conceiving the object in a new way, the metaphor is able to disclose its inner nature; frequently the metaphor, as a sort of a micro-model, expresses the author's individual world outlook: *My verses! Living witnesses of tears that I was shedding for the world* (N. Nekrasov); *The Universe – just only discharges of passion* (B. Pasternak). In contrast to the common "everyday life" metaphor (*he's gone crazy*), an individual metaphor has a high degree of an artistic self-descriptiveness, as it withdraws the object (and the word) from the automatism of perception.

In those case, when the metaphoric image covers several phrases or paragraphs (images of "prematurely ripe fruit" in "The Thought" by M. Lermontov, "triple" in "Dead Souls" by N. Gogol) or even it extends to the whole work (more often expressed in a verse: "Telega of Life" by A. Pushkin), the metaphor is called as developed and turns out to be a figure. In respect of the metaphor such methods of expressiveness as oxymoron, antithesis, and personification can be considered as its varieties or modifications.

The metaphor occurred in the epoch of the mythological consciousness disintegration (See above). In the ancient mythological and pantheistic consciousness with its wholeness of the comprehensible world and the comprehending human being there was no way for the metaphor existence. The occurrence of the metaphor started up the process of abstracting and concrete conceptions and originated the artistic image. The arts and book-learning of the Middle Ages, based on the monotheistic consciousness, wherein the human life is conceived as "being in the offing" with the God and everything in the world turns out to have a mysterious, symbolical sense (the human life, history, natural phenomena, etc.), create a complicated, but uniform and whole symbolic system, which is fully metaphoric. The people's consciousness (as distinct from the bookish one) with its calendar and omens, tokens, and predictions makes its own option of the metaphoric symbolism.

The new time, with the man, not the comprehension of "the beyond-perception world", in the central point, looks for a certain balance between the "self" and the world; and the literature of this new time reflects this process in the so-called "classical styles" of the epoch, deprived of the individual principles and subjective metaphoric character in spite of all their power. The creative works of J. Goethe and A. Pushkin became the standard of such a balance.

A specific "metaphorization" of the world took place in the poetry of the beginning of the 20-th century: the metaphor turned out to be the prevailing method of the extremely intensive expansion of the artist's creative will and freedom; the hypertrophy of the world perceiving "self" destroyed the self-contained sovereignty of the world, altering it into the subjective different being, into the "imagery": "The matter is disclosed only through the metaphor, since there is no existence beyond comparison, as the existence makes the comparison" (O. Mandelshtam). The metaphor comprehended in this way, probably, outgrows the function of the trope. In the modern literature the metaphor does not serve only as a means of the word renewal: the increased metaphoric character of the style can both witness the superfluity of the creative imagination and personal initiative of the artist (as if he surpasses the exposed world) and provide the possibility – to a certain degree artificially cultivated – to uphold the fading expression upon a meeting with him.

The metaphor is not taken to the simple substitution of the word – it is the alteration of the word semantic content, which can be regarded as a result of two operations: adding and reduction of semes. In other words, the metaphor results from the confrontation of two synecdoches. Let us regard the example quoted by J. Dubois.

A poet with the circles of death under his eyes comes down to this wonderland. What will he sow into this furrow, the only one on this sandy shore, wherein once in six hours, like an illiterate maidservant, coming into the room, in order to prepare the paper and the deck set, the sea in a white cap displays and put in again empty letters [literally, an empty alphabet] of seaweeds? What does it give to the world that expects nothing, lying frozen in a gray silence? Coincidence. (M. Deghi)

The esthetic perfection of this text is based on many methods, in particular, on the light coercion of the lexical material. These small semantic "scandals" draw one's attention to the information. From the formal point of view, the metaphor represents a syntactic structure, wherein the identity of two significants and the difference of the corresponding significates exist in the contradictory unity. This challenge to the (linguistic) consciousness requires the reduction performance, which is taken to the fact that the reader tries in a certain way to substantiate the observed coincidence of the significants. It is important that in the process of reduction the linguistic factors are never prejudiced. The reduction is performed owing to the conditions that lie beyond the rhetoric consciousness. The position of the scientific information receiver would be absolutely different. In the scientific text the semantic incompatibility of such kind can be both refused (in case, when the said is recognized to be false or senseless), or accepted. Special modal frames are typical to the utterances of such type, like, for instance: *the experience demonstrates, that...* or *In spite of the adopted point of view, X demonstrated that...* In the framework of the poetical perusal of a text such precautionary measures are superfluous, though, in principle, they can be formulated in the same form, however, then they will bear another semantic burden. A priory, the reader of a poetical text always identifies the code of the given work with the usual linguistic code; immediately he starts arranging the fragments of classification in the form of a "tree" or "pyramid" looking for the level, at which the available significates will be equivalent. When we consider two dissimilar objects, we can always find out a "limiting" class in the pyramid of the nested classes, which will include both of these objects, provided that in all more fractional classes they appear separately (See above).

The following terms as *identical, equivalent and similar* are used exclusively to ascertain approximately the level of the "limiting" class in respect of all those classes, wherein both significates appear as different units. The metaphoric reduction is considered as completed when the reader finds out the third notion that plays the role of a joint between two others (for instance, the linearity – *white uneven edge – black oblong forms on a bright foil*). The process of reduction is taken to the search for this third notion either within the boundaries of a certain tree or a certain pyramid, which either reflects or does not reflect the real state of affairs. Every reader may have his own semantic conception. The main thing is to find out the shortest way that join both objects; the search will continue until all possible criteria of the difference are looked through.

The "limiting" class can be defined as an intersection of two words' senses, as the common part of the aggregate of their semes or parts.

If this common part is necessary to substantiate the postulated identity, nevertheless, their unmatched parts are necessary to provide for the image originality and put the mechanism of reduction in action. The metaphor extrapolates, it is constructed on the basis of real similarity, appearing in the intersection of two senses, and it asserts the full coincidence of these senses. It conferred a characteristic inherent only in their crossing on the combination of two senses.

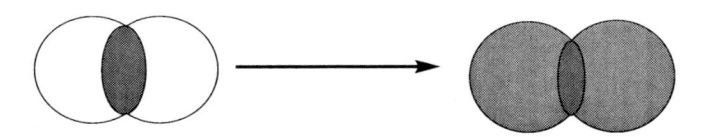

Therefore, the metaphor as if widens the text borders, creates the sensation of its "openness" and makes it more capacious.

The metaphoric process can be described in the following way:

$$I \; a \; (R) \; a \; IM,$$

Wherein *I* is the initial word or expression, *R* is the resulting word, and the transition from the first notion to the second is performed through the intermediate notion *IM*, which is never present in a discourse: depending on the adopted point of view it corresponds either to the "limiting" class or to the intersection of the aggregate of semes.

The metaphor, which is separated into the component parts in this way, can be interpreted as the confrontation of two synecdoches, since *R* represents the synecdoche in respect of *I*, and *IM* appears as the synecdoche in respect of *R*.

As the synecdoche can be either generalizing or narrowing, in order to construct a metaphor we ought to combine (join) two completing each other synecdoches functioning in the way that appears opposite in respect of each other, and they determine the point of crossing between the notions *I* and *IM*: *iron – blade – plain*.

The metaphor can use the general semes *I* and *IM* (*iron* instead of *dagger*) as the basis, the metaphor can be constructed on the foundation of the parts common for *I* and *IM* (*sail* instead of *ship*). The partition between two types of the metaphor: conceptual and referential is performed by this characteristic. The conceptual type is constructed exclusively on the semantic basis; it results from the reduction with addition to semes; the second type, referential, has a purely physical foundation and it can be obtained by the application of the reduction with addition to the material parts (this type of the metaphor can be considered as a linguistic variety of the image metaphor or the metaphor, applied in the painting, which has to be described in the framework of the general rhetoric that covers all kinds of arts).

The compression of the real semantics up to the points of intersection of the semes series, appearing in the process of the metaphor formation, in its turn can be regarded as the emasculation, fabulous contraction and unjustified coercion of the text. In this context a poet or a writer may have a desire to correct one's own metaphor mostly by means of synecdoche that functions within the boundaries of the logical difference of the semes multitudes, or the second metaphor.

We can borrow a noted example of such kind from B. Pascal: "L'homme n'est qu'un roseau, le plus faible de la nature, mais c'est un roseau pensant" – *A man is just a reed, the weakest of the nature's creatures, but he is a thinking reed.*

Let us consider the logical copulas in this sentence: the restricting one just introduces the metaphor in such a way, as if the matter concerns the synecdoche (through the intersection of series in the point that corresponds to the notion of "weakness"), meanwhile the adversative conjunction *but* introduces the generalizing synecdoche (which is always true by definition) in such a way, as if its verity is to be proved. One of the main characteristics typical to the corrected metaphor lies in this deliberate mixture of true and false.

We find out a multitude of simpler examples in the argot or humoristic style of speech. Thus, for instance, a dachshund can be called *a sausage with small legs* (a metaphor corrected by synecdoche). There is one more known metaphor *a crystal breast* (instead of "a jug") and so on.

One can correct the metaphor with the use of the metonymy. This method is often used in the verses of Maeterlinck:

"Les jaunes flèches des regrets…
Les cerfs blancs des mensonges…"
Literally: *Yellow arrows of regrets…*
 White deers of lie…

It is notable that the metaphor is represented here by the name of a flower, i.e. it is one of the rare cases of the monosemantic lexeme, which by this very reason is perceived as a synecdoche.

This method is used also in the collocations like: *a creeping flower of soothing* and *a point of cypress as a frozen spear*.

Bellow there is a triangle in which we have discussed two sides: metaphor and synecdoche. The third side can be presented only by the oxymoron.

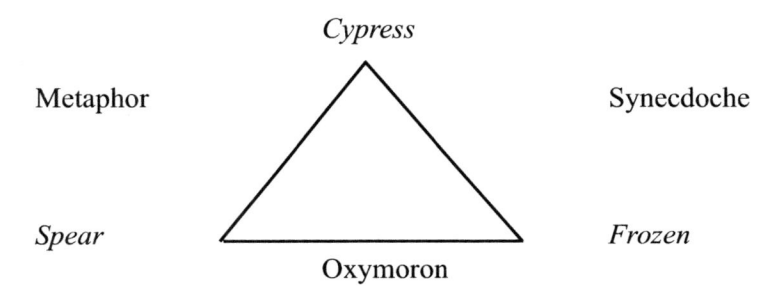

Cypress

Metaphor   Synecdoche

Spear   *Frozen*

Oxymoron

However, the *frozen spear* is presented as an equivalent of the *cypress*, gained by means of a quite admissible transformation. Thus, the cypress, a quiet, well known to everybody tree, receives an internally contradictory definition: one can notice some parts that are incompatible with each other. All this gives us a more precise presentation of the mechanism of the corrected metaphor action: it "blows up" the reality and shocks, illuminating the contradictory sides of the object.

So, the metaphor resulted from the application of the double logical operation. At that, it is important to specify, whether the initial for this figure notion can be present in the text or not. The intelligibility of the text in the given case is ensured either owing to the high level of superfluity in the trope-inclusive sequence, or due to the considerable semantic intersection, between the null stage and the "image-bearing", ("figurative") expression. In fact, only from the context (despite the availability of four metaphors) one can understand what is going on in the following text (an example of J. Dubois):

A nightingale in the wall, an immured spark,
Captivated by lime tender click, a beak (R. Brock) – the matter concerns an electric switch. That is why poets insensibly began applying to the metaphor, which resembles the comparison too much (it differs from it only by the absence of the conjunctive *as*):

Shuddering walls of buildings, cracked puddles of window glasses... (M. Deghi); *Spain is a big whale, stranded on the coast of Europe* (E. Burke).

It is interesting that upon the evident figurativeness of the last example, it resembles the synecdoche (a whale instead of its shape) that underlines the close relationship between these two tropes. Brock's example manifests that metaphors has different degrees of comprehensibility in the speech communication, which is connected with the volume of the semantic units intersection zone that are included into the notions presented in the metaphor.

Let us regard the following example: *You've humbled, stilted dreams of my spring* (A. Pushkin). It is obvious that if a word is used in the meaning, which is more inherent in another word (there is the denotatum behind every word, i.e. that concrete object, which is set by the word), then, of course, the metaphor is constructed on the inner psychological comparison between the objects and phenomena. This connection should be sensible by this very reason that the notion with which the comparison is made, is not named. In the regarded example this connection is clear: *the spring – the youth*. Why? Let us write down the meaning of each of two words through the sequence of semes. The spring represents the post-initial period. It is wise to ask a question: "The post-initial period of what?" (*A* of *B*). "The post-initial period" is defined as a function with the argument presented by one calendar year in the nature: 1) year; 2) singleness; 3) nature.

The conception of the nature can be divided into two notions: *the human being – non-human nature*. Then, the spring appears as the post-initial period of a single year in the human life, as well as in the non-human life of the nature. Let us do the same thing with the conception of *the youth*. The youth represents the post-initial many-years period of the human being. Having compared two semantic writings:

The spring = the post-initial period (year + singularity + the human being + the non-human nature);

The youth = the post-initial period (year + plurality + the human being).

we reveal that these two notions have the similar semantic function ("the post-initial period") and the considerable intersection in the arguments: "Year" and "the human being". The notion of "the spring" has the meaning of singularity, and the notion of the youth – plurality (i.e. these two notions are opposed by the category of singularity/plurality. In addition, the interpretation of the notion of *the spring* has one extra semantic element – *the non-human nature*. Such a metaphor is considered as successful, since it knows the measure of the semantic intersection, which cannot be given formally, but it is intuitively perceived. If the metaphor is constructed on the notions, the semantic interpretations of which have little coincidences (for instance, one common element in an argument), then this metaphor can be incomprehensible to the speech communicants.

If one analyzes some texts, say, Russian poetry of the beginning of the 20-th century, he can feel, first, the supersaturation by metaphors, and, second, the complexity of their decoding. Incomprehensibility of the sense is compensated in a verse by the harmony and form, thus, the form on its own turns out to be the significate of the verse (See above).

So, if in the interpretation of two words there are very little points of crossing, the metaphor won't be comprehensible and, consequently, it is unsuccessful, as any speech conduct is realized in order to transmit information. If a man transmits information and another man is not able to receive it, then such a communicative situation turns out to be inexpedient. There are some writers and poets, who declare that they write for themselves and for other two-three people that can evaluate their text. It is a common point of view. When the author puts his work in other people's judgment, he ought to understand well, whose judgment he is waiting for; may be there is no sense to publish books by large editions, may be one ought to try to distribute them among those few people, who can interpret them in an adequate way, as their mentality is close to the author's mentality, which is the basis for the understanding. There are some texts, which, in fact, can be understood only by little number people, since these texts are constructed on the basis of associations, evoked by a certain joined action. For instance, three persons were sitting by a campfire on the bank of a river and spoke about something – it is a fact of their individual life – only these three men know what they spoke about. Then, one makes a text, which in the semantic sphere leans on this concrete incident. The metaphor appears as the transfer of this concrete sense, as it is founded on the remembrance about that event. Who does remember it? Only those three men, who were sitting on the bank of the river, remember it, nobody else, and only they can decode such a text. In this case one ought to type three copies of the text and distribute among these people. However, when the author puts his own work in the judgment of a great number of people and he publishes it by a considerable edition, he ought to proceed from the fact that there should be a certain level of comprehension, though relative). One ought to consider that a large number of metaphors are founded on the knowledge of other works of art, especially, antic and the Renaissance's; texts with such metaphors are aimed at the erudite readers and listeners.

What happens with the text comprehension, when the level of the senses intersection is considerable, and, say, two notions have a common function and all arguments, except one, are similar?

$$C_1 = f_1 (a_1 + a_2 + A_3 + a_4);$$
$$C_2 = f_1 (a_1 + a_2 + a_3 + a_5).$$

It is evident that such a metaphor will be clear, but will it be successful? Most likely, there will be no metaphoric effect, as C_1 and C_2 will turn out to be close synonyms. How many units of intersection should be enough to make the metaphor, on the one hand, clear and, on the other hand, not banal and to prevent it to become a synonym? There cannot be any formal answer. The author shall apply to his taste and feelings. Every time your reader or listener will find it hard to understand the metaphor, however it will be possible upon a certain mental effort.

The personification represents a special kind of metaphor (In Greek *prósōpon* – face, *poiéō* – making), which is based on the transfer of the human features (in a broader way – the features of a living creature) onto lifeless objects and phenomena. One can trace the gradation of personification depending on the function in the artistic speech and literary creative work. 1. The personification as a stylistic figure, connected with the "instinct" of personification in the living languages and with the rhetorical tradition, inherent in every expressive speech: *the heart speaks, the river plays.* 2. The personification in the folk poetry and individual lyrics (for instance, of H. Heine, S. Esenin) as a metaphor, close by its role to the psychological parallelism: the life of the surrounding world, mainly, of the nature, attracted to the co-operation in the hero's mental life, is endowed with the characteristics of the man-likeliness. The assimilations of natural to human, lying in the basis of such personifications, go back to the mythological and fabulous thinking with that essential difference, that the mythology discovers the "face" of elements through the relationship with the human world (for instance, the relationship between The Uranus – the Heaven and the Gea – the Earth is comprehended through the assimilation to the marriage), and in the folklore and poetic creation of the latest epochs, on the contrary, the "face" and the mental motions of the person are disclosed through the personified manifestation of the spontaneous natural life. 3. The personification as a symbol, directly connected with the central artistic idea and growing up from the system of particular personifications. Thus, the poetic prose of A. Chekhov's novel "Steppe" is full of personifications – metaphors: the handsome poplar feels the burden of its loneliness, half-dead grass sings a plaintiff song and so on. Their aggregate gives rise to the supreme personification: the "face" of the steppe that realizes the wrongful death of its wealth, heroism and inspiration, – a polysemic symbol, connected with the painter's thoughts about his motherland, sense of life and fleetingness. The personifications of such kind are often close to the mythological personification by its common significance, "objectiveness", relative incoherence with the narrator's psychological state, but, nevertheless, it does not cross over the line of the relativity, which always separates the arts from the mythology.

The personification appears as the most expressive one of the available tropes. It is so expressive that sometimes it is dangerous to use it. Why is the personification so powerful? There is the existence of the nature and the existence of the human being, who, on the one hand, represents a part of the nature, and, on the other hand, functions separately, as an observer. The human consciousness is constructed in such a way that everything, which concerns him personally, is always superior to everything, which concerns something else (for instance, stones or trees). This stable human universal appears as general in the human world outlook: the main thing regards that thing, which concerns the people; significant – that which concerns animals; and only then the remaining things go according to their level of significance. Therefore, the human being is represented by those main epithets, which characterize exactly the man, and his most significant actions are those, which exactly the man performs. If one transfers the human characteristics and typical actions onto the lifeless objects, the significance of the latter will increase to the limit. The effectiveness of the sense transfer is maximally expressed in this way. Thus, the personification appears as an "ideal" method of expressiveness. *I'll whistle and the bloody evil will crawl obediently and gingerly to my place. And it will lick my hand and peer at my eyes, reading in them a symbol of my will* (A. Pushkin). Can one express one's thought in a stronger way?

Chapter 21. **Irony in Speech Communication**

> I do not regard myself seriously,
> But I regard my views seriously.
> *G. K. Chesterton*

Irony (in Greek *eirōnéia* literally a pretense; when a man pretends to be more foolish than he is actually) has two interpretations.

1. In the stylistics it regards to a circumlocution that expresses a mockery or craftiness, when a word or collocation gains such a meaning in the speech context, which is opposite to the literal sense, or refutes or prejudices it. Let us cite an example:

> *A powerful masters servant*
> *What kind a noble courage with*
> *Your free speech smashes those*
> *All, whose mouth stopped.*
> F. I. Tyutchev

The irony is defined as a defamation and opposition under the mask of approval and consent; they deliberately attribute to a certain phenomena a characteristic that it cannot have initially. (Where do you, the clever head (an ass), make your way from? – I. A. Krylov) or it is absent; though according to the logic of the author's thought it should be expected. Usually, the irony is referred to tropes, sometimes – to stylistic figures. Usually not the expression hints at a pretense, "a key" to the irony, but the context or intonation, sometimes (especially in prose) – only in the situation of speaking. When an ironical mockery turns out to be a caustic jeer, it is called sarcasm.

2. In the esthetics it regards to the comic type, ideological and emotional evaluation, elementary model or prototype, which applies to the structurally expressive principle of the verbal stylistical irony. The ironical relation assumes deliberately hidden superiority or indulgence, skepticism or mockery, which determine the style of a work of art ("A Praise on the Foolishness" by Erasmus Roterodamus) or the organization of an image-bearing system (characters, plot, the whole work, for instance "Fairy Mountain" by T. Mann). "The secrecy" of a mockery and a mask of the seriousness distinguish the irony from the humor and especially from the satire (See bellow).

An ironic relation is realized in multiple ways: with the use of a grotesque (J. Swift, E. T. A. Hoffmann, and M. E. Saltykov-Shchedrin), paradox (A. France, B. Show), and parody (L. Sterne), wittiness, hyperbola, contrast, combination of various speech styles and so on.

The sense of irony as an esthetic category in various epochs transformed considerably. For the Antiquity it was typical to have, for instance, the so-called "Socratic' irony", which expressed a philosophical principle of doubts and at the same time a means of the truth revealing. Socrates pretended to be an associate of the opponent; he assented to him and insensibly led his view to an absurd, exposing the limited nature of quasi-evident truth. (See above). In the "Socratic" irony the esthetic play and the pleasure of the dialectic of thinking were combined with the searches for the truth and moral values (See Plato's dialog "The Feast"). In the ancient theatre one can come across the so-called tragic irony ("a twist of fate"), however, it turned out to be theoretically comprehended only in the new times: the hero is sure of himself and he does not know (in contrast to the spectator) that it were exactly his deeds, which make ready his own death (a classical example – "Oedipus – the Tsar" by Sophokles, and later on – "Wallenstein" by F. Schiller). Such "a twist of fate" is often called an objective irony. Being skeptical by nature, the irony is a stranger to the literary men, who are directed to the unshakeable hierarchy of values (baroque, classicism), as it was also devoid of the Christian consciousness, including the medieval esthetic thought, being indifferent to the gaming beginning and risorial verge of the existence.

Long ago Cicero, who, however, immediately declared it insoluble, knew the problem of the invariable source of laughter and the actual significance of the laughter connected with it.

The romanticism developed the irony's theoretical substantiation and varied artistic implementation (the notion of a romantic irony in esthetic works of F. Schlegel, C. W. Solger; artistic practice – in works of L. Tieck and E. T. A. Hoffmann in Germany, J. Byron in England, A. Musset in France). German romanticist developed the irony's comprehension up to the ideological principle: the romantic irony shall be universal and infinite, i.e. directed to everything completely both in the sphere of the real, "conditioned" existence, and in the mental vital activity of the subject. In such a comprehensibly ironical position the romanticists saw an absolute expression of freedom – the supreme value of the romantic consciousness. The principle of the universal romantic irony (often identifying the irony with the reflexion in general) dictated to the artist an inner reference: to stop at nothing, to prejudice everything or refute; being not binding upon any finite "truth", freely move from one opinion to another, underlining the relativity and the limited character of all "rules" determined by the human being. This implies a notion of a game that is important for the conception of the romantic irony: the "spirit of a real transcendental buffoonery" should prevail in the work – in his levitation over the "necessity" an artist goes away from any value distinctness, and he consciously makes the serious and feigned, profound and ingenuous be indistinguishable by content and intonation. As a result, the irony turns out to be unfree from the hypertrophy of the purely esthetic game of extremes, which frequently loses the boundaries between good and evil, truth and error, freedom and necessity, "holy" and "vicious" and so on. The irony as the principle of the world outlook also presupposed a composite-artistic game with the extremes in the romanticists' creative work: real and fantastic, elevated and prosaic, reasonable and illogical.

The romantic theory, which exposed the dissention of a dream (ideal) and the real life, undergoes the evolution; in the beginning it appeared as an irony of freedom; the life did not know any insuperable obstacles for its free forces, scoffing at everybody, who tried to make her forms invariable; then it was replaced by the sarcasm of the necessity; the forces of sluggishness and oppression overpowered the free forces of the life, the poet rose high, but they pulled him down, caustically and roughly mocking at him (Byron, Hoffmann and especially Heine, "A knight for an hour" by N. Nekrasov). Then, a tragic and "bitter irony" occurred – the author equally sneers at both the objective evil and his own feebleness to oppose to it. When the mockery at the evil and one's self combines with the doubt in the real character of ideals, the irony turns out to be "obscure" and harmful. The irony in the decadent frame of mind can be considered as "negative" and even "nihilistic", it also pertained to some symbolists, which A. Block wrote about with a bitter feeling. The "nihilistic" irony of some painters and aesthetics of the 20-th century, involved in the modernism (especially "black humor), includes, in particular, the principle of the total parodying and self-parodying of the arts (an American writer J. Barthelm).

T. Mann developed his own conception of an "epic irony" as one of the main principles of the modern realism. Proceeding from the universality of the romantic irony, he underlined that the irony is necessary for the epic arts as a look from the height of freedom, calm and objectiveness, connected with no moralization. At the end of the 19-th century – in the beginning of the 20-th century the irony occupies a noted place also in the works of O. Wild, A. France, B. Show, and C. Chapek. B. Brecht reflected a specific ironic dialectics in the theatrical method of estrangement.

Arthur Schopenhauer gave a very interesting interpretation of the ridiculous and irony. "The paradoxical and therefore unexpected bringing of an object to the definition, which in other respects appears as a heterogeneous, always acts as a source of the ridiculous, and, thus, the phenomenon of laughter seems to be an always unexpected understanding of the discrepancy between such a notion and the real object conceivable in it, i.e. between the abstract and contemplative. The greater and more unexpected is the discrepancy in the perception of the laughing person, the louder will be his laughter. Therefore, in everything that provokes the laughter, there always should be a notion and something singular, consequently, a thing or an event, which could be brought to this notion and conceived in it in this way, however, in another and more significant respect it absolutely does not relate to it, and more over, evidently differs from everything that is conceived in this notion. When, as it frequently occurs upon witty remarks, instead of such a contemplative real, a superordinate concept being subordinate to the supreme or generic concept comes forward and provokes the laughter by this only thing that it is realized by the fantasy, i.e. it substitutes it for that which appears in the contemplation and, thus, arouses the conflict between the conceived and contemplated. In order to understand all this in an explicit way, one can even take the ridiculous to the conclusion by the first form with the doubtless major and, all of a sudden, even the minor introduced in a quasi ticklish way– due to such a combination the conclusion will gain the ridiculous character." And further on: "The source of the ridiculous lies in the discrepancy of the conceivable and contemplative. Depending on the fact, whether we move from the real, i.e. contemplative, to the notion, and vice versa, from the notion to the real, upon the disclosure of such a discrepancy, or not, the ridiculous, appearing as a result of all this, will be either a witty remark or absurdity, but to a higher degree, in particular, in the practical life – a stupidity." As an example of the first kind, i.e. a mockery, we will cite a famous anecdote about a Gascon, whom the king laughed at, seeing him wearing a summer dress in winter cold; the Gascon told the King: " If you, my Lord, wore that which I wore, you would find that it is quite warm in it." And to the King's question about what he dressed up he answered: "All my clothes". Under this one can understand both the boundless wardrobe of the King and the only summer frock coat of a poor fellow, which look on the shivering body does not correspond to the concept of a wardrobe.

A witty remark is often included in a single utterance, only by hinting at the notion, which can be brought to this case that is absolutely heterogeneous (by Schopenhauer) to all other things conceived in the notion. Thus, in Shakespeare's "Romeo and Juliet" cheerful, just now wounded Mercutio tells his friend, who promise to see him on the next day: "Come tomorrow and you will find me a grave man." At this point a dead person is brought to this notion. In the English language a play on words joins this notion, as a grave man means at the same time either a serious or a dead person. A famous anecdote about an actor Unzelmann sounds similar: after any sort of improvisation was prohibited in the Berlin theater, he had to appear on the scene on horseback, at that, exactly at the moment when he was on the proscenium the horse dunged, which on its own aroused the public's laughter; however, the laughter much more increased when Unzelmann directed to the horse with the following words: "What are you doing? Don't you know that we are prohibited from any improvisations?" In this example the bringing of the heterogeneous to a single notion is very clear and therefore the witting remark is extremely ready and the effect of the ridiculous is very strong.

The following example perfectly corresponds to the discussed kind of the ridiculous: Saphire in the literary struggle with actor Andjeli calls him "the mighty spirit and body Andjeli"; in this case due to the weak figure of the actor known to the whole city the unusual minor is brought to the notion of "mighty". The fact that Saphire named arias of a new opera as "old good friends" made the same effect; consequently, exactly the reprehensible characteristics are brought to the notion that in other cases serves as a recommendation. When somebody says about a woman, whose favor depends on a gift, that she is able to combine the useful with the pleasant, they bring something mean in the moral respect to the notion of the rule, which Horace recommends to use in the field of esthetics; in the same way, when they call a bordello as "a modest shelter of quiet pleasures". A descent society in order to reach an absolute vulgarity gets rid of all direct and therefore blunt expressions and applies to the abstracts in order to sooth scandalous or somewhat shocking things; however, in that way more or less heterogeneous is brought to these notions resulting in the effect of ridiculous.

The bringing to a notion of something, which in one respect is heterogeneous, but in other cases corresponds to it, can be also unintentional; for instance, one of the free Negroes in the North America, trying to look similar in everything like white people, wrote to his dead child an epitaph, which began with the following words: "a wonderful, early culled lily". Wherein, quite to the contrary, the real and contemplative is roughly and deliberately brought to the opposite notion, it originates a mean and vulgar irony. For instance, when upon pouring somebody says: *what a nice weather is today* or about an ugly bride: *what a beauty he found*; or about a swindler: *this honest man* and so on. Only children or uneducated people can laugh at it, since here one can see the full convergence between the conceived and contemplated. However, its main character, the noted convergence, appears very clear upon such a rough exaggeration and in the attempt to say something funny. The parody comes close to such kind of the ridiculous due to its exaggeration and evident premeditation. Its method consists in the fact that it attributes the events and words of a serious verse or drama to insignificant and mean persons, or connects them with small-minded motives and deeds. Consequently, it brings the depicted base realities to the high notions given in the theme, which they shall suit in a certain respect, so as for the rest they absolutely do not coincide with; due to which the contradiction between the contemplated and conceived appears very brightly. An address of a certain man, who used the final word of Schiller's ballade "Bail", to the just now married young couple, especially to the female half, whom he liked, sound original and wittily:

> *My friends, forever, from now and on,*
> *Let me be the third in your union!*

In the above example the action of the ridiculous is strong and inevitable, as the banned and immoral relations are brought to the notions, which by Schiller's intention should arouse our thoughts about noble relations in the moral sense; however, they are brought in the correct way and without any change, consequently, the thought about them is aroused by Schiller's words.

In all the above cited examples of witty remarks we can find out that the real is brought to the notion or, in general, to an abstract thought, either directly, or by means of a narrower notion, provided that, strictly speaking, this real relates to this notion, but it is infinitely far from the actual and initial intention and the thought's direction. Therefore, the wittiness as a mental capacity consists in the easiness of finding a notion for every given object, provided that this object can be conceived in this notion, being sharply heterogeneous to all other objects, which relate to the notion.

Another kind of the ridiculous moves in the reverse direction, from the abstract notion to the reality, conceived in this notion, or to the contemplative, which, however, in some respect that was not noticed before does not coincide with the notion, thus making an absurdity and finally leads to a foolish deed. The following facts can serve as examples of the ridiculous of this kind. When a man says that he likes walking alone, the other says in reply: "You like to walk alone, me too. Let us go together". He proceeds from the thought: "The pleasure, which two men liked, can be shared by both of them." – and brings to it exactly the same case, which excludes the compatibility. Soldiers in a guardhouse allow the newly arrested prisoner to take part in a card play, but as he swindles and his swindling provokes a scandal, they turn him out, being governed by the common notion that "bad friends should be turned out", forgetting about the fact that they deal with the prisoner, i.e. with a man, whom they should keep under arrest. Two peasant boys had a gun, loaded with large shot, which they wanted to pull out and replace by small shot without loosing the gunpowder. To do this, one of them put the gun's barrel into his cap, which he gripped by his legs, and told the other boy: "Now, pull the trigger slowly, very slowly, then the shot will go out in the first place". He proceeded from the notion: "The slowing down of the reason will lead to the slowing down of the action". The majority of the Quixote's deeds serve as the examples of such kind; he brings to the notions, taken from the knight's novels, the encountered realities, which are absolutely heterogeneous to these notions, for instance, wishing to help the oppressed people he releases convicts from custody. Generally speaking, the stories about baron Munchausen also relate to this matter: but the matter concerns the deeds, which were not made, it relates to the impossible quasi reality that was pretended to happen. In all these stories the adventures are stated in such a way that the conceivable abstract a priory seems to be possible and probable; however, then, upon the observation of the given individual case, i.e. posteriori, the impossibility and, more over, the absurdity of the stated story is revealed and arouses the laughter by the evident convergence between the contemplated and conceived, for instance, when it is stated that the melodies frozen in the post-horn are thawing down in a warm room. The story about two lions sounds in the same way, when in the night they broke the partition between their cases and gorged each other with rage and in the morning only two their tails were found.

There are some cases of the ridiculous, wherein it is not necessary either to state a notion to which the contemplated is brought, or to hint at it, since it comes to mind by an association of ideas. When a famous actor Garrick while playing a tragic role burst out laughing, since a certain butcher in order to wipe out the sweat put his wig on the head of a big dog, which looked over the theater leaning by the first legs on parterre's barrier, the laughter was aroused by the fact that Garrick proceeded from the spectators' utilitarian notion. It explains the fact that certain animals, like monkeys, kangaroo and groundhogs and so on sometimes look funny, as a certain similarity with the man induces us to bring them to the notion of the human being, due to which we do not notice the discrepancy later on.

The notions, the evident discrepancy of which with the contemplation arouses our laughter, can belong to us or somebody else. In the first case we laugh at another person, in the second case we often feel a pleasant, anyhow, funny amazement. Children and uneducated people laugh by any minor, sometimes even improper reason, if it is sudden, i.e. if it does not correspond to the a priori accepted notion. As a rule, the laughter affords pleasure: we are pleased to see the convergence between the contemplated with the conceived, consequently, in fact, we willingly give ourselves up to the convulsive bursting, initiated by this discovery. The reason lies in the following. Upon such a suddenly appearing contradiction between the conceived and contemplated, the contemplated will be always doubtlessly correct, as in general it is not liable to errors, it does not require any substantiation and supports itself. Finally it arouses a conflict with the conceived due to the fact that the conceived with all its abstract notions is not able to comprehend the infinite multiformity and shades of the contemplated. And we are pleased by this victory of the contemplative consciousness over the thinking. As the contemplation appears as the initial, inseparably linked with the animal nature method of comprehension, which includes everything that directly satisfies the will, this is the environment of the real, pleasure and joyfulness and more over it is not connected with any effort. The opposite is typical to the thinking: it appears as the secondary potential of the comprehension, the performance of which always requires a certain, sometimes, considerable, effort and the notions of which are often opposed to the satisfaction of our direct desires, since they, as the area of the past and the future and the seriousness, serve as an expression of all our fears, repentances and concerns. It is pleasant to see how this strict, tireless, bothersome tutor, the mind, is exposed to be insolvent. Therefore, the expression of laughter is relative to the expression of pleasure.

Seriousness is opposite to the laughter and joke. It represents the consciousness of the full coincidence and equality of the notion or thought with the contemplated or the reality. A serious man is sure of the fact that he conceives the things as such as they are in the reality and he thinks that they look the same as he conceives them. The transition from the deep seriousness to the laughter is so easy that a minor thing can provoke it by this very reason that the more complete is the coincidence accepted with the full seriousness, the easier is the possibility to eliminate it by a minor, unexpectedly revealed discrepancy. Therefore, the more is the man inclined to the real seriousness, the more readily he laughs. The people, who laugh as always affected and look as if forced, are not elevated in the mental and moral respect and, in general, one's manner of laughing and the causes of laughter brightly characterize the man.

We are so wounded when somebody laughs at those things that we do or seriously speak about, since it indicates a considerable discrepancy between our notions and the objective reality. A *ridiculous* epithet is offensive by the same reason. The true mocking laughter gloatingly declares to the defeated opponent how far are the notions, which he was holding to, from the newly disclosed reality. Our own bitter laughter at the sight of the terribly open truth, which demonstrates how illusory were our hopes, serves as a living expression of our discovery about the discrepancy between our thoughts, our naive trust in the people and the destiny and the newly open reality.

The deliberate ridiculous is defined as a joke; it is a desire to bring the reality to the discrepancy with the other person's notions by means of shifting one of its moments; his antithesis, presented by the seriousness, lies, at least by intention, in the exact correspondence of them to each other. If a joke is masked behind the seriousness, then it is an irony; for instance, if we listen to the other person's opinions, which are opposite to ours, with an affected seriousness and at the same time pose that we share them until it is revealed that our interlocutor stops understanding what he says and us. Socrates behaved in this way in his conversation with Hippius, Protagoras, Gorgias and other sophists.

The counter to the irony or the seriousness hidden behind a joke is called the humor. It can be defined as the double counterpoint of the irony. The irony is objective, i.e. it is meant for other people; the humor is subjective; i.e. first of all it means the "Self". Therefore, high examples of the irony can be found in the works of ancient authors and the samples of humor – in the works of new authors. As upon an in-depth analysis it is revealed that the humor is rooted in a subjective, but at the same time a serious and elevated mood that unintentionally comes into collision with the vulgar reality of the outer world, which one cannot avoid, but at the same time one cannot renounce his views. However, in order to make a compromise, one ought to determine his own outlook and the outer world in one and the same notions that gain the double discrepancy of the reality, which is conceived in them, thus being now on that, now on this side. All this results in getting an impression of a deliberate ridiculous, i.e. a joke, in which, however, one can notice a deeply hidden seriousness. If in the beginning the irony is followed by the seriousness and at the end – by a smile, the humor – vise versa. For instance, the above-referred Mercutio's words, as well as the words of Polonium from "Hamlet": "The honorable Prince, I will humbly leave you". And Hamlet's: "There is nothing, my sir, which I could more willingly leave, unless my life…"

As an example we can cite Hamlet's words addressed to Ophelia before the performance began at the court: "What else can a man do if not to be cheerful? Look at this, how my mother joyfully looks, but two hours are not over as my father died".

Ophelia: "No, my Prince, two months are over."

Hamlet: "Such a long time? So let the devil be dressed in black, I will wear the sables."

Henry Heine appears as a true humorist in his "Romancero", in all his jokes and mockeries one can see a deep seriousness, which due to the cheerfulness hides under this mask. Thus, the humor follows from a specific mood; under this notion with all its modifications one ought to conceive a considerable preponderance of the subjective over the objective upon the perception of the outer world. Every poetical or artistic representation of a comic and even a buffoonery scene, wherein in the background one can perceive a serious thought, appears as the humor product, consequently, it is humoristic. Thus, for instance, is the picture of Tischbein: the painter painted an absolutely empty room illuminated only by the fireplace's fire; there is a man dressed in a jacket with high collar standing in front of the fireplace, and his shadow, starting from his legs stretches all over the room. Tischbein comments: "This is a man, who failed to do and reach anything; now he is pleased that he is able to cast such a big shadow." If one needs to express the seriousness, hidden in this joke, he would better do it by means of the lines borrowed from a Persian verse by Anvari Soheili:

> *"If you lose the whole world,*
> *Don't greave; it is nothing.*
> *If you find the whole world,*
> *Don't triumph; it is nothing.*
> *Sorrows and pleasures will go by,*
> *Go along, leaving the world aside,*
> *It is nothing."*

The Russian literature and critics is noted for their multifarious irony (though the ironical position is not so typical to the Russian classics): "the avenger" and "the comforter" by A.I. Hertsen; "mocking critics" by V.G. Belinsky, N.A. Nekrasov, M.E. Saltykov-Shchedrin, N.G. Chernyshevsky (an image of a "penetrating reader" in the novel "What is to do?"); merging with the elements of humor by N.V. Gogol; mock by Koz'ma Prutkov; romantic by A.A. Block. Various types and shades of the irony are inherent in the works of V.V. Mayakovsky, M.M. Zoshchenko, M.A. Bulgakov, Y.K. Olyosha, V.P. Katayev.

The irony as a method shall be applied in the speech with great care, since it is directly connected with the moral aspect in the speech communication. Each of us to this or that extent has the sense of humor, but we rarely think about the fact that addressing jokes to another person sometimes we wound him. You shall address yourself to other people only in the case when you wish them well. No one forces you to be friendly to everybody, but if you have evil feelings in respect of a certain person, you should not address this person with a speech (except the cases of the utmost necessity), especially if it is an ironical speech.

There are many restrictions in respect of the irony. Their strict observance can make your speech communication more humane and corresponding to the esthetical standard. In what situation should one avoid addressing a man with an ironical speech?

1. If you face a man with no sense of humor.
2. f a man stays in the oppressed mood.
3. If you do not know the man.

There are some specific situations wherein the irony is not appropriate. The irony is not appropriate at the funerals in respect of anybody present. Also the irony is not appropriate at the wedding party. Any action, any ritual, which is connected with great emotions, does not allow any irony. Try to venture to say something ironical at the catholic wedding ceremony. You not only won't be understood, but they will look at you strangely and those people, who heard your ironical remark most probably won't socialize with you in the future. They will treat it as a wild thing; however, in this country we consider it (alas!) as a standard.

5. If there is a third person near you, on whom the person that you chose as a subject of your joke depends in some way, provided that he depends both socially, psychologically and emotionally.

Let us analyze it by the following visual demonstration:

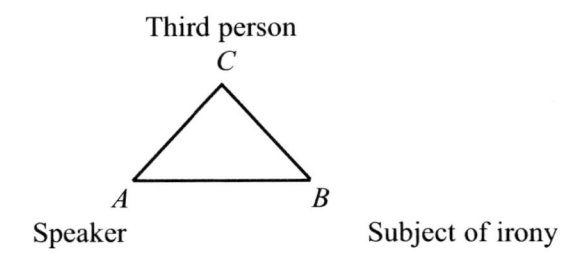

Third person
C

A   B
Speaker   Subject of irony

So, the irony is possible only if the third person is friendly towards *B* and is not connected either hierarchically (socially), or emotionally with him. It is quite a diffused form of irony to sneer at a young person in the presence of a girl, whom he likes. It is not just cruelly; it is disgraceful. Nevertheless, you can see it everywhere. How many times a person's mood was spoiled during a party, wherein he came with a definite emotional mood and after an ironical joke in the presence of a girl, whom he liked, the party turned out to be spoiled. The main communicative objective is not to bring the evil to somebody; and if you spoiled somebody's mood even for a minute, you brought the evil. If the third person socially prevails over B, then in such a situation you'd better avoid any ironical remarks: you should not make fun on the subordinate in the presence of his chief. But you also should avoid sneering at the chief in the presence of the subordinate. Whatever the dependence (social or emotional) is directed to between B and C, one should not venture to mock in their respect.

Of course, it is a certain ideal model and by analyzing the conduct of a concrete man, you will find the multitudes of deviations from the rules. However, one ought to strive for the realization of this model and elaborate a descent system of conduct with other people.

One should not allow oneself to be ironical also in the case when C is a stranger. Thus, the ironical conduct in respect of a man in the presence of a third person is allowed extremely rare. The irony seems appropriate only in a private dialog with a single man.

The cleverer is the man, the more sharp is his language, the more accurate is his strike and the stronger he wounds, therefore, the more restricted should be his irony in the communication.

6. One should not sneer at a person with an evident defect. Only the man with the same defect can venture it, nobody else. It is absolutely evident that you cannot mock, if you have a stronger position. How can you be able to sneer at somebody, who is weaker, sick or cannot counter you? It is one of the reasons according to which you should not sneer at your children; the irony is not the best method of interrelations between the tutor and his pupils, since the communicative positions of the tutor and the pupils differ. First, one ought to reach very confidential and friendly relations and only then he may venture to sneer at any of them.

7. It is categorically not recommended to sneer at such things that are important for the person: his denomination, family, job or a certain work, which he is sincerely devoted to, his system of values, nationality and everything that is connected with the cultural tradition of his nation. The national dignity of the people, especially of small nationalities, should not be ever humiliated. (Such a humiliation causes civil wars, exactly the humiliation!) Everything that to you opinion is dear to the person, something that he is anxious about, should lie beyond the irony.

But it is not all. Imagine, please, a group of friends, whose interrelations are quite friendly, there is no social hierarchy between them and no emotional attachments as well. The irony in such a situation is quite appropriate, however, the first addressee of the irony should be the speaker by himself. First, he ought to sneer at himself, arouse the friends' laughter and only then it is permissible to address another person with an ironical phrase. One ought to learn to laugh at oneself; only a few people, very clever and strong, can do it.

The overcoming of internal complexes and uncertainty, the knowledge about the real value (including oneself), all this represents the signs of the power and intelligence, which enable one to laugh at oneself. When Faina Ranevskaya looked at herself in the mirror and said: "Yes... The beauty is a terrible thing" (and everybody died laughing), it was an example of how one can overcome a complex, which another person is not able to do. As a result she seemed beautiful to those people, who knew her well. No person looks so strikingly, as the one, who can laugh at oneself. It is one of the powerful oratoric methods.

One ought to say that the ability to laugh at oneself is a rare gift (as a high level of intellect as well), presented to a man by the God. But, fortunately, it can be developed. More over, in some countries the pedagogical conception foresees the development of this ability in any child. There are special methods of developing the ability to laugh at oneself. The English people have a delicate sense of humor, however this sense is not genetic, it is a consequence of the national system of children's upbringing. They are so witty, since first of all they can laugh at themselves. Remember English anecdotes: it is always laughter at themselves; however, it is a delicate and elegant laughter.

"A gentleman sits in slippers nearby the fireplace and drinks a tea. A servant comes into the room and says: "Sir, they say that there is flood in the city, the Thames river overflowed the banks." The gentleman answers: "It is the time for a tea, do not bother me." The servant goes out and comes in 5 minutes: "I beg you pardon, Sir, but they say that the flood is so powerful that it reached the street where we live in." "I have told you that I am drinking my tea. Do not bother me, please." A few minutes later the servant comes again and says: "Do you know, Sir, that the water reached the doorway of our house." "Listen to me, please. How long will you bother me? I have told you that now it is time for a tea." Two minutes later the servant widely opens the door and solemnly announces: "The Thames river, Sir!"

It is a typical English joke. In this case it is aimed at the national English characteristic – pedantry. But there is no rudeness, no vulgarity;

it is absolutely not standard, you will never guess what the end it will be.

We can suggest one of the training types, which everybody can do. You go to the bathroom and lock yourself up. You have to be in a closed room, where there is a big mirror and good light. You come close to the mirror and begin a twenty-minutes everyday training. The training goes from the simple to the complicated. First, you look at yourself very attentively, in detail, evaluating and for sure you will find a lot of such things that one can laugh at. And since there are no witnesses of your laughter, this laughter is sincere and it appears as the beginning of your rebirth. You go from the simplest: Look, how "wonderful" is your dress – yellow shirt, blue pants, red tie, dirty boots and so on. "Oh, my God!" Then your speech follows. Loud. You need the voice; therefore you have to be alone. "Only a scarecrow can be so dressed. Only such a man, who has no taste, can wear this tie with this shirt and go like a peacock... I absolutely do not understand how other people can even look at me!" – it is a long speech. Finally, you will find it infinitely funny to look at "something" in the mirror, as every person is quite critical to himself. So, first, you have to examine your dress – it is the simplest method. Then you start examining you appearance. You have to stand up in front of the mirror conditionally dressed and make a good laughter at such a "Perfection", which you represent. It is really funny. Turn around several times before the mirror, examine closely every pimple on your body and laugh at it from the heart. Since nobody sees or hear you, then you are the only witness of you own shame. It is one of the helpful methods to get rid of any psychological complexes, which you can also get rid of. By the way, when you laugh, you do not think that you are funny; it is just funny. Everything that comes through the laughter turns out to be a joy – it is very important to understand. When finally you have estimated the power of your physical "perfection" and laughed at it properly, you start going on to a more serious procedure. You come close to the mirror and start remembering all your small failures for the day, excluding, of course, those critical and serious situations, which brought the pain – they should never become a subject of laughing at. There is no such a man, who at least once a day does not come through blunders and failures. You remember how did you fail in a conversation with a certain person, threw down a cup from the table due to your clumsiness and so on, and start laughing with the full sensation that you look at yourself from a side, and it is not you, but a bear, who overthrew the cup and failed to squeeze into the door (he moves so "masterly" that he cannot distinguish the wall from the door) or forgot absolutely everything, he came late to everywhere he can or something else in the same manner. You start laughing at all daily events, wherein you demonstrated your clumsiness, provided that you do it in words. It must be a mocking speech, at that it should not be castigating and torturing, something like as follows: "What kind of a blunderer you are! You were late everywhere. You scheduled to do five things and you did only one thing – the sixth, and you failed to do properly even this one. Look at yourself. My God, what else do you want from yourself?"

At this point you turn to the more significant problems: you start laughing at your shortcomings, for instance, greediness (which, generally speaking, have quite a great number of people): "Of course, a pitiful miser, you are greedy of a spare banknote. Certainly, there is no such a fool who will go with you to the cinema, when you see whether to buy an ice cream or not". Or you laugh at your laziness: "Well, you are still lying in this bed, it is right, never leave it. If you stay in it for your life – there will be no good." Or you laugh at the peacock's behavior that you recently demonstrated: "Of course, you plumed yourself on it. A peacock is a peacock. Look at your dress, look at yourself. Look at your behavior, at least. The real peacock."

In a while, when going into your bathroom you will start laughing. It will turn out to be your best place, since you will feel joyful in it. And step-by-step the internal habit to laugh at yourself, formed by the everyday training, will enable you to do it in the presence of other people.

Only by mastering the ability to laugh at oneself, one can move to another level of the irony in respect of other people. Can one have a moral right to laugh at other people, if he is not able to laugh at oneself? It is a consequent action: first, to laugh at oneself, then – at other people, at that, both within one's whole life and in a concrete speech episode. A man, who has a real sense of humor, in 90 percent cases laughs at himself; there are people, who can even sneer at their own life. It makes laugh of everybody and never humiliates the man, since there is no element of self-flagellation, but instead there is one of the main specifics of the human mind – understanding of one's own imperfectness. The more primitive is the man, the higher is the position that he places himself to among other people; the cleverer is the man, the more careful is he in the evaluations of his personality, he merely understands the measure of his imperfectness, in particular, intellectual, – it is evident. And if he demonstrates the understanding of his imperfectness, he finds himself at an advantageous point. If a man in the presence of other people proceeds to the self-flagellation, he will get nothing except such a characteristic as "a bore". Nobody wants to hear how you are bad thus revealing your complexes. Only the person, who loves you very much or is so attached to you, is ready to undergo your self-examination. Never expect that other people, who are not so close to you, will do it for you. You should raise their laugh without posing as a clown; it does not mean that you should grimace – it may be one remark, but very witty. A crummy woman comes into the room saying: "Yes, this door seems somewhat narrow to me in the hips", – and by this phrase she takes away the other people's perception of her figure as not beautiful, since the mind is stronger than the beauty. When F. Dostoyevsky wrote: "The beauty will save the world", he meant Sophia, i.e. the wisdom.

If you are a very clever man, you are able to convince somebody that you are attractive and so have a success. However, a beautiful, but stupid woman is not able to convince somebody in something; even her beauty in a while ceases from perception.

There can be any replacement by the opposite in the irony. "Where do you, the clever head, make your way from? – in this example the sign of the subject is replaced by the opposite. The door is narrow for me in the hips – not the door is narrow, but the hips are wide, the object and subject trade places. The irony is constructed not only on the sign transfer, but also on the subject and object transfer.

Do not be afraid of the fact that you will start sneering at yourself; other people will join soon. If you can do it, you will make it in a better, funnier and cleverer way. The one, who will proceed to do it, most probably, will look worse. If you set the upper limit, what is use to try overcoming it. It is a problem of an intellectual priority. The human communication appears as a spectacle, wherein everybody has his own role. Everything lays in the fact who plays the leading role and who is in the crowd in this spectacle – it is very important. If you want to be a leader in your life you have to play the leading party and not to be in the crowd. Laugh at yourself and do not wait until somebody else will do it.

Let us repeat once again that a man, who laughs at himself, does not demonstrate that he has no respect to himself, but quite the contrary, he demonstrates such a powerful mind, which enables him to comprehend his own imperfectness. Of course, they can fail to understand you – it is the matter of choosing the communicants. Some people come to our life naturally, like classmates and colleagues at work. If these people's surrounding affords you pleasure, then you are just a lucky person, if not – sorry. It is beyond our will. However, clever people try to arrange the human surrounding. It is very important whom we choose. A person ought to choose such people, who are either equal to him or surpass him; otherwise it will be boring with them. Bring to your house a few mentally retarded people and become their leader – will you be pleased? No, you won't. There will be no incentive to the self-development. When they do not understand you, it means that you address yourself not to the right people, you did not choose the right people and the right place – it is not your environment for the speech communication. The people intuitively, without any special knowledge, choose those people whom they find interesting, whom they can challenge to a psychological and intellectual duel. Otherwise what is it for? Even in the sphere of intimate relations (however paradoxical it sounds) the psychological rivalry is very important. For whom love is stronger and longer? For the one, who is far from the reach. It is an internal psychological stimulus of the emotional stability. And who is far from the reach? It is the one, who is cleverer and stronger than you.

Let us give a remark. There is one unsuccessful and hard role, which some people choose to play. They are regular cheery fellows. They are expected to make laugh and tell anecdotes and so on in a gathering. One ought to say that it is a very ungrateful position and the person will never meet all the surrounding people's requirements. It does not have anything general with the self-irony, since the sneering man says only a few words in a serious tone of voice and everybody laugh in a long time, wishing that in a while there will be one more remark.

The fact that very often, at the intuitive level in a certain situation, we prohibit ourselves from sneering in the respect of another person, only allowing it in our own respect, means the availability of an internal barrier and this barrier, as a rule, is defined as the humaneness. The caution can also be a barrier: you know by the experience that jokes often come to a bad end. The lesser will you laugh at other people, the more your communicative level will correspond to the common human standard. The constant efforts of every person to win a victory over he arrogance inside, which can be done only at the individual level (almost there is no one who can help in it) appear as the only way to join to the standards of the human social way of life.

Chapter 22. **The Expressive Force of Figures of Speech**

> Everything is in me and I am in everything.
> *F. I. Tyutchev*

Fugures (in Latin *figura* means a shape, appearance and image) are defined as the methods of expressiveness, which are realized in the text that is equal to or bigger than a sentence. Sometimes the figures are considered in a broader sense: as any turns of speech that deviates from a certain (closer to the undefined) standard of the colloquial "naturalness".

The ancient rhetoric elaborated the accentuation and classification of the figures, which were distinguished as the figures of a thought and the figures of a word: the first ones did not alter due to the retelling in other words, the second ones altered.

A. The figures of thought were divided into the specifying: 1) the orator's position – warning, concession (*Even if you did not know about this, but you did it!*); 2) the sense of an object – definition, clarification, antithesis of different kinds; 3) the relation to the object – exclamation on one's behalf, personification in the name of another person; 4) a contact with the listeners – an address or a question. Their verbal expression was intensified (by gradation, contrast and so on) or, vice versa, or it was omitted in a supposed (*I won't tell you that you are a liar, thief and robber, I will just tell you that...*) or in a true way.

B. The figures of words were divided into three types: 1) a figure of addition – a) repetition of various kinds, b) "confirmation" with a synonymic enumerations of various kinds, c) "multi-conjunctionallity" (the repetition of a conjunction, sensed as superfluous, and used as an expressive means: *And the shine, and the noise and the murmur of the waves* – A. Pushkin); 2) a figure of subtracting – an ellipse, asyndeton (the construction of a sentence, wherein the homogenous members or the parts of a complicated sentence are connected without any conjunctions, which attaches the dynamic and saturated character, for instance: *A Swede and a Russian are killing, thrusting and slashing, a beat of drums, cries, shouts and gnashing* – A. Pushkin); 3) a figure of transfer (disposition) – an inversion and, essentially, different kinds of parallelism: accurate and inverted (chiasmus – a disposition of analogical parts if the sequence XY – Y`X`: Everything is in me and I am in everything – F. Tyutchev), non-rhymed and rhymed.

In this classification (in contrast to the one, proposed in this work) tropes also related to the figures and constituted a class of the figures of re-comprehension: with the transfer of the sense (metaphor, metonymy, synecdoche, irony), narrowing of the sense (emphasis), strengthening of the sense (hyperbola) and detailed elaboration of the sense (periphrasis).

Any other classifications are possible, for instance, distinguishing of the figure of extension (adding – subtracting), figures of coherence (combination – separation), figures of significance (equalization – accentuation).

Depending on the abundance of various figures the style is characterized (not terminologically) as objective (figures A2), subjective (A3), lyrical (A4), verbose (B1), dull (B2), image-bearing (B4) and so on. In the epoch of the Renaissance, baroque and classicism the figures were cultivated consciously (the abundance of figures considered to be the sign of a high style); in the 19-th and 20-th centuries their investigation was stopped and they were used spontaneously. Nowadays the representatives of the structural methods, mainly in France and Russia, strive for the processing of the theory of figures on the basis of the modern linguistics.

Let us consider two following texts:

Honorable judges, if I possess even a little of the natural talent – and I realize myself how it is small and insignificant; if I have a certain acquirements in speeches – and here, I am confessing, I have done something; if there is a profit and sense to the public affaires from my studies of the creative works of a thought and a word, from their scientific investigation, – and I have to tell you frankly that for the whole life I have been working on it – so, owing to the everything that I possess, this man, Licinius, is entitled, and one can say, under color of title, to ask me to advocate him (Cicero).

However sad I feel now, whatever gloomy thoughts come to me, however tragic is the surrounding seen around me – still it is worth living.

The rhetoric defines such texts as **periods** (in Greek *períodos* means bypass, gyre) and they represent the developed complex sentence with hypotaxis that is remarkable for the completeness of the though exposure and finality of intonation. Usually, the syntactic construction, open in the beginning of a period, closes only at the end of the period, and subordinate clauses, which comprehensively illustrate the main clause, are framed into it. The melody of the voice divides the period into the ascending protasis and descending apodosis, the pauses divide it into several speech times, the latest time of which is usually prolonged and rhythmic. The periods consisting of one speech time are also possible; in such periods the pressing-in of the intonation is reached due to the disposition of words and stylistic figures. The periodical arrangement of the speech usually is elaborated in the process of the literary language formation (the fourth century B.C. in Greece, the first century B.C. in Rome, the seventeenth century in France and in the period between M. Lomonosov and N. Gogol in Russia).

By using a period as an example one can demonstrate the simultaneous realization of several figures. So, the **period** is defined as a text divided into two unequal parts, the first of them, in its turn, is divided into several homogeneous parts, and the second is a short and conclusive one. The first and second examples include three homogeneous structures; they syntactically and compositionally opposed to the last part, which appears as the resulting by the sense. The period represents a quite diffused kind of the text and it is so by the following reason. The people's efforts to express a complicated and deep thought in a short way have been known from time immemorial. For this reason they elaborated a special literary genre called maxim [from Latin *maxima regula (sentential)* – that means the supreme principle]. The maxim is defined as a kind of aphorism, a moralistic by its content variety of a sentence, which can be expressed in the form of a statement and instruction, but in the framework of a single clause. The clause can be short (*The demonstrative simplicity represents the refined hypocrisy* – F. La Rochefoucauld; *Be victorious over the evil by the use of good* – B. Pascal), but most of all it is a long complicated sentence. Of course, not any big developed sentence represents the maxim, but only that one, which contains a deep thought.

This genre is very diffused in French, and German literatures. One can find plenty of maxims in the works of, say, A. Schopenhauer. La Rochefoucauld introduced this genre into the European literature of the New time, after that this genre became very popular, however, some ancient writers used this genre for making passages. The golden age of the maxim as an independent genre accounts to the 18-th century, however, in Russia it was not popular. It is absolutely evident that the period structure suits very well to represent a serious and deep thought, formulated in the framework of a single sentence.

How can one interpret a syntactic structure that is similar to the period? The first part can perfectly be interpreted as the foundation and the second – as the inference. Or the first part can be interpreted as the argumentation and the second – as the thesis. Or the first part can be interpreted as the condition and the second – as the consequence or result and so on. Any deep thoughts have their inner substantiation and the system of causal effects that is easily representable in the period; therefore, the period appears as a typical form of the maxim's expression.

Let us consider a few rhetoric figures on example 2. The first figure is called anaphora (in Greek *anaphorá*, literally, means removal), uniform beginning – the repetition of a word or a group of words in the beginning of several verses, strophes or phrases:

> *I swear on the first day of Creation,*
> *I swear on its latest day,*
> *I swear on the shame of crime,*
> *And the eternal truth triumph.*
>
> M. Lermontov

Sometimes they say about the phonic anaphora (similar sounds in the beginning of words), thematic anaphora (similar motives in the beginning of episodes) and so on by analogy with the stylistic anaphora. In contrast to the anaphora, as it looks like together with it, there is one more figure, which is called **epiphora** or " a uniform ending" (from Greek *epiphorá* – adding), which represents the repetition of a word or a group of words at the end of several verses, strophes or phrases: *Purl-shells, everything of the purl-shells, the pelerine of the purl-shells, the purl-shells on the sleeves, the epaulettes of the purl-shells, the purl-shells on the lower part of the dress, the purl-shells all over there* or *I would like to know by what reason I am the titular counselor, why I am exactly the titular counselor* – N. Gogol.

The epiphora is applied more occasionally in its pure form than the anaphora, but more frequently in the reduced form (the parallelism of synonyms or grammatical forms in the endings).

The text allows the simultaneous repetition of the initial or final words in adjacent verses or rhythmical parts (i.e. the combination of the anaphora and epiphora). Such a figure is called **simplokḗ** (from Greek *symplokḗ* that means interlacement): *There was a birch standing in the field, there was a leafy birch standing in the field.*

The anaphora is quite frequent in the period. In example 1 it is complete in the first three lines (*if…*), in example 2 it is presented in the first and third lines: each of them begins with *as if…* (the second line resembles the first two lines).

The figure can structure a text of any length. In large texts the anaphora performs a very important semantic task. For instance, one can find a novel compositionally successful, if the author illustrates the destiny of several children, who grew up in one house. Every chapter describes the fate of one of the brothers or sisters and it could begin with the same words. Why so? Sine the uniform beginning of the chapter would correspond to the uniform beginning of these people's life: they grew up together; the beginning of their life was common and similar. Therefore, the chapters begin with the same words and then develop in different directions, as the heroes' destinies differed. It would be a successful application of the anaphora: the method appears as an additional expression of the internal creative task, in particular, the determination of the common origin of life (including genetic). The uniform beginning will manifest itself in the future in the destinies of these people, motivation of their deeds, uniform decision-making and so on. If the novel shows that in complicated life situations the brothers and sisters behave in a similar way, the uniform beginning is taken as a problem. If every chapter began with the anaphora, it would be an extremely successful application of the method of expressiveness.

As to the epiphora (uniform ending), it would suit well the parts of such novels like "Self-murderers' club" by A.C. Doyle, wherein the plot is constructed on the description of destinies of the people, whose end of life is similar – the suicide. The beginning of their lives was different and the destiny absolutely varied, but due to the circumstances the people came to the only result. If every part that corresponds to the description of one hero's destiny ended by one and the same paragraph or clause, or simply by a few similar words, it would be justified from the standpoint of the creative task.

We specially gave not concrete, but speculative examples, in order to facilitate the comprehension of the fact as how to structure the speech. It is not easy. If in some situation you find it important to explain that some people had the equal start, try to tell about them using one and the same beginning. If you find it important to tell that they reached the equal result, try to make the ending similar from the stylistical and purely linguistic point of view. It looks very effective, since herein the form does not work for the sake of the form and not for the outer impression, but it works for the sake of the objective to reflect the inner essence of the given problem.

The following figure is called **parallelism** (from Greek *parállēlos* that means being or walking nearby) is defined as the identical or similar disposition of the speech elements in the adjacent parts of the text, which correlating make a common image. For instance:

> *Ah, if the frost did not fall on the flowers,*
> *And the flowers bloomed in the winter*
> *Oh, if there was no sorrow,*
> *I would not grieve for a single thing*

The parallelism was popular in the folk poetics since olden times (especially, parallel images from the life of the nature and the human being); it was mastered by the written literature long ago (the Bible's poetical style is founded on it in many aspects); sometimes it is complicated by the introduction of the negative (negative parallelism) or the reverse order. Three the most ancient figures of the Greek rhetoric appear as the elaboration of the parallelism: isocolon, antithesis and homeoteleuton (the similarity of the ending in the members, an embryo of a rhyme). By analogy with the described verbal and image-bearing parallelism they say about the verbal-sound (See above: alliteration, rhyme: *A horse-thief prowled along the fence, the grapes get covered with a tan...* – B. Pasternak), rhythmical (a strophe and antistrophe in the ancient Greek lyrics) composition (parallel subjective lines in a novel) parallelism and so on. However, mainly under the parallelism one ought to understand the similar syntactic arrangement of the adjacent clauses or segments of the speech (the correlation between the positions of the subject, predicate and object and etc.). The complete parallelism is presented in the popular phrase: *The young people can go everywhere; the old people are welcomed with respect everywhere.*

The considered examples do not have the complete parallelism, however, one can see the partial parallelism in the first three sentences. Their syntactic structures look similar. In what cases does the parallelism appear as the most effective from the rhetoric point of view? When the author wants to portray the people's destinies, which in some way accompany each other. In this case the parallel constructions will be justified. Let us cite a hypothetic example: a novel describing the life of a woman and her husband. They walked along the path of their life together (in parallel to each other) and therefore, many things in their destinies are set by one and the same scheme. Or, say, a novel about the life of twins, who never separated from each other, seems reasonable to be arranged with the use of parallel constructions. One ought to repeat that the application of figures can be successful only in those cases, when they are internally motivated by the sense.

One more figure can be demonstrated in example 2. It is called **gradation** (from Latin *gradatio* that means a gradual increase) and it is concluded in such disposition of words, upon which every following word has the increased (rarely, reduced) significance, owing to which there is an impression of an increase or fading (of the characteristic). If there is an increase, then the gradation is called **ascending**, for instance: *In the autumn feather-grass steppes absolutely change and get their specific, unique, not similar to anything, look* (A, Chekhov); *Not to call, not to cry, not to help* (M. Voloshin). If there is a fading the gradation is called **descending**, for instance: *All verges of the feelings, all verges of the truth are wiped in hours and years and the worlds* (A. Beliy); *I won't break, I won't waver, I won't get tired* (O. Bergoltz). This method of expressiveness is utterly easy in the comprehension. The ascending gradation is presented in period 2: *It is sad* (*sad* is a key word of the first line) – it is less significant that *it is hard* (*hard* – is a key word of the second line) and *it is hard* is less significant that *it is tragic* (*tragic* is a key word of the third line). The emotional significance increases starting from *sad* through *hard* to *tragic*.

Sometimes they say about the plotline gradation (the sequence of episodes in the fairytale "About the fisherman and the fish" by A. Pushkin), composition gradation (the verse "I came to you to say hello..." by A. Fet) and others by analogy with the rhetoric gradation. Many public speeches are constructed on the principle of gradation: the orator begins with a neutral emotional level, which gradually increases and by the end of the speech it can get the character of an emotional appeal. Of course, the orators uses the descending gradation as well; usually the orator starts from the high emotional note and gradually goes on to a quiet speech; however, it is a rare case.

The increase should be not only emotional, but necessarily semantic: every following conclusion should be more considerable and deeper than the preceding. If you construct your speech with a gradual increase of the semantic effect (for instance, arranging the arguments in the proof you ought to consider the increase of their significance) and at the same time if you increase the emotional nerve-strain in the course of the text, bringing the first and the second to the peak-at-once result, then one can say for sure that it will be a successful speech, which will make a great impression on the listeners.

If one considers the relation between tropes and figures, then he can conclude that the figures represent stronger methods of expressiveness, since they often give a possibility to comprehend the whole text as a single structure, constructed by a definite principle. One-moment impressions, which are produced by epithets, metaphors and etc. (i.e. tropes), are left behind very soon, but the text, constructed by the united scheme structured with the use of figures, makes a strong communicative influence. The modern western literature is presented by a plenty of novels, which consist of a single sentence, sometimes arranged in the form of a single period (there is one point at the end of the novel). The text represents parts of the period, organized in parallel; the semantic and emotional culmination is related to the period's resume. Such experiences were especially popular in the sixties – seventies of the 20-th century in the French literature; some of them are successful. It seems that the figures reflect the reader's esthetic conception by the end of the 20-th century of how a belles-lettres text should look like; therefore the classical literature (not only Russian, but European, as well) practically did not know such spreading of the figures within the framework of the whole text; as usual, the figures extended to a paragraph, to the adjacent clause, and more often in the poetics, than in the prose. The literature appears as a reflection of the inner, intellectual and mental request of the people, who are the potential readers.

Let us examine two more figures: antithesis and oxymoron.

Antithesis (from Greek *antíthesis* – opposite) is defined as a stylistic figure that is founded on the acute confrontation of images and notions. In the modern literary criticism it represents the designation of any substantial and meaningful contrast, though the antithesis, in contrast to it, is almost demonstrated openly (frequently through antonyms), meanwhile, the contrast can be implicit and deliberately hidden. The antithesis and "antitheticity" in the creative work of many writers develop into the principle of poetics and thinking (J. Byron, A. Block). The antithesis, as a striking and effective decoration of the style, was intensively cultivated in the ancient rhetoric. In the literature of the middle ages the antithesis merges with the dualism of the hierarchic mediaeval consciousness, realizing in the opposing pairs: good – evil, light – darkness, earthy – heavenly and others. The antithesis in drama and poetics is used as an esthetic and philosophical principle of representation of the human principle of polarity. This principle gained the most complete and extreme expression in the poetics of the romanticism. The fact of the replacement of some antitheses by others is essential to the poetics of the 19-th and 20-th centuries; it marks a certain shift (or destruction) in the poet's artistic consciousness, or a "removal", cancellation of the antithesis declared by the author, provided that its semantic contrast is not demolished.

> *We are shamefully indifferent*
> *To the evil and good,*
> *We hate and we love accidentally...*
> M. Lermontov

> *You cannot become detached; I am the convict,*
> *You are the escort. The fate is one.*
> M. Tsvetayeva

Here, the antithesis is included into the more complicated "not-antithetic" connections with the world and relations.

Oxymoron (in Greek *oxýmōron* literary means wittily stupid) is defined as a compressed and by this reason paradoxically sounding antithesis, usually presented in the form of antonymic noun and adjective or verb and adverb: *living dead body; bitter joy, sonorous quiet, expressive silence, miserable luxury of dress* (N. Nekrasov); *a lean compromise is better than a fat lawsuit; she is enjoying herself mourning, being such elegantly nude* (A. Akhmatova).

The oxymoron assumes a close vicinity of two words with opposite senses in the syntagma (more often the noun and adjective): *dark light, hot snow* and so on. The matter concerns the absolute contradiction, as the oxymoron is formed on the basis of an abstract vocabulary, which is characterized with the antonymic order of units: *ugly beauty, black sun*. So, the oxymoron is defined as a figure consisting of two words, one of which has a seme in the semantic core, which appears as a negation of the semantic elements of another word. For instance, the noun *light* is compared with the semantic characteristic of the adjective *light*, which is disproved by the adjective *dark*. The oxymoron denies the antithesis, but it fully justifies the contradiction: *Oh! Odious grandeur! A lofty meanness!* (Baudelaire).

The great and elevated on one scale of values can turn out to be odious and low – on the other. As to the phrase: *The dark light emanating from the stars* (Corneille), different objects appear here as the sources of *darkness* and *light*, two adjacent zones in the sky, if we do not consider herein the *darkness* as a hyperbola of *colorless*.

The oxymoron breaks the rules of the lexical code. It is true, in particular, for the presented bellow example: *But, madam, so if we have to be rude, please, tell me, what will happen with your mind, with your charm [literally, amenities], if in the surroundings of Your Highness, there will be hard to find a half-dozen of noble persons, who are able to estimate you at your true worth?* (Voltaire)

The words mind and amenities have no choice to be considered as rude and in order to make certain of it, one should not consult with an adviser or a context: it is enough to look through the dictionary. This example is interesting also by the fact that when being addressed to a simpleton this phrase will turn out to be an irony. In other case there is only the oxymoron here.

In the phrase: *Wherein was the table of viands, but now the coffin stands* (A. Pushkin), the food appears as a symbol of life and a coffin appears on the same place as a symbol of death.

Thus, the antithesis is defined as a turn of speech, in which contrast notions are opposed in order to increase the expressiveness, and the oxymoron represents a rhetoric figure, which is included in the combination of two opposite notions. It is obvious that the antithesis and oxymoron represent the pair figures: both methods have included the opposition of certain creatures in the surrounding world, but in the antithesis this opposition is brought to its maximum and in the oxymoron it is combined into a third creature, which is common to both of them. In a certain sense these methods of expressiveness are similar. L. Sellie wrote that " the tragically discovered opposition of the antithesis is opposed to the natural smooth opposition of the oxymoron". But, of course, the oxymoron appears as a more delicate method, since it sets the so-called dialectic triangle:

```
                    Synthesis
                       /\
                      /  \
                     /    \
              Thesis ------ Antithesis
```

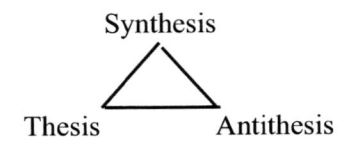

It is very important to understand that the dialectic triangle is the standard and for any opposed notions one can find a certain third notion, in which this opposition is neutralized. If it were not so, there would be no cognitive movement from now on. The matter concerns the fact that the neutralization happens not at the level where both opposite notions are placed, but at a higher level. How is a scientific investigation constructed, in general? Almost all scientific discoveries were made in the following way. A certain idea, thesis A, was recognized by the science during a certain period of time. Then it was proved that this idea did not meet the requirements of the truth, it did not reflect the surrounding reality. Then they proposed a new interpretation, which was opposite to conception A. Sometimes this simple idea, which was evidently closer to the truth, than A, belonged to the scientific thought for many centuries. Thus, some time ago there was a popular idea among the scientists that the Sun rotates around the Earth. Then it was proved that actually the Earth rotates around the Sun. From the standpoint of the science it was a deadlock, until a new investigator with no evident reasons felt himself doubtful, at the purely emotional level, about the opposition of $A - not\text{-}A$. He felt an intellectual anxiety: "I read about this thesis from my youth and I do not like something in it. And more frequently I read, I do not like it more and more". The scientific thought starts working from this exact moment of the internal anxiety and doubts. The recognition of the mental and intellectual doubt as a mental standard gives the man an incentive to move in his perception ahead (See above). As a rule, such a doubt results in searching for certain accidental and peripheral conditions, wherein the confrontation of two positions turns out to be invalid under specific conditions, i.e. the confrontation (opposition) is taken away. For instance, the opposition of "man – woman" is taken away in the people – hermaphrodites. Of course, the positions of neutralizations are rare and peripheral, however, one can reveal them. The finding out of these positions usually forms the basis for a deeper view on the problem, as a whole, for instance, today's science came to the understanding that every man has both male and female chromosomes. The cases of scientific discoveries made as a result of this mechanism action, is much more significant, than those, which were made upon other circumstances (accidental discoveries and co on). In other words it is a typical dialectic development of the mental process. When the man inside refuses any of the opposite positions and he wants to formulate the third, more nonstandard point of view, which does not lie on the surface (and he looks for its substantiation) – he is on the eve of a scientific discovery.

The following example is one of the most demonstrable in this respect. Every elementary particle in different situations demonstrates opposite characteristics from the standpoint of the true sense: in some cases it manifests itself as a particle, in other cases as a wave. It is the physics' contradiction.

At first it was I. Newton's corpuscular theory of the light, according to which the light is considered as a set of particles (the 18-th century). Later on many experiments showed that the light demonstrated wave characteristics (the 19-th century), which could not be explained from the standpoint of the corpuscular theory. At the same time the light had a number of characteristics that could be explained only by the corpuscular theory and could not be explained from the standpoints of the wave conceptions. A new scientific theory – quantum physics (the 20-th century N. Bohr and others) for the first time gave the possibility to combine these conceptions in the noncontradictory way, in particular, to demonstrate in what cases the light (and other elementary particles) manifests the corpuscular characteristics and in what cases – wave. It is a new level of understanding.

If even elementary particles – the basis of the material world, manifest such contradictory characteristics, then the availability of the contradiction appears as a standard of the surrounding world at all its levels and the task of every scientific description is to combine the inconsistent.

If you face a statute you can look at it from the front, you can look at it from the back; you can go upstairs and look at it from above. The scientific perception goes in the same way from the lower lever to the higher, at which there is the point of neutralization.

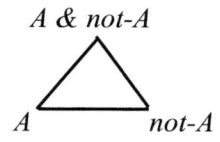

A & not-A

A   *not-A*

The dialectic triangle belongs to the intellectual thought not only in the science: any deep reflection leads us to the comprehension of the availability of peripheral cases, which do not correspond to any categorical position. It is a dialectic compromise (in a good sense of this word).

It is not a moral compromise, but intellectual, which enables us to combine the inconsistent.

The synthesis is presented in the arts, life and human relations – in everything. The understanding of this fact, nevertheless, does not manifest itself as so trivial – to achieve it one needs a developed mind and observation, the ability to mix black and white paints, light and dark colors and see how these mixed paints and colors demonstrate the color of the surrounding world. As soon as you desire to occupy a categorical position in some respect, just remember, please, about the dialectic triangle: probably, somebody else, who is cleverer than you (or you by yourself in a while) will reach the possibility to combine your categorical position with the opposite position – and, for sure, it will be a more accurate knowledge.

Every neutralization can be considered as a new thought (*B*), for which an antithesis (*not-B*) will be found, that consequently will bring the confluence of *B* and *not-B* and so on, It is a tree that grows up.

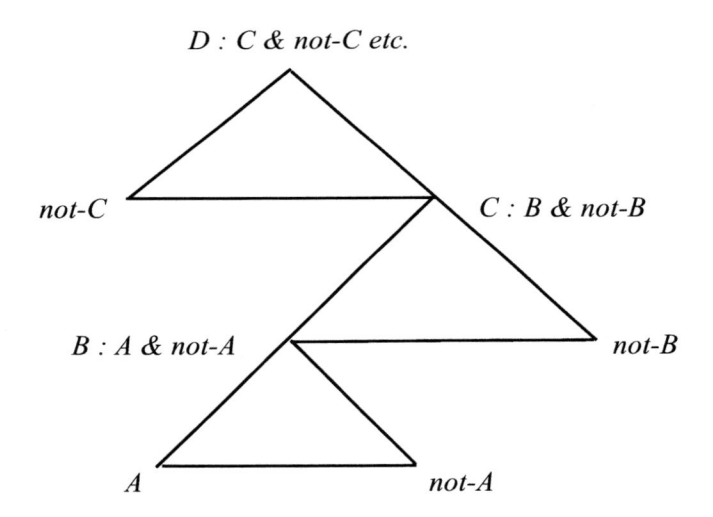

D : C & not-C etc.

not-C   *C : B & not-B*

B : A & not-A   *not-B*

A   *not-A*

In the collocation of *living dead body* the contrast between the life and death diminishes, in the collocation of *eloquent silence* the opposition of speech, eloquence and oratory combines with the full absence of the speech (silence).

The oxymoron as a method of expressiveness represents a dialectic synthesis and its historical significance lies in it. The oxymoron verges on the logical and verbal paradoxes and it produces a strong impression in the speech. If one apply the oxymoron upon the estimation of the human personality it will be very effective. Of course, to do this one will need an in-depth analysis of a concrete person. If it is a man full of internal contradictions, one can estimate his personality through the antithesis and demonstrate the contrast features of his character, i.e. say: "There are some people with whom this man behaves as a noble, soft and kind person, and there are the people with whom he is cruel up to the sadism". But one can say in another way: "It is such a strange personality, which cannot be determined by other words except cruel mercy". If one thinks it over, he will notice that the personality of any man is contrast, therefore we have two elements inside: divine and devilish. At some stages one of them surpasses, at some stages – another. Therefore, the oxymoron is very appropriate in the estimation of the human personality.

In the conclusion, let's consider a specific method of expressiveness – **a figure of omission**. As it was said above, the rhetoric is defined not only as the science of how to speak, but in many respects it is the science of how not to speak and what not to speak about. The figure of omission sets this principle by its very name. The **omission** appears as a turn of speech, which is included in the fact that the author deliberately does not express a thought up to the end, giving the reader or listener a chance to guess about the unexpressed thing. "What did both of them think and feel? Who will know it? Who will tell this" There are such moments in one's life, such feelings – one can only point to them and pass over..." (L. N. Tolstoy). It is not said what kind of feelings he meant, they are only pointed at and finished by the omission points. As it was said above, it is very hard to express the emotional sphere of a man by words. The emotions are better transmitted through the body language: expression of one's eyes, look, posture and so on. Of course, they can be transmitted by means of the energetic method. We let another person feel our emotional state, which we are not able to explain, at the non-verbal level. One's very strong inner anxiety is always transmitted to the surrounding people; it is evident and every person feels it so strongly that it can "be contagious".

The speech distorts the emotional sphere and it is connected with several reasons. First of all it is up to the words decemantization. The point is that there are quite a few emotions and all of them have their own accurate names. There are no complicated synonymic series. We know the word *shame* and its inaccurate synonym *disgrace*; the word *despair* has the following inaccurate synonyms *grief* and *tragedy*. In other words every emotion is set by one or some adjacent by sense words. Since the emotions lay in the sphere of the unconsciousness (and the speech appears as a symbolic system of the consciousness), the consciousness badly orients itself in the chaos of emotions and it transmits the information about them in a distorted way. The man often is not able to comprehend what he feels. For instance, it seems to him that he feels a sense of awkwardness, but in fact he feels irritation. Sometimes he feels irritation, disappointment, despair and pleasure at the same time and very often by one and the same reason. Since the emotional elements, lying in the sphere of the unconsciousness and badly penetrating into the consciousness, are inadequately transmitted by the speech, then the figure of omission in a definite situation turns out to be the most accurate method used to transmit an emotion.

What is the structure of a segment borrowed from the work of L.N. Tolstoy? The situation is specified and the reader can mentally place himself into it and feel a definite state. It is not important whether Tolstoy meant exactly the same feeling or some one else. He meant a nonstandard, specific state and each of us cam memorize such moments in his life, such episodes, wherein we felt something that it was hard to express, but it is memorized for the whole life as something deep and significant. If you feel something similar once again in your life, you will remember your first impression, you will find the difference and you will be able to compare. Such states belong to the category of states unspecified at the linguistic level, but recognized well inside. What can be better in this situation than the figure of omission? In order not to distort the information, one ought to explain to the man a definite situation; he will psychologically place himself to this situation and will name his own feelings in his internal emotional language.

The figure of omission enables you to hide everything that you do not want to disclose to your interlocutors. Everybody has the right to keep silence, the right not to transmit any information. You have to stand upon your right and prevent other people from changing you into the source of information. Every time you ought to think to what extent you consider it appropriate to say or not to say something, and you will feel soon that often it is more expedient to keep silence. It is reasonable to keep silence in all such situations, when you understand that you will cope with the problem by yourself. In such a case you need no interlocutors and the figure of omission with no doubt plays here its main role.

The figure of omission is connected with an oratoric method, which is called *to sustain a pause.* **To sustain a pause** means to keep silence for a long time (but to keep silence in such a way that other people won't be shocked with you silence and regard it as a strange one), holding the listeners in that emotional state, into which you, as the orator, are able to lead them, and letting them feel this state for quite a long time. It requires certain skills, which you can learn.

The second sense of the term *to sustain a pause* means a time-out, which another person gives you in the speech. When you stay in a complex situation (for instance, you do not know how to answer and whether it is worth answering or not, or you want to hide your first reaction to the interlocutor's speech). Very often it happens in the situation wherein you are asked a question and the answer to it is polysemic or undesirable (it can be an unexpected question) and you take a time-out to find out such an answer, which will be the most expedient to you. By sustaining a pause you can come to a conclusion that it is expedient to sustain it up to the infinity and that you should not to answer it at all. However, it also needs a time. When during an exam you are asked a certain question, it is recommended to sustain a pause in order to analyze the sense of the question and avoid the substitution for the thesis (See above). Considering the nervousness, which is usual at the examinations, no one will blame you for this pause, only try to sustain it physiognomically in a definite way: do not open your eyes wide, do not show the tongue and so on – you are to be silent and by all your look demonstrate the mental work. You have to be lost in thoughts in such a way that your entire look will demonstrate that you are thinking exactly over the question, which was asked.

Chapter 23. **The Body Language**

> We should be careful with personality's secrecy: don't burst into his inner sanctum forgetting about respect!
>
> *T. Carlyle*

The natural language is closely contiguous to (and sometimes it even merges with) another semiotic system, which is the one of the closest to it, a system of gestures (body language – BL). "Every feeling has its peculiar gestures, intonation and mimics; the impression that they produce, either good or bad, pleasant or not, is the reason of the fact that the people either win our favor or repel." (F. La Rochefoucauld). Upon the choice of the means of expression the speaker sometimes chooses not among the purely linguistic means of expression, but between the linguistic, on the one hand, and non-linguistic, on the other. Thus, the expression (*Go away!*) can be included into two different symbolic systems, the members of which have pair-wise correspondence between each other.

Sound language	Leave the room, please	Take yourself off	Go out
BL	Polite gesture, pointing at the exit	Polite ironical gesture, pointing at the exit	Rude gesture

The second series of symbolic systems that follow or complete (compensate) the speech, in case if for some reasons it turns out to be not adequately effective, is investigated in a specific field of the linguasemiotics, called kinesics.

In the kinesics the investigators of gestures and postures single out the simplest (cannot be divided into smaller parts without loosing the sense) posture of the human body, the so-called **kinemorph**. The class of interchangeable postures composes a kinemorpheme. The investigator regards it as the main objective to single out such postures, which actually mean something in the given culture, i.e. appear as symbols. They are called **isolates**. Every pair of postures has its own structural distinguishing characteristics. When the isolates are allocated, one ought to describe the limitation of the frequency of their occurrence, i.e. to introduce the principle of equivalency. One also ought to describe the situations (contexts), in which they appear.

The investigation of the human body language is connected with the fact, in what way the information at the non-verbal level is transmitted from the speaker to the listener, and, actually, not to the listener, but to the spectators. In a certain sense, when a man is subjected to the speech, he appears as the spectator and listener at the same time. The BL system is slaved to the natural language, i.e. to the speech and the influence as if a double impact is directed to those, who are chosen as its subject. The problem lies in the fact that the symbolic system of the natural language represents the symbolic system of the conscious (See above), it realizes in the speech, as a rule, that thing, which you consciously are going to realize in it; and the BL symbolic system represents the semiotics of the unconscious, it realizes those motives, which lay in the unconscious. To a certain extent the zone of the unconscious contradicts the zone of the conscious. It should be understood well, as according to one of the main theses of the psychoanalytical theory, the unconscious strives for the attainment of pleasure. Therefore, all inner conflicts of a person are determined by this striving for the pleasure and joy; the ethical conception of the hedonism declares the thesis about the attainment of pleasure as the main incentive and goal of the human life (See above). The conscious appears as the voice of the sociability and penance, which restrict this internal striving for pleasure or joy in those cases, wherein the attainment of pleasure and joy contradicts the ethical or legal standards of the society.

Thus, the human intellect appears as the constantly functioning field of the battle between the conscious and unconscious and therefore, as a rule, the man does not receive any inner psychological satisfaction: he is a contradictory structure by his nature. Exactly proceeding from this point, the psychoanalytical conception declares the existence of the human being on the Earth as the existence full of suffering, as there is a strong inner contradiction between the needs in pleasure and inner personal restrictions of the human being in the attainment of this pleasure. These inner restrictions are more important then social. They are more significant for the human personality. So, one can make a natural conclusion that two zones, which realize the conscious and unconscious, contradict each other at the level of realization. Therefore, the BL symbolic system often contradicts the real speech. At the verbal level the man tries to convince his listeners in something, but the BL symbolic system contradicts his thesis, appearing as the so-called incongruency. Thus, the verbal perception, i.e. the perception of words turns out to be utterly contradicting. On the one hand, the man perceives and conceives the argumentation, and, on the other hand, by the interlocutor's look, posture and motions he understands that there is something wrong. Such a speech has another purpose. And the comprehension takes place at the unconscious, not conscious level. There is a certain anxiety appearing in respect of the heard speech. Very often you felt certain dissatisfaction in the situation, wherein somebody told you warm and gentle words, but his entire look, notwithstanding his efforts to hide this, told about the fact, that this man was not sincere. You cannot catch him, but at the same time you feel yourself dissatisfied. What does the listener's inner dissatisfaction mean? It means that the speech was constructed in vain, as it did not reach the objective. It arouses the necessity to slave the BL unconscious symbolic system to a concrete speech, which lies in the deliberate arrangement of the similarity, i.e. an attempt to arrange at the level of the body, face, hand and etc. those symbols, which confirm the verity of your truth. It is hard to do, since by doing this you have to break the unconscious. It can be reached by certain training (often, it is a professional training, for instance, in a fixed-post spy's activity) as a result of the many-year hard work, and it never finishes by a full victory. One can win partial victories on this path, since the BL is a traitor of the man's consciousness, i.e. the traitor of the man; it is something that betrays him. Sometimes it happens that you very attentively look at a person and listen to what he is speaking about, but you do not penetrate into the words and make the only one inference: this man treats me badly – and you do not make any other substantial inferences from his speech (but may be he suggests you something expedient and profitable). Unfortunately, it happens because the unconscious had more priority-driven information, than the conscious.

The hands are the most important part of the human body.

> *Palm*
> *Palms! (a reference book*
> *For the youths and maids.)*
> *They kiss the right*
> *They read on the left.*
>
> *The one, who joined*
> *The midnights plot, be aware*
> *They show the right*
> *They hide the left*
>
> *The Sybil is the left:*
> *Far away from the glory.*
> *The right is enough,*
> *But no one to be Scaevola.*
>
> *Still in the hatred*
> *In the infinite hour*
> *We give to the world*
> *Our left from the heart*
>
> *And still, being full*
> *Of the righteous hatred,*
> *We cut the veins*
> *Of our left by the right.*
>
> M. Tsvetayeva

Gestures of hands.

1. Rubbing of hands symbolizes the expectation for the victory.

However, one ought to remember that sometimes the demonstration of this sign is not appropriate (for instance, a waiter should not do it waiting for tips), as a slow rubbing of hands puts the interlocutor on his guard.

2. Rubbing the thumb and the index finger or the tips of other fingers symbolizes "money". It is a vulgar gesture; it should not be always used.

3. Interlaced fingers symbolize one's frustration and the man's desire to hide his negative relation to you, especially if the hands are raised vertically. It is very important to know about one wonderful characteristic of the BL as the symbolic system of the man's psychological state. If a man feels something, he transmits it by conventional signs (it is evident). The other thing seems strange: if a man by force is deprived of the possibility to demonstrate these signs, his psychological state changes due to the absence of these signs. So, not only the sign turns out to be the consequence of a certain psychological state, but the psychological state as well can be the consequence of a certain sign (the law of the symbol (sign) reversibility). Therefore, if a man symbolizes his negative relation to you by his gestures, try to deprive him of his physical possibility to demonstrate this relation and, probably, the situation will change in a better way. The following recommendation is founded, in particular, on this phenomenon: during negotiation force the sitting man to uncouple the hands and to stretch them with open palms; to achieve this you can afford a book or a cigarette.

4. Spire-wise position of hands represents the sign of assured and "all-knowing" position. It is a gesture of subordination; it is often followed with the up-raised head, which symbolizes the arrogance and self-satisfaction. These gestures can lead you to both positive and negative result depending on the other gestures followed.

5. Placing hands on the back appears as the gesture of self-assurance and the sense of superiority (in stressful situations it helps to be self-controlled and feel self-reliance, for instance, in front of the doctor's office. It enables one to open fearlessly all his vulnerable areas of his body: stomach, heart and throat. If the hands are locked on the back it means merely the assurance. If one hand holds another hand's wrist it means that the man is frustrated and tries *to keep himself in hands*. The position of hands looks as if one hand holds the other preventing it from thrusting a blow. The higher is the place of the grip, the more evident is the nervousness.

6. Accentuation of thumbs. The thumbs in the chiromancy signify the power of the character and personality. In the non-verbal language they have the same meaning. The putting out of thumbs symbolizes the imperiousness, superiority and aggressiveness. This sign is very effective, if the words are contrary to the arrogance of the gesture. It suggests an idea that two coexistent symbolic systems – the natural language and the body language can increase the impression of each other, in particular, owing to the contrast. In this situation the listener usually feels distrust. Thumbs exposed out of the pockets appears as a frequent posture of the

female dominance, at that, the woman usually stands up on the toes.

The crossing of hands on the chest (negative, defensive signal) and waving on the heels frequently follows the accentuation of thumbs.

Pointing at a man with a thumb represents a mockery, at that, it is very offensive and is applicable mostly by men.

7. Position of hands as a barrier (an attempt to protect one's heart).

Hands on the chest. In the childhood we frequently hide ourselves from the danger behind a certain object (a cupboard, large stone, etc.). It is also a barrier to protect oneself from the appearing threat and unwished circumstances. If a man crossed his hands, it means that he is nervous and feels a threat. It is a defensive posture. In such a posture the man conceives less amount of information. There is some information about a very interesting experiment, carried out with students. The students were asked to cross hands and listen to a text that included N number of symbols and then to write down everything that they were able to memorize (at the level of lexical units, i.e. to write down the words, which to their point were present in the text). Then the same students listened to another text with the same N number of symbols, at that they were asked to release their hands. When they wrote down by heart the lexical units of the second text, it turned out that there were 38 percentages of units more than of the first text. Therefore it is recommended to have armchairs in auditoriums.

Even if a man feels himself comfortable with the crossed hands (a habit), nevertheless it reflects his state. In addition one ought to know that this man has a slowed-down reaction. We often use this gesture in a crowd of unknown people, in a turn, in a lift, in every place, where we feel unsafe. Sometimes it is a posture of disagreement (for instance, when somebody swears at a person, whom you respect). The orator should try to worm up the auditorium and obtain the releasing of hands; otherwise, his speech will be doomed to failure. You ought to force the interlocutor to release his hands and he will stop feeling distrust towards you (even partially). Force him to stretch his hands or ask him to bend forward in order to examine something in detail. You can ask him a question: "What do you think about this?" If upon the crossed hands the fingers are clenched into the fists it symbolizes the hostility. You are facing an offensive position. If at the same time you see the clenched teeth and redden face, be aware of an immediate assault. If a man holds the crossed hands it means that he tries to cope with the negative emotions. You have to help him.

The crossed hands from bellow. The gesture enables the man to reconstruct the sense of the emotional security, like in the childhood, when parents hold your hand upon any danger.

If a man holds his forearms (incomplete barrier) it means the diffidence (during a speech or getting an award).

The man's crossed hands, which he wants to hide, symbolize the desire to hide the nervousness; for instance, when you go across the auditorium wherein everybody looks at you, – it also includes such gestures as to adjust the watch, collar buttons or hold flowers, a handbag or a glass with both hands.

The position of legs also transmits important information together with the position of hands.

The crossed legs (an attempt to protect the genitals) symbolize one's negative or defensive relation. The crossed hands are more negative than crossed legs, which should be interpreted with care just keeping in mind that "ladies sit in this way".

The leg on the leg with formation of the four (in an American way) symbolizes the rivalry and competitive spirit. In this situation one ought to ask a question: "What do you think about this?"

If the legs are crossed and hands lean on them it symbolizes a steadfast and stubborn person; in this situation you will need a special approach.

Crossed legs and hands in the up-right position in a company of unknown people symbolize the self-defense even if there is a smile on the face. In the course of the conversation the defensive posture can be transformed into an open posture (open palms); alcohol facilitates it.

Clenched fists + crossed legs + bitten lip – all this symbolizes an attempt to cope with one's negative relation, unpleasant emotions, fear or anxiety. In order to help someone to cope with the anxiety and change the posture, just sit down nearby. During the talks this posture means that the partner does not want to take off.

The fixing up of the foot on the shin of the other leg means the strengthening of the defensive position of a woman.

If the postures of this group became habitual, first, remember, please, that the surrounding people misinterpret you and, second, if you are nervous, such postures aggravate your emotional state.

The human eyes are able to tell more, they can transmit the finest shades of thoughts, feelings and sensations. The mankind estimated at its true worth the significance of this source of the psychological information transceiving; it was praised in the paintings, sculptures and poetics.

The eyes appear as the strongest symbols of the BL, first, since they occupy the central position in the human organism, second, since 87 percentage of the entire information, received by the man, goes through the visual analyzer (9 percentage – through the auditory analyzer and 4 percentage through other analyzers). The pupils of the eyes are absolutely independent; they widen upon positive emotions and narrow – upon negative. If a man is exited his pupils widen four times, if he is angry – they narrow (in such cases such eyes are called as *snake's eyes*). Children's pupils are physiologically bigger, than adults', in addition, they are widened, as children want to win the attention of adult people.

When speaking with a man try to answer three following questions:
1. In what way does he look at you?
2. How long does he look at you?
3. How long can he sustain your stare?

If a man is dishonest with you and tries to hide something, his eyes meet yours less than one-third of your communication time. If his eyes meet yours more than two-thirds of the communication time, you can interpret it in the following way: a) he finds you attractive (the pupils will be widened); b) the man feels hostility towards you, he challenges you. (His pupils are narrowed). If you want to arouse somebody's trust and love you ought to look almost into his/her eyes (not less than 70 percentage of the communication time) and your success will be more certain. A stiffed and shy person with the lowered down gaze rarely enjoys other people's confidence. Never wear sunglasses during business talks, as the partner will think that you scrutinize him. One ought to be aware that there are national peculiarities of the duration of gazing; Japanese people usually gaze at the neck and Europeans look into eyes.

The gaze can and should be trained and chosen. Depending on the obstacles there are three types of gazing:
1. Business gazing is directed to the triangle on the interlocutor's forehead.
2. Social gaze is directed to the triangle, formed by the interlocutor's eyes and mouth.
3. Intimate gaze is directed to the triangle, formed by the interlocutor's eyes and solar plexus.

Looking asquint means an interest or hostility (in the second case it is followed by dropped brows, frowning forehead and/or dropped corners of the mouth). In all affairs with subordinate people only the business gaze is permissible.

Upon an intimate gaze men are usually more frank, than women, but his lowered eyelids means the break of his interest towards the woman. If the man's eyelids are lowered and are followed with the head leaned back and a long gaze, be careful: it is a signal that you provoked a negative reaction.

Male gestures of courting:
1. He tries to touch his neck (he make attempts to tie his necktie, adjust a tiepin, sleek his hair).
2. He fixes his hands on the hips or put his thumbs under the belt.
3. An intimate look (a bit longer than usual).
4. The tip of his boot is directed towards the woman.
5. Widened pupils.

Female gestures of attraction:
1. She pulls down her dress.
2. She touches her hair.
3. She fixes her hands on the hips and puts the thumb under the belt.
4. She turns her feet or body towards the man.
5. A long intimate gaze.
6. More frequent eye contact.
7. Widened pupils.
8. Blushing.
9. Shaking hairs.
10. Demonstration of her wrist.
11. Slightly spread legs.
12. Waving by hips.
13. Looking asquint.
14. A slightly open mouth and moistened lips.
15. Lipstick.
16. Low voice.
17. A glance over the raised shoulder (that accentuates the breast).
18. Open knees.
19. Playing with a taken off shoe.
20. Stroking of hips.

Yes, the symbolic system of our unconscious did not skimp in empowering the woman with the whole arsenal of means to attract men's attention. None of the human internal psychological purpose is realized so differently and comprehensively, which indirectly proves the priority of libido in the unconscious and thus the verity of S. Freud's conception.

Territorial claims.
The BL system is indirectly connected with the energetic channel of information transceiving that determines the territorial claims of every man. It is extremely important aspect of the human communication. The matter concerns the fact that the man tries to subdue the surrounding space and he perceives everything in this space as a part of himself or his property. Say, coming to his car or staying nearby his car the man demonstrates this car as his property and if he wants to specify the title to the

car, he leans on the car. It is a symbol of the title to the object. The same thing happens with a person, who turns out to be a part of our space. This fact underlies the man's need to hold his beloved "object's" hand. You make a mistake if you think that it is just an erotic component in this gesture: in fact it is the man's necessity to declare the title to this person. Therefore, men prefer hold the hand or waist of the bellowed woman, who is not merely beloved, but who is belonged to him. At least, he touches her by his fingers. In this way the man demonstrates everybody his title. So, other people perceive this information and either do not want or refuse to claim for another man's property.

No one putting his hand on the girl's shoulder thinks that at this moment he demonstrates his title to her; and other people, who see this gesture also do not think so. Since this information, as any other information in the BL is transferred at the unconscious level. Nevertheless, the people behave correspondingly, since they received the signal: *Do not come. It is not yours*. It was an important scientific achievement to comprehend the fact that the man in the space (from the standpoint of his energetic state and his mentality) occupies not only the place, which corresponds to the dimensions of his body, he occupies a bigger place (in a radius of a stretched hand) and when moving he bears this space as a part of himself. It takes place at the utterly unconscious level.

One can easily check it in a speech communication, which has three levels of approaching. The distance of four feet represents such a zone, into which the man does not allow unknown people to get in; otherwise he feels a great discomfort. This zone is called as *personal*. The second zone is approximately three feet in a radius. It can be called *social*. This zone is comfortable for the communication with known people. The third level approximates to one and a half feet. It is an intimate level and the man allows only very close relatives: children, parents and a spouse, the one whom he can embrace. The figures are approximate, since they slightly vary for different people. In particular it depends on the nationality and place of residence. In cities radius of zones is less than in villages. Probably, the communicative zone is connected not only with the nationality, but also with the energetic capacities of people.

So, the man feels himself being in a space that exceeds the dimensions of his body. It is an internal genetic characteristic of people. If the man does not sense the communicative space, it means that he is mentally sick. The mentally healthy person feels that he should not approach to the people closer than a definite distance. A mentally sick person often violates these genetic-psychological laws of the human conduct and that is why the society designates him as a sick person.

The understanding of the importance of the fact how the person senses himself in a space enables one to comprehend how often we get into the state of a nervous stress due to the breach of our territorial claims. One can confirm that serious personal and social dramas and conflicts take place due to the pressed space, as it is true for the public transport (buses and metro) and small premises. The man not only transfers himself in the space together with his private space (field), he acts as if leaves this field in those places, where he often attends. The man considers the physical place that he occupies to be his own. Of course, it is true first of all for his private premises. In the house everybody, who lives in it, has his own territory, which is psychologically marked. Any encroachments on "his" territory provoke a reciprocal negative reaction in the man, as an infringement of the property.

In the same way as in his own house, the man can "mark" a territory in other places. A classical example is to have a favorite place in a cafй. In many countries, in particular, in France the notion of "my cafй" is typical. One can see that intuitively the cafй owners perfectly understand it. If in every morning you come to the cafй at a definite time with a newspaper and always occupy one the same table, the owner will know your table and he won't let anybody else to occupy it (if he is such a man, who knows how to deal with his clients).

There are such cases (quite often) when moving to another house the man feels himself uncomfortable by unknown reasons. In fact, he had his own private territory in the previous house and has not found yet the same in the new house. You cannot by force make a certain place be your own physiologically, it is inside you, something inside you looks for this place and finds it, it is practically beyond your power. In some houses you may fail to find such a place. When moving from one house to another you for sure loose something that you had in the old place: you territory. Therefore, any move, even to a better place, is stressful, as the man looses his private territory in the old place and looks for the substitution in a new place.

These problems are absolutely dim to the people. They are not investigated, however they deserve a closer look, they deserve that every person analyzes and understands where is his place on the earth and where is the place on the earth of those people, who are close to him and let them to be nearby. Then the interrelations between people and simply the speech and merely human communication will become incomparably happier. It relates to all relations, including business relations.

Bodily manifestations – it is something absolutely spontaneous. The one, who mixes up too many conscious control and evaluation with his manifestations, lowers down his influence as compared with the possible one. The greatest power of the influence outside and the highest emotional feeling inside are kept always there, where the conscious "self" and the bodily manifestations are united, where the reason and unconsciously governed body interact and equally influence on each other.

What are the reasons of the bodily manifestations and what do they base on? The relationship between the spirit (soul) and body always yields to one and the same regularity: we receive a certain perceptible sensation (impression), which immediately provokes a certain inner feeling that leads to an incentive.

The law of manifestation is determined by three theses:

1. Every bodily movement in its action is directed to the goal of the mental feeling.

2. Every bodily movement is directed by the unconscious (mainly) expectations for a success.

3. Every bodily movement is directed by his individual basic (leading) method.

Let us discuss a number of manifestations.

The preparedness for actions, a will for a mental work – acute uprising of one's head, earlier relaxed body gets some evident signs of tension, for instance, the upper part of the body moves from the comfortable position to the up-right posture.

Concentration – vertical wrinkles on the forehead, narrowed and at the same time steady look into the distance, pronouncedly covered forehead.

Concentrated direction to something – tensely stretched index finger.

Statement of thoughts upon one's internal involvement – straightening of one or both palms, open bottom-up to the partner with a gesture of persuasion.

Strained waiting (for instance an answer to the question) – widely open eyes and steady visual contact.

Reached understanding – horizontal wrinkles on the forehead obove widely open, attentive, goggle eyes followed by an evident nodding.

A waiting petitioner – an open palm stretched towards and up.

Voluntarily devoting or bestowing something – open bottom-up palms slowly move up-towards-down.

"I see through you" – squinting of only one eye, then a steady, frequently asquint look of the other.

Purposeless passive state appears in accordance with the following rule: the more your partner "covers" or "hides" parts of his body, the more he moves back or turns aside, the more is his abstraction, if not a refusal or defense. It includes, in particular, the movement to the back, bending of the upper part of the body and the head. "Closed" posture of the hands (contradictious motion of the hands, turning the head aside) slowing down of motions, the changing of the active participation in the conversation by a certain rhythmical playing of hands, legs and feet, the same – in a demonstratively lazy posture, for instance, the partner drums his finger on the table, changes the free up-right posture into a comfortable posture, leans back and bends his head (or the upper part of the body) aside with an uncertain specification or accentuation, slows down speed of the speech and gestures.

Internal anxiety – evident nervousness, nerve-strained look, continuous movements of fingers, legs, feet or hands, often distinguished by a small amplitude (which means that the anxiety is not negative), rhythmically infringed repetitive motions (wiggling on the chair, unequally drumming fingers, rotation of a cigarette package and so on), squinting.

Astonishment, fear, shock, impossibility to comprehend, helplessness due to a certain fear – horizontal wrinkles with widely open eyes, open mouth and paleness.

Suppressed mood, helplessness, full indecision, passive mood – "empty" look directed into the distance with the bent head and released tension, highly raised shoulders, clasped elbows, widely open eyes, puckered up nose or "a full of suffering wrinkles".

Doubts, thoughts (indecision, scepsis, distrust – alternate raising and lowering of shoulders, bending of the head from side to side, frequently followed with the slightly raised shoulders, asquint look.

Internal indecision, confusion, fear, shame – the upper part of the body is supported by hands that lean on something down, closed sitting posture, the posture manifests the preparedness to stand up, one or two hands are in the pockets, the motion of the hand that covers the face of a part of the face, straightened index finger touches the borders of lips, blushing.

The lost of confidence – low tension, bent head, slow movement of the hand (hands) outward-down with a palm turned down, "squinted" eyes, slightly open mouth, slowing down speed of the speech and gestures.

Somewhat helpless searching for a support, a needed word, good thought – meanwhile, with the increasing relaxation inside, the hands make holding motions.

The tendency of expectancy, searching for help – biting of the lips or the tongue.

The reciprocal construction of "a defensive wall" – clasping or crossing of the hands on the chest, especially, if they stay for a while motionless in this position.

Often hidden careful observation – motions of the hands that cover the face of its parts, narrowed and at the same time asquint look, a look underbeneath upon a strong tension and slight vertical wrinkles, a quick glance from the corners of the eyes upon a quiet posture of the head, a smile – in a positive sense.

Reverie, in-depth reflection – a look to the distance upon a certain relaxation, hands on the back, slow rubbing of the forehead with a wiping motion, slightly open fingers touch the forehead and mouth, upon this a lock to a certain distance. Shut for a while eyes, the tongue touches the borders of lips.

Increasing abstraction, neglect, defense of an active or passive kind – turning the face out from the partner, moving the body back with stretching hands with the palms directed towards.

Astonishment, unwillingness, dissuasion, anger and fury – more or less strong tension, powerful strikes by palms or fingers on the table, vertical wrinkles on the forehead, showing teeth, "a gesture of a protest", "a gesture of a shock", clenched teeth, flushing, increasing of voice.

Decisiveness, preparedness to struggle, aggressiveness – a decisive tension (up-right, raising up), force – in a tensed preparedness to stand up, hand acutely and tensely put into the pockets with the following tension of shoulders, hands are clenched into fists, vertical wrinkles on the forehead, frowning look, steady look at the partner, closed of pressed mouth.

A strive for caution, supplanting, holding unpleasant things under control – a hand or hands with stretched fingers move towards the floor with palms down.

Strong reproach or warning – widely open eyes upon a rigorously tensed face.

Evident displeasure – squinted eyes, "a full of suffering wrinkle" (unpleasant taste reaction, puckered up nose).

We ought to emphasize once again that postures, gestures and looks represent the symbols of "living content": feelings, sufferings, trust.

In every language and in every culture the signs and symbols vary. In China they smile when they tell about a sad event; it means that the listener should not be upset. Even classical nodding, which means "yes" – in Bulgaria means "no". Greeks raise brows, it means a negative answer, however, a European man will regard it as an astonishment. If one does not know this, he will face a communicative inadequacy in the communication with the people from other countries: you do not understand their mimic gestures – symbols.

It is an important question whether these symbols – signs appear as just national forms of one and the same feelings or the outward difference of traditions (symbols) expresses a deep difference between feelings and experiences of various social groups and various nations.

Most probably, the BL symbols can be divided into three groups: common to the mankind (for instance, widening of pupils), civilization (for instance, nodding) and individual (for instance, motion of tongue tip at the moment of a nervous tension).

The symbols common to the mankind can be considered as semiotic universals; they are inherent in any man from the nature and they are of interest from the standpoint of the Homo sapiens investigation.

The civilization symbols belong to definite cultures or sub-cultures (communities). It is important to understand that their division does not coincide with the word map. For instance, Austria and Switzerland have different national languages (Austria – German; Switzerland – mainly, French), but the BL symbolic system is similar in the territory of these countries. The division takes place not according to the languages, but culturological regions. Hence, it is an actual task to make a polysemiotic dictionary of the BL, wherein the literary article would begin with a picture and then this picture would be interpreted by various possible in different cultures means. The scientists have not started working on it yet – it is a problem of the 21-st century. However, we have to make one caution. The human being is created with a certain restriction of the cognitive possibilities. There are secrets, which he is not able to know: the secrecy of conception, elements of people's consciousness and so on. However, the people exceeded their authority, vested by the Creator. And the punishment is obvious. The works on the correction of the future child's genotype are close to the elaborations in the field in the nuclear energy. Making a H-bomb, the mankind acquired a weapon of self-destruction and people live under this threat for dozens of years. The elaborations in the sphere of the BL, which finally will lead to the penetration into other people' consciousness and unconsciousness, can run into sufferings of the mankind: the communicative system, which has been arranging for thousands of years, will be destroyed, as it is founded on the secrecy that every human personality bears. If a person loses the secrecy, will he still have the possibility to keep his personality?..

Summing up, one ought to say that in the communication a person uses five different symbolic systems: 1) verbal text, 2) intonation. 3) signature (timbre of voice), 4) gestures and postures, 5) energetic impulse. The first three traditionally relate to the competence of the linguistics (auricle symbolic systems), the fourth – to the BL (visual symbolic systems) the fifth – to the extra sensory perception.

Bibliography

A. Sources:
Aristotle. Poetics. V.4. A., 1984
Cicero Mark Thulium. Three treatises on the oratory. M., 1972
Demosthenes. Speeches. A., 1954
Plato. Dialogs, M., 1986
Seneca. Moral letters to Lucilly. M., 1977
Tacitus P. A conversation about orators. SPb., 1905

B. Literature:
Adler A. Practice and theory of individual psychology. M., 1995
Arnold W. E., McClure C. Communication. N. Y. 1989
Asmus V. F. Logic. M., 1947
Bakhtin M. M. Esthetics of the literary creation. M., 1979
Bart R. Semiotics. Poetics. M., 1994
Berdyaev N. A. The destiny of Russia. M., 1970
Bibler V. S. Thinking as creation. Introduction into the logic of a mental dialog. M., 1975
Bourbaki N. Theory of multitudes. M., 1965
Carnap R. The significance and necessity. M., 1959
Casagrande D. O., Casagrande R. D. Oral communication. California, US. 1986
Chomsky N. Aspects of the syntax's theory. M., 1972
Church A. Introduction in the mathematical logic. V1. M., 1960
Descartes R. Selected works. M., 1950
Diderot D. Collected works. V7. M.-L., 1939
Dubois J. and others. General rhetoric. M., 1986
Feuerbach L. Selected philosophic works. V1-2. M., 1955
Frege G. The sense and denotatum//Semiotics and informatics. 8st edition. M., 1977
Freud S. Psychoanalysis. Religion. Culture. M., 1992
Goldin V. E. Speech and etiquette. M., 1983
Hegel. G. Encyclopedia of philosophical sciences. Collected works. V1. M., 1929
Heidegger M. Time and existence. M., 1993
Helvetius. About the mind. Collected works. M., 1938
Hilbert D., Bernays P. Grundlagen der Mathematic, Bd.1. Berlin, 1934

Hjelmslev L. Prolegomenas to the theory of language. SL, 1st ed. M., 1960
Hubbard L. R. Dianetics. The modern science of the mental health. M., 1993
Humboldt V. Language and philosophy. M., 1985
Husserl E. Logival investigations. P.1. Prolegomenas to the pure logic. SPb., 1909
Ivanov Vyach. Vsev. Odd and even. M., 1978
Jakobson R. Works on poetics. M., 1987
James W. Pragmatism. SPb., 1910
Jung C. G. Psychological types. M., 1995
Kant I. Crytics of the pure reason. M., 1994
Karcevskij S. Du dualisme assymetrique du signe linguistique. TCLP. I. Prague, 1929
Karinsky M. N. Classifications of conclusions. SPb., 1880
Katz J., Folor J. The structure of a semantic theory. Vol.39. Language, 1963
Klinie S. Mathematical logic. M., 1973
Kony A. F. Selected works. M., 1956
Koshansky N. F. General rhetoric. SPb., 1824
Kozarzhavsky A. C. The arts of polemics. M., 1972
La Rochefoucauld F. Memoirs. Maxims. M., 1993
Lamettrie J. Selected worcs. M., 1925
Leibniz G. W. New experiments on the human rationality. Collected works in 4 volumes. V2. M., 1982
Levi-Strauss C. Primitive thinking. M., 1994
Lomonosov M. V. A compendium to rhetoric in favor of the funs of or tory. Full collected works in 10 volumes. V7. M., L., 1952
Losev A. F. Philosophy. Mythology. Culture. M., 1991
Lotman Y. M. Analysis of a poetical text. L., 1972
Luria A. R. Attention and memory. M., 1975
Mel'čuk I. A. The Ryssian language in the model "sense-text". M., Vena, 1995
Meletinsky E. M. Poetics of the myth. M., 1995
Nietzsche F. Power urge. Kiev, 1994
Ozhegov S. I. Lexicology. Lexicography. Culture of speech. M., 1974
Pascal B. Thoughts. World literature library. M., 1974
Pierce C. S. Collected Papers of Charles Sanders Pierce. Vol. 1-8. 1931 1958
Potebnya A. A thought and the language. Kharkov. 1982

Propp V. Y. Morphology of a fair tail. L., 1928
Revzin I. N. Language models. M., 1962
Rousseau J. J. Selected works in 3 volumes. M., 1961
Russel B., Whitehead A. Principia Mathematica. L., 1913
Sapir E. Selected works on the linguistics and culturology. M., 1993
Saussure F. Works on the linguistics. M., 1977
SchopenhauerA. Aphorisms and maxims. L., 1991
Shaff A. Introduction in the semantics. M., 1963
Shiller F. Letters about the esthetic education. Collected works in 7 voumes. V6. M., 1956
Spencer G. Composition. SPb., 1900
Stanislavsky K. S. Collected works in 8 volumes. V3. M., 1955
Stoll R. R. Multitudes. Logic. Axiomatic theories. M., 1968
Sussman L., Deep S. The communication experience in human relations. Cincinnati, 1989
Tarski A. Logic, semantics, metamathematics. Oxford, 1956
Toporov V. N. Myth. Ritual. Symbol. Image. M., 1995
Turner V. W. Ritual Process. Structure and Antistructure. Chicago, 1969
Vauvenargues L. Thoughts and maxims. L., 1988
Vekker L. M. Psychic processes. Collected works in 3 volumes. L., 1981
Vinogradov V. V. Poetics and rhetoric: About the language of belles-lettres prose. M., 1980
Volkov A. A. The structure of a lecture. M., 1986
Vygotsky L. S. Psychology of arts. M., 1968
Wiener N. Cybernetics. M., 1983
Wittgenstein L. About authenticity: Philosophic works in 2 volumes. V1. M., 1994
Yaglom I. M. Boolean structure and its models. M., 1980
Zaliznyak A. A. The Russian nominative inflection. M., 1967
Zholkovsky A. K. Wandering dreams. M., 1994
Zvegintsev V. A. Problems of the language symbolism. M., 1956